EARLY CHILDHOOD EDUCATION 91/92

Twelfth Edition

A Annual Editions E

A Library of Information from the Public Press

Editor

Karen Menke Paciorek
Eastern Michigan University

Karen Menke Paciorek is an assistant professor of Early Childhood Education at Eastern Michigan University. Her professional training is in Early Childhood Education with a B.S. from the University of Pittsburgh, an M.A. from George Washington University, and a Ph.D. from Peabody College of Vanderbilt University. She is the vice president of the Michigan Association for the Education of Young Children, and she serves on the advisory board for many community groups. Her workshops and presentations focus on quality programming, teacher training, and curriculum development.

Editor

Joyce Huth Munro
Centenary College

Joyce Huth Munro is Chair of the Education Division at Centenary College. She received her Ph.D. from Peabody College of Vanderbilt University. In addition to administration and teaching, she directs the Children's Center at Centenary College. Regionally and nationally, she presents seminars on curriculum design and teacher education. Currently, she is coordinator of a research project on case studies in teacher education for the National Association for Early Childhood Teacher Educators.

Cover illustration by Mike Eagle

The Dushkin Publishing Group, Inc.
Sluice Dock, Guilford, Connecticut 06437

The Annual Editions Series

Annual Editions is a series of over fifty volumes designed to provide the reader with convenient, low-cost access to a wide range of current, carefully selected articles from some of the most important magazines, newspapers, and journals published today. Annual Editions are updated on an annual basis through a continuous monitoring of over 200 periodical sources. All Annual Editions have a number of features designed to make them particularly useful, including topic guides, annotated tables of contents, unit overviews, and indexes. For the teacher using Annual Editions in the classroom, an Instructor's Resource Guide with test questions is available for each volume.

VOLUMES AVAILABLE

Africa
Aging
American Government
American History, Pre-Civil War
American History, Post-Civil War
Anthropology
Biology
Business and Management
Business Ethics
Canadian Politics
China
Comparative Politics
Computers in Education
Computers in Business
Computers in Society
Criminal Justice
Drugs, Society, and Behavior
Early Childhood Education
Economics
Educating Exceptional Children
Education
Educational Psychology
Environment
Geography
Global Issues
Health
Human Development
Human Resources
Human Sexuality

Latin America
Macroeconomics
Management
Marketing
Marriage and Family
Microeconomics
Middle East and the Islamic World
Money and Banking
Nutrition
Personal Growth and Behavior
Psychology
Public Administration
Race and Ethnic Relations
Social Problems
Sociology
Soviet Union and Eastern Europe
State and Local Government
Third World
Urban Society
Violence and Terrorism
Western Civilization, Pre-Reformation
Western Civilization, Post-Reformation
Western Europe
World History, Pre-Modern
World History, Modern
World Politics

Library of Congress Cataloging in Publication Data
Main entry under title: Annual Editions: Early Childhood Education. 1991/92.
    1. Education, Preschool—Periodicals. 2. Child development—Periodicals. 3. Child rearing—United States—Periodicals. I. Paciorek, Karen Menke, comp.; Munro, Joyce Huth, comp. II. Title: Early Childhood Education.
ISBN 1–56134–018–9   372.21′05   77–640114
HQ777.A7A

Twelfth Edition

Manufactured by The Banta Company, Harrisonburg, Virginia 22801

Editors/ Advisory Board

To the Reader

In publishing ANNUAL EDITIONS we recognize the enormous role played by the magazines, newspapers, and journals of the *public press* in providing current, first-rate educational information in a broad spectrum of interest areas. Within the articles, the best scientists, practitioners, researchers, and commentators draw issues into new perspective as accepted theories and viewpoints are called into account by new events, recent discoveries change old facts, and fresh debate breaks out over important controversies.

Many of the articles resulting from this enormous editorial effort are appropriate for students, researchers, and professionals seeking accurate, current material to help bridge the gap between principles and theories and the real world. These articles, however, become more useful for study when those of lasting value are carefully *collected, organized, indexed,* and *reproduced* in a *low-cost format,* which provides easy and permanent access when the material is needed. That is the role played by *Annual Editions.* Under the direction of each volume's *Editor,* who is an expert in the subject area, and with the guidance of an *Advisory Board,* we seek each year to provide in each *ANNUAL EDITION* a current, well-balanced, carefully selected collection of the best of the public press for your study and enjoyment. We think you'll find this volume useful, and we hope you'll take a moment to let us know what you think.

After a long and often frustrating battle lasting more than twenty years, the Child Care and Development Block Grant was passed and funded by Congress and signed by President Bush in the fall of 1990. In the final hours of the budget negotiations, there was cause for a major celebration as the United States finally had legislation and funding to assist in providing for quality education and care for young children. As with all new legislation and appropriations, it will take time for the benefits to be realized by local communities. Families, child care professionals, and children will definitely benefit, but it will take time as much of the responsibility for the distribution of funds lies with individual states. A survey of existing programs will be made to determine the greatest need, and plans for implementation will be developed.

The role of professionals and others concerned for the education and welfare of young children is to capitalize on the renewed societal interest in the field, while bringing to light the contradictory tapestry of attitudes and actions regarding young children and their families. A second purpose is to stimulate awareness, interest, and inquiry into the historical trends, issues, controversies, and realities of the field.

Four central themes are evident in the articles chosen for this *Annual Editions: Early Childhood Education 91/92.* First, collaborative efforts are critical if changes are to be made in the lives of many young children in America for whom the future appears bleak. No one group can do all the work or provide all the necessary skills for change to be implemented. Second, the benefits of play in all areas of a child's development provides strong evidence that play is a fundamental organizer of life in the child's early years. The third theme focuses on the affective self and underscores the benefits of a positive self-esteem. Finally, there is common belief among professionals that if steps are not taken immediately on issues related to young children and their families, we are headed for a disastrous future.

A major purpose of the twelfth edition of *Annual Editions: Early Childhood Education 91/92* is to highlight the progress that has been made on issues facing young children and their families, and to outline the hard work that lies ahead. We have made tremendous strides in quality programming, teacher training, and collaborative efforts, but much still needs to be done. We should encourage more developmentally appropriate programs and environments both at the preschool and elementary level, increased availability of child care for families, improved compensation for teachers, and expanded accessibility for all who need quality child care.

Given the diversity of topics included in the volume, it may be used with several audiences: with parents as an available resource in an Early Childhood center; with undergraduate or graduate students studying Early Childhood Education; or with professionals pursuing further development. It is also useful in many ways as an anthology of primary and secondary sources; as supplementary readings correlated with textbooks in developmental or child psychology, human development, special education, family life, pediatrics, or child care; as a source book for individual term papers, oral presentations, or projects; or for class discussions, group work, panel discussions, or debates. Some topics are addressed in two or more articles. One article may be more appropriate for the beginning student, while another will challenge an advanced student or professional.

Long-time users of *Annual Editions: Early Childhood Education* will notice a change in editors. Judy Spitler McKee, who has been an editor for the first eleven editions, decided it was time for a well-deserved break. She has closely followed the many changes in the profession over the past 20 years and made significant contributions.

A new editor has joined the team and the selection of articles for the twelfth edition has been a cooperative venture between the two editors, the members of the advisory board, and other professionals. Your comments on this edition are welcomed and will serve to modify future anthologies. Please fill out and return the article rating form on the last page. Continue to work diligently for young children, their families, and teachers. Our future depends on it.

Karen Menke Paciorek

Karen Menke Paciorek

Joyce Huth Munro

Joyce Huth Munro
Editor

Contents

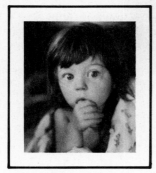

Unit 1

Perspectives

Seven selections provide a brief history of the development of early childhood education, consider the importance of continuity between early education and elementary education, and look at the value of child-initiated activities in the early childhood learning setting.

The concepts in bold italics are developed in the article. For further expansion please refer to the Topic Guide and the Index.

Unit 2

Child Development and Families

Seven selections consider the effects of family life on the growing child, and the importance of parent education.

The concepts in bold italics are developed in the article. For further expansion please refer to the Topic Guide and the Index.

Unit 3

Appropriate Educational Practices

Seven selections examine how various educational programs meet the needs of the growing child.

The concepts in bold italics are developed in the article. For further expansion please refer to the Topic Guide and the Index.

Unit 4

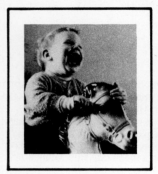

Guiding Behavior

Five selections examine the importance of establishing self-esteem in the child and consider the effects of stressors and stress reduction on behavior.

The concepts in bold italics are developed in the article. For further expansion please refer to the Topic Guide and the Index.

Unit 5

Curricular Applications

Ten selections consider various curricular choices. The areas covered include creating, inventing, emergent literacy, motor development, and conceptualizing curriculum.

The concepts in bold italics are developed in the article. For further expansion please refer to the Topic Guide and the Index.

Unit 6

Teaching

Five selections discuss teaching as an art, and the
importance of program evaluation for the effective
professional.

Unit 7

Reflections

Three selections consider the present and future of early childhood education.

The concepts in bold italics are developed in the article. For further expansion please refer to the Topic Guide and the Index.

Topic Guide

This topic guide suggests how the selections in this book relate to topics of traditional concern to students and professionals involved with early childhood education. It can be very useful in locating articles that relate to each other for reading and research. The guide is arranged alphabetically according to topic. Articles may, of course, treat topics that do not appear in the topic guide. In turn, entries in the topic guide do not necessarily constitute a comprehensive listing of all the contents of each selection.

TOPIC AREA	TREATED IN:	TOPIC AREA	TREATED IN:
Academics	18. Why Not Academic Preschool?	Developmentally Appropriate Practice	15. Programs for 4- and 5-Year-Olds 16. Developmentally Appropriate Practice 18. Why Not Academic Preschool? 30. Thinking, Playing, and Language Learning 31. Emergent Literacy 32. Early Childhood Physical Education 33. State of American Preschool Playgrounds 34. Transition Time 35. Conceptualizing Today's Kindergarten Curriculum 40. Excellent Early Education
Advocacy	4. Early Care and Education 22. How Well Do We Respect the Children in Our Care? 42. Promise at Risk		
Affective Development	6. Schools and Classrooms as Caring Communities 10. Guns and Dolls 15. Programs for 4- and 5-Year-Olds 24. Children's Self-Esteem 26. Understanding and Altering Aggression		
Child Care: Half Day/Full Day	3. Economic Issues Related to Child Care and Early Childhood Education 5. Head Start 12. Working Parents 37. Who Cares? 43. Day Care Generation 44. Cost of *Not* Providing Quality Early Childhood Programs	Discipline	12. Working Parents 25. Avoiding "Me Against You" Discipline
		Divorce	13. Single-Parent Families
		Dual-Income Families	12. Working Parents
		Emergent Literacy	31. Emergent Literacy 39. Learning to Read in New Zealand
Child Development	8. First Year Milestones 10. Guns and Dolls	Equipment/ Materials	28. Creative Play 33. State of American Preschool Playgrounds
Child Development Associate	38. Child Development Associate Program	Ethics	1. New Code of Ethics for Early Childhood Educators!
Children at Risk	2. Children of Poverty 5. Head Start 42. Promise at Risk	Evaluating	7. Preschool Children with Mild Handicaps
Cognitive Development	30. Thinking, Playing, and Language Learning	Families	7. Preschool Children with Mild Handicaps 11. What Birth Order Means
Collaboration	2. Children of Poverty 4. Early Care and Education 5. Head Start 6. Schools and Classrooms as Caring Communities 42. Promise at Risk 44. Cost of *Not* Providing Quality Early Childhood Programs	Federal Government's Role	44. Costs of *Not* Providing Quality Early Childhood Programs
		Head Start	5. Head Start
Creativity	27. Learning to Play 28. Creative Play 29. "Put Your Name on Your Painting, But . . . the Blocks Go Back on the Shelves"	Health and Safety	33. State of American Preschool Playgrounds
		Homeless	2. Children of Poverty
		Infants and Infant Care	8. First Year Milestones 9. First Friends
Curriculum	16. Developmentally Appropriate Practice 21. Synthesis of Research on Grade Retention 22. How Well Do We Respect the Children in Our Care? 35. Conceptualizing Today's Kindergarten Curriculum 36. How Good Is Your Kindergarten Curriculum?	International Perspectives	39. Learning to Read in New Zealand 40. Excellent Early Education 41. Learning, Chinese-Style

Perspectives

- **Conditions Today (Articles 1-3)**
- **Collaborative Efforts (Articles 4-7)**

As we begin the 1990s there has been a major cause for celebration among those who care for our nation's children. During the fall of 1990, Congress passed the long-awaited Child Care and Development Block Grant. For years legislators and business leaders had been joining ranks with early childhood professionals in calling for greater funding and the establishment of partnerships among varied constituencies to ensure high quality programs for America's young children. Inadequate support from the federal government during the 1980s, greater numbers of families living in poverty, and an increase in the percentage of working mothers and dual-income families who need child care services were the reasons for these collaborative efforts. Previous government, business, and educational collaboration has occurred in the past—during the Depression, World War II, and Head Start. The lessons learned from those interagency efforts have clearly shown both the necessity and effectiveness of early childhood programs that are comprehensive and high quality.

Public perceptions about society's investment in young children in general and helping at-risk and minority children in particular are gradually changing. Today, millions of working parents need quality child-care programs that are consistently and adequately funded, comprehensive in nature to meet the basic needs of children and families, and operated by dedicated and specially educated staffs of professionals. The day-to-day stresses parents that face in their jobs have become more intense and complex, and they often have to cope with them alone due to lack of support from employers, colleagues, family, and friends. This is where alliances formed among home, school, and business can be extremely helpful and comforting.

It is unrealistic to expect the passage of the child care bill to solve all of the problems faced by parents looking for quality child care, or of teachers and directors who provide care for young children. But this legislation could lead to significant changes. The majority of child-care centers struggle to be self-supporting, receive only a fraction of their operating budget from outside sources,

pay low wages to their staff, and cannot provide comprehensive services to either children or parents. Consequently, millions of young children under six years of age are inadequately cared for by untrained, uncaring, or indifferent persons. Many children are transported to the homes of relatives, friends, or to two different programs in a single day. Uncounted numbers of "latchkey" children are left to fend for themselves. This patchwork of alternative child-care arrangements is having significant developmental effects on today's young children who will be tomorrow's adolescents. Disturbing questions must be raised about what these vulnerable young children are experiencing in these varied settings during their formative years.

Of greater concern are the 12 million young children who live in poverty and do not receive health care, proper nutrition, shelter, or educational opportunities necessary for survival in America today. Parents or guardians of these children are confronted with a multitude of concerns, but few resources. They are faced with finding a safe place to sleep for the night or a church offering a meal and a box of used clothing. Their children receive so little of quality.

Head Start, one of the few government-funded programs for young children and their families, has been praised for the progress made by the children. But it has also received criticism because the program does not serve more children. Less than 20 percent of the children eligible are actually enrolled in a Head Start program. The program is now being embraced by many as the best avenue to take as we look to the twenty-first century. Head Start just celebrated its 25th anniversary and a Silver Ribbon Panel comprised of prominent educators has detailed ideas and plans to lead the program into the future.

Federal legislation (P.L. 99-457) had led to more services available for handicapped preschool children and their families. This legislation may present some new challenges for teachers not used to working with handicapped children. Teachers and other school personnel need to work cooperatively as children are evaluated and services are provided to assist them in their education.

As we examine the living and learning conditions for children today we see many problems, but there are educators, parents, and community groups standing by ready to assist children and their families. Unfortunately, the number of people requiring assistance is growing at a rapid pace. Preventing problems from occurring in the first place seems to be the one key to ensuring a safe, nurturing, and successful educational experience for all our country's children.

Looking Ahead: Challenge Questions

How are children from families headed by young, poor, and single parents at jeopardy for failure in school and society in general? What steps can be taken to assist these children who face poverty every day of their lives?

What can schools do to assist children and their families as they struggle to walk the thin line between economic disaster and a safe and secure life?

How could collaborative efforts among business, industry, government, and communities better serve the pressing needs of young children and their changing families? Why is it necessary that early education efforts reach beyond the schoolhouse doors to families, communities, and other social institutions?

What events have caused state legislators to provide financial support for child-care services, especially children who are considered to be at risk? What guiding principles must be considered for children, parents, and the early childhood ecological systems if quality is to be achieved for all?

What steps need to be taken if the recommendations made by the Silver Ribbon Panel addressing the achievements and challenges of Head Start are followed? What recommendations do you see as achievable in your community?

How can professionals assist in the screening and evaluation process of mildly handicapped preschool children?

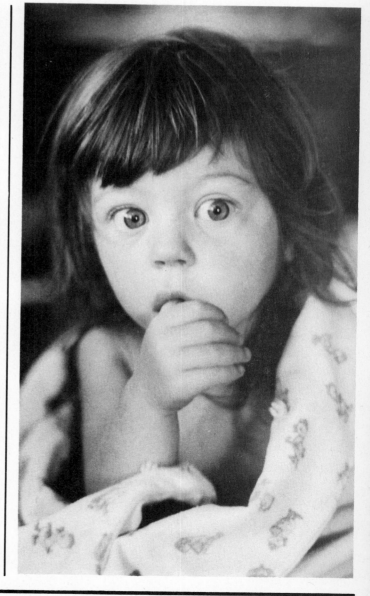

A New Code of Ethics for Early Childhood Educators!

Code of Ethical Conduct and Statement of Commitment

Stephanie Feeney and Kenneth Kipnis

Stephanie Feeney, *Ph.D., is Professor and Early Childhood Education Specialist at the University of Hawaii at Manoa. She is a former member of NAEYC's Governing Board.*

Kenneth Kipnis, *Ph.D., Professor of Philosophy at the University of Hawaii at Manoa, has written on legal philosophy and ethical issues in law, medicine, engineering, and other professions.*

Editor's Note:

Under the leadership of Stephanie Feeney, appointed by the Governing Board in 1984, and a Board-established Ethics Commission, NAEYC began a process in which members would explore and clarify the early childhood profession's understanding of its own ethics. This process has entailed

● *a survey of members to learn concerns* (Young Children *March 1985),*

● *numerous workshops in various locations with early childhood educators to identify and explore dilemmas, and*

● *another survey of members to help formu-*

Financial assistance for this project was provided by NAEYC, the Wallace Alexander Gerbode Foundation, and the University of Hawaii.

late principles of ethical action (Young Children *May 1987).*

Written reports summarizing readers' contributions served as the basis for three more articles published in Young Children: *"The Working Mother" November 1987 with commentary by Lilian Katz; "The Aggressive Child" January 1988 with commentary by Bettye Caldwell; and "The Divorced Parents" March 1988 with commentary by Sue Spayth Riley. Kenneth Kipnis wrote a commentary from the philosopher's perspective to all three articles.*

With the additional resources of ethicists and relevant codes of ethics developed by other groups, the process next produced a "Draft Code of Ethics and Statement of Commitment." That was presented to the membership at the NAEYC Conference in November 1988, resulting in further refinements.

The final document, presented below, was approved by NAEYC's Governing Board in July 1989.

The Statement of Commitment accompanying the Code is a recognition that the ultimate strength of the Code rests in the adherence of individual educators.

From *Young Children,* Vol. 45, No. 1 (November 1989), pp. 24-29. Copyright © 1989 by the National Association for the Education of Young Children, 1834 Connecticut Avenue, N.W., Washington, DC. Used by permission.

The National Association for the Education of Young Children
Code of Ethical Conduct

Preamble

NAEYC recognizes that many daily decisions required of those who work with young children are of a moral and ethical nature. The NAEYC Code of Ethical Conduct offers guidelines for responsible behavior and sets forth a common basis for resolving the principal ethical dilemmas encountered in early childhood education. The primary focus is on daily practice with children and their families in programs for children from birth to 8 years of age: preschools, child care centers, family day care homes, kindergartens, and primary classrooms. Many of the provisions also apply to specialists who do not work directly with children, including program administrators, parent educators, college professors, and child care licensing specialists.

Standards of ethical behavior in early childhood education are based on commitment to core values that are deeply rooted in the history of our field. We have committed ourselves to:

- Appreciating childhood as a unique and valuable stage of the human life cycle
- Basing our work with children on knowledge of child development
- Appreciating and supporting the close ties between the child and family
- Recognizing that children are best understood in the context of family, culture, and society
- Respecting the dignity, worth, and uniqueness of each individual (child, family member, and colleague)
- Helping children and adults achieve their full poten-

tial in the context of relationships that are based on trust, respect, and positive regard

The Code sets forth a conception of our professional responsibilities in four sections, each addressing an arena of professional relationships: 1) children, 2) families, 3) colleagues, and 4) community and society. Each section includes an introduction to the primary responsibilities of the early childhood practitioner in that arena, a set of ideals pointing in the direction of exemplary professional practice, and a set of principles defining practices that are required, prohibited, and permitted.

The ideals reflect the aspirations of practitioners. The principles are intended to guide conduct and assist practitioners in resolving ethical dilemmas encountered in the field. There is not necessarily a corresponding principle for each ideal. Both ideals and principles are intended to direct practitioners to those questions which, when responsibly answered, will provide the basis for conscientious decision making. While the Code provides specific direction for addressing some ethical dilemmas, many others will require the practitioner to combine the guidance of the Code with sound professional judgment.

The ideals and principles in this Code present a shared conception of professional responsibility that affirms our commitment to the core values of our field. The Code publicly acknowledges the responsibilities that we in the field have assumed and in so doing supports ethical behavior in our work. Practitioners who face ethical dilemmas are urged to seek guidance in the applicable parts of this Code and in the spirit that informs the whole.

This Code of Ethical Conduct and Statement of Commitment was prepared under the auspices of the Ethics Commission of the National Association for the Education of Young Children. The Commission members were Stephanie Feeney (Chairperson), Bettye Caldwell, Sally Cartwright, Carrie Cheek, Josué Cruz, Jr., Anne G. Dorsey, Dorothy M. Hill, Lilian G. Katz, Pamm Mattick, Shirley A. Norris, and Sue Spayth Riley.

Section I: Ethical responsibilities to children

Childhood is a unique and valuable stage in the life cycle. Our paramount responsibility is to provide safe, healthy, nurturing, and responsive settings for children. We are committed to supporting children's development by cherishing individual differences, by helping them learn to live and work cooperatively, and by promoting their self-esteem.

Ideals:

I-1.1—To be familiar with the knowledge base of early childhood education and to keep current through continuing education and in-service training.

I-1.2—To base program practices upon current knowledge in the field of child development and related disciplines and upon particular knowledge of each child.

I-1.3—To recognize and respect the uniqueness and the potential of each child.

I-1.4—To appreciate the special vulnerability of children.

I-1.5—To create and maintain safe and healthy settings that foster children's social, emotional, intellectual, and physical development and that respect their dignity and their contributions.

I-1.6—To support the right of children with special needs to participate, consistent with their ability, in regular early childhood programs.

Principles:

P-1.1—Above all, we shall not harm children. We shall not participate in practices that are disrespectful, degrading, dangerous, exploitative, intimidating, psychologically damaging, or physically harmful to children. *This principle has precedence over all others in this Code.*

P-1.2—We shall not participate in practices that discriminate against children by denying benefits, giving special advantages, or excluding them from programs or activities on the basis of their race, religion, sex, national origin, or the status, behavior, or beliefs of their parents. (This principle does not apply to programs that have a lawful mandate to provide services to a particular population of children.)

P-1.3—We shall involve all of those with relevant knowledge (including staff and parents) in decisions concerning a child.

P-1.4—When, after appropriate efforts have been made with a child and the family, the child still does not appear to be benefitting from a program, we shall communicate our concern to the family in a positive way and offer them assistance in finding a more suitable setting.

P-1.5—We shall be familiar with the symptoms of child abuse and neglect and know community procedures for addressing them.

P-1.6—When we have evidence of child abuse or neglect, we shall report the evidence to the appropriate community agency and follow up to ensure that appropriate action has been taken. When possible, parents will be informed that the referral has been made.

P-1.7—When another person tells us of their suspicion that a child is being abused or neglected but we lack evidence, we shall assist that person in taking appropriate action to protect the child.

P-1.8—When a child protective agency fails to provide adequate protection for abused or neglected children, we acknowledge a collective ethical responsibility to work toward improvement of these services.

Section II: Ethical responsibilities to families

Families are of primary importance in children's development. (The term *family* may include others, besides parents, who are responsibly involved with the child.) Because the family and the early childhood educator have a common interest in the child's welfare, we acknowledge a primary responsibility to bring about collaboration between the home and school in ways that enhance the child's development.

Ideals:

I-2.1—To develop relationships of mutual trust with the families we serve.

I-2.2—To acknowledge and build upon strengths and competencies as we support families in their task of nurturing children.

I-2.3—To respect the dignity of each family and its culture, customs, and beliefs.

I-2.4—To respect families' childrearing values and their right to make decisions for their children.

I-2.5—To interpret each child's progress to parents within the framework of a developmental perspective and to help families understand and appreciate the value of developmentally appropriate early childhood programs.

I-2.6—To help family members improve their understanding of their children and to enhance their skills as parents.

I-2.7—To participate in building support networks for families by providing them with opportunities to interact with program staff and families.

Principles:

P-2.1—We shall not deny family members access to their child's classroom or program setting.

P-2.2—We shall inform families of program philosophy, policies, and personnel qualifications, and explain why we teach as we do.

P-2.3—We shall inform families of and, when appropriate, involve them in policy decisions.

P-2.4—We shall inform families of and, when appropriate, involve them in significant decisions affecting their child.

P-2.5—We shall inform the family of accidents involving their child, of risks such as exposures to contagious disease that may result in infection, and of events that might result in psychological damage.

P-2.6—We shall not permit or participate in research that could in any way hinder the education or development of the children in our programs. Families shall be fully informed of any proposed research projects involving their children and shall have the opportunity to give or withhold consent.

P-2.7—We shall not engage in or support exploitation of families. We shall not use our relationship with a family for private advantage or personal gain, or enter into relationships with family members that might impair our effectiveness in working with children.

P-2.8—We shall develop written policies for the protection of confidentiality and the disclosure of children's records. The policy documents shall be made available to all program personnel and families. Disclosure of children's records beyond family members, program personnel, and consultants having an obligation of confidentiality shall require familial consent (except in cases of abuse or neglect).

P-2.9—We shall maintain confidentiality and shall respect the family's right to privacy, refraining from disclosure of confidential information and intrusion into family life. However, when we are concerned about a child's welfare, it is permissible to reveal confidential information to agencies and individuals who may be able to act in the child's interest.

P-2.10—In cases where family members are in conflict we shall work openly, sharing our observations of the child, to help all parties involved make informed decisions. We shall refrain from becoming an advocate for one party.

P-2.11—We shall be familiar with and appropriately use community resources and professional services that support families. After a referral has been made, we shall follow up to ensure that services have been adequately provided.

Section III: Ethical responsibilities to colleagues

In a caring, cooperative work place human dignity is respected, professional satisfaction is promoted, and positive relationships are modeled. Our primary responsibility in this arena is to establish and maintain settings and relationships that support productive work and meet professional needs.

A—*Responsibilities to co-workers*

Ideals:

I-3A.1—To establish and maintain relationships of trust and cooperation with co-workers.

I-3A.2—To share resources and information with co-workers.

I-3A.3—To support co-workers in meeting their professional needs and in their professional development.

I-3A.4—To accord co-workers due recognition of professional achievement.

Principles:

P-3A.1—When we have concern about the professional behavior of a co-worker, we shall first let that person know of our concern and attempt to resolve the matter collegially.

P-3A.2—We shall exercise care in expressing views regarding the personal attributes or professional conduct of co-workers. Statements should be based on firsthand knowledge and relevant to the interests of children and programs.

B—*Responsibilities to employers*

Ideals:

I-3B.1—To assist the program in providing the highest quality of service.

I-3B.2—To maintain loyalty to the program and uphold its reputation.

Principles:

P-3B.1—When we do not agree with program policies, we shall first attempt to effect change through constructive action within the organization.

P-3B.2—We shall speak or act on behalf of an organization only when authorized. We shall take care to note when we are speaking for the organization and when we are expressing a personal judgment.

C—*Responsibilities to employees*

Ideals:

I-3C.1—To promote policies and working conditions that foster competence, well-being, and self-esteem in staff members.

I-3C.2—To create a climate of trust and candor that will enable staff to speak and act in the best interests of children, families, and the field of early childhood education.

I-3C.3—To strive to secure an adequate livelihood for those who work with or on behalf of young children.

Principles:

P-3C.1—In decisions concerning children and programs, we shall appropriately utilize the training, experience, and expertise of staff members.

P-3C.2—We shall provide staff members with working conditions that permit them to carry out their responsibilities, timely and nonthreatening evaluation procedures, written grievance procedures, constructive feedback, and opportunities for continuing professional development and advancement.

P-3C.3—We shall develop and maintain comprehensive written personnel policies that define program standards and, when applicable, that specify the extent to which employees are accountable for their conduct outside the work place. These policies shall be given to new staff members and shall be available for review by all staff members.

P-3C.4—Employees who do not meet program standards shall be informed of areas of concern and, when possible, assisted in improving their performance.

P-3C.5—Employees who are dismissed shall be informed of the reasons for their termination. When a dismissal is for cause, justification must be based on evidence of inadequate or inappropriate behavior that is accurately documented, current, and available for the employee to review.

P-3C.6—In making evaluations and recommendations, judgments shall be based on fact and relevant to the interests of children and programs.

P-3C.7—Hiring and promotion shall be based solely on a person's record of accomplishment and ability to carry out the responsibilities of the position.

P-3C.8—In hiring, promotion, and provision of training, we shall not participate in any form of discrimination based on race, religion, sex, national origin, handicap, age, or sexual preference. We shall be familiar with laws and regulations that pertain to employment discrimination.

Section IV: Ethical responsibilities to community and society

Early childhood programs operate within a context of an immediate community made up of families and other institutions concerned with children's welfare. Our responsibilities to the community are to provide programs that meet its needs and to cooperate with agencies and professions that share responsibility for children. Because the larger society has a measure of responsibility for the welfare and protection of children, and because of our specialized expertise in child development, we acknowledge an obligation to serve as a voice for children everywhere.

Ideals:

I-4.1—To provide the community with high-quality, culturally sensitive programs and services.

I-4.2—To promote cooperation among agencies and professions concerned with the welfare of young children, their families, and their teachers.

I-4.3—To work, through education, research, and advocacy, toward an environmentally safe world in which all children are adequately fed, sheltered, and nurtured.

I-4.4—To work, through education, research, and advocacy, toward a society in which all young children have access to quality programs.

I-4.5—To promote knowledge and understanding of young children and their needs. To work toward greater social acknowledgment of children's rights and greater social acceptance of responsibility for their well-being.

I-4.6—To support policies and laws that promote the well-being of children and families. To oppose those that impair their well-being. To cooperate with other individuals and groups in these efforts.

I-4.7—To further the professional development of the field of early childhood education and to strengthen its commitment to realizing its core values as reflected in this Code.

Principles:

P-4.1—We shall communicate openly and truthfully about the nature and extent of services that we provide.

P-4.2—We shall not accept or continue to work in positions for which we are personally unsuited or professionally unqualified. We shall not offer services that we do not have the competence, qualifications, or resources to provide.

P-4.3—We shall be objective and accurate in reporting the knowledge upon which we base our program practices.

P-4.4—We shall cooperate with other professionals who work with children and their families.

P-4.5—We shall not hire or recommend for employment any person who is unsuited for a position with respect to competence, qualifications, or character.

P-4.6—We shall report the unethical or incompetent behavior of a colleague to a supervisor when informal resolution is not effective.

P-4.7—We shall be familiar with laws and regulations that serve to protect the children in our programs.

P-4.8—We shall not participate in practices which are in violation of laws and regulations that protect the children in our programs.

P-4.9—When we have evidence that an early childhood program is violating laws or regulations protecting children, we shall report it to persons responsible for the program. If compliance is not accomplished within a reasonable time, we will report the violation to appropriate authorities who can be expected to remedy the situation.

P-4.10—When we have evidence that an agency or a professional charged with providing services to children, families, or teachers is failing to meet its obligations, we acknowledge a collective ethical responsibility to report the problem to appropriate authorities or to the public.

P-4.11—When a program violates or requires its employees to violate this Code, it is permissible, after fair assessment of the evidence, to disclose the identity of that program.

POVERTY

CHILDREN OF

THE STATUS OF 12 MILLION YOUNG AMERICANS

Sally Reed and R. Craig Sautter

SALLY REED and R. CRAIG SAUTTER are writers and editors based in Chicago.

T IS 9 a.m. on a November morning, and Terrence Quinn, principal of Public School 225 in Rockaway, Queens, New York, is serving breakfast. But he's not in the school cafeteria. He's in the lobby of a ramshackle welfare hotel where homeless parents and their children have come to seek shelter. With a social worker in tow, Quinn has cruised the hotel corridors, knocking on doors, inviting what is an ever-changing group of parents to share coffee and break bagels and doughnuts with him while he tries to persuade them to send their children to his elementary school six blocks — and a world — away.

Quinn first tried his pied piper approach to drawing poor children into his school in November 1988, and he repeats the effort periodically. His aim is to make the parents and children feel welcome in his school. Last spring, Jacqueline, a sixth-grader who had lived at the hotel, was selected as the school's valedictorian. One month before the official announcement, she entered Quinn's office and asked to speak to him in private.

"Can someone on welfare actually be the valedictorian?" she asked.

Quinn reassured Jacqueline, a youngster who has overcome many obstacles. Each day millions of others like her are trying to do likewise. And it's not fair. While the last decade became known in the media for its rampant greed, it left millions of poor people (and their children) literally out in the cold. The outcomes are heartbreaking. Why should a child such as Jacqueline feel so humiliated and ashamed of her predicament?

Jacqueline doesn't know it, but she's not alone. We've all been numbed by the horror stories we've heard of late — stories of homeless families sleeping in cars and of crack babies abandoned to hospital nurseries. Meanwhile, the mind-boggling statistics paint a dreadful picture of what life in this nation is like for far too many children. Once you gather all the figures — from con-

ferences, from government agencies, and from scores of reports — the result is frightening. As a nation we're talking about setting goals for fire safety while a wildfire rages out of control all around us. What can educators, politicians, and individual citizens do? People's lives are at stake, and we can't wait any longer.

WAR WITHOUT END

A generation after President Lyndon Johnson declared an official War on Poverty, nearly one-fifth of America's youngest citizens still grow up poor; often sick, hungry, and illiterate; and deprived of safe and adequate housing, of needed social services, and of special educational assistance. Millions of these youngsters are virtually untouched by the vast wealth of the nation in which they begin their fragile and often painful lives.

It didn't take long to lose the War on Poverty. Only a decade after President Johnson's bold declaration, his antipoverty offensive had been lost for millions upon millions of children. By 1975, after the cutback of the Great Society programs by the Nixon and Ford Administrations and after spiraling inflation hit the economy, the interests of children slid lower on the list of economic priorities than even the interests of the elderly. The youngest Americans became the poorest Americans.

During the Great Depression, most Americans were poor. At the end of World War II, about one-third were still poor, but the industrial output of the U.S. was rapidly expanding. By August 1964, when the first antipoverty legislation was enacted, 32 million Americans (about 15% of the population) were materially impoverished. About 13 million of those poor people were children. More of them were elderly.

The one front that has at least received sustained reinforcements since the War on Poverty was scaled back is the fight to improve the lot of the elderly poor. By 1990, 90% of the elderly poor were receiving significant benefits through Social Security cost-of-living adjustments, through housing assistance, through Medicaid, and through other federal and state safeguards.

As a result of this triumph of social policy for senior citizens, many child advocates, including educators and politicians, insist that we can do the same for our most vulnerable citizens, our children. This persistent band is finally making progress toward changing the way society treats youngsters who are the innocent victims of accidents of birth or family misfortune.

But the scale of the problem is overwhelming. Over the past 15 years the incidence of poverty among children has increased and become complicated in ways that portend catastrophic consequences, not only for the children themselves, but also for our schools, our economy, and our social well-being.

Since 1975 children have been poorer than any other age group. By 1989 young people accounted for 39.5% of America's poor. The official U.S. poverty rate for all citizens in 1989 edged slightly downward to 13.1% — only a 2% decline from the Johnson era. Yet in raw numbers more Americans are poor today than before the War on Poverty. Nearly 40 million people of all ages live in families with income levels below the official poverty line of $7,704 for a family of two, $9,435 for a family of three, and $12,092 for a family of four. The current poverty rate is higher than during the worst recession years of the 1970s.

Actually, the real crisis for children and families is even worse than it first appears. Income for the average poor family in 1988 was $4,851 *below* the poverty line. For poor families headed by females, that gap was $5,206. Levels of family income this low mean that some serious family needs — such as food, clothing, medicine, early learning assistance, and housing — are not being met. The result for the children of these families is sickness, psychological stress, malnutrition, underdevelopment, and daily hardship that quickly takes its toll on their young minds and bodies.

Even though the postwar baby boom has long since subsided, nearly as many young people are poor today as when the War on Poverty was launched. However, the percentage today is higher. More than 12.6 million U.S. youngsters — nearly 20% of all children under the age of 18 — are poor.

From *Phi Delta Kappan*, June 1990, pp. K1-K12. Reprinted by permission of *Phi Delta Kappan* and the authors.

Thus one in five American children goes to bed hungry or sick or cold.

And when these children wake each day, they face little prospect that the economic plight of their families will improve enough to make their lives better. Often they internalize the bleakness of their situation and blame themselves for it. Their lives become bitter and humorless or filled with anxiety and fear. Of course, many poor children retain their dignity, and their character is tempered by the Spartan battle for subsistence. But millions of others, permanently damaged, are unable to recover and fall victim to the vicious social pathology of poverty.

And the future seems even grimmer. U.S. Secretary of Education Lauro Cavazos has estimated that, by the year 2000, "as many as one-third of our young people will be disadvantaged and at risk."

Some American youngsters will never even have the chance to see the turn of the century. As has happened in other wars, they will perish. More than 10,000 children in the U.S. die each year as a direct result of the poverty they endure. Often they die during the first weeks of their lives because simple and inexpensive prenatal health care was unavailable to their mothers.

The U.S. has the highest rate of child poverty among the industrialized nations, nearly three times that of most other economically advanced nations. Moreover, the Children's Defense Fund, a leading Washington-based child advocacy group, has sadly noted that only the U.S. and South Africa, among the advanced industrial nations, do not provide universal health coverage for children and pregnant women and do not provide child care to foster early development.

THE YOUNGER, THE POORER

And the picture gets worse. The younger a child is in America today, the greater are his or her chances of being poor. According to the U.S. Census Bureau, the Americans most likely of all to be poor are those age 3 and under. Officially, 23.3% of this age group are poor. During the early years so critical to development, nearly one-fourth of U.S. children lack medical, nutritional, and early-learning assistance. Thus many poor children are needlessly condemned to physical and psychological deficiencies for the rest of their lives.

Further down the road, the social cost of this neglect will almost certainly be extravagant. Physical and mental damage that could have been prevented by inexpensive prenatal checkups or by nutritional programs in early childhood haunts our society in expensive educational, medical, welfare, and correctional costs that can reach into the hundreds of thousands of dollars.

For example, 11% of children end up in special education classes because of cognitive and developmental problems, many of which could have been prevented by prenatal care. Even a pragmatist can count. The willful neglect of America's poor children is not only immoral; it is just plain stupid.

Children of poverty who make it through their earliest years relatively unscathed face new hardships later on. Nearly 22% of 3- to 5-year-olds are poor. Then, after six years of material want, most poor children enter school and make their first significant contact with a social institution. Indeed, the largest group of poor children ranges between the ages of 6 and 11. More than four million of these children — 19.9% of the age group — continue to grow up in unremitting destitution.

Schools should be equipped to help these children gain skills to cope with and ultimately to escape from their economic circumstances. But far too many schools fail far too many poor children. And poor communities tend to get stuck with poor schools as patterns of taxation make a bad situation worse.

Only as children enter their teenage years — and begin to confront a new set of social and biological problems — does the poverty rate actually dip. But even among young people between the ages of 12 and 17, more than 16% live below the poverty line. That figure is higher than the poverty rate for the general population.

The Carnegie Council on Adolescent Development has emphasized that, between the ages of 10 and 15, young people are extremely volatile. For poor teens, the match is even closer to the fuse, since these youngsters are often besieged by problems of school failure, pregnancy, substance abuse, and economic stress.

These young people suffer not only the immediate physical and psychological damage of economic and social adversity; the long-term effects of their childhood deprivation and neglect also manifest themselves in a growing complex of social ills. One-fourth of young black men are reported to have trouble of some kind with correctional authorities. Illiteracy among poor dropouts is endemic. And the personal tragedy of broken homes and a future of perpetually low-paying jobs feeds young black men into the drug trade — and the morgue. The popular appeal of Jesse Jackson's slogan, "Up with Hope," demonstrates just how many young people are growing up in the hopelessness that poverty breeds.

YOUNG FAMILIES, POOR CHILDREN

Then there is the matter of family circumstances. Almost 50% of all U.S. children living in a family headed by a person 25 years of age or younger are poor. One-third of all children living in a family headed by a person 30 years of age or younger are poor. In fact, while the nation's overall poverty rate slowly declined from 1967 to 1987, the poverty rate for children living in a family headed by a person 30 years of age or younger shot up from 19% to 35.6%.

Likewise, if a child lives in a family headed by a woman, the chances are better than 50/50 that the child is poor. More than 56% of families headed by single black women are poor. The poverty rate for families headed by Hispanic women is 59%. Yet single-parent families do not necessarily cause poverty. Half of the nation's poor children live with both parents.

Contrary to popular perception, child poverty is not a phenomenon confined to the inner cities. Fewer than 9% of America's poor people live in the nation's core cities. The largest number of poor people still live in semi-isolation in towns and hamlets across the country. About 17% of these people are hidden in rural America. Just as in the inner cities, poverty rates in some rural areas have reached 50% and higher. And some rural regions have been poor for generations. Surprisingly, 28% of America's poor struggle amidst the affluence of suburban communities, shut out from most of the benefits that their neighbors enjoy. Westchester County, New York, one of the 11 wealthiest suburban areas in the country, now has more than 5,000 homeless people looking for shelter.

Another inaccurate perception about poverty is that being poor is directly related to race. Two-thirds of poor Americans are white. The Children's Defense Fund calculates that one white child in seven is poor. However, the *rate* of poverty is considerably higher for minorities, who are fast becoming majority demographic groups in the 10 largest states. Four out of nine black children are poor; three out of eight Hispanic children are poor. Poverty in America knows no racial boundaries, no geographic borders. The only common denominator for the children of poverty is that they are brought up under desperate conditions beyond their control — and, for them, the rhetoric of equal opportunity seems a cruel hoax, an impossible dream.

THE FLIP SIDE OF PROSPERITY

During the "get-rich-quick" decade of the 1980s, when the number of U.S. billionaires quintupled, child poverty jumped by 23%. More than 2.1 million children tumbled into poverty as the stock market first soared, then plummeted, and finally rebounded. The bull market, with its leveraged buyouts, $325 billion savings-and-loan ripoffs, tax cuts for the wealthy, and junk bond scams, did little to drive up the value of children on the domestic agenda.

"The story of child poverty has become a story of American decline," a congressional staffer who works on poverty-related legislative issues recently lamented. "People have a vague sense that we are doing something wrong nationally, that we are going to be in trouble in the near future. The plight of children is related to this feeling. In addition to being immoral, our treatment of children is profoundly shortsighted. It is economically and socially shortsighted to allow children to grow up with unhealthy bodies and lousy educations and poor nutrition and inadequate health care. We all know that, but now it looks like it will kill us in the 21st century."

What makes matters worse is that the poor are getting poorer. According to the U.S. House of Representatives' Select Committee on Children, Youth, and Families, the income gap between families with the highest incomes and those with the lowest was wider in 1988 than in any year since 1947. The poorest 20% of families received less than 5% of the national income, while the wealthiest 20% received 44%, the largest share ever recorded. Maurice Zeitlin, a sociologist at the University of Caliornia, Los Angeles, recently concluded that the richest 1% of families own 42% of the net wealth of all U.S. families — a staggering proportion that has changed little since the 19th century. This super-rich elite owns 20% of all real estate, 60% of all corporate stock, and 80% of family-owned trusts. These huge disparities make the familiar excuses about budget deficits and tax burdens standing in the way of helping children seem feeble at best.

The vast and ongoing transformation of the U.S. economy from manufacturing to service jobs and from local to global markets has also harmed poor families. When the unemployment of the recession of the 1980s finally began to ease, many of the new jobs were service jobs that paid half as much as manufacturing jobs. According to Michael Sherraden, a professor at Washington University in St. Louis, "The overwhelming reality is that most new jobs being created today are very low-skilled service jobs with low pay and no benefits, not high-tech jobs."

Statistics from the U.S. Department of Labor show that, although the unemployment rate has fallen steadily since 1983, the poverty rate has remained high. Since 1983 unemployment has dropped by 4%. Meanwhile, the overall poverty rate has fallen only 2% — and has actually increased for children.

WORKING HARDER, GETTING POORER

U.S. Census Bureau figures reveal that nearly half of the heads of all poor households are employed. In 1988 the proportion of poor heads of households who worked full-time increased by 1.8%. But that was accompanied by a decline in the average earnings of full-time male workers. A low minimum wage offers one explanation for this stubborn trend. For example, full-time work at the minimum wage by the head of a family of three leaves that family $2,500 below the poverty line.

In nearly 42% of poor households headed by females, the women are employed. About 10% work full-time, year-round. And 87% of poor children live in a family in which at least one person is employed at least part of the time. However, from 1979 to 1987 income for young families with children dropped by nearly 25%.

"The public has a misconception about who the poor are," Sherraden observes. "Most people who live below the poverty line are not welfare recipients and members of the underclass. They are people who have jobs or are members of a household in which someone has a job." He adds, "What kind of message are we delivering if people work hard and still do not make it?"

Some of the workers in poor families are children and teenagers. In 1989 the U.S. Department of Labor discovered 23,000 minors working in violation of the Fair Labor Standards Act. In fact, child labor violations have doubled in the last five years. Most such violations have involved young teenagers working too many hours or under unsafe conditions. Unlike the sweatshops of the past, many violators of child labor laws today are hamburger joints and fast-food establishments. Many teenagers work long hours because they must do so in order to survive, not because they are trying to buy designer jeans or are exploring future careers in food services. And, as teachers know, working often becomes a reason for classroom failure.

CUTBACKS AND REDUCTIONS

To add to an already bad situation, government cutbacks and the perpetual budget crisis have increased children's woes. The House Select Committee on Children, Youth, and Families found that, since 1970, the median grant through Aid to Families with Dependent Children (AFDC) has fallen 23%, from $471 to $361 in constant dollars. In 1987 AFDC reached only 56% of children in poverty, a lower proportion than in 1964 when the first volley was fired in the War on Poverty.

"Child poverty is Ronald Reagan's legacy to the 1990s," according to Rep. George Miller (D-Calif.), who chairs the Select Committee on Children, Youth, and Families. Between 1980 and 1988, during President Reagan's military build-up, the U.S. government spent $1.9 trillion on national defense, while cutting $10 billion from programs aimed at protecting poor children and families.

According to the Center for the Study of Social Policy, AFDC benefits and food stamps for a family of four amounted to only 66.3% of the 1988 poverty line, down from 70.9% in 1980. Meanwhile, participation in the food stamp program has declined 14% since 1982.

At the same time, federal assistance for low-income housing tumbled 76% when adjusted for inflation. In *The Same Client: The Demographics of Education and Service Delivery Systems*, a recent report from the Institute for Educational Leadership, Harold Hodgkinson concluded that many dropouts and school failures can be attributed directly to such basic factors as the high cost of housing that eats up most of a family's available and limited income. Children living on the edge of homelessness are prevented from finding the stability that usually makes successful schooling possible.

"If low-income children were living in economically and socially secure housing with some rent protection, there is little doubt that most of them could stay out of poverty and in school, while their parents stay on the job and off welfare," Hodgkinson advised in the report. He argued that national housing strategies to increase the availability and reduce the cost of housing are essential, if we wish to limit poverty. So are preventive social strategies that help people who are facing financial emergencies to stay out of poverty.

NO PLACE TO CALL HOME

Poor housing or no housing — those seem to be the options facing most poor children. Homeless children are one more distressing by-product of the new poverty that plagues this nation. The U.S. Department of Education estimates that 220,000 school-aged children are homeless and that 65,000 of them do not attend school. About 15,600 homeless children live in publicly operated shelters, 90,700 live in privately operated shelters, 55,750 stay with relatives or friends, and 63,170 live "elsewhere." The greatest number of homeless children live in Los Angeles, New York, Chicago, Minneapolis, and Houston. Homelessness among children in the nation's capital has increased by a factor of five in recent years.

A report from the General Accounting Office estimated that, on any given night, 186,000 children who are not actually homeless are "precariously housed," living on the verge of homelessness. The Department of Health and Human Services calculates that, over the course of a year, as many as one million youngsters under age 18 lack a permanent home or live on the streets.

Despite the $1.7 billion in federal funds expended through the Stewart B. McKinney Homeless Assistance Act of 1987 and the millions more spent through the Runaway and Homeless Youth Act of 1974, homelessness continues to grow — a disturbing reminder that not all is well in the land of the free.

The future also looks bleak for those categories of young people who no longer live at home, according to the House Select Committee on Children, Youth, and Families. Its late 1989 report, *No Place to Call Home: Discarded Children in America*, concluded that by 1995 nearly a million children no longer living with their parents will cause serious problems for the schools. The study found that between 1985 and 1988 the number of children living in foster care jumped by 23%, while federal funding for welfare services for children rose only 7%.

Foster children are only one of the categories of displaced children, most of whom come from poor families. The number of children in juvenile detention centers rose 27% between 1979 and 1987, while funding fell from $100 million to $66.7 million. The number of children in mental health facilities also soared by 60% between 1983 and 1986. Meanwhile, federal block grants for mental health services declined by $17 million.

Drug and alcohol abuse by parents contributed to these dangerous trends. From 1985 to 1988 the number of children born with drug exposure quadrupled, reaching 375,000 in 1988. Add to that the number of abused or neglected children, which climbed 82% between 1981 and 1988. Of course, not all of these children are poor, but needy children fall into these categories much more frequently than their not-needy counterparts.

Rep. Miller warned that the nation's schools could be "overwhelmed" by such problems in the 1990s. He noted that teachers, counselors, and social workers are already overworked and that none of them "receives the training needed to deal with the complex and difficult problems confronting children and families today."

Clearly, no social problem operates in isolation. Poverty breeds personal and social disintegration. Difficulties in the areas of health, housing, and education are all linked. For example, significant numbers of homeless children suffer a wide range of health disorders. Many risk hearing loss because of untreated ear infections. That in turn leads to serious learning problems. In many homeless shelters, such infectious diseases as tuberculosis and whooping cough run rampant among uninoculated youngsters. Poverty is more than a social label; it is a disease that weakens and often destroys its victims.

HEALTHY GOALS, UNHEALTHY RESULTS

At first glance, it seems that the U.S. has a comprehensive health-care system. For example, we spent $551 billion on health care in 1987. But 37 million Americans, including more than 12 million children, have no health insurance. Uninsured children have a 20% greater chance of poor health and are less likely to have proper immunization against infectious diseases.

Nearly half of all poor children do not receive benefits from Medicaid, despite recent congressional action ordering states to provide more extensive coverage to poor children and pregnant mothers. The National Commission to Prevent Infant Mortality has found that the U.S. ranks 20th among the nations of the world in infant mortality and has urged Congress to take over Medicaid to insure that it reaches *all* infants and pregnant mothers.

This year the Pepper Commission, a bipartisan group of congressional representatives, urged a massive overhaul of the national health system, which is "in total crisis." Among other reforms, the commission called for universal protection for poor children and families. But the $66 billion a year price tag has scared off many potential supporters.

One pregnant woman in four receives no prenatal care during the critical first trimester. Such a mother is three to six times more likely to give birth to a premature, low-birth-weight baby who will be at risk for developmental disability or even death. Ultimately, 10.6 of every 1,000 newborns in the U.S. die — the highest rate in the developed world.

In 1980 Dr. Julius Richmond, then surgeon general of the U.S., published a list of 20 health-care goals for infants and children to be achieved by 1990. Like the recent list of educational goals promulgated by President Bush and the National Governors' Association, the health-care targets were ambitious and essential to heading off social and economic crisis. But by late 1989 the American Academy of Pediatrics, an organization of 37,000 experts on children's medical health, concluded that only one of the 20 goals had been achieved.

That one success was in reducing neonatal mortality: the death rate for infants in the first 28 days after birth has dropped from 9.5 to 6.4 deaths per 1,000. However, other goals, such as improving birth weights and prenatal care and narrowing the gap between racial groups in infant mortality, remain unfulfilled. The mortality rate for black infants is still twice that for white infants, about the same as it was 26 years ago; the infant mortality rate for the entire U.S. population stands at 10.1%, while the rate for African-Americans is 17.9%. (By contrast, the infant mortality rate in Japan is just 4.8%.) Moreover, surviving black infants have nine times more chance than white infants of being neurologically impaired.

Dr. Myron Wegman of the University of Michigan School of Public Health, who conducted the study for the pediatricians, discovered the existence of two separate medical nations within this land. One nation is prosperous, with the latest in health technology and knowledge at its disposal; the other nation is deprived, with death rates and health problems that match those commonly found in the Third World. Dr. Wegman blamed government cuts in health programs and social services during the Reagan Administration for a slowdown that prevented reaching the goals.

IMPACT ON SCHOOLS

What do the mountains of statistics and a heritage of damaged lives mean for educators in the public schools? Surveys of teachers have found disturbing news. The Metropolitan Life Insurance Company's annual *Survey of the American Teacher* discovered that in 1989 American teachers were greatly alarmed at the health and social problems of their students.

Other surveys show that teachers worry about constant pupil turnover, about students' health problems, and about students' preoccupation with family problems. Once again, such concerns are more common among teachers of children from low-income families. Guidance counselors report that, even at the elementary level, they find themselves "dealing with one crisis after another" in a child's life.

Teachers also report that they are seeing more children with learning disabilities. In fact, over the last 10 years the number of children diagnosed as learning disabled has increased 140% — to about 1.9 million children. While educators argue over the meaning of the term and debate possible reasons for the increase, veteran teachers claim that they have never before seen so many children with problems of comprehension and basic skills in their classes.

According to Verna Gray, a veteran teacher in the Chicago schools, poverty leads to more problems than just the lack of the basic academic skills needed to succeed in school. "Many of these youngsters don't have any self-esteem or even the belief that they can achieve," she notes.

The effects on the schools of increasing numbers of children living in poverty may not be completely clear, and the details are certainly debatable. But no one disputes that there are serious effects — or that the effects are negative.

WHAT SOCIETY MUST DO

No single individual or group can successfully tackle all the factors that contribute to child poverty. The lack of jobs that pay a decent wage, for example, is the biggest contributor to poverty in small towns, cities, and suburbs. Clearly, this is a national problem that can be addressed only by a comprehensive economic policy that gives top priority to the creation of jobs that pay a living wage. A number of family experts believe that an even greater increase in the minimum wage than the one recently passed by Congress is essential to help the working poor escape a lifetime of poverty.

Some effective programs already exist to deal with almost every aspect of the cycle of child poverty. But the programs that work have never been properly funded. Head Start is the classic example. Head Start was created by the antipoverty legislation of the 1960s, and a number of studies have documented its positive impact. One study found that nearly 60% of the Head Start graduates were employed at age 19, compared to just 32% of a control group. Only 49% of the control group had graduated from high school, while 67% of the former Head Start students had earned high school diplomas. Nearly 40% of the Head Start graduates had taken some college courses, while just 21% of the control group had taken any coursework beyond high school.

Such statistics add up to lives and money saved. One dollar invested in Head Start saves $7 in later social services that are not needed. Numbers of this kind have convinced many, but Head Start, which celebrates its 25th birthday this year, still serves only one in five eligible students.

That situation might be about to change. There are hopeful signs that some basic services for poor children could improve in the next few years if the federal government reasserts its leadership in child care, health coverage, and education.

Major political players are lining up in favor of a vastly extended support system for early care and education. The National Governors' Association has made early childhood learning a top goal, and President Bush's education budget called for a modest increase of $245 million for Head Start. Most important, the mammoth child-care bill hammered out by Congress over the last two years will bolster Head Start by as much as $600 million over the next five years. At press time, only a veto by President Bush, who wishes to shift to the states more of the burden of funding the program, can block what has become the most important piece of antipoverty legislation in the last 25 years.

Educators worry that, as the number of children in poverty grows, education for those children — without sharp increases in funding for Chapter 1 and Head Start — can only get worse, not better. Susan Frost, executive director of the Committee for Education Funding, says that "there is no alternative to Chapter 1 and Head Start, which are estimated to serve only one-half and one-fifth respectively of eligible children." The needs of such children, she adds, are not going to be met by restructuring.

Meanwhile, there is growing public support for offering a wider array of social and health services in the schools. In September 1989 a survey by the *Washington Post* and ABC News found widespread support for a variety of nontraditional services in the schools: the dissemination of information about birth control, counseling for psychiatric and drug-related problems, more nutrition information, and so on. Likewise, the 21st Annual Gallup Poll of the Public's Attitudes Toward the Public Schools (published in the September 1989 *Kappan*) found 74% of the public willing to spend more tax dollars to screen children for health programs, 69% willing to spend more money for Head Start, and 58% willing to spend more for day care for young children whose parents work.

WHAT SCHOOLS CAN DO

The prevalence of child poverty in the U.S. is enough to make any educator shudder — and not just because of the damage to the children. All too often the public schools are given the burden of overcoming economic and social inequities, usually without adequate resources to confront these difficult problems. Indeed, children who have been maimed by such new social epidemics as homelessness and crack use by pregnant women are already testing the resources and tolerance of the schools. Many reformers believe that, instead of another add-on program, the schools need a coordinated and concerted societal effort to deal with these problems.

Still, all across the nation, educators are struggling to meet the crisis with innovative solutions and more of their legendary dedication. The many examples of their efforts fall into two major categories: mobilizing parents and integrating community and health resources into the school.

PARENT INVOLVEMENT

Some educators are reexamining the roles parents can play in the schools. But poor parents face significant obstacles to becoming involved. According to the National Committee for Citizens in Education, "A parent who speaks limited English or who was herself a school dropout is unlikely to volunteer as a member of a school improvement council. A poor parent who has no automobile may not be able to send his child to a better public school located outside the attendance area — even when the option is available — unless transportation is provided by the school district. These barriers to full participation can be removed with training, encouragement, and resources that insure equal access."

Nevertheless, many educators are putting their energies into parent solutions — and getting results.

• The Center for Successful Child Development, known as the Beethoven Project, is a family-oriented early childhood intervention program at the Robert Taylor Homes, a public housing project on the south side of Chicago. Sponsored by the Chicago Urban League and by the Ounce of Prevention Fund, the Beethoven Project opened in 1987. Some 155 families now benefit from a variety of educational, social, and medical services for young children who will ultimately enroll in the Beethoven Elementary School.

• In Missouri, Parents as Teachers combines an early childhood component with an education program for parents. It began as a pilot program in 1981, and today all 543 Missouri school districts are required to provide certain services to families, including parent education, periodic screening through age 4 to detect developmental problems, and educational programs for those 3- and 4-year-olds who are developmentally delayed. The program is not restricted to poor children, but it can catch their problems early, and results have been encouraging.

• James Comer, director of the School Development Program at Yale University, is working with 100 inner-city schools across the country to create management teams made up of parents, teachers, and mental health professionals. The aims are to improve the teachers' knowledge of child development, to involve parents, and to provide children with community resources normally found outside the school.

• In California and Missouri a new approach, known as the Accelerated Schools Program, is trying to change parents' attitudes toward their children. The Accelerated Schools Program attempts to raise parents' expectations about what their children can do, while it also focuses on giving literacy training to the parents. The goal is to empower parents so that they can become involved in their children's education. The program currently operates in two schools in California and in seven schools in Missouri.

A number of researchers and scholars have endorsed the idea of parent involvement. For example, Harold Stevenson of the University of Michigan released a study in 1989 that found that, contrary to popular belief, black and Hispanic mothers are keenly interested in their children's education and want to be involved despite the economic and social barriers to their doing so.

Parents can play a key role in many aspects of a school, providing a sense of community that can nurture as well as protect children in a school setting. During a cold Boston winter, for example, parents noticed that some children at David A. Ellis School in Roxbury did not have warm jackets. The parents established a clothing exchange to make sure that the children were warm on their way to school.

"The parents are part of the everyday life of the school," says Owen Haleem of the Institute for Responsive Education (IRE) at the Boston University School of Education. Two years ago the IRE organized a Schools Reaching Out Project. In January 1990 it organized a national network to increase parent and community involvement in urban public schools serving low-income communities. Known as the League of Schools Reaching Out, the network now includes 37 schools in 19 urban school districts.

"New relationships with low-income parents must be fashioned in order to break the link between poverty and school failure," according to Don Davies, president of the IRE. Two schools were part of a two-year pilot study of ways to develop these new relationships. The David A. Ellis School in Roxbury and Public School 111 in District 2 on the west side of Manhattan each converted one classroom near the principal's office into an on-site parents' center and initially paid a full-time "key teacher" to serve as a link between the school, the students' families, and the community. P.S. 111 offered classes in English as a second language (ESL) for Spanish-speaking parents and organized a lending library for educational toys and games. Parents at Ellis

School offered ESL and formed a support group to study for the high-school-equivalency exams. Both schools send trained parents and community members to visit other parents at home and organize collaborative projects between teachers and parents.

The IRE pilot study was modeled, in part, on a similar program in Liverpool, England, where each school has a coordinator of social services. The IRE programs at P.S. 111 and at Ellis School try to combat the idea that parents need only to come to school for meetings. According to Haleem, "Our goal was to work with regular public schools to build fundamentally different relationships with low-income parents." And both schools have recorded achievement gains, which, Haleem notes, may not be connected to the parent involvement program. But then again they might be.

To some child advocates, *family* literacy is the key both to involving parents and to improving student achievement. A Department of Defense study conducted in the 1980s found that the most important variable in determining the educational attainment of 16- to 23-year-olds was the educational level of their mothers. Indeed, Thomas Sticht of Applied Behavioral and Cognitive Sciences, Inc., in San Diego argues that federal programs need to work with families.

Next year the Department of Education will spend $10,477,000 for Even Start, a program of financial assistance to local agencies that conduct projects in family-centered education. Privately funded and family-centered literacy projects, such as the Kenan Family Literacy Project in Louisville, Kentucky, also teach basic skills to parents while their children attend a preschool. Operating in seven schools in Kentucky and North Carolina, the Kenan Family Literacy Project teaches parents to read and to teach their children to read. This program was a model for the Foundation for Family Literacy, initiated by First Lady Barbara Bush.

For poor children whose parents remain uninvolved, schools may have to come up with other answers. An increasing number of social scientists argue that just one relationship between an adult and a disadvantaged child in stressful conditions can make a significant difference.

Public/Private Ventures, a nonprofit organization based in Philadelphia, examined five programs involving adults in the community and at-risk students. It found that the bonds that formed between the generations helped the youngsters weather crises, gave them a sense of stability, and improved their sense of their own competence.

SCHOOLS AS SOCIAL CENTERS

Indeed, many educators feel that they'll be able to address the needs of poor children only if the community works with the schools.

"The most urgent task is to regenerate families deep in the inner cities," Roger Wilkins, a professor of history at George Mason University, argued in the *New York Times* last year. "While employment, early childhood education, and child-care programs are critical parts of such an effort, it is essential that the public schools become the focus of special remedies," Wilkins asserted. "In addition, the schools would become centers of the community for the children they serve and for their parents and grandparents."

Indeed, more and more schools are designing programs that link social services and academic programs. But such ventures require schools and communities to overcome the instinct to protect their own turf and to agree to work together as one entity.

A number of states — including New York, Oregon, South Carolina, and Florida — have initiated new efforts to coordinate services for children. The problem is that child services are so spread out. In California, for example, 160 state programs for children operate out of 45 agencies. Schools must organize the services in ways that funnel them directly toward the complex needs of poor youngsters.

One initiative that helps not only poor children but all children coming of age today was started by Edward Zigler, Sterling Professor of Psychology and director of the Bush Center in Child Development and Social Policy at Yale University. Zigler has touted "Schools for the 21st Century" — schools that function as community centers, linking a host of family-support services to help children overcome social, psychological, and health problems. The approach includes home visitations, assistance for parents with infants, day care for 3- to 5-year-olds, before- and after-school care for school-age children, teen pregnancy prevention programs, and adult literacy classes. Zigler's program began in Independence, Missouri, and has spread to five states.

One educator who agrees that the school needs to take on a broader role in the lives of children is Allan Shedlin, Jr. In 1987 the Elementary School Center that Shedlin directs called for a reconceptualization of the elementary school as the locus of advocacy for all children.

"Traditional sources of support for the child — the family, the neighborhood, schools, social and religious organizations, nutritional and health care programs — are fragmented or do not exist at all for many children," says Shedlin. School has become the only agency that deals with every child, every day. Thus the school should serve as the center of advocacy for children.

The National School Boards Association (NSBA) argues that school officials cannot wait until all the desired elements are in place before taking action, and it suggests a number of remedies. Schools should:

• establish a local policy to help all children learn — perhaps by means of counseling programs, tutoring programs, or parent involvement;

• examine the needs of a community and determine whether parents need day-care services, health services, job skills, or the help of volunteers;

• develop a demographic profile of the school system — find out whether families are in poverty and whether there are single-parent families, migrant families, immigrant families — and communicate this information to all people in the school system;

• define and identify all youth at risk — considering such factors as student absenteeism, poor grades, low test scores in math or reading, chemical dependency, boredom, and family mobility;

• follow student progress in school by keeping comprehensive records;

• evaluate programs that have already been implemented;

• give administrators and teachers flexibility in helping students at risk and make use of student mentors, faculty advisors, teaching teams, and tutoring;

• involve parents in children's schooling; and

• work with local businesses, agencies, and organizations to develop and fund programs.

Carol Pringle didn't believe that she could wait any longer to help the poor children in her Seattle community. In April 1989 the mother of three and former schoolteacher organized a two-room schoolhouse called First Place. It is now one of a dozen programs in the country designed for homeless children. Technically it is a nonprofit agency, but it works in cooperation with the Seattle School District, which provides buses each day to round up children (kindergarten through grade 6) from homeless shelters all over the city.

Two salaried teachers and a number of volunteers have adapted the regular school curriculum for this new clientele. But the school also finds shoes for the children and, in addition to basic academics, provides breakfast, lunch, and a safe environment. Students stay an average of four to five weeks, but some attend for only a single day. They come from shelters for battered women or live with mothers who can't afford housing. Some are from families that move constantly in an effort to find work.

Other school systems have different programs. The Harbor Summit School in San Diego is near the St. Vincent de Paul Joan Kroc Center. The Tacoma (Washington) School District and the Tacoma YWCA run the Eugene P. Tone School.

However, some school officials believe that homeless children should not be placed in separate programs. Yvonne Rafferty, director of research with Advocates for Children, claims that all children should be in regular programs. New York City prohibits any separate programs for homeless children, and Minneapolis tries to provide homeless children with transportation to their former school.

Essentially the solution to the problem of schooling for homeless children is a state responsibility. The McKinney Act of 1987 grants money to states to develop plans so that homeless children can gain access to the schools.

Like Carol Pringle, Carol Cole couldn't wait any longer. Just as the first wave of crack babies was hitting school systems across the nation, she was hard at work creating a special program for such children. The Salvin Special Education School in Los Angeles is a two-year-old program designed to aid children born to crack-addicted mothers. Eight 3- and 4-year-olds work with three teachers, who give the children as much individual attention as possible. The school has a pediatrician, a psychologist, several social workers, and a speech and language specialist. According to Cole, the home lives of the children are "chaotic." Salvin School reaches only eight children at a time. But 375,000 drug-exposed babies are born annually.

A survey released by the NSBA in February 1990 found that urban school districts face an "awesome challenge" in trying to provide more social services when federal aid for such programs has declined in real dollars. The survey of 52 urban school districts found that the proportion of resources devoted to attacking social and health programs puts "a severe strain on local school districts' budgets, draining their coffers."

Jonathan Wilson, chairman of the NSBA Council of Urban Boards of Education, argues that local resources are running dry. If urban schools are to improve their performance, he maintains, they need dramatic hikes in state and federal funding and in Chapter 1.

IN THE END the Children's Defense Fund calculates that the key investments to help rescue children from poverty are not prohibitively expensive. The CDF estimates that universal health care for children and pregnant women is a relatively inexpensive prevention measure and is a far better social policy than trying to remediate social ills later. In addition, the CDF figures that the costs of eliminating poverty and child poverty are not as high as many people think. Good nutrition, basic health care, and early education can make a big difference.

"We must shed the myth that all poor children need massive, long-term public intervention," Marian Wright Edelman told those attending the annual meeting of the CDF in Washington, D.C., in March 1990. "Certainly, some children are so damaged that they need such help," Edelman allows. "But millions of poor children need only modest help. They need child care, not foster care; a checkup, not an intensive-care bed; a tutor, not a guardian; drug education, not detoxification; a scholarship, not a detention cell. But it has been hard to get them what they need — even when we know what to do and when it saves us money."

According to CDF estimates (based on 1987 figures), the cost of eliminating child poverty is $17.22 billion; the cost of eliminating poverty in families with children, $26.874 billion; the cost of eliminating poverty among all persons, $51.646 billion. That last figure is equivalent to only 1% of our gross national product. Eliminating poverty in families with children would cost only about 1.5% of the total expenditures of federal, state, and local governments combined.

Indeed, if the nation's largest bankers are capable of writing off billions of dollars in debts owed by developing nations, if the U.S. Congress can almost nonchalantly commit $325 billion dollars to bailing out the unregulated and marauding savings-and-loan industry, if the public can live with military excesses and a variety of foreign affairs ventures, then surely we can renegotiate the terms of the escalating human debt embodied by the children of poverty.

Congress, the states, and local communities must rewrite the options of opportunity for *all* our children, but especially for our poor children. We must be willing to write the checks that guarantee poor children a real chance of success from the moment they are conceived until the moment that they receive as much education as they can absorb. Only then will the tragedy of children deprived from birth of a dignified life be banished forever from this land.

A Resource Guide

Numerous organizations, foundations, and education groups are currently focusing on the plight of children in America. Listed below are a few sources of more information on the subject.

ORGANIZATIONS

☑ *Children's Defense Fund* is a private, nonprofit child-advocacy group that offers extensive research, information, and publications. Among the CDF publications are: *CDF Reports* ($29.95 a year); *Children 1990: A Report Card, Briefing Book, and Action Primer* ($2.95); and *The Health of America's Children* ($12.95). For a free listing of materials, write to: CDF, 122 C St. N.W., Washington, DC 20001.

☑ *Family Resource Coalition* is a national membership organization that publishes a variety of materials. Individual membership is $30; agency/organization membership, $60. For information, write to: Family Resource Coalition, 230 N. Michigan Ave., Suite 1625, Chicago, IL 60601.

☑ *Hispanic Policy Development Project* publishes the *Research Bulletin*, a free newsletter. To obtain a copy, write to: Hispanic Policy Development Project, Suite 310, 1001 Connecticut Ave. N.W., Washington, DC 20036.

☑ *Institute for American Values* is a nonpartisan, nonprofit policy organization concerned with issues affecting the American family. It publishes *Family Affairs*, a free newsletter. To obtain a copy, write to: Institute for American Values, 250 W. 57th St., Suite 2415, New York, NY 10107.

☑ *Institute for Responsive Education* is a 17-year-old nonprofit public interest group that publishes a variety of reports, as well as the magazine *Equity and Choice* (one-year subscription, $15) and *Building Parent-Teacher Partnerships: Prospects from the Perspective of the Schools Reaching Out Project*, by Jean Krasnow ($6). For more information, write to: Institute for Responsive Education, 605 Commonwealth Ave., Boston, MA 02215.

☑ *National Committee for Citizens in Education* is a 16-year-old nonprofit organization dedicated to parent involvement and local action. It produces and distributes publications and operates a toll-free hotline (800/Network). For more information, write to: NCCE, 10840 Little Patuxent Parkway, Suite 301, Columbia, MD 21044.

☑ *Southern Education Foundation* publishes studies on southern states. For more information, write to: Southern Education Foundation, 135 Auburn Ave., Atlanta, GA 30303.

☑ *Youth Policy Institute* publishes *Youth Record*, a semimonthly report on federal policy ($75 a year). For more information, write to: Youth Policy Institute, 1221 Massachusetts Ave. N.W., Suite B, Washington, DC 20005.

BOOKS AND ARTICLES

☑ Jonathan Kozol, *Rachel and Her Children: Homeless Families in America* (Crown Publishers, 225 Park Ave. S., New York, NY 10003, 1988).

☑ Lisbeth B. Schorr, *Within Our Reach: Breaking the Cycle of Disadvantage* (Doubleday, 666 Fifth Ave., New York, NY 10103, 1989).

☑ James P. Comer, "Educating Poor Minority Children," *Scientific American*, November 1988, pp. 42-48.

REPORTS

☑ *An Imperiled Generation: Saving the Urban Schools* (Princeton University Press, 3175 Princeton Pike, Lawrenceville, NJ 08648, 1988). The price is $7.50.

☑ *A Proper Inheritance: Investing in the Self-Sufficiency of Poor Families* (Center for Social Policy Studies, George Washington University, 1730 K St. N.W., Suite 701, Washington, DC 20006, July 1989). The price is $2.05 for postage; include a 9" x 12" self-addressed envelope.

☑ *A Survey of Public Education in the Nation's Urban School Districts, 1989* (Special Program Services Department, National School Boards Association, 1680 Duke St., Alexandria, VA 22314, 1990). The price is $35.

☑ *Children in Need: Investment Strategies for the Educationally Disadvantaged* (Committee for Economic Development, 477 Madison Ave., New York, NY 10022, 1988). The price is $10.50 plus $3 postage.

☑ *Conditions of Children in California* (Policy Analysis for California Education, School of Education, University of California, Berkeley, CA 94720, 1989). The price is $20.

☑ *Family Support, Education, and Involvement: A Guide for State Action* (Council of Chief State School Officers, Resource Center on Educational Equity, 379 Hall of the States, 400 North Capitol St. N.W., Washington, DC 20001, 1989). The price is $10.

☑ *Kids Count: Data Book, State Profiles of Child Well-Being* (Center for the Study of Social Policy, 1250 I St. N.W., Washington, DC 20005, 1990). The price is $10.

☑ *Making the Grade: A Report Card on American Youth* (National Collaboration for Youth, 1319 F St. N.W., Suite 601, Washington, DC 20004, 1990).

☑ *Our Future and Our Only Hope: A Survey of City Halls Regarding Children and Families* (National League of Cities, Publications Sales, 1301 Pennsylvania Ave. N.W., Washington, DC 20004, 1989). The price is $10.

☑ *Partners in Growth: Elder Mentors and At-Risk Youth* (Public/Private Ventures, 399 Market St., Philadelphia, PA 19106, 1989). Single copies are free.

☑ *State of Black America* (National Urban League, Communications Department, 500 E. 62nd St., New York, NY 10021, 1989). The price is $19.

☑ William Braden et al., "The Critical Years: City Kids Left Behind at the Start." This is a five-part series that ran in the *Chicago Sun-Times* from 26 June through 30 June 1988; it is available through ERIC.

☑ William T. Grant Foundation Commission on Work, Family and Citizenship, *The Forgotten Half: Pathways to Success for America's Youth and Young Families* (William T. Grant Foundation Commission on Youth and America's Future, Dept. K, Suite 301, 1001 Connecticut Ave. N.W., Washington, DC 20036, 1988). Single copies free.

☑ Harold L. Hodgkinson, *The Same Client: The Demographics of Education and Service Delivery System* (Institute for Educational Leadership, Publication Department, 1001 Connecticut Ave. N.W., Suite 310, Washington, DC 20036, 1989). The price is $12.

☑ Michael A. Sherraden and Isaac Shapiro, *The Working Poor: America's Contradiction* (George Warren Brown School of Social Work, Washington University, St. Louis, MO 63130, 1990).

VIDEOS

☑ "Joining Forces: Educating Every Child for a Healthy and Productive Future" is a videotape of a teleconference held on 21 February 1990. It is available from the National Association of State Boards of Education, 1012 Cameron St., Alexandria, VA 22314. The price is $65.

☑ "Learning to Change: Schools of Excellence for At-Risk Students" is a videotape released in 1990 about schools serving low-income students that have turned themselves around. It is available from the Southern Regional Council, 60 Walton St. N.W., Atlanta, GA 30303-2199. The price is $30.

Economic Issues Related to Child Care and Early Childhood Education

Marian Wright Edelman

Children's Defense Fund, Washington, D.C.

Seeing the economy and social structure of America as inexorably linked, Edelman explores the benefits of adequate child care to the family, the child, and the nation. She takes seriously the slogan, today's child is tomorrow's worker.

There are many false dichotomies in our perceptions of what constitutes public policy in the United States today. Nowhere is this more evident than in the way in which we assign separate categories to "social policy" and "economic policy" and fail to take into account the interrelationship and synergy between the two.

One glaring and critical example is our failure to recognize the connections between safe, affordable, quality child care and the barriers that prevent tens of thousands of Americans—present and future—from working to maximize the productivity of our society and our economy. The child of today is the worker of tomorrow. We say and hear this phrase over and over again—so often that we barely consider its implications. The opportunities available to a child help determine not only his or her eventual self-sufficiency or lack thereof, but also the degree to which that child becomes a productive adult who contributes to building the nation's economy.

The care and education of preschool children is an issue that has arrived fairly recently on the national policy agenda. Twenty years ago relatively few mothers of young children worked outside the home and quality child care was a luxury for a wealthy minority. Today, it is essential for the economic health and stability of millions of American families. This dramatic change has been stimulated by the inexorable march of mothers of young children into the work force, the increase in single-parent families, the decline in real wages of young families, and the recognition that too many of our children are growing up ill-equipped to succeed in the world economy, let alone to

generate the level of income supports that will soon be needed by aging parents and grandparents.

Just what is this connection between the availability of day care and early childhood education and the future of the U.S. economy? By examining three key elements in the equation—the family, the individual, and the nation as a whole—we can arrive at some answers.

THE FAMILY

The most important factor in a child's healthy development is the existence of a nurturing, positive family environment. A family in which parents are losing the struggle to find work and to pay the rent and food bills may also be losing the fight for the healthy development of their children. Currently, economic uncertainty and poverty pose a constant threat to millions of American children. Particularly hard hit are the newly formed, young families with children who, despite the economic recovery of the 1980s, have actually lost economic ground compared with their peers in the 1970s. While real median family income for households headed by individuals forty-five to fifty-four rose 3 percent between 1973 and 1986, it actually declined more than 10 percent for families with a twenty-five to thirty-four-year-old head of household, and 24 percent for those with a household head under age twenty-five.[1]

Equally disturbing is the increasing incidence of births to unmarried, teenage mothers. Although total births to teen-agers have declined since 1970, the percentage of all teen births that are to unmarried teens rocketed from 13.9 in 1950 to 30 in 1970 to 58.7 in 1985.[2] Both these young mothers and their children face high risks of failure in the educational system and of living in poverty.

According to Census Bureau projections, the decade beginning in 1990 will mark a watershed in the demographic evolution of the American family:

From *Teachers College Record*, Vol. 90, No. 3, Spring 1989, pp. 342-351. Copyright © 1989 by Teachers College, Columbia University.

The 1990s will be the first decade to begin with a majority of mothers of young children (55 percent) in the work force, representing an increase of over 80 percent since 1970.

The population of children under 10 from single-parent households will have risen from 6 million to 8.9 million—a 48 percent increase from the 1980s.

The population of children under six will have increased 3.3 million to 23.0 million in 1990 (and will then begin to decline).[3]

In addition, the Department of Labor predicts that by 1995, more than 80 percent of women between the ages of twenty-four and forty-four will be in the work force. This compares with about half of the women in that age group in 1970.[4]

BUFFER AGAINST WELFARE DEPENDENCY AND POVERTY

For many of the still-growing population of single parents, child care is the only thing that stands between them and welfare dependency. If teen mothers, for example, do not have access to reliable and affordable child care, they are unlikely to return to high school or to find some other way of completing their education and prepare for the work force—a crucial step toward becoming independent and productive adults and avoiding additional pregnancies.

In a 1983 census bureau report on child-care arrangements among working mothers, single mothers cited difficulties with child-care arrangements as a major problem in seeking and keeping jobs. Forty-five percent of these women reported that they would be able to take a job if affordable child care were available.[5]

Similar results were reported in a study conducted by the General Accounting Office, which found that some 60 percent of respondents thought that lack of child care prevented their participation in work-training programs.[6] One of these parents, Annie Bridgers, a Washington, D.C., mother of three, told a congressional committee that access to subsidized day care enabled her to complete a job-training program, get off public assistance, and secure a job that generates income to support the family.[7] In the same hearing, another witness recounted: "Divorce took me from the upper middle class to complete poverty." With assistance from a social services program, she was able to enroll her young daughter in child care, attend college, and earn the bachelor's and law degrees that now make her a productive member of society.[8]

Such individual success stories are echoed in the collective experience of participants in initiatives such as Massachusetts's ET program, an employment, skills training, and education program including a substantial day-care component, that has placed over 30,000 welfare recipients in jobs since 1983.[9]

Experience shows that providing child care does

make it possible for more parents to work to support their families and that making child care available to low-income working families costs less than maintaining them on welfare.[10] For many two-parent families, the second income, made possible by the availability of child care, is the only thing that stands between them and poverty.[11] Child care helps such families close the door on dependency and become economically self-sufficient in several ways: It enables them to replace welfare checks with salary checks and to stay on the job without the loss of work hours stemming from uncertain (or even dangerous), undependable, and discontinuous child-care arrangements; and it permits one or both adults in a family to work additional hours, thus increasing the family income.

HOW MUCH CHILD CARE AND FOR WHOM?

There is abundant evidence that lack of reliable, affordable child care is a major obstacle to parents' finding work, remaining employed, and increasing family income by working additional hours. More than a third of the women interviewed for a study reported in the *American Journal of Sociology* stated that they would like to work additional hours but are prevented from doing so by lack of available child care.[12] Research by University of Miami economists on the links between child care and economic self-sufficiency among low-income families living in public housing revealed that a 50 percent increase in the size of an on-site child-care center would result in a 13.5 percent rise in hours worked by residents and a 19.5 percent increase in their earnings.[13]

While availability and dependability of child-care services influence families' ability to use and benefit from them, an equally critical factor in access is cost. "Child care costs, the newest major expense for families, now consume nearly 10 percent of the average family's income and 20 percent of the income for poor families," noted Representative George Miller (D.-Calif.) in a congressional hearing.[14] This increase in the proportion of income needed for child care is occurring at a time when the average income for young families with children has declined and other costs, such as paying for housing, are increasing.

Because of the cost factor, the families whose youngsters most need child care are the least able to afford it. In 1985, fewer than one-third of four-year-olds and 17 percent of three-year-olds in families with incomes below $10,000 a year were enrolled in preschool programs. In that same year, however, 67 percent of four-year-olds and 54 percent of three-year-olds whose families had incomes of $35,000 a year or more attended preschool programs.[15]

If poor families do figure out a way to pay for child care from their low or sporadic incomes, all too often the care they can afford may be in an unsafe or inadequately staffed facility, such as a neighbor's home. Few are able to afford the cost of developmentally enriching child-care programs that would increase the chances of poor and at-risk children to overcome the health, environmental, and other disadvantages that accompany poverty. Currently, the highly successful, federally supported Head Start Program serves less than 20 percent of eligible children.[16]

This brings us to the second element of the equation: the relationship of child care and early childhood experience to the child's future role and competence in society and in the economy.

THE CHILD

Just as the availability of safe, affordable child care is linked to the ability of low-income parents to move from dependency to self-sufficiency, there is also linkage between quality child care and preschool programs and the nation's future.

At the most basic level, a child requires protection from a health- or life-threatening environment. The sad litany of accidents and other tragedies such as burning to death in a clothes dryer, drowning in a well, or being caught in a home fire that have taken the lives of children in inadequate care (or at home alone because of lack of access to care) will continue to unfold until we commit ourselves to providing safe, adequate care for all who need it. Our vision for our children must, however, go far beyond mere physical survival.

The first high school graduating class of the twenty-first century entered first grade in September 1988. These preschoolers are future leaders, workers, parents, college students, taxpayers, soldiers, and the hope of the twenty-first century. Many of them and their young siblings are off to a healthy start, but millions are not:

One in four of these children is poor.

One in three is nonwhite, of whom two in five are poor.

One in five is at risk of becoming a teen parent.

One in six is in a family in which neither parent has a job.

One in seven is at risk of dropping out of school.[17]

For these children and those that will follow them, access to quality child-care services may determine not only their prospects for success in school, but their prospects for success in life, for example, the risk of falling prey to dependency, handicapping conditions, psychological problems, and even crime.

LONG-TERM EFFECTS

Success in school depends on a foundation of psychological development and social skills as well as on intellectual factors. Researchers and others have found that youngsters who lack access to quality child care may arrive at school ill-prepared to succeed. Two decades of experience with Head Start and other quality early childhood programs, however, show that poor and other at-risk youngsters can be helped by such programs to overcome their disadvantages and become successful in school, work, and social roles. Among the education-related benefits cited for children who attend preschool compared with those who do not are the following:

Better grades, fewer failing marks, fewer retentions in grade, and fewer absences in elementary school.

Less need of special education services and fewer placements in special education classes.

Improved literacy and curiosity in school.

Greater likelihood of completing high school and of continuing education beyond high school.[18]

Examples abound. Participants in South Carolina's half-day child-development program for four-year-olds arrived in school better prepared to learn to read than those who did not have the experience. Participants in Syracuse, New York's early education program were studied ten years later and found to have higher academic achievement and less school absence than peers who did not participate. The Perry Preschool Program in Michigan was found to have "increased the percentage of persons who were literate, employed and enrolled in postsecondary education, whereas it . . . reduced the percentages who were school dropouts, labelled mentally retarded, on welfare or arrested for delinquent and criminal activity."[19] In sum, the effects of quality child care and preschool education endure long beyond a child's entry into kindergarten or first grade.

At the same time, it is important to realize that the need for child care does not end when a child goes to kindergarten or first grade. The importance of providing after-school care was exhibited dramatically when the editors of *Spring*, a magazine for fourth, fifth, and sixth graders, asked their readers to write to them about a situation they found "scary." The editors were stunned to discover that nearly 70 percent of the seven thousand letters that poured in dealt with fear of being home alone, most while parents were working.[20] In interviews with more than one thousand teachers, the Metropolitan Life Insurance Company found that the majority cited isolation and lack of supervision after school as the major reason children have difficulty in school.[21]

THE NATION

In 1978, young people between the ages of sixteen and twenty-four made up 27 percent of the working-age population, but, by 1995, they will account for only 18 percent.[22] The rapid decline in the percentage of young people and children in the population makes it essential that we devise ways to maximize the competence of our future work force. As this demographic trend plays itself out, the value of each individual young worker to business and industry increases.

Research is beginning to demonstrate what common sense had told us for many years. In addition to the social benefits of high-quality child care, such as less delinquency and fewer dropouts, there are also measurable economic benefits:

> The value of benefits to participants and to the nation far exceeds the initial cost of the program. In the case of the Perry Project, it is estimated that a $1 investment in preschool education returns $6 in taxpayer savings because of lower education costs, lower costs of public welfare and crime, and higher worker productivity.[23]

> The "head start" afforded by quality child care or preschool enhances a child's prospects of being employable as an adult, and of earning more (and paying more taxes) than he or she would have without the strong foundation built in the early years.[24]

> Employers are more likely to be spared the cost and difficulties associated with hiring workers who lack basic skills and of training or retraining them.[25]

> Employers and the economy benefit from quality, dependable child care since the working parents who use the child-care services are more productive on the job.[26]

A *Fortune* magazine survey of 405 employed parents in dual-earner families identified several ways in which lack of child care detracts from the ability of parents to carry out their work effectively. For parents who lacked child care, the absence of such service was one of the most significant predictors of job absenteeism. In addition, parents who had access to some child care but had to contend with breakdowns in the system were more likely to arrive at work late, leave early, and exhibit stress-related symptoms, all of which undermine their effectiveness on the job.[27]

Employers who have provided child-care services or assisted employees to find them think that they have been rewarded. Harry L. Freeman of the American Express Company describes the benefits of employer-sponsored child care in this way: "When employees know their children are in good hands, tardiness and absenteeism are lower . . . recruitment and retention are easier . . . morale and self-esteem are better . . . and productivity is higher."[28]

The experience of American Express is not unique. Between 1983 and 1987, the number of employers providing some type of child care assistance to their employees increased 400 percent.[29] Assistance ranges from sponsoring seminars on parenting, to helping employees find child care, to increasing the supply of family day-care centers, to sponsoring on-site centers. Few employers, however, offer a full-scale program or actually help their employees pay for child care. Of those that do, the form of assistance most often provided is a "salary reduction plan" in which up to $5,000 in child-care expenses may be deducted from the employee's salary, thus reducing his or her tax liability. This system, obviously, tends to benefit more highly paid employees.

Despite the increase in the number and variety of employer-sponsored child-care services, they are the least frequently offered of all employee benefits. It is estimated that only three thousand of the nation's six million employers offer some type of child-care service; the majority of employers that offer on-site child care are hospitals, using the service as an incentive for recruiting nurses. Expenditures for early education in the 1985–1986 school year were $1.5 million—a tiny fraction of the $140 billion spent on education preschool through secondary.[30] Thus, despite some progress, child-care assistance appears to remain a low priority in both government and industry.

THE PUBLIC ROLE

In the twenty years since we began debating the value of early childhood programs, the chorus of voices calling for a commitment to quality care has expanded to include representatives of many segments of our society, from parents and social-program advocates to economic and business leaders, to religious organizations and public officials. This chorus of voices representing so many disparate segments of our society is sending a clear message that our increasing need for child care and early education can be met only through a partnership of the federal government, state and local governments, and the private sector.

In recent years, business and government have endorsed the concept of "early investment" in children, a concept that places child care and education of youth at the heart of the country's future economic well-being and involves government, education, and industry in partnership to sponsor educational improvement. The nation's governors espoused this viewpoint in their 1986 report *Time for Results*.[31] The concept is articulated by the Committee for Economic Development, a group of 225 corporate officers and university presidents, in the introduction to *Children in Need*: "This nation cannot continue to compete and prosper in the global arena when more than one fifth of our children live in poverty and a third grow up in ignorance. And if the nation cannot compete, it cannot lead."[32] In 1988, more than 130 national organizations united to form the Alliance for Better Child Care to work for congressional passage of the Act for Better Child Care (S. 1885, H. 3660), a measure that will help provide safe, affordable, quality child care for the low-income families who so desperately need it.

As the 1980s draw to a close, we are struggling to increase productivity and restore our competitiveness in world markets. We are experiencing the pain that comes from being bested by nations that have placed a higher priority on preparing all of their children for productive roles in the national economy. We must act now to reverse the effects of the trends that are crippling our future work force at an early age. A commitment to providing early childhood education is more than a logical extension of the commitment we already make to children from five to eighteen, and to college students. It is a national imperative. As the population of youth declines, every one of our children becomes more precious to us, not just to our families but to our economy.

Until we as a nation commit ourselves to starting at the beginning, we will always be playing catch-up. Our business leaders know this. Many of our political leaders are saying it. Now it is time to do something about it. Our nation cannot afford, morally or economically, to continue to waste this most precious of resources.

NOTES

1. *Children's Defense Budget, FY 1989* (Washington, D.C.: Children's Defense Fund, 1988), p. 85.

2. *Teenage Pregnancy: An Advocate's Guide to the Numbers* (Washington, D.C.: Adolescent Pregnancy Prevention Clearinghouse, Children's Defense Fund, January/March 1988), p. 11.

3. U.S. Department of Commerce, Bureau of Census, *Current Population Reports*, Series P-25, No. 952, "Projections of the Population of the United States by Age, Sex, and Race: 1983 to 2030" (May 1984), Table 6, Middle Series.

4. "American Families in Tomorrow's Economy" (Hearing before the Select Committee on Children, Youth, and Families, U.S. House of Representatives, July 1, 1987), p. 11.

5. U.S. Bureau of Census, *Current Population Reports*, Series P-23, No. 129, "Child-Care Arrangements of Working Mothers, June 1982" (Washington, D.C.: U.S. Government Printing Office, 1983), Table H.

6. U.S. General Accounting Office, *Work and Welfare: Current AFDC Work Programs and Implications for Federal Policy*, GAO/HRD 87–34 (Washington, D.C., January 1987), p. 86.

7. "Child Care: Key to Employment in a Changing Economy," Hearing before the Select Committee on Children, Youth, and Families (Washington, D.C.: U.S. House of Representatives, March 10, 1987), p. 8.

8. Ibid., p. 9.

9. Ibid., p. 17.

10. *Children's Defense Budget*, p. 178. As an example of the extent of the savings involved, the State of Colorado found that it costs 38 percent less to provide day care for working parents than to maintain the same families on the public assistance and Medicaid benefits they would require if unemployed.

11. Sheldon Danziger and Peter Gottshalk, "How Have Families with Children Been Faring?" (Presentation to the Joint Economic Committee, Washington, D.C., November 1985). The committee found that the 1984 earnings for two-parent families were 23.4 percent higher than they would have been had wives not worked.

12. Harriet Presser and Wendy Baldwin, "Child Care as a Constraint in Employment: Prevalence Correlates Being on the Work and Fertility Nexus," *The American Journal of Sociology* 85 (1980): 5.

13. "Child Care: Key to Employment in a Changing Economy," p. 149.

14. "American Families in Tomorrow's Economy," p. 1. Note: The cost of child care now averages over $3,000 per year, and infant care often costs $100 per week per child.

15. *State Child Care Fact Book* (Washington, D.C.: Children's Defense Fund, 1987), p. 24. From data supplied to the U.S. Department of Education Center for Educational Statistics by researchers Sheila Kamerman and Alfred Kahn of Columbia University.

16. *Project Head Start Statistical Fact Sheet*, Fiscal Year 1988 (Washington, D.C.: Administration for Children, Youth, and Families, Office of Human Services, Department of Health and Human Services).

17. *Child Care: The Time Is Now* (Washington, D.C.: Children's Defense Fund, 1987), p. 6.

18. "Opportunities for Success: Cost-Effective Programs for Children, Update 1988" (Hearing before the Select Committee on Children, Youth, and Families) (Washington, D.C.: U.S. House of Representatives, 1988), p. 39.

19. Ibid., p. 40.

20. As cited by Dale B. Fink in "Latch Key Children and School Age Child Care," Background briefing prepared for the Appalachian Educational Laboratory School Age Child Care Project (Wellesley, Mass.: Wellesley College Center for Research on Women, 1986), p. 4.

21. Louis Harris and Associates, "Strengthening the Links between Home and School" (Survey of the American Teacher sponsored by the Metropolitan Life Insurance Company, 1987).

22. Ellen Galinsky, Testimony before the Subcommittee on Children, Families, Drugs and Alcoholism, U.S. Senate, March 15, 1988, p. 11.

23. J. R. Berreuter-Clement et al., *Changed Lives: The Effects of the Perry School Program on Youths through Age 19* (Ypsilanti, Mich.: Monographs of the High/Scope Educational Research Foundation, 8, 1984), p. 90.

24. Ibid., p. 88.

25. Ibid.

26. "Child Care: Key to Employment in a Changing Economy," p. 56. This survey of 405 employed parents in dual-earner families suggests that this benefit accrues to employers of workers at all income levels, not just those living on the economic margin.

27. Ibid., p. 4.

28. Ibid., p. 56.

29. *State Child Care Fact Book*, p. 27.

30. "Child Care: Key to Employment in a Changing Economy," p. 217.

31. *Time for Results: Task Force on Readiness* (Washington, D.C.: National Governors' Association Center for Policy Research and Analysis, August 1986).

32. *Children in Need: Investment Strategies for the Educationally Disadvantaged* (New York: Committee for Economic Development, 1987), p. 1.

Early Care and Education: Beyond the Schoolhouse Doors

SHARON L. KAGAN

SHARON L. KAGAN is associate director of the Bush Center in Child Development and Social Policy at Yale University, New Haven, Conn.; a member of the governing board of the National Association for the Education of Young Children; co-editor of Early Schooling: The National Debate *(Yale University Press, 1987); and editor of the forthcoming yearbook on early care and education of the National Society for the Study of Education.*

In order to reform and improve education significantly, schools must reach beyond the schoolhouse doors to families, to communities, and to other social institutions that serve children and their families, Ms. Kagan reminds us.

Illustration by Kay Salem

THOUGH SOME of us have grown wary (and others weary) of efforts to reform education, there is little doubt that "restructuring" is this era's main contribution to improving America's schools. More than just a buzz word or a new twist on old concepts, *restructuring* refers to not-so-subtle changes that alter the balance of power within schools. Our growing experience with efforts to restructure schools suggests that teachers, parents, and communities must be more involved in school decision making and that children must be allowed more choice in curricular decisions.[1] At the heart of the restructuring movement, as at the heart of early childhood education, is a commitment to engage children, adults, and communities more actively and meaningfully in the decisions that affect education.

My aim in this article is simple. I wish to suggest that, in order to reform and improve education significantly, schools must reach beyond the schoolhouse doors to families, to communities, and to other social institutions that serve youngsters and their families. I will show that a similarly open and holistic approach to classroom pedagogy and program practice has historically characterized the care and education of young children and suggest that early childhood education may have some lessons to share with those who are concerned about the general restructuring of our education system. Finally, I will extract the lessons learned from two

From *Phi Delta Kappan*, October 1989, pp. 107-112. Reprinted by permission of *Phi Delta Kappan* and Sharon L. Kagan.

25

olicy makers are calling for the strengthening not only of family ties but also of ties among agencies that serve young children.

promising early childhood efforts (family resource and support and cross-program collaborations) and shape them into 10 "commandments" that may be useful in our efforts to restructure general education practice and policy.

SCHOOLS AND SOCIAL REFORM

The current efforts to expand early care and education and to restructure schools, though they use different nomenclature and appeal to different audiences, share common roots, goals, and strategies. Each stems from a concern that children are entering an increasingly pressured and technologically advanced world that will require complex social and cognitive skills. To ready children for the demands imposed by such a world and to enable them to cope with the effects of pervasive drug use, increasingly fragmented family structure, and widespread poverty, educators recognize that schools must do more than simply teach the basics. Motivated by changes in demographics, in values, and in perceptions of social responsibility, schools are addressing the problems of society and are becoming effective agents of social reform.

Such responsibility forces schools to realize that they cannot remain isolated from other social institutions. Unquestionably, moving beyond the basics to embrace social and cognitive competences broadens education's mission and expands its perspectives and strategies.

Broadened mission. Throughout the history of American education, debate has focused on the purposes of schooling. To be sure, those working in the field have changed their visions of the aims of education radically over the centuries. The role of schools in Colonial times was narrowly defined: teaching the basics of reading, writing, and arithmetic. Totally separate from schools, the family and the church were responsible for the ethical and moral development of children. By the time of Horace Mann in the 19th century, these aims were deemed narrow and dysfunctional. Encouraged by women activists, schools broadened their mission in order to improve life for new immigrants and children of the poor. Gradually, many par-

ents formed coalitions and pressed for the introduction of play gardens and kindergartens; formal parent/school organizations were established to improve education. By the 1930s the community school movement had emerged. Though not widely accepted at the time, it advocated more active learning for children, greater involvement for parents, lifelong learning for adults, and the redefinition of the school as a hub of community services.

Over the past 25 years, three separate forces have hastened the realignment of relationships among schools, parents, and communities. First, the force of mandate — enunciated through the *Brown* v. *Board of Education* decision, through Head Start policy, through Title I of the Elementary and Secondary Education Act of 1965, and through the Education for All Handicapped Children Act (P.L. 94-142) — moved the spirit and molded the structure of various programs. Opportunities arose for more equitable and community-sensitive strategies. A second force, research in education and child development — guided by Urie Bronfenbrenner and others — provided an ecological perspective that underscored the interdependence of parent, child, and community.

Emerging more recently, the final force is perhaps the most potent. Steeped in a growing uneasiness about the quality of family life in the U.S., liberals and conservatives alike have become concerned about the state of the nation's children and about the high cost of delivering public services in uncoordinated and fragmented ways. Concerned policy makers recognize that today's complex problems often cut across the rigid lines drawn to separate the authority of education, health, mental health, and social service agencies, and they are calling for the strengthening not only of family ties but of ties among agencies as well.

For most early childhood educators, commitments to uniting children, parents, families, and communities are hardly novel. Early educators have for a long time loudly proclaimed that parents are the first and most important teachers of their children. The long-standing commitment to involving parents in early care

and education programs is manifest in the very structure of those programs, be they parent cooperatives for the children of the affluent or Head Start programs that mandate parent participation in decision making. The presence of parent coordinators and family and community workers in high-quality early childhood programs — particularly those for low-income youngsters — underscores the field's commitment to a linked mission: serving families and children together.

Equally important, early childhood educators recognize that the domains of development are intertwined. Fostering cognitive development in young children necessarily involves a simultaneous commitment to social, emotional, and physical growth. Consequently, the language of early childhood education is the language of the "whole child" and of integrated learning.

Although part and parcel of early care and education, such beliefs can pose considerable challenges for many educators and policy makers.[2] Burdened by tight budgets or overloaded agendas, some parties are reluctant to make more than rhetorical commitments to the whole child and to educating the child in the context of family and community. Understandably, others are unclear about the strategic consequences of such commitments.

Expanded perspectives and strategies. What do such commitments to the whole child in an ecological context really require in terms of altered perspectives and strategies? Clearly, they entail a vision of education as a shared responsibility: shared with parents, with businesses, and with other agencies and providers of services. When education is viewed as a cooperative venture, with mandatory and meaningful input from the community, closed schoolhouse doors, barred gates, a quest for the one best system, and other forces that keep families, schools, and communities apart are excluded. Within this perspective, shaping the culture of the program so that it is sensitive to parents, teachers, and the community is not only a democratic ideal but also an imperative for effectiveness. At a minimum, such a perspective demands a dedication to forging links between the school and its community, a revamped training program for school staff members, the establishment of vehicles for shared decision making, and regular communication with other service providers in the community.

Just as commitments to the child within the context of family and community have strategic implications for programs, so a commitment to the whole child has implications for pedagogy. Young children don't separate their learning by topic; they don't distinguish science or math as disciplines, distinct from one another or distinct from play. Blocks and sand, venerable tools of integrated learning, know no disciplinary boundaries. Withstanding decades of curricular fads in upper levels of education, integrated experiential learning has been the constant cornerstone of early care and education. With Dewey, Froebel, Piaget, and Pestalozzi as its pedagogical pioneers, early childhood education espouses the development of social competence, embracing and integrating children's physical, social, emotional, creative, and cognitive development.

Paradoxically, the very principles that have been treasured by early childhood education and that have traditionally set it somewhat apart from elementary education — extensive commitment to family, to community, to student choice, and to integrated learning — are now considered hallmarks of reform. As such, they are being incorporated into a variety of reform reports, projects, and laws, including *Right from the Start*, from the National Association of State Boards of Education; the Casey Foundation's New Futures Project; the Joining Forces initiative; school-business partnerships; Schools Reaching Out, from the Institute for Responsive Education; and P.L. 99-457. Indeed, a new ethos is developing, one that supports integrated learning, interagency collaboration, and partnerships between schools and families.

Two promising efforts that are closely related to early childhood education — the family resource and support movement and early care and education collaboratives — are examples of important new approaches emerging from this ethos. Though distinct in purpose and structure, family resource and support programs and early care and education collaboratives both see schools as key levers in shaping services designed to improve child development, in enhancing the functioning of families, and in improving the delivery of social services to children and families. Both movements acknowledge the schools' potential as direct deliverers of service to parents and children. Finally, both movements, whether their programs are rooted within or outside the school walls, see themselves as potential vehicles for positive change.

Just what are these movements? What can we learn from them? And how do they further school reform?

FAMILY RESOURCE AND SUPPORT PROGRAMS

Family resource and support programs are inventive responses to changes in the lives of families. Propelled into existence by changes in our social fabric that have left families more stressed, more isolated, and often poorer than ever before, thousands of family resource and support programs throughout the country offer services for parents (parent education, job training, respite care, adult education, employment referral, and emotional support) and services for children (health and developmental screening, home-based programs, and child care).

Recognizing the importance of this movement in its own right, as well as its importance to the education system, schools across the nation have begun to take part in it. To date, nearly one-third of the states include some form of parent education — an important component of family resource and support services — within their early childhood programs.[3] Not all of these efforts offer the complete array of services listed above. Indeed, many do not even call themselves "family resource and support programs." However, it is clear that educators are increasingly recognizing parents' substantial influence on their youngsters and are seeking innovative and practical ways to involve parents as educational partners.

This thinking has emerged, in part, from research on the relationship between children's home environments and family characteristics and their subsequent school performance. From James Coleman's work that suggested the important relationship between family status and student achievement to more recent studies that explore the differential effects of parenting styles on school performance, the case for closer ties between the home and the school has continued to grow. While research may not be sufficiently sophisticated to explain why such relationships occur or to pinpoint precisely which behaviors affect which outcomes, the evidence supports the critical role of families in the educational process.[4] Evaluations of early intervention programs that work directly with parents indicate that, despite variations in intent and strategy, they can have a considerable positive impact on children's lives, both in school and out.

Beyond their roots in research, family resource and support programs owe a debt to the self-help and parent education/parent involvement movements.[5] From the self-help movement, family resource and support programs have learned the importance of empowering

individuals to improve their own lives. From the parent education and parent involvement movements, family resource and support programs have developed a strong commitment to enhancing the competence and confidence of parents.

Yet, in important ways, family resource and support programs are quite distinct from their historical antecedents. Family resource and support programs are not like the old-fashioned kinds of parent involvement that asked parents to bake cookies or accompany children on field trips; nor are they like more recent and often confrontational kinds of parent involvement that asked parents to concentrate not on themselves or their own families but on school reform in general. While family resource and support programs may remind us of many earlier efforts to link families and schools, they construe past lessons in new ways and represent the next frontier in home/school relations.

Two characteristics that distinguish family resource and support programs from past efforts are particularly important for schools. First, family support is seen as a developmental service for all parents. Family resource and support programs recognize that, even though families of all economic levels share such common concerns as drug abuse or sibling rivalry, not all families need precisely the same support at the same time. Thus, to meet the changing needs of families, family resource and support programs must be individualized, adaptive, and flexible. In addition, they must respect parents' values and schedules. Gone are the days when two daytime parent meetings per year constituted parent involvement. In their place, family support substitutes ongoing flexible programs that encourage parental input in planning.

Second, family resource and support programs stress egalitarian relationships between parents and school staff members. Parents are respected for their rich knowledge of their children, their culture, and their community, while teachers contribute knowledge of educational processes and systems. Working together as equals, parents and teachers plan and execute programs. Such realignment of relationships and roles alters the balance of power in schooling and challenges conventional working arrangements. Indeed, new job descriptions and new training programs may become necessary.

However, the greatest challenge, practically and financially, is integrating family resource and support programs into the mainstream of school life. Such pro-

Like tugboats, family resource and support programs are small but mighty. They have the power to move entities many times their own size.

grams report that, while acceptance is growing, they are still seen as *in* but not *of* the schools.[6]

Part of this separation stems from the lack of a well-defined place for the programs in the educational bureaucracy. They may be part of early childhood education, or of vocational or adult education, or even of the social-service division of a school system. These tenuous links are further weakened by the precarious funding that characterizes many of the programs. The stability of family resource and support programs is sometimes threatened annually, a situation that requires staff members to devote valuable program time to fund-raising activities — perhaps even in competition with the school district. In some cases, funds for family support have been diverted from other funded programs, a practice that generates considerable animosity within school systems.

In spite of these challenges, school-based family resource and support programs are gaining currency in cities and states throughout the nation because they make important contributions to school life and to school reform. In addition to generating much community support, school-based family resource and support programs have rendered important services to children and families. They have demonstrated that it is possible and beneficial for schools to collaborate with community service agencies, and they have opened the schoolhouse doors a little wider, promoting the meaningful involvement of parents and other community members.

Likened to tugboats by David Seeley, family resource and support programs are small but mighty. They have the power to move entities many times their size. Just as tugs steer mighty ocean liners out of congested harbors toward open seas, family resource and support programs are one vehicle for guiding schools toward educational practices that are more open and responsive to the needs of families and communities.

COLLABORATION IN EARLY CARE AND EDUCATION

As schools embrace a more comprehensive vision of the nature of the child and of their own role in society,

the schoolhouse doors swing open ever wider. To meet the comprehensive needs of children, contacts with agencies rendering health, welfare, and social services have become routine. Special education legislation has propelled interagency collaboration to a new level, and the need to meet the before- and after-school child-care needs of children has fostered many connections between schools and communities. Collaborations between university scholars and school personnel have also helped mend town-gown schisms. And the existence of 40,000 partnerships between businesses and schools clearly indicates that the conventional vision of schools as isolated entities is outdated.[7]

Interestingly, such collaborations often involve agencies that deliver services that augment, but are clearly distinct from, the primary services offered by schools. For example, in addition to "special project" dollars, the private sector often brings new fiscal and management strategies to schools. Health agencies and the schools collaborate to provide health education, screening for health problems, and services to meet youngsters' specific health needs. Although each agency's raison d'être is distinct, through collaboration each enriches the services offered by the other.

A second type of collaboration that is beginning to emerge in early care and education could have a dramatic impact on schools and school reform. These new collaborations involve agencies that share the same goals and missions and provide direct services to young children. In communities throughout the country, early care and education collaboratives are being established to bring together child-care programs, Head Start programs, profit and nonprofit programs, and the public schools.

Though still fragile, these collaborations in early care and education take the form of community councils, advisory groups, and resource and referral centers. In some communities, ad hoc councils have been converted into permanent bodies. Some collaborations have full-time staff members and funding; others have neither. But whatever their structure, these collaborations typically aim to: 1) increase the quantity and quality of available services, 2) insure more

equitable distribution of services, 3) minimize expenses, 4) address shortages of staff and space, 5) equalize regulations across early childhood programs, 6) improve training opportunities, and 7) insure continuity for children. Many early childhood collaborations sponsor joint training for staff members in Head Start programs, child-care programs, and schools; others encourage cross-site visitation by staff members; still others join forces to buy materials and supplies. Collaborations often engage in community-wide data collection, cooperate in short- and long-term planning, and participate in advocacy efforts.

Given that public schools have played a comparatively minor role in the provision of preschool services and given that preschool services have remained quite distinct from one another, we might wonder why such interest in collaborations has arisen now and what schools might gain from getting involved. Interest in collaboration has peaked for several reasons. First, funding for early care and education has increased. Second, because no empirical evidence has indicated a single "best" system and because of our national commitment to diversity, schools, child-care centers (public and private), and Head Start programs are all potential recipients of the new benefits that have been earmarked for early childhood education.

Inevitably, this situation fosters competition. The stakes, after all, are quite high. To the victor go not only more slots for children but also typically the authority to control program regulations and staff requirements. Meanwhile, the losers lose doubly: they do not get program dollars, and, because of shortages of professionals in the field, their existing programs often lose staff members to better-funded programs. In truth, though they are conceived as separate entities, early care and education programs function on common pedagogical and physical grounds, a fact that makes collaboration all the more necessary.[8]

And finally, more important though less apparent, early care and education collaborations are emerging because communities are rejecting the segregated approach to funding and regulation that has yielded an inequitable system. Even the most cursory review of early care and education in the U.S. today reveals vast inequities and discontinuities for children, parents, and programs.[9] The children of the rich and of the poor do not have equal access to services. And even those youngsters who do receive services are blatantly segregated by income, with low-income children in subsidized programs and middle- and upper-income children in fee-for-service programs. Inequities exist, too, for providers of early care and education; those who work in public schools typically receive better salaries and benefits for fewer workdays per year and fewer working hours per day. Consequently, new school-based programs often act as magnets, attracting children and staff members away from other programs. Paradoxically, such competition for children, for staff, and for space, which is now well documented,[10] has spurred the drive for collaboration.

Interestingly, the challenges inherent in implementing early care and education collaborations are similar to those faced by public schools when they collaborate with community-based agencies. Often the goals and strategies of the collaboration are ill-defined, staff members and funds are not adequate to the task, and the participants remain committed to agendas of their own agencies rather than to any overarching goal of the collaboration.

Yet early care and education collaborations are even more complex than public school collaborations because they involve more parties, many of which have longstanding acrimonious relationships. In addition, these collaborations can be somewhat suspect because they often act as external agents of change, initiating reform outside the school. Though this may sound ominous because the schools appear to forfeit control, such collaborations have been remarkably successful in broadening the schools' understanding of their important role within the early childhood system. Collaborations legitimate the sharing of responsibility. They do not allow any of the parties to avoid accountability, but they free schools to act as equal partners in crafting an equitable system of service delivery. Collaborations give schools options: they can improve their own early childhood services, they can add services, or they can join forces with community agencies. Furthermore, these collaborations give schools the opportunity to work in extremely productive ways with communities and providers who have tended to see the schools as rivals in the scramble for funding.

Whatever the motives, communities, cities, and states are embarking on collaborative strategies to influence the delivery of educational services. For example, Florida is notable for its cooperative agreement between the departments of education and health and rehabilitative

services; for its work on P.L. 99-457; for its prekindergarten Early Intervention Program, which was passed by the state legislature; and for its Central Agency system, which establishes city, county, and state collaborations that offer training, engage in joint planning and siting of programs, and coordinate service delivery. New Jersey's Urban Prekindergarten Program links Head Start, child care, and the schools. In New York City, the Mayor's Office of Early Childhood Education, the board of education, and the Agency for Child Development plan the implementation of services for 4-year-olds.

Moreover, efforts such as these are not unique. They are taking root throughout the country, as services for preschoolers expand. Meanwhile, such efforts will increase as many pieces of federal legislation and most state legislation related to children and families call for establishing local or state-level collaborations or committees to address these issues.

GUIDING EDUCATION REFORM

Clearly, we need more experience with the programs before we can draw definitive conclusions regarding the efficacy of school-based family resource and support programs and early care and education collaborations. Yet each provides a stunning glimpse of the "restructuring" of American education. While neither effort originally set out to reform schools directly, each views education as a collective responsibility, each seeks equity for children and adults, and each recognizes the value of families and communities. Both efforts challenge conventional strategies, both ask schools to open their doors a bit wider, and both have altered the nature and amount of contact with parties one step removed from the schools.

However, more important than common intentions or creative strategies, family resource and support programs and early childhood collaborations share with each other and with advocates for reform a set of beliefs about the future of education in general and about the future of early care and education in particular. Though the following 10 "commandments" are not delivered from on high or carved indelibly in stone, they encapsulate lessons to be learned from these efforts.

1. *We cannot separate care and education.* Together with the schools' involvement with young children and their families must come the recognition that high-quality care and education are in-

separable. Whether labeled *care* or *education*, high-quality programs for preschoolers provide both. In spite of the similarity of services, we have seen that, within a community, different qualifications and salaries for teachers and different regulations for programs exist, diminishing the quality of care and education for children. To mitigate such differences, we must strive to link care and education.

2. *We cannot segregate children according to family income.* In many communities young children have unequal access to care and education, and, once in programs, youngsters are segregated according to family economic status. Thus our reforms will need to include strategies to foster access to programs and to integrate services more equitably. Such is the spirit and the law of the land.

3. *We cannot expect too much from poorly funded services.* As discussed above, the inconsistent — and consistently low — funding of family resource and support programs has been one factor limiting their success. To permit early childhood services to achieve their proven potential, we must insure the stability and high quality afforded by sufficient and stable funding.

4. *We must improve the infrastructure of early care and education along with increasing the number of slots.* Because the expansion of services can exacerbate shortages of staff and space and because new slots and new needs generate increased demands for a coordinated system, funds must be devoted to planning and collaboration.

5. *We must honor parents.* Parents have a great influence on their children's development. Whether through Head Start's mandate for parent involvement or through family resource and support programs, educators must incorporate the family and the home culture into programs for children.

6. *We must honor staff members.* In early care and education programs, staff members are perhaps the most crucial component of program effectiveness. They facilitate learning, nourish active thinking and doing, and create environments in which children are cherished. We must support staff members by providing opportunities for continued professional growth, by involving them in decision making at the levels of program and school, and by compensating them fairly.

7. *We must serve the whole child, within the context of family and community.* Meeting children's needs demands that we address social, cognitive, emotional,

and physical domains in an integrated fashion. Thus health, nutrition, psychological, social, special education, and parent support services must be included in early childhood programs.

8. *We must foster developmentally appropriate pedagogy.* Classroom practices that respect individual differences, that give children choices, and that foster the development of lifelong learning should be implemented. In addition to advancing the acquisition of skills, we must craft programs that foster social and cognitive growth and the development of curiosity, motivation, and other dispositions toward learning.

9. *We must strive for the involvement of business, industry, and other groups.* Recognizing that education is a shared responsibility, we need to make use of strategies that actively involve community members and organizations in school life. Although we should not allow the financial support of business to substitute for public responsibility, we must allow business to take its place along with other community organizations in our efforts to improve school effectiveness.

10. *We must work together, not coveting the resources or children of other programs.* Because policy strategies and funding have been largely categorical, early childhood education, like education in general, has matured in isolation. However, tighter resources, coupled with growing needs, make cooperation a necessity today. We must acknowledge that, as our problems transcend institutions and domains, so must their solutions. Reaching out is *the* key to reaching reform.

1. Richard F. Elmore, *Early Experience in Restructuring Schools: Voices from the Field* (Washington, D.C.: National Governors' Association, 1989).

2. For discussion of the challenges and strategies inherent in linking families and schools, see Donald Davies, ed., *Schools Where Parents Make a Difference* (Boston: Institute for Responsive Education, 1976); Hope Jensen Leichter, ed., *Families and Communities as Educators* (New York: Teachers College Press, 1979); Sara Lawrence Lightfoot, *Worlds Apart: Relationships Between Families and Schools* (New York: Basic Books, 1978); Milbrey Wallin McLaughlin and Patrick M. Shields, "Involving Low-Income Parents in the Schools: A Role for Policy?," *Phi Delta Kappan*, October 1987, pp. 156-60; David Seeley, *Education Through Partnership: Mediating Structures and Education* (Cambridge, Mass.: Ballinger, 1981); and Cynthia Wallet and Richard Goldman, *Home, School, Community Interaction* (Columbus, Ohio: Merrill, 1979).

3. Fern Marx and Michelle Seligson, *The Public School Early Childhood Study: The State Survey* (New York: Bank Street College of Education, 1988).

4. James Coleman et al., *Equality of Educational Opportunity* (Washington, D.C.: U.S. Government Printing Office, 1966); Ann Henderson, *Parent Participation and School Achievement: The Evidence Mounts* (Columbia, Md.: National Committee for Citizens in Education, 1981); and Douglas R. Powell, *Families and Early Childhood Programs* (Washington, D.C.: National Association for the Education of Young Children, 1989).

5. Bernice Weissbourd, "A Brief History of Family Support Programs," in Sharon L. Kagan, Douglas R. Powell, Bernice Weissbourd, and Edward Zigler, eds., *America's Family Support Programs: Perspectives and Prospects* (New Haven, Conn.: Yale University Press, 1987).

6. Heather B. Weiss, "Family Support and Education Programs and the Public Schools: Opportunities and Challenges," paper prepared for the Early Childhood Task Force of the National Association of State Boards of Education, 1988.

7. Susan D. Otterbourg and Michael Timpane, "Partnerships and Schools," in Perry Davis, ed., *Public-Private Partnerships: Improving Urban Life* (New York: Academy of Political Science, 1986).

8. Sharon L. Kagan, "Early Schooling: On Common Ground," in Sharon L. Kagan and Edward Zigler, eds., *Early Schooling: The National Debate* (New Haven, Conn.: Yale University Press, 1987).

9. Sandra Scarr and Richard Weinberg, "The Early Childhood Enterprise: Care and Education of the Young," *American Psychologist*, October 1986, pp. 1, 140-46.

10. Irene F. Goodman and Joanne P. Brady, *The Challenge of Coordination: Head Start's Relationship to State-Funded Preschool Initiatives* (Newton, Mass.: Education Development Center, May 1988).

Recommendations for Head Start in the 1990s

Head Start:
The Nation's Pride, A Nation's Challenge

Joan Lombardi

A Report on the Silver Ribbon Panel
sponsored by
The National Head Start Association

Joan Lombardi, Ph.D., served as the Project Director of the Silver Ribbon Panel for the National Head Start Association. She is a member of NAEYC's Governing Board.

Head Start celebrates its 25th anniversary with an impressive record of achievement and a new set of challenges. Over the years Head Start has proven to be a significant and sound investment in our nation's future. It has received widespread support from parents, policymakers, and the business community.

Since 1965 however, the world has changed dramatically. Over the past 25 years the percentage of children living in poverty has escalated at an alarming rate. Today, American children are much more likely to have families in which both parents are working away from home, or which are headed by single parents. Child care needs and educational reform have resulted in an increased supply and demand for early childhood programs. At the same time, problems such as substance abuse and homelessness pose serious threats to child development and family life. These changes, coupled with the demands on limited funds, have created a new social context within which the Head Start of the 21st century will emerge.

To help meet these new challenges, as part of the 25th Anniversary the National Head Start Association (NHSA) convened a panel of experts to develop policy recommendations for the future of the program. This article, based on the Silver Ribbon Panel report released in May 1990, provides background on the panel, summarizes Head Start's successes and challenges, outlines the panel's recommendations, and discusses implications of the panel report.

Background

NHSA is a membership organization that represents the parents, staff, directors and friends of Head Start programs across the country. In the Fall of 1989, NHSA convened a panel of distinguished advisors to examine what has made Head Start a success and how the program should be expanded and improved. The panel was composed of leaders with expertise in Head Start, other early childhood programs, health services, policy and business (see Members of the Silver Ribbon Panel).

The panel met to hear expert opinion and to review various task force reports and relevant policy documents. The panel process was based on the Head Start philosophy which values the opinions of those most directly affected by the program. Panel members therefore reached out and listened to the concerns expressed by the Head Start community.

More than 70 witnesses, including Head Start parents, staff and other early childhood experts, testified at three hearings held in Washington, D.C., Atlanta and Phoenix. More than 1,400 people (including 900 Head Start parents

From *Young Children*, Vol. 45, No. 6, September 1990, pp. 22-29. Copyright © 1990, NAEYC, National Association for the Education of Young Children, 1834 Connecticut Avenue, N.W., Washington, D.C. 20009.

and 500 staff) responded to an open-ended questionnaire soliciting their opinion on program success and future issues. Finally, a score of national organizations provided material and input to the panel's deliberations.

Celebrating 25 years of success

Head Start enjoys a long list of accomplishments. Over the years Head Start has provided comprehensive services including health, education, and social services to more than 11 million children and extensive involvement opportunities for parents and families. It has provided a model of parent participation by including parents in key roles as decision makers and as staff. It has served as a national laboratory for early childhood innovation by launching such efforts as Parent and Child Centers, Child and Family Resource Programs, and the Child Development Associate Program. It has provided critical leadership in bilingual/multicultural programming, parent education, and the mainstreaming of children with special needs.

Research has provided abundant evidence that Head Start is an investment, not an expense. Organizations calling for the expansion of Head Start and other effective early childhood programs include the National Governors' Association, the National Conference of State Legislatures, and the Committee on Economic Development.

Data collected by the Silver Ribbon panel confirm Head Start's success. Testifying before the panel and responding to the panel survey, parents expressed overwhelming satisfaction with the program. In the survey, ninety percent of the parents spontaneously indicated a positive program effect on their children, and many spoke of improvements in the parent-child relationship. One parent put it this way:

Head Start has helped build my family's

Members of the Silver Ribbon Panel

Eugenia Boggus, Silver Ribbon Panel Chair and President, National Head Start Association

Susan S. Aronson, M.D. F.A.A.P., American Academy of Pediatrics

Mattie Brown, Utica Head Start

Gail Christopher, Gail C. Christopher Enterprises

Raul Cruz, Head Start Parent

Marian Wright Edelman, Children's Defense Fund

Sandra Kessler Hamburg, Committee for Economic Development

Betty L. Hutchison, Chicago City-Wide College

Sharon Lynn Kagan, Bush Center in Child Development and Social Policy, Yale University

Sister Geraldine O'Brian, East Coast Migrant Head Start

Katie Ong, National Alliance of Business

Shelby Miller, Ford Foundation

Evelyn Moore, National Black Child Development Institute

Roszeta Norris, Total Community Action, Inc.

Mary Tom Riley, Texas Tech University

Winona Sample, Consultant Early Education and American Indian Programs

Tom Schultz, National Association of State Boards of Education

Jule Sugarman, Special Olympics International

self–esteem. It has given my children the opportunity and experience that I could never afford to give them. It has helped me learn better ways to use and acquire resources available in the community. After being a Head Start parent for 3 years, I have learned that I am just as good as anybody else; my opinion does matter, and if I apply myself and work toward a goal, I can make it.

In a world in which people are poor not only in material goods, but often lack critical social supports as well, Head Start helps establish important relationships. Head Start directors and staff

"Head Start has helped build my family's self-esteem."

spoke about the many ways that the program helps to build the self–esteem of children, parents and staff. Testifying before the panel in Atlanta, Arvern Moore, a Head Start Director from Mississippi, expressed the sentiment of many when he said:

Once Head Start touches the lives of people, it makes you a new person and that impacts the family and community in which one lives.

Parents and staff attributed Head Start's success to the involvement of parents, parent–staff relations, the comprehensive nature of the services, and the commitment of the staff.

Facing new challenges

Addressing the Head Start Conference in 1977, Dr. Edward F. Zigler said:

This basically positive view of Head Start does not mean that we should rest on our laurels. I prefer to think of Head Start not as a static program but as an evolving concept, an effort that must continue to grow and develop (1978, p. 6).

This statement is more timely today than ever before. Head Start's record of achievement and experience makes it an ideal program to address the challenges of rising poverty and the increasing changes in the family, provide critical comprehensive services to children and supports for families, and serve as a model for the entire early childhood field. However, in order to meet the challenges of a changing world, the panel identified three conditions that must be addressed: the need to protect quality, to expand enrollment and service delivery, and to encourage collaboration and research.

Quality

To be effective in the future, Head Start must continue to provide good early childhood services. Yet the panel heard repeated concerns about Head Start's ability to provide quality services, due to inadequate funding, at a time when demands on program effectiveness are increasing. The National Head Start Association (1990) reports that even with moderate inflation rates, funding per child in constant dollars has declined during the 1980's.

Like most early childhood programs, Head Start faces increased difficulty attracting and retaining qualified staff due to inadequate salaries. According to a 1988 survey by the Administration for Children, Youth and Families (ACYF), 47% of Head Start teachers earn less than $10,000 per year (National Head Start Association, 1989). The overall average salary of a Head Start teacher was $12,074. Furthermore, salaries are low for staff working in all aspects of the program. Inadequate salaries often force Head Start staff (many of whom are former Head Start parents) to live in or near poverty, affecting overall program morale.

At the same time, Head Start must respond to increasing numbers of multiple-problem families. However, programs report that they lack sufficient numbers of qualified staff to provide family support. In addition, despite the demands for additional training to respond to new issues, Head Start training funds have not kept up with program expansion (NHSA, 1990).

Along with staffing needs, Head Start parents and directors talked about the need to improve facilities and transportation. Head Start programs reported that they have had to vacate space due to increased rents and the rising cost of renovations. Lack of adequate space often affects the program's ability to

expand services. Similarly, the rising costs of purchasing and maintaining vehicles has caused cutbacks in transportation services. Head Start parents mentioned lack of transportation as a disincentive to parent involvement and a barrier to obtaining both medical services and job training.

Expansion

The panel heard stories of long waiting lists for Head Start programs, especially where no other services exist. They heard concerns about recent policies which

hours and days of operation. At a time of increasing employment among parents, Head Start has been moving away from directly using Head Start dollars to meet the extended-day needs of working families. Only 6% of Head Start programs use Head Start funds to provide full-day services that run nine hours or more (Congressional Research Service, 1990). Although many programs use other funds to supplement Head Start dollars and extend the day, the panel heard reports that outside funds are often inadequate to meet Head Start needs and directors often face conflicting regulations and fiscal requirements.

Head Start has provided comprehensive services including health, education, and social services to more than 11 million children, and extensive involvement opportunities for parents and families.

---

target four-year-olds and appear to limit multiple years of service. Parents and staff spoke of the critical need to serve children three years old and younger, particularly to provide continuity of services and to respond to family needs.

In addition to the need to expand Head Start to include programs for younger children, many Head Start staff and parents raised issues regarding the income guidelines for eligibility. Head Start eligibility guidelines are more stringent than many other federal programs. In fact, local costs of living and family circumstances put many families at risk who are above the federal poverty level.

Finally in the area of expansion, the panel heard a repeated need to expand service delivery, particularly to provide full-day services. Responding to the Silver Ribbon Panel questionnaire on improvement and expansion, parents most often listed the need for extended

Collaboration and research

As the importance of early childhood programs has grown and the funding has become more diversified, there is a need for federal leadership to establish a more cohesive and effective early childhood system by promoting collaboration and new research. New programs such as those provided by recent state early childhood initiatives, the Education of the Handicapped Act and the Family Support Act, provide new challenges for coordination. The panel found that additional incentives are needed to promote collaboration between Head Start and other early childhood and human service programs, to ensure continuity with the public schools, and to provide linkages with new funding sources and with the business community. In addition, new research efforts are needed to influence practice and inform policy.

The panel survey and testimony

revealed that although many Head Start programs are making tremendous progress towards collaboration, they often lack incentives due to limited public awareness of Head Start, barriers to launching creative funding initiatives with other programs already serving low-income children, the need for more flexibility in programming and limited paid time for collaboration. When collaboration does not occur, programs may compete for children, space and staff (Goodman and Brady, 1988).

have been few systematic efforts to disseminate promising practices both within Head Start and to the larger early childhood and human service field.

A renewed vision: Silver ribbon panel recommendations

The Silver Ribbon Panel provides a renewed vision of Head Start. Its recommendations are based on the founding principles that Head Start should be a model of compre-

to protect program quality in seven key areas.

Staff compensation. Immediate steps should be taken to provide equitable salaries to all staff and a responsive portion of all new funds should be earmarked for such increases. Furthermore, new initiatives should be explored to supply health benefit packages and retirement funds to all staff. In addition, working with the Head Start community and appropriate professional organizations, a career ladder should be developed and implemented.

Training and technical assistance. Additional funds should be earmarked for training and technical assistance to adequately reflect program expansion. Further guidance should be provided to promote training which is long-term, competency-based, supervised and focused on staff/child and staff/parent interaction. College credit should be provided.

Head Start's record of achievement and experience makes it an ideal program to address the challenges of rising poverty and the increasing changes in the family, provide critical comprehensive services to children and supports for families, and serve as a model for the entire early childhood field.

There is also increasing concern that as Head Start children move on to pubic schools, their progress may be lost if there is not a continuation of comprehensive services for them and appropriate support for their families. The panel found that there is a need for better collaboration between Head Start and federal education programs serving low-income children such as Chapter I.

In the area of research, the panel found that the percentage of the Head Start budget devoted to research, demonstration and evaluation has decreased over the past 15 years (NHSA, 1990). Furthermore, new research is needed to explore the ingredients for delivering effective services for various types of children and families. Finally, the panel found that although Head Start has been a leader in launching local innovations, there

hensive services, should be flexible enough to meet emerging local needs and should provide leadership in serving low-income children and their families. To build on Head Start's success, the panel made three recommendations to federal policymakers.

Investments should be made in the quality of Head Start to ensure that the program provides effective comprehensive services to children and families.

The panel recommended that the protection of quality be the top priority. They warned that program expansion should never occur at the expense of quality. They urged Congress to establish a quality set aside as an integral part of any new funds. Below are some of the strategies suggested by the panel

Developmentally and culturally responsive practice. A formal Education Coordinators Task Force should be convened to identify issues facing the education component and to develop recommendations for improvements. Efforts should be made to upgrade the Head Start Program Performance Standards to reflect new knowledge, younger children and new settings. In addition, new materials and training should be provided on multicultural/bilingual programming and on developmentally appropriate practice.

Parent involvement. New initiatives should be launched to provide more extensive training to parents, to establish clearer policies on parent involvement and to develop new approaches that reflect the current life circumstances of individual families. For example, further training should be provided to parents for their role as both volunteer and decisionmaker in the program and new innovations should focus on parent involvement for different types of families (teens, fathers, working parents, hard-to-reach families, etc).

Family support and health services. There should be an increase in the number of family support staff and new efforts to provide case management and service integration. Furthermore, a national symposium should be convened on new directions for family support and additional strategies should be developed to respond to children and families affected by substance abuse.

Facilities and transportation. New funding should include a targeted amount to improve facilities and transportation. In addition, the feasability of building permanent multi-use Head Start facilities should be explored.

Program oversight. Additional qualified staff, training and travel funds should be made available to the national and regional offices. New efforts should be made to improve the collection and reporting of Head Start program information.

Funds should be increased so that all eligible children who need Head Start can participate and local programs can provide services that meet the needs of today's families.

The panel envisioned a Head Start expansion that allows much more flexibility for local programs to meet the specific needs of the children and families in a particular community. This view of expansion calls for increased enrollment and for allowing programs to decide the age and scope of services provided. Below are some of the strategies suggested by the panel in three key areas.

Enrollment and program options. The panel recommended two enrollment targets. By 1994,

Funding per child in constant dollars declined during the 1980s . . . members of the early childhood community must join together to increase funding for Head Start and the other early childhood programs struggling with similar issues.

quality programs should be provided to all eligible three- to five-year-olds in need of Head Start services. By the year 2000, substantial progress should be made to build the capacity and serve children in need younger than age three. Expanded enrollment should be accompanied by the implementation of new program options such as Parent and Child Centers, Family Resource Centers, and Head Start Family Day Care.

Full-day services. Head Start programs should be encouraged to provide full-day services for those families in need. Clearer policies should be established for the use of Head Start funds for full-day services. While supporting the use of non–Head Start funds to supplement Head Start operations, the panel urged that such policies should be implemented in a way that provides continuous developmental services across a child's day rather than promoting a false distinction between care and education.

Flexibility in income criteria. While the panel strongly recommended that Head Start give priority to families with greatest need, it suggested that a working group and demonstration effort be launched to explore issues related to flexibility of income guidelines.

Leadership should be provided to build a more coordinated and effective system of services for children and families

through collaboration and research.

The panel believes that the Head Start Bureau, ACYF, as the administrator of the largest early childhood system in the country, should reaffirm its leadership role, not only by ensuring that Head Start is a model of quality, but also by continuing to promote collaboration efforts and new research. Below are some of the strategies in each of these two areas.

Collaboration. The panel recommended that collaboration accomplish four goals: encouraging the continuation of quality comprehensive services to children as they move on to public schools, fostering linkages with other early childhood programs, encouraging the development and utilization of services for low-income children, and securing stronger commitments from the business community. The panel applauded recent efforts by ACYF to promote collaboration and suggested several new initiatives including, among others:

• materials and support to help establish state and local early childhood councils to foster continuity among programs and to serve as a coordinating and planning body;

• additional projects with Head Start feeder schools to continue comprehensive services;

• a high-level summit on the future relationship of Head Start and state-funded early childhood programs;

• a new demonstration effort to promote linkages at the state level between the Head Start community and other state programs serving young children and families;

• a study to explore the feasibility of establishing State Resource Centers to network the Head Start and early childhood community and encourage collaborative training;

• new and ongoing initiatives to encourage the business community to invest in Head Start and other early childhood programs and to advocate for comprehensive services for young children.

Research. The panel commended ACYF for recent efforts to launch a new wave of research. They suggested that future research efforts explore such issues as the effects of quality variables, particularly those related to staffing; the impact of Head Start on the whole family; and the effects of more than one year of participation. They also suggested new demonstration and evaluation efforts to explore such areas as Head Start public school linkages, family day care, and economic integration of Head Start eligible and middle–class children. Finally they recommended new initiatives to disseminate information on local innovations.

Implications and conclusions

The Silver Ribbon Panel Report was released in the midst of unprecedented attention and support of the program by both Congress and the Administration. In early 1990, President Bush demonstrated a strong commitment to Head Start by requesting a $500 million increase. Throughout the spring and summer of 1990, Congress moved forward on a Head Start reauthorization bill that called for more than seven billion dollars by 1994 to serve all eligible children

ages three to five (Human Services Reauthorization Act of 1990).

Along with the strong voice of the Head Start community and the many longstanding supporters in the early childhood field and in Congress, the Silver Ribbon Panel Report lent support to the movement to ensure that expansion will be accompanied by the protection of program quality. The new Head Start reauthorization bill provides that funds be set aside for salaries, training, facilities and transportation. It also includes some limited expansion to younger children and

exciting new initiatives for Head Start research and demonstration.

The implications of the Silver Ribbon Panel Report, however, go beyond any contribution to the current Head Start debate. Even after this reauthorization is passed, Congress and the Administration face important issues on how best to spend limited federal Head Start dollars and how Head Start relates to other programs. At the same time, state and local policymakers will continue to plan new early childhood initiatives that will often serve Head Start eligible children.

Summary of Recommendations for Head Start in the 1990s

I. Investments should be made in the quality of Head Start to ensure the program provides effective comprehensive services to children and families. Specifically, investments should

• provide equitable salaries for all staff

• increase funds for training and technical assistance

• improve the education component to ensure that it is developmentally appropriate and culturally responsive

• enhance parent involvement

• increase family support

• improve facilities and transportation

• support program supervision

II. Funds should be increased so that all eligible children who need Head Start may participate, and local programs can provide services that meet the needs of today's families. Specifically, funds should

• provide, by 1994, programs for all eligible three- to five-year-olds in need, and provide programs for children younger than three years by the year 2000

• encourage full-day programs for those in need

• consider flexibility in income guidelines

III. Leadership should be provided to build a more coordinated and effective system of services for children and families through collaboration and research. Specifically, leadership should

• focus collaboration efforts to encourage continuation of comprehensive services in elementary grades, to foster linkages with other ECE programs, to encourage more services for young children and their families, and to secure commitments from the business community

• increase research, demonstration, evaluation, and dissemination efforts.

To influence decisionmaking, partnerships among the various segments of the early childhood community are becoming more important than ever. Below are some of the implications of the panel report for each of these groups.

Congress

As the reauthorization process draws to a close, the critical issue facing Congress is the appropriation of sufficient funds to meet the goals for expansion and improvement. The Silver Ribbon Panel recommended that Head Start become a priority in the national budget and that expenditures be adequate enough to provide quality. Bipartisan program support must be translated into new dollars. Head Start must not become a victim of looming budget problems.

At the same time, Congress must show support for other federal programs so critical to children and families. The Silver Ribbon Panel endorsed the principle that Head Start expansion must be accompanied by the continuation, improvement and expansion of other early childhood and human services needed by low-income families. Head Start's comprehensive services cannot fill in the gaps for a system plagued by inadequate housing, health, and other family supports.

The Administration

As the Head Start program expands, the importance of its role in the early childhood community increases. Head Start policies and practice should be carefully designed to reflect important changes in the field and within families. Decisions about policies should include input from the Head Start community and other early childhood experts. The Silver Ribbon Panel therefore recommended an ongoing Head Start Advisory Panel to review and develop future Head Start policies.

State and local policymakers

Although the Silver Ribbon Panel report was directed at federal policymakers, its message has important implications for policy planners at the state and local level. As early childhood programs move forward in the states and municipalities, they should be planned to ensure quality comprehensive services, to provide linkages with Head Start and other existing programs, and to respond to the needs of the total family. Inadequate and unrealistic costs per child and reliance on half-day programs that target only one age, are not responsive to these needs.

The early childhood community

The early childhood community faces new challenges as the supply and demand for our services grow. No one segment of this community can meet all the needs of today's families. In order to be effective advocates, we must join together to increase funding for Head Start and the other early childhood programs struggling with similar issues.

The many voices of the early childhood community are critical to the policy process. The stories collected by the panel make the statistics on Head Start come alive. In order to ensure that program expansion is broadly defined, that local programs have the flexibility to tailor services to their particular communities, that quality is protected, and that other critical human services are available to low-income families, advocates for Head Start and other early childhood programs must continue to share their wisdom with policymakers at all levels.

Head Start has made significant contributions to our country and our field. Upon releasing the Silver Ribbon Panel Report on May 18, 1990, the official day of the 25th anniversary, Eugenia Boggus, President of the National Head Start Association and Chair of the panel, called Head Start "an American success story for millions of children and their families." The panel report sets forth ways to sustain and extend this success in an increasingly challenging environment.

References

Congressional Research Service. (1990). *Head Start program: Background information and issues.* Washington, DC: Author.

Goodman, I. & Brady, J. (1988). *The challenge of coordination.* Newton, MA: Education Development Center.

Human Services Reauthorization Act of 1990. (H.R. 4151). *Congressional Conference Report of the 101st Congress.* Committee on Education and Labor. Washington, DC: U.S. Government Printing Office.

National Head Start Association. (1990). Draft paper on the full cost of Head Start. Alexandria, VA: Author.

National Head Start Association. (1989). Highlights from Part I of the 1988 ACYF Head Start Salary Study. *NHSA Newsletter, 7*(4), 22.

Zigler, E.F. (1978). America's Head Start program: An agenda for its second decade. *Young Children, 33*(5), 4–11.

Copies of *Head Start: The nation's pride, a nation's challenge, the final report of the silver ribbon panel* may be obtained from NHSA (1220 King Street, Alexandria, VA 22314) for $6 a copy, prepaid.

Schools and Classrooms as Caring Communities

When students feel they are valued members of the school family, the school becomes more effective at fostering all aspects of their development—intellectual, social, and moral.

ERIC SCHAPS AND
DANIEL SOLOMON

Eric Schaps is President, and **Daniel Solomon** is Director of Research, Developmental Studies Center, 111 Deerwood Pl., Suite 165, San Ramon, CA 94583.

How can schools encourage social responsibility in their students? They can teach the behaviors that constitute being "socially responsible," but social responsibility is more than a set of learned skills or acquired habits—it is anchored in the development of deeply personal commitments to such core social values as justice, tolerance, and concern for others. We cannot expect our children to develop commitments of this kind in a vacuum. They must be able to see and experience these values in action in their daily lives, including their lives in school. This is why schools must strive to become "caring communities," imbued with these values, in which all children become contributing, valued members.

Creating such communities has not, unfortunately, been a priority in Amer-

ican education, but a few schools are succeeding at developing them. We would like to describe a program presently in place in seven elementary schools in two California districts.[1] This program, the Child Development Project (CDP), fosters the creation of a caring community within each school and each classroom.

Toward More Optimistic Assumptions

Although students spend their academic careers in groups, schools often ignore the potential benefits of this group life. Teachers and administrators, when they organize students to work individualistically or competitively, actually undermine a sense of community. An emphasis on competition guarantees that school life will become a series of contests, with some students winners and some losers. And the current enthusiasm for "time-on-task" often condemns students to spend inordinate amounts of time working alone on narrowly defined cognitive exercises.

In our view, the assumptions about student learning and motivation that underlie these approaches are misguided. We view students as partly self-interested, of course, but also as well intentioned and concerned about their fellows, curious and interested, and capable of using and responding to reason.

The Child Development Project is based on these optimistic assumptions. We designed it to promote children's *prosocial development*: their kindness and considerateness, concern for others, interpersonal awareness and understanding, and their ability and inclination to balance consideration of their own needs with consideration for the needs of others. What we have tried to do is to structure conditions in schools and classrooms that bring out the best in teachers, administrators, and students alike.

The CDP classroom contains three major elements that work together to foster prosocial development: cooperative learning, "developmental discipline," and a literature-based approach to reading instruction. The CDP version of cooperative learning emphasizes:

- extensive interaction among group members;
- collaboration toward group goals;
- division of labor among group members;
- mutual helping;
- use of reason and explanation;
- explicit consideration and discussion of values relevant to the group activity.

This approach stresses two major types of experience that we consider essential for promoting children's prosocial development: collaboration and adult guidance. It is through their collaboration with equal-status peers that children learn the importance of attending to others, supporting them, and working out compromises. Then, because peer interaction is not *always* equal-status, collaborative, and benevolent, the teachers act as values advocates, pointing out the importance and relevance of helpfulness, fairness, concern and respect for others, and responsibility. They show students the meaning of doing one's best, one's part, one's fair share, and how these values can be effectively applied in their group work. In "setting up" cooperative activities and in "processing" them with the students afterwards, teachers routinely lead discussions about the relevant values and their applications, after first focusing on the academic task at hand.

"Developmental discipline" is a classroom management approach that encourages children to take an active role in classroom governance, including participating in the development of classroom rules. They meet periodically to discuss issues of general concern, enjoy as much autonomy as is appropriate for their age level, and work collaboratively with the teacher to develop solutions to discipline problems. The teachers treat the children with respect—as capable people who can respond to reason. They help students to think about and understand the importance of common values, rather than imposing values by virtue of their authority or power. Further, these teachers avoid extrinsic incentives (rewards as well as punishments) so that children will develop their own reasons for positive actions other than "what's in it for me." Teachers work to help children develop and tap their own intrinsic motivation by emphasizing the inherent interest in and importance of the academic activities.

We want each student to feel that the school is a large family and that he or she is an important and valued member. It is the feeling of belonging and contributing that motivates children to abide by and uphold the norms and values that the school community has decided are important.

We try to ensure that students' emerging sense of community is not achieved through a process of isolating and distancing their communities from others. To discourage such isolation, we change the membership within class groups, so that by the end of the year each student will have worked in groups with most, if not all, the other students in the class. And in the school at large, students often work outside their own particular classrooms, particularly in the "buddies" program. For this program, classes of older students are paired with classes of younger students for activities such as reading to each other, planting a vegetable garden, or holding a bake sale to raise money for an earthquake relief fund.

As with other literature-based reading programs, ours is designed to help students become more skilled in reading and more inclined to read. Ours is also designed to develop children's understanding of prosocial values and how those values play out in daily life. In much the way that cuisinaire rods provide examples of mathematical

> # A feeling of belonging and contributing motivates children to abide by and uphold the norms and values that the school community has decided are important.

processes, good literature shows how values "work." For example, the touching story *The Hundred Dresses* by Eleanor Estes (about a poor girl who claims to have 100 dresses at home) helps children to see how damaging and hurtful teasing can be. Similarly, other stories and books show concretely and vividly how such values as fairness and kindness make the world a better place. Still others reveal the inner lives of people from other cultures, ages, and circumstances as they deal with universal issues and concerns— they help children to empathize with people who are both like them and not like them and to see the commonalities that underly diversity.

Encouraging Results

To find out how well the program was actually implemented in the project classrooms and what effects it had on participating students—to see whether what *should* work in theory actually works in practice—we conducted a comprehensive evaluation of the project. Our evaluation has followed a cohort of children who participated in the project from kindergarten through 6th grade.[2]

Our findings show that the project was well implemented in most participating classrooms and that it produced a broad range of positive effects on students. It helped them to improve in social competence, interpersonal behavior in the classroom, interpersonal understanding, endorsement of democratic values, and higher-level reading comprehension. They also reported themselves to be significantly less lonely in class and less socially anxious. Overall, we believe the program is fostering a healthy balance between children's tendencies to attend to their own needs and to attend to the needs and rights of others.

In this article, we want to focus on our attempt to assess students' perceptions of their classrooms as caring communities and the impact of such perceptions. We included a measure of this perception in questionnaires that we administered to project students when they were in the 4th, 5th, and 6th grades. This instrument included items representing two major components in our conception of the sense of community: (1) students' perceptions that they and their classmates care about and are supportive of one another and (2) their feeling that they have an important role in classroom decision making and direction.

The first of these components was represented by 7 items, including: *Students in my class work together to solve problems, My class is like a family,* and *The children in this class really care about each other.* The second component was measured by 10 items, including: *In my class the teacher and students plan together what we will do, In my class the teacher and students decide together what the rules will be,* and *The teacher in my class asks the students to help decide what the class should do.* Students in the three project schools scored significantly higher on this combined measure than those in three comparison schools each year of the three years we administered the questionnaires. Thus, as we had hoped, the program was successful in creating caring communities in the classrooms, at least as seen by the students in those classrooms.

We also found, in general, that the

A Circle of Friends in a 1st Grade Classroom

Susan K. Sherwood

Ann. Age 6. Severe multiple disabilities. Birth trauma. Head injured. Moderate to severe mental disabilities. Hemiplegia to right side of body but ambulatory. No right field vision. Small amount of left peripheral and central vision. Color-blind. Verbal.

Pacing back and forth in the entryway, I pondered the details in my mind. As I anticipated Ann's arrival on the area agency education bus, I vacillated between calm conviction and near panic. Three days before, the special education teacher had greeted me with a request for a full-time integration placement. In light of my conviction to meet the needs of all students, my answer was instantaneous. Now I wasn't quite so sure.

As a teacher of young children for 18 years, I know that *every* class has a wide range of abilities and problems. This particular group of 21 students was no different. Their intelligence range, as measured by the Cognitive Abilities Test was 137–68 (excluding Ann's evaluation). Shane was reading at the 8th grade level; Sara had been diagnosed as learning disabled, James as hyperactive; Mike was adept at mathematics problem solving; Erica was a 6-year-old in puberty; and so on. Indeed, Ann was not so different. *All* needed to belong to our classroom community and to accept their own strengths and limitations before they could freely accept others. To develop confidence, instill love of learning, and enhance self-concept, the teacher builds on each child's uniqueness— creating a motivating and challenging atmosphere where all children are free to work cooperatively, learn from mistakes, take risks, and rejoice in accomplishments. Such a classroom community is a support system for each of its members.

Special educators coined the term "a circle of friends" to describe the framework of peers, friends, and adults in the natural environment that surrounds a child with severe multiple disabilities and offers mainstream support (Perske 1988, Stainbeck and Stainbeck 1987). Only the term itself, however, is new to the classroom teacher who has worked to build these relationships in his or her classroom all along.

Just as circles of friends draw the lives of children together, networking within the classroom links special educators and regular educators together in common goals. Our objectives for Ann were to help her (1) develop normal relationships and friendships with her peers; (2) build functional skills through normal 1st grade routines; and (3) continue work at her level toward functional academic life skills.

In social interactions, nonhandicapped children are good role models. By observing what they see, the handicapped imitate appropriate social behaviors and engage in fewer inappropriate ones (Donder and Nietupski 1981, Stainbeck et al. 1983). I was amazed at the ability of my students to provide structure for Ann's activities in the absence of an adult aide. For example, when Mike noticed that Ann needed assistance, he would gather the necessary materials, quietly approach her, and firmly direct her task. On one occasion, when she flatly refused to participate, he unemotionally prodded her, "You have to because you're a 1st grader, and these are the things 1st graders do." Then, without a pause, with the same sense of purpose as an adult, he directed her to trace the letters.

Of course, to promote Ann's independence, we had to adapt basic 1st grade materials to enable her to follow directions and participate routinely. For example, to allow her easy access to her supplies, we affixed a wooden block to the top of her desk to hold pencils, crayons, and her name stamp in an upright position.

On some academic tasks, such as rote counting by one's and five's to one hundred, Ann was capable of full participation. At other times, we struggled creatively to supply her with parallel activities so that she could still feel part of the group.

We also initiated the "facilitator of learning" role for each supporting adult on our classroom team. This means that their primary purpose was to assist Ann's integration; however, each team member was to support *any* child when not directly involved with Ann. In this way, the other children did not perceive Ann as having a special helper.

As I reflect on this past year, I know that Ann's life has been touched in many ways by her peers and teachers because she was afforded a free and public education in a regular classroom. Yet the integration process isn't easy. At times, it can become all-consuming. With no right answers, however, we cannot allow ourselves to be constrained by past practice. Don't be afraid to try. We can capitalize on mistakes and transform them into learning experiences and opportunities to creatively solve problems. My vision for education is students, parents, educators, and administrators working cooperatively to make learning positive and empowering for each student within a *regular* classroom.

References

Donder, D., and J. Nietupski. (1981). "Nonhandicapped Adolescents Teaching Playground Skills to Their Mentally Retarded Peers: Toward a Less Restrictive Middle School Environment." *Education and Training of the Mentally Retarded* 16: 270–276.

Perske, R. (1988). *Circles of Friends.* Nashville: Abingdon Press.

Stainbeck, W., and S. Stainbeck. (1987). "Educating All Students In Regular Education." *The Association for Persons with Severe Handicaps Newsletter* 13, 14: 1, 7.

Stainbeck, S. B., W. C. Stainbeck, and C. W. Hatcher. (1983). "Nonhandicapped Peer Involvement in the Education of Severely Handicapped Students." *The Journal of the Association for Persons With Severe Handicaps* 8: 39–42.

Susan K. Sherwood taught 1st grade for 18 years at Hansen Elementary in Cedar Falls, Iowa. She is presently instructor in the Education Department at Wartburg College, 222 - 9th St. NW, Waverly, IA 50677.

greater the sense of community among the students in a program class, the more favorable their outcomes on measures of prosocial values, helping, conflict resolution skill, responses to transgressions, motivation to help others learn, and intrinsic motivation.

These findings indicate that the program produces its best effects on students when it succeeds in creating caring communities in classrooms. We believe that students who feel themselves to be part of such communities are strongly motivated to abide by the norms of the communities, as they see them. When these norms include the maintenance of prosocial values and the development of and reliance on intrinsic motivation, these are the characteristics that children in such classrooms will display.

Creating Caring Communities

Because of fundamental changes in American family and community life, today's children often lack close, stable relationships with caring adults. Schools cannot ignore this reality—it cuts across all class and ethnic categories, and it shows no sign of abating— nor can they avoid the problems it causes. Schools have little choice but to compensate by becoming caring communities, by becoming more like supportive families.

Our experience in the Child Development Project shows that, with effort and dedication, schools *can* become such communities. What's more, when they do, they become measurably more effective at promoting all aspects of children's development—intellectual, social, and moral.

All too often, meeting children's needs for belonging and contributing is the missing variable in the school improvement equation. Systematic attention to their human needs holds high promise for both children and society, as children and adults thrive in caring communities and develop their personal commitments to each other, to the world around them, and to abiding human values.

---

[1] In the San Ramon Valley Unified School District, the project schools are Neil Armstrong, Bollinger Canyon, Country Club, Walt Disney, and Rancho Romero; in the Hayward Unified School District, the project schools are Longwood and Ruus.

[2] The research described here was conducted in six schools, three that implemented the program and three "comparison" schools in the same district. We have focused on a cohort of children who began kindergarten in the fall of 1982 and finished 6th grade in the spring of 1989.

During each of these years we have conducted classroom observations to assess program implementation and student behavior and have assessed characteristics of the children with interviews, questionnaires, and small-group activities. From 300 to 350 students have taken part in our research assessments each year. For further information about our findings, see Watson et al. 1989, Solomon et al. 1990, and Battistich et al. in press.

References

Battistich, V., M. Watson, D. Solomon, E. Schaps, and J. Solomon. (In press). "The Child Development Project: A Comprehensive Program for the Development of Prosocial Character." In *Handbook of Moral Behavior and Development: Vol. 3. Application*, edited by W. M. Kurtines and J. L. Gewirtz. Hillsdale, N.J.: Erlbaum.

Solomon, D., M. Watson, E. Schaps, V. Battistich, and J. Solomon. (1990). "Cooperative Learning as Part of a Comprehensive Classroom Program Designed to Promote Prosocial Development." In *Cooperative Learning: Theory and Research*, edited by S. Sharan. New York: Praeger.

Watson, M., D. Solomon, V. Battistich, E. Schaps, and J. Solomon. (1989). "The Child Development Project: Combining Traditional and Developmental Approaches to Values Education." In *Moral Development and Character Education*, edited by L. Nucci. Berkeley, Calif.: McCutchan.

Identification of Preschool Children with Mild Handicaps:

The Importance of Cooperative Effort

Ronald L. Taylor, Paula Willits and Nancy Lieberman

Ronald L. Taylor is Professor of Exceptional Student Education and Paula Willits, Doctoral Student, Florida Atlantic University, Boca Raton. Nancy Lieberman is Preschool Coordinator, Broward County Public Schools, Florida.

Public Law 99-457 was passed, in part, to assist school districts in providing appropriate services for preschool handicapped children. This mandate requires that school districts must identify and serve *all* preschool children who are handicapped, including those with mild handicaps. Identification of children who display minor speech/language, cognitive/learning or emotional/behavioral problems presents a unique challenge to the educator.

Because of the nature of the preschool population, traditional evaluation procedures used with school-age students will be largely ineffective and of questionable validity (Peterson, 1987). It is clear that school districts will have to make many modifications to their current assessment process. Among other changes, it will be necessary that preschool teachers and child care workers become more involved in the initial identification of these children. In addition, the parent must become a more active participant throughout the evaluation process. A number of specific concerns must also be addressed, including those related to screening, planning the evaluation and interpreting/communicating evaluation results. The central theme of all these concerns is the need for a cooperative, coordinated effort.

CONCERNS WITH SCREENING

Appropriate screening information enables school districts to make intelligent decisions about the need for further evaluation. It is probable that the individuals most directly involved with initial screening (at least on an informal basis) will be the preschool teacher/child care provider and the parents of the child (Lerner, Mardell-Czudnowski & Goldenberg, 1987). These individuals are in the best position to observe a child, gather pertinent information and make the appropriate referral. Another method in which a child might be referred is through some formal screening effort by the school district or community agency. It is therefore important that communication and coordination be emphasized among teachers/parents, those involved with formal screening, and the school district evaluation team responsible for determining eligibility for preschool handicapped programs.

Another issue relates to making incorrect decisions at the screening stage. Most professionals agree that it is probably better to make a false positive than a false negative error (Peterson, 1987). This means that if there is any question, a child should be referred for further testing at this point. It is better to overidentify at the screening stage than to risk missing a child who would benefit from early intervention. The more in-depth evaluation procedures should help clarify which children truly need services. This also has implications for selection of the screening test to be used. Some instruments (e.g., the Denver Developmental Screening Test) lack sensitivity and subsequently tend to lead to false negative errors (Wolery, 1989).

PLANNING THE EVALUATION

How To Evaluate

Certain characteristics related to the typical preschool child will influence the choice of evaluation procedures. For example, it is typical for young children's behavior to be variable during the preschool years (e.g., Lidz, 1983; Paget & Nagel, 1986). Performance on any one day may not give a true picture of a child's abilities. In addition, a clinical testing setting is often a very unnatural, anxiety-producing one for a young child. Finally, typical preschool behaviors such as separation anxiety, fear of strangers and lack of compliance may contribute to the very real possibility of making false assumptions about a child's abilities or disabilities (Martin, 1986; Torrey & Rotatori, 1987).

As a result of these factors, it is important that the child be evaluated on more than one occasion. This is not limited to formal testing, but could and should include observation and informal evaluation. In fact, it is a good idea to observe or informally evaluate the preschool child prior to any formal testing. This information can be used to determine the appropriate procedures/instruments, as well as provide another "sample" of behavior on which to base decisions. Consistent with an ecological assessment model, it is preferable to observe the child in more than one setting to provide additional information.

Even after observing the child, selection of appropriate procedures can be problematic, particularly due to the general lack of acceptable standardized tests for this age range. It is extremely important to investigate a test's technical characteristics related to the preschool population (Sheehan, 1989). Were preschoolers adequately represented in the standardization sample? Is the test-retest reliability acceptable for this age group? Does the test have adequate predictive validity? Unfortunately, the majority of tests used with this population fail to meet acceptable criteria (Lehr, Ysseldyke & Thurlow, 1986). In addition, the choice of instruments should be made with the curriculum of the preschool program in mind; information collected during the evaluation should serve the dual purposes of determining eligibility and helping to plan educational programs (National Association for the Education of Young Children, 1988).

Administration of standardized tests is also challenging with young children. Preschoolers' short attention spans, lack of test wiseness, and normal fears and apprehensions due to unfamiliarity with the testing situation can make assessment sessions quite difficult (Lichtenstein & Ireton, 1984). Examiners must be allowed to adapt administration of standardized tests if needed. Of course, examiners should carefully document any procedural changes found necessary to get the child to respond.

With the limitations of formal testing, it is both necessary and beneficial to rely heavily on more informal procedures. Information from such procedures can help validate the formal test results and provide meaningful additional information. Again, the preschool teacher and/or parent will play a crucial role in providing this information. Such procedures might include use of developmental histories and interviews that will allow input from the parents. Also, language samples and observation of the child in both structured and unstructured settings will provide valuable data.

What To Evaluate

It is necessary to determine the evaluation domains that must be assessed to meet local or state eligibility criteria. Although PL 99-457 does not require use of specific labels, many states have adopted a categorical approach similar to that used with school-age children (Sheehan, 1989). In Florida, for instance, mildly handicapped preschoolers must qualify for programs for learning disabilities, emotional handicaps, educable mental handicaps or speech/language impairments. By carefully analyzing eligibility criteria for programs that will serve preschool children, appropriate assessment areas can be determined.

If a categorical approach is used, parents and teachers must be informed that the label is not always permanent, but is the best descriptor of the child's needs at that time. In addition, parents must clearly understand that the instructional needs of two children with the same label may be the same or quite different (Sheehan, 1989).

Whom To Evaluate

It is extremely important to involve the parent throughout the assessment process. Many instruments designed for preschool children use the parent as an informant. In addition, informal techniques such as interviews and developmental histories will require input from parents. Other significant family members should also be included when appropriate. In some families, for example, grandparents who assume primary child-rearing responsibilities might be in the best position to provide relevant information.

Who Will Evaluate

One very important decision involves the choice of evaluators who will work with a given child and the manner in which they will operate. Among the possible evaluation models are the unidisciplinary, multidisciplinary, interdisciplinary and transdisciplinary models (Wolery & Dyk, 1984). In the *unidisciplinary* model, the child is evaluated by only one person. In the *multidisciplinary* approach, a team is used but communication is limited. There is more role-identification and increased communication in the *interdisciplinary* approach, while the most carefully planned, integrated model is the *transdisciplinary*.

In general, the more communication and cooperative planning among the team members, the better the evaluation will be. This might involve the child being simultaneously evaluated by a team consisting of a psychologist, a speech/language clinician, a teacher and appropriate therapists. Team members should be familiar with both their own areas of expertise and those of other team members. Determination of who comprises the team for a given child should be an individual decision based on referral/screening information, observational data and the evaluation domains that are subsequently identified.

Where To Evaluate

Another decision that must be made is the choice of the evaluation setting. It is hoped that the child will be observed and evaluated in more than one setting (Peterson, 1987). Any formal testing may need to be scheduled in a large room that allows for gross-motor activities. If furniture is used (as opposed to testing on the floor), it should be age-appropriate (Paget, 1983).

CONCERNS WITH INTERPRETATION/ COMMUNICATION

Interpretation of evaluation results becomes easier if multiple sources of information have been used to document behavioral and developmental trends (Florida Department of Education, 1989). A child's developmental strengths and weaknesses should become obvious if relevant procedures and instruments have been chosen for the evaluation process. What is not so obvious is how to convey that information both in written and oral form to parents and future preschool special education teachers (if the child is found eligible for services).

Parents may react with shock, fear, guilt or denial when confronted with negative information at post-evaluation meetings (Peterson, 1987). For these reasons, they should be informed at every step in the evaluation process. Team members should also realize that when a final "diagnosis" is stated, the parents may not be "taking in" the rest of what is being said during the meeting. The following suggestions may help ease a rather painful stage in the evaluation process (Biggs & Keller, 1982; Hooper, 1977):

1) First inform parents of four or five positive things about their child.
2) Encourage parents' questions and acknowledge their feelings.
3) If labels are required, remind parents of their transient nature at this age.
4) Inform parents of future re-evaluations.
5) Avoid technical terms and concepts; use everyday terminology.
6) Organize evaluation results in a logical fashion, with test scores and observations grouped to show patterns in the child's abilities and behaviors.
7) If possible, include another parent of a handicapped child as a team member to provide support and answer questions.

Along with orally presenting evaluation results to parents, evaluation team members must convey the child's results in written form. Final evaluation reports should be written in a meaningful way. One recommended format is the "translated report" developed by Bagnato (1980). Translated reports focus on the child's performance relative to specific preschool curriculum objectives. They are organized by developmental or functional domains, not by tests given. A child's developmental strengths and weaknesses are described in behavioral terms, linked to specific curriculum objectives with functional levels listed and

instructional needs delineated to facilitate development of an Individual Education Program. Quite specific recommendations are made for behavioral and instructional management.

Another approach that might be used is the *System To Plan Early Childhood Services* (Bagnato, Neisworth, Gordon & McCloskey, 1990). This approach provides a systematic method of linking screening, evaluation, program planning and progress monitoring. Results of the evaluation are presented in a meaningful way that addresses various service options.

A PROPOSED MODEL

A number of "best practice" suggestions have been discussed. These include the following:

■ Make sure there is a link between screening and evaluation.
■ Gather information from the parent and the home environment.
■ Use multiple evaluators/evaluation sessions.
■ Consider child characteristics in test selection.
■ Observe/discuss the child prior to the formal evaluation.

The Broward County School District in Florida has developed a model of preschool evaluation that incorporates these best practice suggestions (see Figure 1). This approach minimizes the time needed to evaluate the child and maximizes the communication between team members. Two points should be made before the model is described. First, categorical labels (educable mentally handicapped, learning disabled, emotionally handicapped, speech and language impaired) are required for preschool children in Florida. Analysis of eligibility for those categories resulted in the nine evaluation domains noted in the model. Second, because Broward County is a large county, a transdisciplinary approach is feasible with an evaluation team

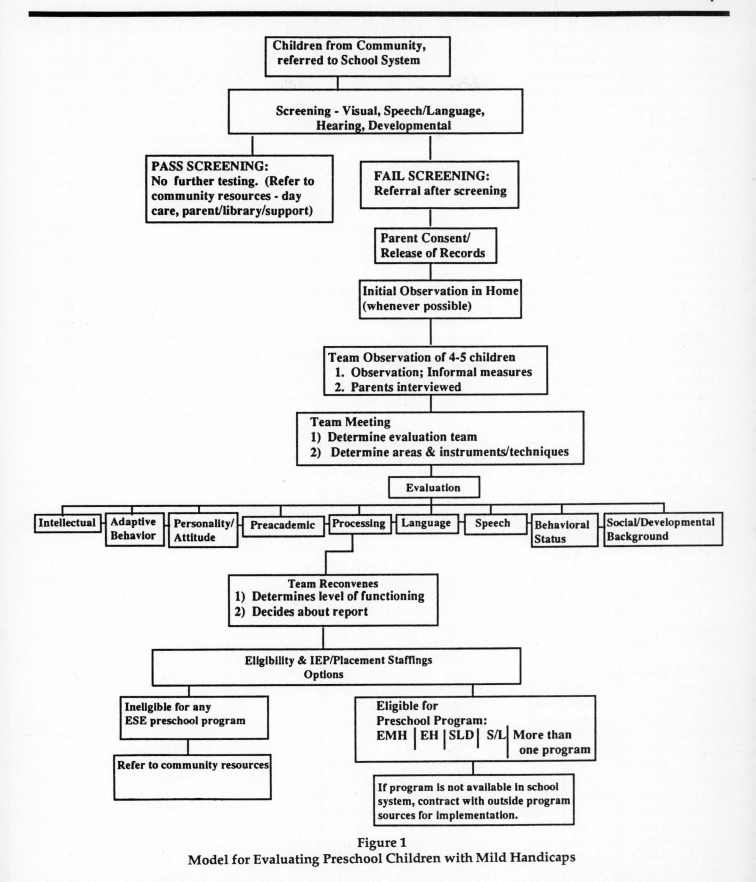

Figure 1
Model for Evaluating Preschool Children with Mild Handicaps

housed together within a school or center. Smaller districts might have to modify this model somewhat. The flowchart in Figure 1 can be divided roughly into three phases: screening, planning the evaluation and conducting the evaluation.

Screening

With this model, initial screening procedures are conducted through Child Find Services. The process begins when groups of children who have been referred for screenings (usually from parents and preschool teachers) are gathered at one location and given individual vision and hearing acuity screenings, along with speech/language and developmental screening. Parents are immediately informed by screening team members as to whether further testing may be indicated; consent and release of records are obtained for those children who will continue to be evaluated.

Because it is important that the evaluation team be familiar with screening procedures to avoid duplication of effort, one person from the evaluation team is designated to mutually plan and coordinate the screening with the Child Find designee. Those individuals also share information with parents and preschool teachers about the services available and the characteristics of children who might qualify.

Planning the Evaluation

Children who fail initial screenings are observed at home when possible by at least one evaluation team member. The child is then given a preliminary evaluation by a team consisting of a school psychologist, a speech and language clinician, a preschool special education teacher and any other appropriate professional. A developmental instrument (usually the Battelle Developmental Inventory) is used for this preliminary evaluation. While the child is being evaluated, the parent is interviewed. A team meeting is held once this information has been collected. Team members review all screening and preliminary evaluation information and determine the nature of the formal evaluation. Decisions made at this point are:

- Which team members will evaluate the child?
- Will the child be evaluated individually by the chosen members or simultaneously by the team?
- What domains need to be evaluated?
- What instruments/procedures should be used?

A formal assessment session is then scheduled if necessary. Because of the nature of the criteria for speech and language impairment, determination for eligibility for that category can be made at this point.

Conducting the Evaluation

Once the decision regarding the nature of the evaluation has been made, testing is scheduled and conducted. After the evaluation, the team reconvenes to determine the child's levels of functioning and to write the final evaluation report. An eligibility staffing is later held with the parents to share evaluation outcomes and decide what placement options, if any, will be employed based on the child's results. Built into this system is a "transition reevaluation" prior to the child's entering kindergarten to update his/her developmental status and provide information for program changes if necessary.

This model highlights the importance of observing preschoolers prior to formal testing and emphasizes the importance of gathering as much information as possible from a variety of sources, including the family. It also emphasizes the practicality and efficiency of a team approach. Districts must be sure to choose a delivery system that does not result in delays in identification and placement for mildly handicapped youngsters. Pooling the knowledge of a variety of experts, while involving them in a cost-efficient, time-efficient system, works extremely well with the preschool population.

In summary, prekindergarten evaluation of mildly handicapped children is a multifaceted, specialized endeavor. Assessment of young children with mild handicaps requires a number of skills and procedures not involved when older youngsters are evaluated. Individuals from a variety of disciplines must be willing to share their expertise with a team of informed professionals, as well as parents. Special skills, creative thinking and patience are required to discover the developmental strengths and weaknesses of such very young children. It is imperative that educators and parents work together in a cooperative and coordinated fashion to meet that goal.

References

Bagnato, S. (1980). The efficacy of diagnostic reports as individualized guides to prescriptive goal planning. *Exceptional Children, 46,* 554-557.

Bagnato, S., Neisworth, J., Gordon, J., & McCloskey, G. (1990). *System to plan early childhood services.* Circle Pines, MN: American Guidance Service.

Biggs, D., & Keller, K. (1982). A cognitive approach to using tests in counseling. *Personnel and Guidance Journal, 59,* 528-532.

Florida Department of Education. (1989). *Preschool assessment and training for the handicapped manual.* Tallahassee: Author.

Hooper, G. (1977). Parental understanding of their child's test results as interpreted by elementary school teachers. *Measurement and Evaluation in Guidance, 10,* 84-88.

Lehr, C., Ysseldyke, J., & Thurlow, M.

(1986). *Assessment practices in model early childhood education projects* (Research Report #7). Minneapolis: University of Minnesota.

Lerner, J., Mardell-Czudnowski, C., & Goldenberg, D. (1987). *Special education for the early childhood years* (2nd ed.). Englewood Cliffs, NJ: Prentice-Hall.

Lichtenstein, R., & Ireton, H. (1984). *Preschool screening: Identifying young children with developmental and educational problems.* Orlando, FL: Grune & Stratton.

Lidz, C. (1983). Issues in assessing preschool children. In K. Paget & B. Bracken (Eds.), *The psychoeducational assessment of preschool children* (pp. 17-28). New York: Grune & Stratton.

Martin, R. (1986). Assessment of the social and emotional functioning of preschool children. *School Psychology Review, 15,* 216-232.

National Association for the Education of Young Children. (1988). NAEYC position statement on standardized testing of young children 3-8 years of age. *Young Children, 44,* 42-47.

Paget, K. (1983). The individual examining situation: Basic considerations for preschool children. In K. Paget & B. Bracken (Eds.), *The psychoeducational assessment of young children* (pp. 51-62). New York: Grune & Stratton.

Paget, K., & Nagel, R. (1986). A conceptual model of preschool evaluation. *School Psychology Review, 15,* 154-165.

Peterson, N. (1987). *Early intervention for handicapped and at-risk children.* Denver: Love.

Sheehan, R. (1989). Implications of PL 99-457 for assessment. *Topics in Early Childhood Special Education, 8,* 103-115.

Torrey, C., & Rotatori, A. (1987). Assessment practices for young handicapped children. In A. Rotatori, M. Banbury, & R. Fox (Eds.), *Issues in special education* (pp. 38-54). Mountain View, CA: Mayfield.

Wolery, M. (1989). Child find and screening issues. In D. Bailey & M. Wolery (Eds.), *Assessing infants and preschoolers with handicaps* (pp. 119-143). Columbus, OH: Merrill.

Wolery, M., & Dyk, L. (1984). Arena assessment: Description and preliminary social validity data. *Journal of the Association for Persons with Severe Handicaps, 9,* 231-235.

Child Development and Families

- Development (Articles 8-10)
- Family Trends (Articles 11-14)

This unit is divided into two sections. The first section contains three articles that examine child development and the factors that influence development. The second group of articles covers family trends, especially those that affect the education of young children.

More and more research is being conducted that focuses on infants and toddlers. The capacity of infants to do and understand is far greater than was known even five years ago. This area of knowledge is quickly expanding as is the care of children under the age of three outside of the home. The article "First Friends" looks at the social development of infants and toddlers and provides information that will assist parents and teachers in providing opportunities for children to interact with peers.

Families and their child-rearing beliefs and strategies have changed in the last few decades, and so must parent education in its varying forms. More than one-half of all American children can be expected to spend part of their childhood in some type of nontraditional family. They may have two working parents; they may have been in several substitute child-care arrangements; their parents may be divorced; they may have a female head of household; their parents may be teenagers; they may have minimal or no contact with the father; they may live in a stepfamily or in a protective foster family. These nontraditional families need to be recognized; moreover, they have special needs that require early childhood educators to be especially vigilant to potential complications and problems that may affect the children's learning processes.

The changes taking place in American families have been one of the reasons the field of early childhood education has grown so rapidly in the past decade. Along with more dual-income families and single-parent families in our communities comes the need for quality early childhood programs. Specially trained caregivers and teachers will enable the school setting to be a consistent force in the lives of young children and will provide them with a safe, exciting, and nurturing environment. The nuclear family can no longer depend on an extended family network to provide care, assistance, or daily support. Families frequently relocate and do not have direct access to family resources. Therefore, it is increasingly necessary for educators to assist children and their parents as they strive to work and learn together. Professionals who are aware of the enormously varied life circumstances children and parents experience today are mindful not to offer magic formulas, quick remedies, or simplistic suggestions to complicated, longstanding problems of living and growing together. What many parents do seem to appreciate is a sense that they are respected and given up-to-date objective information about their child. The problem educators face is that some families are neglecting their responsibility of assisting the schools in educating their children. Parents are not available to meet with school personnel, requests for materials from home are unanswered, and most importantly, children are not coming to school prepared to learn. This lack of cooperation occurs at all socioeconomic levels.

Several decades ago educators were deeply concerned with families. As a result, professional organizations such as the Parent-Teachers' Associations and the American Association of University Women often undertook extensive programs aimed at providing information on parenting to families. Teachers of kindergarten children in the 1920s and 1930s would teach in the morning and spend the afternoon on home visits and working with parents so they could better understand their children and their development. Also during this period, women who received mother's pensions, or welfare as it is called today, were required to take classes in child-rearing techniques. Proper nutrition, language stimulation, and activities for children were taught. We need to reexamine these earlier efforts.

Two articles in this unit address issues not traditionally found in education texts. The effects of birth order on social, academic, professional, and creative activities have captured the attention of scholars for over a century. Recognizing the unique personality differences in each child can assist parents in better relating to their children. The article "Guns and Dolls" also explores an issue often discussed by parents and teachers but always surrounded by controversy. The way teachers establish the environment and provide activities for students can affect the learning experiences of children. Much has been written concerning the ways in which teachers relate to girls and boys in the classroom, or the skills possessed by girls in math and science. Shapiro's article reports on recent findings on gender research and assists parents and teachers in providing experiences for and communicating with girls and boys.

Looking Ahead: Challenge Questions

What are some of the special considerations necessary when caring for and teaching infants and toddlers?

How has child care changed to keep pace with the changing American family? What do parents, employers and caregivers need to do to meet future challenges?

What are some normal developmental milestones for babies during their first year?

What role do parents play in helping their children form relationships with other children?

Do parents really treat girls and boys differently? What can parents do to ensure equal treatment for all their children?

Is being a firstborn in a family a burden many find hard to bear? Why is it important for teachers to be familiar with birth order characteristics?

What attitude changes have taken place among many parents in the past twenty years? How have these changes affected the ways in which parents and teachers relate?

What are the effects of divorce on children of different age levels? Why are boys especially vulnerable to divorce?

First Year Milestones

JENNY FRIEDMAN

Jenny Friedman has a PhD in learning disabilities with a specialty in preschool language and cognitive development. She is the mother of two.

FIRST WEEK

- *Arm, leg, and hand movements controlled primarily by reflexes.*
- *Sleeps 70 to 80 percent of day, in about eight naps.*
- *Requires seven to eight feedings a day.*
- *Sensitive to location of sound.*
- *Focuses about eight inches away.*
- *Is individual in looks, feelings, activity level, and reaction to stimulation.*

Parenting books are meant to be encouraging, certainly to be helpful—but to cause despair? That's what one mother of a healthy eight-month-old girl recently felt after reading a popular book on child rearing. The author had written that by eight months most children were pulling up on furniture and crawling. Her child was doing neither. Although embarrassed to admit it, this mother worried that her daughter's development might be slow.

Babies don't come with instructions. So in the first one or two years of our baby's life, most of us are hungry for information. We want to know when and how to feed our child, how to get her to sleep, and how to comfort her when she cries. And we want to know that she's developing into a bright, happy child. To get some answers, parents turn to the many child-development books available. In them we may find a great deal of helpful information but encounter some pitfalls as well.

Many parenting books describe the stages of growth for the "average" baby and sometimes provide a chart, such as the one that accompanies this article, that lists when parents can expect developmental milestones, such as crawling, walking, and uttering a first word. But many times this information leads parents to believe that their child should conform to these norms.

Bob Brancale, director of the Minneapolis Early Childhood Family Education program, has heard such concerns many times. "Even though we believe development happens in a systematic fashion, it doesn't always happen when the book says it's going to," he says.

Most books caution parents about comparing their baby's development with the norms listed in the charts. For instance, Frank Caplan, in the popular book *The First Twelve Months of Life* (Bantam, 1984), writes, "Please do not re-

"First Year Milestones," by Jenny Friedman, *American Baby,* August 1989, pp. A17-A21. *American Baby,* The Cahners Publishing Company, a division of Reed Publishing.

gard this chart as a rigid timetable. Babies are unpredictable." In fact, the phrase "no two babies are alike" is common in these books, but it is human nature to want our offspring not only to meet developmental expectations but also to surpass them.

A deeper concern among some parents, however, is that their child's deviation from a norm may signal a real problem. Or—and this is something even the most self-assured parents experience—there is concern that if children are behind where the chart says they

FIRST MONTH

- Lifts head briefly
- Usually keeps hands fisted.
- Stares at faces and objects.
- Indicates response to human voice.

- Reflexes becoming more efficient.
- Daily patterns of sleeping, crying, and eating are very disorganized.
- Is alert about one out of every ten hours.

should be, they will lag in that particular area their whole life.

A child who talks early is described by everyone as "very bright." The infant who's walking before her first birthday is dubbed "a track star." So when a child shows no interest in walking until well after her first birthday or says few words before her second birthday, what does that portend for her future? "At 13 months," one mother wrote to a popular

SECOND MONTH

- Reflex control begins to disappear as actions become voluntary.
- Can hold head at 45-degree angle for a few seconds.
- Coordinates senses: looks for sound; sucks at sight of bottle or breast.

- Studies own hand movements.
- Is able to express distress, excitement, or delight.
- Quiets in response to being held or to person's voice or face.

newsletter for parents, "our first child said only three words. I was worried. Even if I subtracted one-and-a-half months for her prematurity, she was only 'average.' To me 'average' meant an IQ of 100—not likely to make it through college."

Is there a measure of truth in these predictions? Are the roots of intelligence apparent in the behavior of infants? Can a parent—or indeed a highly trained infant-behavior researcher with sophisticated tests

and measures—tell with any degree of certainty how bright a child will be or what talents she will possess as an adult by considering her rate of development in the early years?

PREDICTING THEIR FUTURE

No, says Robert McCall, director of the University of Pittsburgh office of child development and author of *Infants* (Harvard University Press, 1979). He believes that the evidence indicates "unequivocally" that mental performance in the first 18 months does not predict later intelligence "to any practical extent." Furthermore, says McCall, "there is no evidence that a child who walks earlier runs faster at age eight."

Researchers measure "mental performance" in babies by administering infant-intelligence tests. These gauge many of the skills described in the familiar milestone charts—age of crawling, standing, walking, talking, build-

THIRD MONTH

- When on stomach, holds chest up and head erect for a few seconds.
- Begins to recognize and differentiate family members.
- Gurgles and coos.

- Visually follows a slowly moving object.
- Views fingers individually instead of in fisted position.
- Smiles easily and spontaneously.

ing block towers, and so forth. What researchers have found is that infants who perform well at these tasks in their first two years are not necessarily those who do well on IQ tests as preschoolers or who do well in school in later years.

Also, development can be lopsided. The baby who toddles before a year is not necessarily the one who will be putting words together at 18 months. Furthermore, a child's "strengths" might shift. The child who talks late but walks early may be verbal and poorly coordinated by age three.

Although research continues, scientists have been unable to find a measurable behavior, manifested in the first two years, that accurately predicts how smart a child will be or what talents she will possess. No one is sure why intelligence, which tends to be fairly stable by the preschool years, predicts so little when measured in the first two years of life. Some think that infant-intelligence tests measure different behaviors (such as motor skills) than later tests do. Many believe, in fact, that the nature of infant intelligence is fundamentally different (i.e., sensorimotor) from childhood intelligence, which is symbolic in nature.

KNOWLEDGE IS CRITICAL

The best way for parents to be reassured about their child is to gain a good understanding of the nature of development. "Parents who have little knowledge of child development are much more anxious about the rate [at which] their children develop skills," says Kate Horst, a Minneapolis parent educator and specialist in early-childhood development. "If their child isn't walking somewhat early, then they will really work hard to push

The first year of a child's life is full of exploration and a hunger for information. Developing the ability to walk is of enormous importance to the young child. (EPA Documerica)

FOURTH MONTH

- *When on stomach, rolls from side to side.*
- *Holds head steady and erect for a short time.*
- *Can now focus at different distances.*
- *Bats at objects.*
- *Follows source of sound.*
- *Laughs while socializing.*
- *Is interested in making new sounds and imitating others.*

that child. They feel the child's rate of development is a reflection on them, and late walking means their child is not very smart." Parents with an understanding of development, she says, know children progress at different rates; these parents are not as likely to be concerned.

Ironically, reading those milestone charts can help. Although the rate of development has little predictive value in general, severe delays in skill development or unusual milestone patterns may indicate a problem. Parents who are aware of the general pattern of development are more likely to catch potential problems early. Although many such problems may not have a "cure," early detection may mean greater understanding—and less frustration—if and when the child encounters difficulties. "Once you know there are certain limitations," says McCall, "you can get about the business of coping by developing alternative strategies and not expecting as much."

Most experts agree that there is enormous variation in the age at which children acquire each stage of speech—babbling, using first words, and producing sentences. Even children in the same family may show remarkably different patterns of speech development. Jessica, now five years old, began talking before her first birthday and was putting

FIFTH MONTH

- *Rolls from back to stomach or vice versa.*
- *Reaches for objects with one or both hands.*
- *May transfer objects from hand to hand.*
- *Can squeal, grunt, blow "raspberries."*
- *Vocalizing takes on adult inflections and intonations.*
- *When seated or pulled to sit, head is balanced steadily and held erect.*
- *Smiles at faces and voices.*

words together at 15 months. Her sister, Rachel, spoke few words until her second birthday. Yet by age three their verbal skills exhibited few differences. What researchers have discovered, however, is that a child's understanding of language is a more critical indicator of development than his expression of it.

WARNING SIGNS

How can parents know at what point

SIXTH MONTH

- *Can roll from stomach to back.*
- *Sits with support.*
- *Eyes now direct hands for reaching.*
- *Reaches quickly and without jerkiness for any-*
- *thing he sees.*
- *Creeps, forward or backward, by propelling self with legs and steering with arms.*
- *May be disturbed by strangers.*

developmental delays signal a serious problem that requires intervention? First, consider the warning signs described below. If you are still concerned, check with your pediatrician. He or she can refer your child to the appropriate specialist. In the end, trust your intuition. If it feels as though something might be wrong, have the child checked.

- Are your child's skills consistently delayed

SEVENTH MONTH

- *Sits alone steadily for several minutes or more.*
- *Pushes up on hands and knees and rocks back and forth.*
- *Grasps, manipu-*
- *lates, mouths, bangs objects.*
- *Explores body with mouth and hands.*
- *Is more able to concentrate attention.*
- *Understands first words.*

in a *number* of areas—motor, language, and self-help?

- If your one-year-old has not started to *understand* some words, there may be a problem.
- Do you have any questions about your child's hearing? If so, act immediately. No

EIGHTH MONTH

- *Crawls, either forward or backward at first.*
- *Sits alone steadily for several minutes.*
- *Is developing pincer grasp with thumb and forefinger.*
- *Claps and waves hands.*
- *Retains small series of immediate past events.*
- *Babbles with a variety of sounds.*
- *Enjoys games such as "peekaboo" and "so big."*

child is too young for a hearing screening. Consider whether your child is awakened by loud noises, turns toward voices behind him, hears when you call from another room, and notices such things as the doorbell's ringing.

- Is your child's motor development significantly delayed in a *variety* of tasks, such as sitting, crawling, standing, and walking?

Knowledge of child development is important even for parents of children with no serious problems. A unique parent-education project in Missouri trained parents in the basics of child development. A subsequent evaluation found a strong correlation between a parent's knowledge of development and a child's achievement. "The more knowledgeable a parent was," researchers concluded, "the better the child performed on measures of intelligence, achievement, and language ability."

The awareness of what children are capable of at various ages allows parents to enhance

NINTH MONTH

- *May crawl up steps.*
- *May be able to stand, with or without support.*
- *Approaches small*
- *object with finger and thumb.*
- *Follows simple instructions.*
- *Can keep a series of ideas in mind.*
- *Initiates play.*

their growth at each stage without rushing them into areas they are not ready for. Parents who know that children understand language long before they are able to speak are more likely to talk with their infant. Exposure to conversation will help the child develop expressive language skills.

At the same time, knowledge of child development assures parents that it is appropriate and healthy for a two-year-old to be more interested in playing with dolls, trucks, and blocks, for example, than reading flashcards. These parents can provide appropriate toys and make adjustments in the environ-

TENTH MONTH

- *Stands with little support.*
- *Sidesteps along furniture (cruises).*
- *Sits down from standing position.*
- *Enjoys water play.*
- *Is interested in fitting things together.*
- *Searches for hidden object if she sees it hidden.*
- *Understands and obeys some words and commands.*

ELEVENTH MONTH

> • *Stands alone.*
> • *Takes a step or two without holding on.*
> • *Climbs up stairs.*
> • *Deliberately places objects.*
> • *Aware of own ac-*
> *tions and some of their implications.*
> • *Seeks approval and avoids disapproval.*
> • *Obeys commands; understands "no."*

ment as her skills develop. They realize that rushing a child into early academics not only is unproductive but often can be detrimental if it makes the child feel worth is based on performance.

ENJOY, ENJOY

The most important reason for learning about development, says McCall, is that "it makes having children more fun." It is "more intellectually interesting and emotionally fulfilling," he says, when you understand the normal process of development. We live in a society in which parents are not content to let their children be merely average and certainly not to let them be below average. Thus children are often rushed into formal learning. Everything we know about development tells us that this is not appropriate. When parents understand the wonder and uniqueness of each child's development, they will relish each stage of childhood—whenever it occurs.

TWELFTH MONTH

> • *Displays some combination of standing, walking, and cruising.*
> • *Can reach accurately for something as he looks away.*
> • *Can put things back*
> *together instead of just taking them apart.*
> • *Gives affection to humans and favored objects, such as toys.*
> • *Distinguishes self as separate from others.*

First Friends

*Baby friends can help each other learn, play, and develop; mostly,
though, they seem to make each other happy.*

Ruth Mason

Ruth Mason, a free-lance writer, lives in New
York City with her husband and two children.

It's a winter morning, and the members of my mothers' group and I are drinking coffee and tossing around ideas for getting more sleep. Our babies, all around six months old, are lying on a big quilt on the living room floor, gurgling over rattles. I see my daughter, Ilana, gaze at Beth's son, Matthew, the one baby in the group whom she has "known" since birth. Ilana drops her rattle and starts kicking her legs, squealing with excitement. Matthew returns the look and chortles. That afternoon, I write in the book I keep for Ilana, "She seems to have a thing for Matthew—and I think it's mutual."

Abby and Nancy, who met in a prepared-childbirth class, jokingly call their kids, Leah and Elliot, Lamaze siblings. For two years Abby and Nancy spent many afternoons together with their babies, and the families would often get together on weekends. At two and a half, Elliot and Leah are best friends. They speak to each other on real and toy telephones, greet each other with hugs, and ask to play together every chance they get.

Refuting old research.

For decades it was assumed that very young children did not form significant attachments to one another, but Matthew and Ilana, Leah and Elliot, and others like them are teaching the experts a thing or two. Jean Piaget, the grandfather of child-development research, had determined that preschoolers were egocentric, and subsequent thinking about their relationships flowed from that assumption. Until recently, experts believed five was the minimum age for making friends. But with increasing numbers of young children in group care, psychologists have had the opportunity to observe their interactions more closely. And they are beginning to see something new. When given the opportunity to socialize regularly, children under three can move beyond parallel play—in which two toddlers play near but not with each other—to a mutually rewarding friendship.

"We've documented friendships as early as ten months," says Carollee Howes, Ph.D., a developmental psychologist at the University of California at Los Angeles and a leading expert in the field. "They do exist."

Howes calls the relationship between two toddlers a friendship when they prefer each other above all other peers, engage in ongoing play, and show a lot of "positive affect"—that is, they smile and giggle a lot—when they play together.

But toddler friendships apparently go beyond play. "These friends don't just play together, they have an emotional connection to each other," says Edward Mueller, Ph.D., a clinical and developmental psychologist at Boston University. It was Mueller's landmark 1975 study of toddler interaction that began to change psychologists' and other researchers' thinking on early friendships. He became interested in the subject after watching his son, Loren, form a strong attachment to Robert, the son of family friends.

"Robert's mother is Danish, and the Danes have long believed that young children are capable of friendship," Mueller says. "She suggested getting the kids together regularly when Loren was eight months old and Robert was six months. Christmas break came about six months later, and the kids didn't see each other for a couple of weeks. When they met again, they played a greeting game showing their joy at being back together. Robert walked in the door and, gesturing to Loren, said, "Da!" and laughed. Loren laughed back. Robert gestured, said, "Da!" and laughed again, and Loren laughed back again, sustaining the game. This went on for about seventeen rounds.

"We realized then that this was more than a peer relationship," says Mueller. "It was a true friendship. We were amazed because it went against everything the textbooks said."

Mueller's federally funded three-year study of twelve-month-old to two-year-old children in play groups confirmed what he had seen in his own home. He found not only that the children developed relationships

From *Parents*, October 1990, pp. 83-86, 88. Copyright © 1990 by Ruth Mason. Reprinted by permission of the author.

but that a few of the pairs clearly had strong emotional ties.

Frequent contact.

Some parents who watch their little ones' developing friendships are amazed that children as young as one year of age will show a preference for playing with a particular child. Deborah Lowe Vandell, Ph.D., a psychologist at the University of Wisconsin—Madison who has studied friendship patterns among preschoolers, points out that even for the youngest children, "friendship implies some element of choice, just as it does for us."

However, the element that seems to have an even greater bearing on friendships is regular, sustained contact. "Kids have to have the opportunity to be with each other on a regular basis," says Vandell. She stresses that meeting in a gym or playground doesn't provide fertile ground for fostering friendships. Visits in each other's home, where the children can focus on each other and where they feel safe, are more conducive to making friends. But, she cautions, "If two kids are really different temperamentally, it won't necessarily work."

Hildy Ross, Ph.D., professor of psychology at the University of Waterloo, in Ontario, Canada, and Susan Lollis, Ph.D., assistant professor of child studies at the University of Guelph, also in Ontario, agree. They studied 32 pairs of toddlers, ages 20 and 30 months, who were brought together for play sessions several times a week over a period of four months.

Was there a special quality between some pairs of toddlers that was not there between others? "The kids all saw one another under the same circumstances, yet different relationships emerged," Ross says. The researchers found that in general, attractions were mutual. "If Michael loved Max, Max tended to love Michael. If Sarah ignored Jennifer, Jennifer ignored Sarah," Ross says. But Ross and Lollis, like other researchers, were stumped when asked *why* Michael liked Max. They have not yet been able to analyze scientifically the magic that happens when two toddlers click.

The mother connection.

Toddlers are virtually assured of the regular contact needed to foster friendship when their own mothers share a friendship. Researchers are just beginning to look at the influ-

---

ENCOURAGING FRIENDSHIPS: WHAT PARENTS CAN DO

Young friendships bloom when parents provide regular, sustained contact in an environment where children feel safe and secure.

1. Be a friend to your child. The roots of friendship are in a responsive, secure parent-child relationship. Early communication skills that infants learn with parents—like smiling and vocalizing—are later used with peers.

2. Interaction takes practice. Provide your infant or toddler with frequent and regular contact with a small number of peers (even one may be enough) in your home or theirs. Try to find mothers whose company you enjoy.

3. Choose the right materials. The younger the children, the bigger the toys should be: Dress-up items, large blocks, empty boxes, an exercise mat, and other household items contribute to cooperative play. Stay away from puzzles and small stacking toys, which kids tend to fight over.

4. Don't hover. Researchers notice that the presence of an intrusive adult inhibits interaction and conversation.

Toddlers play in more sophisticated ways when adults are not in control. Your quiet presence, however, is reassuring.

5. If possible, stay out of conflicts. Unless you see violence brewing, step back and give children over two years of age a chance to resolve the conflict. If you have to intervene, try the problem-solving approach. Say, "There's one doll and you both want it. What can we do?" You'd be surprised at how early on children are able to participate in solving their problems.

6. Don't take their words too literally. At two and three years of age, "You're not my friend" can simply mean "I'm mad at you right now."

7. Relax and enjoy yourself. Nurture and support your child's friendships, but don't push. Some toddlers are attracted to other children and connect with them easily. Others may not make friends until much later. —R.M.

---

ence of parents on babies' and toddlers' relationships. Whether or not they realize it, mothers who are friends seem to encourage their young children to become friends. I remember wanting Ilana and Matthew to be friends in part because I knew their developing friendship would cement the growing bond between his mother, Beth, and me. Elliot's mother, Nancy, says, "I probably encouraged his friendship with Leah by the way I talked about getting together. It was such a treat for me to see Abby."

It's not always mothers who bring two toddlers together. For two years, Vandell's daughter, Ashley, now five, shared a daytime baby-sitter with another child. Their friendship blossomed. "To this day, Ashley and Lila are incredibly close," Vandell says.

When friends come later.

In her studies of infant-peer relationships, Vandell noticed that firstborns were significantly more interactive than were other children. She says that the more babies are around older children, such as brothers and sisters, the less likely they are to interact with peers.

Other factors may also explain why second children seem to be less "friendship-prone." First-time mothers who seek out other mothers for companionship, and in the process provide playmates for their children, often don't have the time to do this once number two comes along. One mother I know says that her five-year-old has had a special friend since he was nine months old but that her two-year-old does not. "It's harder when you're on your older child's schedule," she says. "With the first, I sought friends for myself so I wouldn't go crazy. Now I already have my friends with children."

Of course, some toddlers, whether firstborn or not, just don't show much interest in other children until much later. One mother told me that she regularly invites other kids over to play with her two-and-a-half-year-old, but he just ignores them. Although my daughter, now five, has had two good buddies since infancy, my three-and-a-half-year-old son is only now just beginning to develop an interest in having friends.

"Friendships are important if

they're there, but it's not harmful *not* to have a friend," Mueller notes. "The key friendship at this stage should be with the parent."

How young friends play.

A friendship with someone their own age, however, gives toddlers opportunities they might not have otherwise. How many parents can sustain a game of run-around-the-dining-room-table-laughing 25 times and then want to do it again? That's what the very earliest games are like: repetition and imitation. A one-year-old shakes her head, and her friend imitates her. Two eighteen-month-olds take turns hiding behind a chair and then running out and scaring each other amid shrieks of laughter. Giving each other something—a ball, a stuffed animal—and then taking it back is also a favorite activity of one-year-old friends.

"Some parents don't think of these as games," says UCLA's Howes. "But to a fifteen-month-old, they definitely are. They have rules, a format, and the participants enjoy them."

Benefits of early friendship.

Aside from the sheer enjoyment of play, early friendships provide toddlers with other advantages. Vandell goes so far as to say that it's time to revise our concept of quality time. "There's so much emphasis—especially for children in day care—on spending quality time with a parent," she says. "In fact, when children stay home with their mothers, they also need quality time with peers. What we're learning is that both parents and peers are important."

Peers can sometimes play a role in development. One- and two-year-olds, for example, often are inspired by their friends to take the next developmental step. "The slightly more advanced toddler can provide a model that the less advanced child can match," says Dennie Palmer Wolf, Ed.D., a senior research associate at the Harvard Graduate School of Education, in Cambridge, Massachusetts. "If you have a friend who can climb stairs and you can't, that's a powerful incentive."

A toddler's friendship with someone who not only is willing to climb up and down a step 50 times but is enthusiastic about it also eases some of the pressure on the parents. "Especially with twos, it helps if you're not the only social outlet for your child," Mueller says.

Friends also tend to bring out each other's tolerance, generosity, and affection. Jon and Rebecca have been close since they were infants, when their mothers met at a local mothers' workshop. Sheila and Joan were both new mothers looking for companionship. They found it in each other, and their children's friendship has survived five years as well as Jon's move with his family to a neighboring state. At five, Jon is into Ghostbusters, and Rebecca likes to draw. When they get together, "Jon will tolerate Rebecca's coloring and even color with her, and then he'll want to play Ghostbusters. And even though she's not into that on her own, she'll play it with him," says Joan, Rebecca's mother. "She's more tolerant of him than of her other friends. There's something very special here."

Joan has seen how important Jon's friendship has been to Rebecca. She best articulates what is probably the most important benefit young children—and all of us—derive from having a close friend: "It's important to feel you're very special to someone outside your family. It makes you feel safe. It makes you feel loved."

Guns and Dolls

Alas, our children don't exemplify equality any more than we did. Is biology to blame? Scientists say maybe—but parents can do better, too.

LAURA SHAPIRO

Meet Rebecca. She's 3 years old, and both her parents have full-time jobs. Every evening Rebecca's father makes dinner for the family—Rebecca's mother rarely cooks. But when it's dinner time in Rebecca's dollhouse, she invariably chooses the Mommy doll and puts her to work in the kitchen.

Now meet George. He's 4, and his parents are still loyal to the values of the '60s. He was never taught the word "gun," much less given a war toy of any sort. On his own, however, he picked up the word "shoot." Thereafter he would grab a stick from the park, brandish it about and call it his "shooter."

Are boys and girls *born* different? Does every infant really come into the world programmed for caretaking or war making? Or does culture get to work on our children earlier and more inexorably than even parents are aware? Today these questions have new urgency for a generation that once made sexual equality its cause and now finds itself shopping for Barbie clothes and G.I. Joe paraphernalia. Parents may wonder if gender roles are immutable after all, give or take a Supreme Court justice. But burgeoning research indicates otherwise. No matter how stubborn the stereotype, individuals can challenge it; and they will if they're encouraged to try. Fathers and mothers should be relieved to hear that they do make a difference.

Biologists, psychologists, anthropologists and sociologists have been seeking the origin of gender differences for more than a century, debating the possibilities with increasing rancor ever since researchers were forced to question their favorite theory back in 1902. At that time many scientists believed that intelligence was a function of brain size and that males uniformly had larger brains than women—a fact that would nicely explain men's pre-eminence in art, science and letters. This treasured hypothesis began to disintegrate when a woman graduate student compared the cranial capacities of a group of male scientists with those of female college students; several women came out ahead of the men, and one of the smallest skulls belonged to a famous male anthropologist.

Gender research has become a lot more sophisticated in the ensuing decades, and a lot more controversial. The touchiest question concerns sex hormones, especially testosterone, which circulates in both sexes but is more abundant in males and is a likely, though unproven, source of aggression. To postulate a biological determinant for behavior in an ostensibly egalitarian

Girls' cribs have pink tags and boys' cribs have blue tags; mothers and . . .

NEWBORNS

. . . fathers should be on the alert, for the gender-role juggernaut has begun society like ours requires a thick skin. "For a while I didn't dare talk about hormones, because women would get up and leave the room," says Beatrice Whiting, professor emeritus of education and anthropology at Harvard. "Now they seem to have more self-confidence. But they're skeptical. The data's not in yet."

Some feminist social scientists are staying away from gender research entirely—"They're saying the results will be used against women," says Jean Berko Gleason, a professor of psychology at Boston University who works on gender differences in the acquisition of language. Others see no reason to shy away from the subject. "Let's say it were proven that there were biological foundations for the division of labor," says Cynthia Fuchs Epstein, professor of sociology at the City University of New York, who doesn't, in fact, believe in such a likelihood. "It doesn't mean we couldn't do anything about it. People can make from scientific findings whatever they want." But a glance at the way society treats those gender differences already on record is not very encouraging. Boys learn to read more slowly than girls, for instance, and suffer more reading disabilities such as dyslexia, while girls fall behind in math when they get to high school. "Society can amplify differences like these or cover them up," says Gleason. "We rush in reading teachers to do remedial reading, and their classes are almost all boys. We don't talk about it, we just scurry around getting them to catch up to the girls. But where are the remedial math teachers? Girls are *supposed* to be less good at math, so that difference is incorporated into the way we live."

No matter where they stand on the question of biology versus culture, social scientists agree that the sexes are much more alike than they are different, and that variations within each sex are far greater than variations between the sexes. Even differences long taken for granted have begun to disappear. Janet Shibley Hyde, a professor of psychology at the University of Wisconsin, analyzed hundreds of studies on verbal and math ability and found boys and girls alike in verbal ability. In math, boys have a moderate edge; but only among highly precocious math students is the disparity large. Most important, Hyde found that verbal and math studies dating from the '60s and '70s showed greater differences than more recent research. "Parents may be making more efforts to tone down the stereotypes," she says. There's also what academics call "the file-drawer effect." "If you do a study that shows no differences, you assume it won't be published," says Claire Etaugh, professor of psychology at Bradley University in Peoria, Ill. "And until recently, you'd be right. So you just file it away."

The most famous gender differences in academics show up in the annual SAT results,

which do continue to favor boys. Traditionally they have excelled on the math portion, and since 1972 they have slightly outperformed girls on the verbal side as well. Possible explanations range from bias to biology, but the socioeconomic profile of those taking the test may also play a role. "The SAT gets a lot of publicity every year, but nobody points out that there are more women taking it than men, and the women come from less advantaged backgrounds," says Hyde. "The men are a more highly selected sample: they're better off in terms of parental income, father's education and attendance at private school."

Girls are encouraged to think about how their actions affect others . . .

2-3 YEARS

. . . boys often misbehave, get punished and then misbehave again

Another longstanding assumption does hold true: boys tend to be somewhat more active, according to a recent study, and the difference may even start prenatally. But the most vivid distinctions between the sexes don't surface until well into the preschool years. "If I showed you a hundred kids aged 2, and you couldn't tell the sex by the haircuts, you couldn't tell if they were boys or girls," says Harvard professor of psychology Jerome Kagan. Staff members at the Children's Museum in Boston say that the boys and girls racing through the exhibits are similarly active, similarly rambunctious and similarly interested in model cars and model kitchens, until they reach first grade or so. And at New York's Bank Street preschool, most of the 3-year-olds clustered around the cooking table to make banana bread one recent morning were boys. (It was a girl who gathered up three briefcases from the costume box and announced, "Let's go to work.")

By the age of 4 or 5, however, children start to embrace gender stereotypes with a determination that makes liberal-minded parents groan in despair. No matter how careful they may have been to correct the disparities in "Pat the Bunny" ("Paul isn't the *only* one who can play peekaboo, *Judy* can play peekaboo"), their children will delight in the traditional male/female distinctions preserved everywhere else: on television, in books, at day care and preschool, in the park and with friends. "One of the

things that is very helpful to children is to learn what their identity is," says Kyle Pruett, a psychiatrist at the Yale Child Study Center. "There are rules about being feminine and there are rules about being masculine. You can argue until the cows come home about whether those are good or bad societal influences, but when you look at the children, they love to know the differences. It solidifies who they are."

Water pistols: So girls play dolls, boys play Ghostbusters. Girls take turns at hopscotch, boys compete at football. Girls help Mommy, boys aim their water pistols at guests and shout, "You're dead!" For boys, notes Pruett, guns are an inevitable part of this developmental process, at least in a television-driven culture like our own. "It can be a cardboard paper towelholder, it doesn't have to be a miniature Uzi, but it serves as the focus for fantasies about the way he is going to make himself powerful in the world," he says. "Little girls have their aggressive side, too, but by the time they're socialized it takes a different form. The kinds of things boys work out with guns, girls work out in terms of relationships—with put-downs and social cruelty." As if to underscore his point, a 4-year-old at a recent Manhattan party turned to her young hostess as a small stranger toddled up to them. "Tell her we don't want to play with her," she commanded. "Tell her we don't like her."

No matter what their parents do, girls and boys will enthusiastically . . .

4-5 YEARS

. . . embrace the male/female stereotypes they find all around them

Once the girls know they're female and the boys know they're male, the powerful stereotypes that guided them don't just disappear. Whether they're bred into our chromosomes or ingested with our cornflakes, images of the aggressive male and the nurturant female are with us for the rest of our lives. "When we see a man with a child, we say, 'They're playing'," says Epstein. "We never say, 'He's nurturant'."

The case for biologically based gender differences is building up slowly, amid a great deal of academic dispute. The theory is that male and female brains, as well as bodies, develop differently according to the amount of testosterone circulating around the time of birth. Much of the evidence rests on animal studies showing, for instance, that brain cells from newborn mice change their shape when treated with testosterone. The male sex hormone may also account for the different reactions of male and female rhesus monkeys, raised in isolation, when an infant monkey is placed in the cage. The males are more likely to strike at the infant, the females to nurture it. Scientists disagree—vehemently—on whether animal behavior has human parallels. The most convincing human evidence comes from anthropology, where cross-cultural studies consistently find that while societies differ in their predilection toward violence, the males in any given society will act more aggressively than the females. "But it's very important to emphasize that by aggression we mean only physical violence," says Melvin Konner, a physician and anthropologist at Emory University in Atlanta. "With competitive, verbal or any other form of aggression, the evidence for gender differences doesn't hold." Empirical findings (i.e., look around you) indicate that women in positions of corporate, academic or political power can learn to wield it as aggressively as any man.

Apart from the fact that women everywhere give birth and care for children, there is surprisingly little evidence to support the notion that their biology makes women kinder, gentler people or even equips them specifically for motherhood. Philosophers—and mothers, too—have taken for granted the existence of a maternal "instinct" that research in female hormones has not conclusively proven. At most there may be a temporary hormonal response associated with childbirth that prompts females to nurture their young, but that doesn't explain women's near monopoly on changing diapers. Nor is it likely that a similar hormonal surge is responsible for women's tendency to organize the family's social life or take up the traditionally underpaid "helping" professions—nursing, teaching, social work.

Studies have shown that female newborns cry more readily than males in response to the cry of another infant, and that small girls try more often than boys to comfort or help their mothers when they appear distressed. But in general the results of most research into such traits as empathy and altruism do not consistently favor one sex or the other. There is one major exception: females of all ages seem better able to "read" people, to discern their emotions, without the help of verbal cues. (Typically researchers will display a picture of someone expressing a strong reaction and ask test-takers to identify the emotion.) Perhaps this skill—which in evolutionary terms would have helped females survive and protect their young—is

the sole biological foundation for our unshakable faith in female selflessness.

Infant ties: Those who explore the unconscious have had more success than other researchers in trying to account for male aggression and female nurturance, perhaps because their theories cannot be tested in a laboratory but are deemed "true" if they suit our intuitions. According to Nancy J. Chodorow, professor of sociology at Berkeley and the author of the influential book "The Reproduction of Mothering," the fact that both boys and girls are primarily raised by women has crucial effects on gender roles. Girls, who start out as infants identifying with their mothers and continue to do so, grow up defining themselves in relation to other people. Maintaining human connections remains vital to them. Boys eventually turn to their fathers for self-definition, but in order to do so must repress those powerful infant ties to mother and womanhood. Human connections thus become more problematic for them than for women. Chodorow's book, published in 1978, received national attention despite a dense, academic prose style; clearly, her perspective rang true to many.

Harvard's Kagan, who has been studying young children for 35 years, sees a different constellation of influences at work. He speculates that women's propensity for caretaking can be traced back to an early awareness of their role in nature. "Every girl knows, somewhere between the ages of 5 and 10, that she is different from boys and that she will have a child—something that everyone, including children, understands as quintessentially natural," he says. "If, in our society, nature stands for the giving of life, nurturance, help, affection, then the girl will conclude unconsciously that those are the qualities she should strive to attain. And the boy won't. And that's exactly what happens."

Kagan calls such gender differences "inevitable but not genetic," and he emphasizes—as does Chodorow—that they need have no implications for women's status, legally or occupationally. In the real world, of course, they have enormous implications. Even feminists who see gender differences as cultural artifacts agree that, if not inevitable, they're hard to shake. "The most emancipated families, who really feel they want to engage in gender-free behavior toward their kids, will still encourage boys to be boys and girls to be girls," says Epstein of CUNY. "Cultural constraints are acting on you all the time. If I go to buy a toy for a friend's little girl, I think to myself, why don't I buy her a truck? Well, I'm afraid the parents wouldn't like it. A makeup set would really go against my ideology, but maybe I'll buy some blocks. It's very hard. You have to be on the alert every second."

In fact, emancipated parents have to be on

GIRLS

All children have to deal with aggression; girls wield relationships as . . .

6-7 YEARS

. . . weapons, while boys prefer to brandish water pistols.

BOYS

the alert from the moment their child is born. Beginning with the pink and blue name tags for newborns in the hospital nursery—I'M A GIRL/I'M A BOY—the gender-role juggernaut is overwhelming. Carol Z. Malatesta, associate professor of psychology at Long Island University in New York, notes that baby girls' eyebrows are higher above their eyes and that girls raise their eyebrows more than boys do, giving the girls "a more appealing, socially responsive look." Malatesta and her colleagues, who videotaped and coded the facial expressions on mothers and infants as they played, found that mothers displayed a wider range of emotional responses to girls than to boys. When the baby girls displayed anger, however, they met what seemed to be greater disapproval from their mothers than the boys did. These patterns, Malatesta suggests, may be among the reasons why baby girls grow up to smile more, to seem more sociable than males, and to possess the skill noted earlier in "reading" emotions.

The way parents discipline their toddlers also has an effect on social behavior later on. Judith G. Smetana, associate professor of education, psychology and pediatrics at the University of Rochester, found that mothers were more likely to deal differently with similar kinds of misbehavior depending on the sex of the child. If a little girl bit her friend and snatched a toy, for instance, the mother would explain why biting and snatching were unacceptable. If a boy did the same thing, his mother would be more likely to stop him, punish him and leave it at that. Misbehavior such as hitting in both sexes peaks around the age of 2; after that, little boys go on to misbehave more than girls.

Psychologists have known for years that boys are punished more than girls. Some have conjectured that boys simply drive their parents to distraction more quickly; but as Carolyn Zahn-Waxler, a psychologist at the National Institute of Mental Health, points out, the difference in parental treatment starts even before the difference in behavior shows up. "Girls receive very different messages than boys," she says. "Girls are encouraged to care about the problems of others, beginning very early. By elementary school, they're showing more caregiver behavior, and they have a wider social network."

Children also pick up gender cues in the process of learning to talk. "We compared fathers and mothers reading books to children," says Boston University's Gleason. "Both parents used more inner-state words, words about feelings and emotions, to girls than to boys. And by the age of 2, girls are using more emotion words than boys." According to Gleason, fathers tend to use more directives ("Bring that over here") and more threatening language with their sons than their daughters, while mothers' directives take more polite forms ("Could you bring that to me, please?"). The 4-year-old boys and girls in one study were duly imitating their fathers and mothers in that very conversational pattern. Studies of slightly older children found that boys talking among themselves use more threatening, commanding, dominating language than girls, while girls emphasize agreement and mutuality. Polite or not, however, girls get interrupted by their parents more often than boys, according to language studies—and women get interrupted more often than men.

Despite the ever-increasing complexity and detail of research on gender differences, the not-so-secret agenda governing the discussion hasn't changed in a century: how to understand women. Whether the question is brain size, activity levels or modes of punishing children, the traditional implication is that the standard of life is male, while the entity that needs explaining is female. (Or as an editor put it, suggesting possible titles for this article: "Why Girls Are Different.") Perhaps the time has finally come for a new agenda. Women, after all, are not a big problem. Our society does not suffer from burdensome amounts of empathy and altruism, or a plague of nurturance. The problem is men—or more accurately, maleness.

"There's one set of sex differences that's ineluctable, and that's the death statistics," says Gleason. "Men are killing themselves doing all the things that our society wants them to do. At every age they're dying in accidents, they're being

When girls talk among themselves, they tend to emphasize mutuality . . .

GIRLS

9-10 YEARS

BOYS

. . . and agreement, while boys often try to command and dominate

Where Little Boys Can Play With Nail Polish

For 60 years, America's children have been raised on the handiwork of Fisher-Price, makers of the bright plastic cottages, school buses, stacking rings and little, smiley people that can be found scattered across the nation's living rooms. Children are a familiar sight at corporate headquarters in East Aurora, N.Y., where a nursery known as the Playlab is the company's on-site testing center. From a waiting list of 4,000, local children are invited to spend a few hours a week for six weeks at a time playing with new and prototype toys. Staff members watch from behind a one-way mirror, getting an education in sales potential and gender tastes.

According to Kathleen Alfano, manager of the Child Research Department at Fisher-Price, kids will play with everything from train sets to miniature vacuum cleaners until the age of 3 or 4; after that they go straight for the stereotypes. And the toy business meets them more than halfway. "You see it in stores," says Alfano. "Toys for children 5 and up will be in either the girls' aisles or the boys' aisles. For girls it's jewelry, glitter, dolls, and arts and crafts. For boys it's model kits, construction toys and action figures like G.I. Joe. Sports toys, like basketballs, will be near the boys' end."

The company's own recent venture into gender stereotypes has not been successful. Fisher-Price has long specialized in what Alfano calls "open gender" toys, aimed at boys and girls alike, ages 2 to 7. The colors are vivid and the themes are often from daily life: music, banking, a post office. But three years ago the company set out to increase profits by tackling a risky category known in the industry as "promotional" toys. Developed along strict sex-role lines and heavily promoted on children's television programs, these toys for

ages 5 and up are meant to capture kids' fads and fashions as well as their preconceptions about masculinity and femininity. At Fisher-Price they included an elaborate Victorian dollhouse village in shades of rose and lavender, a line of beauty products including real makeup and nail polish, a set of battery-operated racing cars and a game table outfitted for pool, Ping-Pong and glide hockey. "The performance of these products has been very mixed," says Ellen Duggan, a spokesperson for Fisher-Price. "We're now refocusing on toys with the traditional Fisher-Price image." (The company is also independent for the first time in 21 years. Last month longtime owner Quaker Oats divested itself of Fisher-Price.)

Even where no stereotypes are intended, the company has found that some parents will conjure them up. At a recent session for 3-year-olds in the Playlab, the most sought-after toy of the morning was the fire pumper, a push toy that squirts real water. "It's for both boys and girls, but parents are buying it for boys," says Alfano. Similarly, "Fun with Food," a line of kitchen toys including child-size stove, sink, toaster oven and groceries, was a Playlab hit; boys lingered over the stove even longer than girls. "Mothers are buying it for their daughters," says Alfano.

Children tend to cross gender boundaries more freely at the Playlab than they do elsewhere, Alfano has noticed. "When 7-year-olds were testing the nail polish, we left it out after the girls were finished and the boys came and played with it," she says. "They spent the longest time painting their nails and drying them. This is a safe environment. It's not the same as the outside world."

LAURA SHAPIRO *in East Aurora*

shot, they drive cars badly, they ride the tops of elevators, they're two-fisted hard drinkers. And violence against women is incredibly pervasive. Maybe it's men's raging hormones, but I think it's because they're trying to be a *man*. If I were the mother of a boy, I would be very concerned about societal pressures that idolize behaviors like that."

Studies of other cultures show that male behavior, while characteristically aggressive, need not be characteristically deadly. Harvard's Whiting, who has been analyzing children cross-culturally for half a century, found that in societies where boys as well as girls take care of younger siblings, boys as well as girls show nurturant, sociable behavior. "I'm convinced that infants elicit positive behavior from people," says Whiting. "If you have to take care of somebody who can't talk, you have to learn empathy. Of course there can be all kinds of experiences that make you extinguish that eliciting power, so that you no longer respond positively. But on the basis of our data, boys make very good baby tenders."

In our own society, evidence is emerging that fathers who actively participate in raising their children will be steering both sons and daughters toward healthier gender roles. For the last eight years Yale's Pruett has been conducting a groundbreaking longitudinal study of 16 families, representing a range of socioeconomic circumstances, in which the fathers take primary responsibility for child care while the mothers work full time. The children are now between 8 and 10 years old, and Pruett has watched subtle but important differences develop between them and their peers. "It's not that they have conflicts about their gender identity—the boys are masculine and the girls are feminine, they're all interested in the same things their friends are," he says. "But when they were 4 or 5, for instance, the stage at preschool when the boys leave the doll corner and the girls leave the block corner, these children didn't give up one or the other. The boys spent time playing with the girls in the doll corner, and the girls were building things with blocks, taking pride in their accomplishments."

Little footballs: Traditionally, Pruett notes, fathers have enforced sex stereotypes more strongly than mothers, engaging the boys in active play and complimenting the girls on their pretty dresses. "Not these fathers," says Pruett. "That went by the boards. They weren't interested in bringing home little footballs for their sons or little tutus for the girls. They dealt with the kids according to the individual. I even saw a couple of the mothers begin to take over those issues—one of them brought home a Dallas Cowboys sleeper for her 18-month-old. Her husband said, 'Honey, I thought we weren't going to do this, remember?' She said, 'Do what?' So that may be more a function of being in the second tier of parenting rather than the first."

As a result of this loosening up of stereotypes, the children are more relaxed about gender roles. "I saw the boys really enjoy their nurturing skills," says Pruett. "They knew what to do with a baby, they didn't see that as a girl's job, they saw it as a human job. I saw the girls have very active images of the outside world and what their mothers were doing in the workplace—things that become interesting to most girls when they're 8 or 10, but these girls were interested when they were 4 or 5."

Pruett doesn't argue that fathers are better at mothering than mothers, simply that two involved parents are better than "one and a lump." And it's hardly necessary for fathers to quit their jobs in order to become more involved. A 1965-66 study showed that working mothers spent 50 minutes a day engaged primarily with their children, while the fathers spent 12 minutes. Later studies have found fathers in two-career households spending only about a third as much time with their children as mothers. What's more, Pruett predicts that fathers would benefit as much as children from the increased responsibility. "The more involved father tends to feel differently about his own life," he says. "A lot of men, if they're on the fast track, know a lot about competitive relationships, but they don't know much about intimate relationships. Children are experts in intimacy. After a while the wives in my study would say, 'He's just a nicer guy'."

Pruett's study is too small in scope to support major claims for personality development; he emphasizes that his findings are chiefly theoretical until more research can be undertaken. But right now he's watching a motif that fascinates him. "Every single one of these kids is growing something," he says. "They don't just plant a watermelon seed and let it die. They're really propagating things, they're doing salad-bowl starts in the backyard, they're breeding guinea pigs. That says worlds about what they think matters. Generativity is valued a great deal, when both your mother and your father say it's OK." Scientists may never agree on what divides the sexes; but someday, perhaps, our children will learn to relish what unites them.

What Birth Order Means

A child's place in the family can't explain
everything about him, but it
can yield important clues to his personality.

Jean Marzollo

Jean Marzollo is the author of many books for children and adults, including *Your Maternity Leave: How to Leave Work, Have a Baby, and Go Back to Work Without Getting Lost, Trapped, or Sandbagged Along the Way* (Poseidon).

I have two teenage sons. My older son has many of the characteristics researchers attribute to firstborns. He is organized, is a serious list maker, and is driven in accomplishing the goals that he sets for himself. On the other hand, when it comes to his schoolwork, "driven" hardly describes him. He's one of the most laid-back people I know. And believe me, if he's supposed to be a perfectionist, you wouldn't know it by looking in his closet.

My second child, and last-born, is, typically, a real charmer. When it's said that the baby of the family tends to get away with murder, I can relate. My younger son can talk me out of punishments and into privileges much too easily. Yet like his older brother, he's driven to accomplishment. At one point in their lives, the older one was quiet and responsible, as a firstborn is wont to be, while the younger one was chatty and irre-

sponsible. But as my sons have grown older, these distinctions have blurred or largely disappeared. The older one talks more; the younger one is more responsible. In fact, although my sons have many of the characteristics attributed to firstborn and second- or last-born children, it has become clearer that while their personalities are surely influenced by their position in the family, there's more to it than that.

Where birth order fits in.

In 1923, the renowned psychiatrist Alfred Adler, M.D., wrote that a person's "position in the family leaves an indelible stamp" on his or her "style of life." Subsequent research has shown that although birth order does affect a child, it does not automatically shape personality. If it did, life would be much more predictable and a good deal less interesting. Along with other critical factors—including heredity, family size, the spacing and sex of siblings, education, and upbringing—birth order provides clues about our children that we can use to help them feel good about who they are. "The point is not to put people in boxes but to

add to our general understanding of them," says Kevin Leman, Ph.D., author of *Were You Born for Each Other?* (Delacorte) and *The Birth Order Book* (Dell).

The danger of putting too much stock in birth-order analysis is that we may stereotype our children solely on the basis of their position in the family. We expect our firstborn to be John Glenn and our baby to be Paul Newman. "Our negative expectations can turn out to be self-fulfilling prophecies," warns psychologist Linda Musun-Miller, Ph.D., associate professor of psychology at the University of Arkansas at Little Rock. If we expect our last-born to be manipulative, we may unconsciously encourage that trait. If we expect our middle child to be insecure, we may treat her as an insecure person regardless of her true nature. Also, depending on the size of the family and the spacing of siblings, birth-order descriptions may not really apply. For example, according to Leman, if there are more than five years between a child and his closest brother or sister, he may be more like an only child than like a sibling. And in very large families, everything changes.

From *Parents*, December 1990, pp. 84-86, 88, 91. Copyright © 1990 by Jean Marzollo.

Your One and Only

"Only children may have high self-esteem and be more self-sufficient than all other children except those with one sibling," says Norval D. Glenn, Ph.D., professor of sociology at the University of Texas at Austin.

In many ways the only child is like the firstborn child. He benefits greatly from his parents' enthusiastic attention, as long as it isn't too critical and invasive. Because of their isolation, only children often develop agreeable ways of relating to adults—their parents and their parents' friends. They may also develop admirable skills for entertaining themselves when they are alone. "Because only children never have to compete with siblings for parental affection, they can develop a deep sense of security and self-worth," says Glenn.

On the downside, only children miss out on forming bonds and alliances with siblings. They may not have much opportunity at home to learn how to compete, negotiate, and compromise. As a result, they may have trouble sharing with other children and will have to wait until they're in school to learn to lead, cooperate, and follow.

Raising an only child is similar to bringing up a firstborn. In addition, though, it's important to make the most of your child's freedom to be himself by encouraging individual pursuits at home. Make sure you have art materials, books, records, tapes, and toys for him to explore. Take time to share in these activities with him.

Be patient if your child has problems making friends at school. Realize that your child is learning the people skills that children with siblings get a head start on at home. Help your child solve problems with friends just as you would help him learn any set of skills. —J.M.

"In families with four or more kids, there is a change in dynamics," explains Leman. "Large families tend to divide the children into two 'families'—the big ones and the little ones. And each of these 'families' will have its own firstborn, middle child, and baby."

We need to keep birth-order research in perspective. As Leman explains, each position in a family has its advantages and disadvantages, and knowing this gives parents some important guidance for maximizing their children's strengths and minimizing their problems.

The first child: the achiever.

"Firstborn," says Leman, can be used to describe either the first child or the first male or female child. These kids are typically the ones "who [as adults] are driven toward success and stardom in their given fields." Many choose a demanding career in science, engineering, medicine, or law. Of the first 23 astronauts, 21 were firstborn or only children.

In general, firstborn children have higher IQs than younger siblings have—not because they're innately more intelligent but, say researchers, because of the amount of attention eager new parents pay to their first child. The firstborn's audience of parents and caregivers is enthusiastic, so she takes pride in her accomplishments and develops a deep sense of self-worth. Because the first child is taken seriously, she responds seriously—by making a responsible inner commitment to personal achievement and growth. Often a firstborn child is conscientious and well organized—a list maker. "These wonderful traits are the perks of being first," explains Norval D. Glenn, Ph.D., professor of sociology at the University of Texas at Austin. "But there are also problems with being first out of the cradle."

Firstborns often suffer from a type of pseudomaturity, explains Leman. "They may act grown-up throughout childhood, because their role models are grown-ups rather than older siblings, only to reject the role of leader in early adulthood." A firstborn is also not the most gracious receiver of criticism, and adults' constant critical comments of his performance may cause the child to become a worried perfectionist. He may fear making mistakes before eyes that he feels are constantly watching him and may grow to hate criticism because it emphasizes the faults that he's trying to overcome.

True to their reputation for excelling, firstborns will rise to the challenge of competition, especially within the family. The arrival of a sibling, for example, may lead a firstborn to wonder, Why is this little crying baby, who can't do anything, getting so much attention? And what happened to all the attention I used to get? Concluding that babyish behavior is the way to go, the youngster may try to reclaim center stage by imitating the baby.

If this doesn't work, she may shift tactics and try to imitate her parents by being helpful in caring for the baby. The child-as-parent role can be overdone, however. The firstborn needs, and deserves, her full share of childhood. Parents can reassure her that she is not being displaced and that she needs to be neither a baby nor a parent to continue to receive love; she can just be herself.

Raising the first.

Encourage your child's development without demanding perfection. "In particular, the parent of the opposite sex of the firstborn [mother of son, father of daughter] should avoid excessive criticism," says Leman. "Children especially want to please opposite-sex parents. If they conclude that they can't, they may give up." In general, both parents should welcome a firstborn's willingness to achieve, and at the same time should convey the message not only that mistakes are permissible but that everyone makes them.

It's also important to help your child realize for himself that he doesn't have to do everything perfectly. "Teach him to take smaller bites of life and to work on saying no," advises Leman. "And please, encourage his sense of humor. Help him enjoy life."

The middle child: the diplomat.

Middle children are "born too late to get the privileges and special treatment that firstborns seem to inherit by right," says Leman. And when another child arrives, middle children lose the bonanza that lastborns enjoy—the relaxing of the disciplinary reins, which is sometimes translated as "getting away with murder."

"It's important for all children to feel special in their parents' eyes and to have a quality they feel is valued in the family," explains Jeannie Kidwell, Ph.D., an adjunct professor of psychology at Florida State University and a family therapist in Tallahassee. "In the case of the middle child, it's especially hard to carve out that niche in the family." Neither the achiever nor the baby, the middle child may feel that he has no particular role in the family. Consequently, he may look outside the family to define himself.

"Friends become very important to children in the middle," says Leman. "In outside groups, they find it easier to carve their own identities. They develop friendship skills that firstborns may lack, and they learn to be good team players and club members."

Lacking the benefit of the exceptions parents make for their firstborns and their last-borns, middle children may learn to negotiate, to compromise, to give and take—valuable life skills that will help them succeed. They can become effective managers and leaders because they are good listeners and can cope with varying points of view. By necessity, "middle children get better training for real life than firstborns and babies," says Leman.

Researchers who study birth order say that the middle child is the hardest to describe because she is influenced by so many variables, especially the personalities of her older and younger siblings and the number of years between them. Kidwell finds that middle children suffer the lowest self-esteem if there is a two-year difference between them and their siblings, because they're competing with both the older and the younger child and, in their estimation, they don't measure up to either. If siblings are closer in age (say, a year apart)—and, therefore, more alike—or further apart (say, three years)—and, consequently, quite different—the middle child's self-esteem is stronger. She also finds that middle children have more self-confidence if their siblings are of the opposite sex, because there is less competition. These characteristics hold true throughout childhood, but they're especially noticeable in early childhood, when competition for their parents' attention and affection is at its peak, and in early adolescence, when teenagers are searching for themselves.

How to raise kids in the middle.

Help your middle child develop self-esteem by recognizing her talents and individuality. You may be less of a cheerleader for your middle child without being aware of it. If your child is developing a competitive sense, help her channel this drive into age-appropriate sports and other competitive activities. If she displays a talent for listening and mediating, show your appreciation of these skills and encourage your "peacemaker" to speak her mind, to bring her ideas to family discussions, and to share them with others. Make an effort to give your middle child a little extra attention so that she doesn't have to fight for it within the family. If your middle child is two years older and younger than her siblings, be especially sensitive to this child's need to establish her value in your eyes.

Because middle children often feel it necessary to establish themselves through friendships outside the family, help fulfill this need by supporting group activities.

As they try to decide what they want to be when they grow up, "middle children are most likely to become whatever their older siblings are not," says Kidwell. "They bounce off the kids directly above them, deliberately taking on traits and interests that will save them from having to compete with big brother or sister. This is particularly true with an older sibling of the same sex."

If the oldest boy is a good athlete, the second may try hard to get a good report card. As parents, we can understand this natural tendency of a child to go in the opposite direction of an older sibling as a way of carving out a personal identity. And while we support our children's efforts to be what they want to be, we also should refrain from typing them "the jock" and "the brain." Instead, we can let our children know that we think of each of them as a whole, lovable child whose many talents can develop over the years.

The second-born child.

Because slightly more than one third of American families today have only two children, many parents find themselves thinking in terms of the firstborn and the second-born. The second-born child, however, does share some characteristics with the middle child. Like the middler, the second-born is likely to search for ways to be different from the firstborn child. If the firstborn is neat, the second-born may be messy. The second-born also shares characteristics with the last-born, the "baby."

"A lot depends on the family dynamics, particularly family spacing," says Kidwell. "Two children spaced two years apart may develop a particularly intense rivalry, feeling they can't play the same role in the family." When there are more years between the children, the second not only may look up to his big brother or sister but may fruitlessly spend a good portion of his childhood trying to catch up to the older sibling.

How to raise a second child.

Let your second child choose his own role—whether it's the same as or different from that of the older sibling. Be flexible in your expectations of your kids and whatever roles they select. If one chooses to be involved in sports or drawing while the other spends every free moment in the school library, accept it, but also be aware of, and support, the activities they enjoy together (say, listening to music, having you read to them).

Make sure that each child gets one-on-one time with you. When you're with both children, find ways to treat them equally, yet as individuals, too.

The last-born child: the baby.

The baby of the family is often given an extra dose of affection and attention, as well as a dispensation from rules. Seasoned parents know how fast childhood goes by, so they often justify their permissiveness by telling themselves, He's our last, so let's enjoy him as long as we can.

The positive consequences of this more permissive upbringing are that many last-borns are fun-loving, affectionate, and persuasive. They often grow up to become successful salespeople, counselors, and teachers.

On the negative side, the endless fawning over and praise of these youngsters—primarily because of their place in the family—may leave them feeling that their families do not take them seriously. "And," says Leman, "there's another difficult aspect to the charming last-born's life. She grows up being coddled one minute as a darling little baby, but the next minute she's compared unfavorably with an older sibling. She can't clear the table without spilling something. She can't clean up her room by herself. She can't walk as fast as everyone else through the amusement park. As a result of such conflicting experiences, last-borns can be extremely self-confident in some ways and insecure in others."

Having learned that, as the baby of the family, they cannot *insist* on anything, some last-borns have learned to beg and cajole very effectively—sometimes through smiles, sometimes through tears. The effect is the same: They get their way.

Bringing up baby.

Since he is the youngest, the last-born may be introduced by his parents as "our baby" even when he is an adult. Let your child grow up when it's time to grow up. Teach him to accept age-appropriate responsibilities. Praise him for carrying out reasonable chores. Avoid doing his chores yourself simply because it's

easier on you. Don't let him get away with murder.

Though your baby is adorable, beware of setting him up to perform whenever anyone visits. Display your love for him at times when he is not being adorable, when he's not the center of attention. If you worry that you don't pay enough attention to your child or that it fluctuates, make an effort to give attention to your last-born consistently. This way your baby will learn that he doesn't have to be charming or a cutup to catch your eye, that he can count on it "for free."

Appreciating kids for themselves.

Birth order—along with gender, the child's temperament, and parental influence—is certainly a contributing factor in a youngster's personality, but it's important to focus on your child as a unique individual. By making judgments primarily on the basis of "where the chips fall," parents may lose the opportunity to appreciate their children for who they really are and what each child has to offer. Regardless of whether they were born first, last, or somewhere in between, they're special.

Working Parents

One of America's leading pediatricians tells how
to cope with the stresses of jobs and family life

DR. T. BERRY BRAZELTON

The question I'm asked most frequently these days is, "Has child rearing changed since you started working with families in the 1950s?" I become almost speechless. The changes have been so great, and the new stresses on families so real and so apparent. What hasn't changed is the passion that parents have for doing a good job in raising their children. We in the '50s were passionate. But we were somber, undecided, retiring. We turned for advice to Dr. Spock. We brooded about whether we were doing the right things for our children.

The degree of stress that new parents feel about child rearing hasn't changed, but the focus for their anxiety has. We are in a period of real pressure on families. Parents have as much concern today about keeping the family together as in doing well by their children. At a time when nearly 50 percent of all marriages end up in divorce, maintaining family life is a high-risk venture. Single parents struggle against the dual demands of providing financial and emotional support for their children. Two-career couples face the conflicts of trying to balance work and family life—and trying to do both well.

These "new" families are searching for guidelines for rearing their children. As I talk with working parents around the country, they ask similar questions about how to cope with work and home—how to care for their children in a changing world, how to deal with the limited time they have for family life, how to live with the anxieties they have about child care, how to handle the inevitable

competition they feel with their mates and caregivers. Yet for all their doubts and fears, there is a new force in the air that I feel in my contact with young families. The parents of this generation are beginning to feel empowered. They are asking hard questions, demanding answers, and they are ready to fight for what they need for their children and for themselves. "Parent power" is the new catch phrase.

Roles and Rivalries

In our culture, we live with a deep-seated view that a woman's role is in the home. She should be there for her children, so the theory goes, and both she and they will suffer if she's not. I felt that way for a long time myself, and it took constant badgering from my three militant daughters, who all work, as well as from a whole succession of working parents in my practice, to disabuse me of my set of mind. This bias prevents us from giving working women the support they need. It keeps us from realizing that 52 percent of women whose children are under 3 are in the work force, and it prevents us from providing them with choices for adequate child care. Many working women have no alternative but to leave their infants and small children in conditions none of us would trust. These women are as certain as you and I that their babies are at risk. But they have no choice.

Because of their double roles, women face a costly, necessary split within themselves. Can they invest themselves in a successful career and still be able to nur-

ture a family? Can they cope with the guilt and the grief that they feel when they leave their children every day? Will women feel threatened as men get closer to the children? Their worries are understandable. A parent who must leave her small baby before she has completed her own work of attaching to him can't help but grieve. It's hard to free up energy for the workplace if a mother spends her time wondering whether her child is being adequately cared for. Women who choose to stay home with their children are equally conflicted. They wonder whether they should continue their careers out of self-protection—and whether the family can manage on one salary instead of two.

Upsetting as they may be, such concerns can be put to positive use. Women should allow themselves to feel anxious and guilty about leaving their children—those feelings will press them to find the best substitute care. Women can also find strength in their double roles. Lois Hoffman, a professor at the University of Michigan, has demonstrated in a study that working mothers who feel confident and fulfilled in their jobs bring that sense of competence home to their children.

For men, greater involvement in the work of family life has forced them to confront the same conflicts women do—trying to balance working and caring. And as fathers accept nurturing roles within the family, competition with women is bound to emerge. There is an inevitable rivalry for the baby that will spring up between caring parents. Women may unconsciously act

Bringing up Baby: A Doctor's Prescription for Busy Parents

Juggling work and family life can often seem overwhelming. Dr. Brazelton offers some practical advice for easing the strain on harried parents:

1 Learn to compartmentalize—when you work, be there, and when you are at home, be at home.

2 Prepare yourself for separating each day. Then prepare the child. Accompany him to his caregiver.

3 Allow yourself to grieve about leaving your baby—it will help you find the best substitute care, and you'll leave the child with a passionate parting.

4 Let yourself feel guilty. Guilt is a powerful force for finding solutions.

5 Find others to share your stress—peer or family resource groups.

6 Include your spouse in the work of the family.

7 Face the reality of working and caring. No supermom or superbaby fantasies.

8 Learn to save up energy in the workplace to be ready for homecoming.

9 Investigate all the options available at your workplace—on-site or nearby day care, shared-job options, flexible-time arrangements, sick leave if your child is ill.

10 Plan for children to fall apart when you arrive home after work. They've saved up their strongest feelings all day.

11 Gather the entire family when you walk in. Sit in a big rocking chair until everyone is close again. When the children squirm to get down, you can turn to chores and housework.

12 Take children along as you do chores. Teach them to help with the housework, and give them approval when they do.

13 Each parent should have a special time alone with each child every week. Even an hour will do.

14 Don't let yourself be overwhelmed by stress. Instead, enjoy the pleasures of solving problems together. You can establish a pattern of working as a team.

like "gatekeepers," excluding men from their babies' care. A new mother will say to her inexperienced, vulnerable husband, "Darling, that's not the way you diaper a baby!" or "You hold a baby *this* way." Working families need to be aware of this competition, which can disrupt family ties unless it is recognized. If parents can discuss it, the rivalry can motivate each person to become a better parent.

How can working men and women make the time they have with their children "quality time"? It's difficult when parents see their children for only an hour or two in the morning and a few hours in the evening. The whole concept of quality time can feel like a pressure. But if parents can concentrate on getting close to their children as soon as they walk in the door, then everything that follows becomes family time—working, playing, talking. Parents can involve children in their chores, teaching them to share the housework. Children who participate in the family's solutions will be competent to handle the stresses of their own generation. Even if time is short during workdays, parents can set aside time on the weekend for family celebration. Each parent should have a special time alone with each child at least once a week. An hour will do. But talk about it all week to remind the child—and yourself—that you will have a chance to cement your special relationship.

Conflicts

All parents worry about the same kinds of problems—sleep, feeding, toilet training, sibling rivalry. But there are some issues that seem especially troublesome for working parents, in part because the limited time they have with their children makes each problem seem twice as difficult. Some of the more perplexing issues—and suggestions for coping with them:

Going back to work: I am often asked when women should go back to work. I don't like to advocate one period of time over another, because for economic reasons some women don't have a choice about how long they can stay home. I am fighting for a four-month period of unpaid parental leave for both fathers and mothers, however, because I believe we must provide parents with the time to learn how to attach both to the baby and to each other. By 4 months, when colic has ended, and when the baby and parent know how to produce smiles and to vocalize for each other, the baby feels secure enough to begin turning away to look at other adults and to play with his own feet and his own toys. For the parent, it is marked by the sure knowledge that "he knows *me*. He will smile or vocalize at *me.*"

℞: Regardless of how much time new parents can take off from work, it's important to recognize that the process of learning to attach to a new infant is not a simple

one. Everyone who holds a new baby falls in love. But while falling in love is easy, staying in love takes commitment. A newborn demands an inordinate amount of time and energy. He needs to be fed, changed, cuddled, carried and played with over endless 24-hour periods. He is likely to cry inconsolably every evening for the first 12 weeks. Much of the time his depressed, frightened parents are at a loss about what to do for him. A new mother will be dogged by postpartum blues; a new father is likely to feel helpless and want to run away. Their failures in this period are a major part of the process of learning to care. When new parents do not have the time and freedom to face this process and live through it successfully, they may indeed escape emotionally. In running away, they may miss the opportunity to develop a secure attachment to their baby—and never get to know themselves as real parents.

Separation: Leave-taking in the morning can be a problem. Children will dawdle. They won't get dressed and they won't eat. Parents feel under pressure to get going; children resist this pressure. Everything goes to pot. The parent is faced with leaving a screaming child, and ends up feeling miserable all day.

℞ : Get up earlier. Sit down to talk or get close with the children before urging them to get dressed. Help them choose their clothes. Talk out the separation ahead. Remind them of the reunion at the end of the day. When you're ready to go, gather them up. Don't expect cooperation—the child is bound to be angry that you're leaving. And don't sneak out: always tell a child when you're going. Say goodbye and don't prolong your departure.

Discipline: The second most important parental job is discipline. Love comes first, but firm limits come second. A working parent feels too guilty and too tired to want to be tough at the end of the day. Of course parents would rather dodge the issue of being tough. But a child's agenda is likely to be different. When a child is falling apart, as children tend to do at the end of the day, he needs you most. He gets more frantic, searching for limits. Children need the security of boundaries, of knowing where they must stop.

℞: Discipline should be seen as teaching rather than punishment. Taking time out, physically restraining and holding the child or isolating him for a brief period breaks the cycle. Immediately afterward parents can sit down and discuss the limits with firm assurance. No discipline works magically. Every episode is an opportunity to teach—but to teach *over time*. Working families need more organization than other families to make things work, and discipline gives a child a sense of being part of that organization.

Sleep issues: Separation during the day is

On Competing With Caregivers

A child can adjust to two or more styles of child rearing if each of the adults cares about him as an individual

so painful for working parents that separating at night becomes an even bigger issue, and putting their children to bed is fraught with difficulty. The normal teasing any child does about staying up is so stressful that working parents find it tough to be firm. Then a child's light-sleep episodes, which occur every three or five hours, become added conflicts. If the child cries out, parents often think they must go in to help her get back into a deep sleep. But learning to sleep through the night is important for the child's own sense of independence.

℞: Teaching the child to get to sleep is the first goal. A child is likely to need a "lovey" or a comfort object, an independent resource to help her break the day-to-night transition. Learning to get herself to sleep means having a bedtime ritual that is soothing and comforting. But a child shouldn't fall asleep in her parent's arms; if she does, then the parents have made themselves part of the child's sleep ritual. Instead, after she's quiet, put her in bed with her lovey and pat her down to sleep. When she rouses every four hours, give her no more than five minutes to scrabble around in bed. Then go in and show her how to find her own comfort pattern for herself.

Feeding: Parents often believe that feeding is the major responsibility they have in taking care of their children. "If a child doesn't eat properly, it's the parent's fault," goes the myth. "A good parent gets a well-rounded diet into a child." Yet this myth ignores the child's need for autonomy in feeding. Each burst of independence hits feeding headlong, and food becomes a major issue. But because they are away most of the day, parents feel a need to become close to their children at mealtimes.

℞: Try to ease up on the struggle. Leave as much as possible to the child. Steps to create autonomy in feeding: start finger-feeding at 8 months. Let her make all of her own choices about what she'll eat by 1 year. Expect her to tease with food in the 2nd year. Set yourself easily attainable goals. If a child won't eat vegetables, give her a multivitamin every day. A simple amount of milk and protein covers her other needs for the short run. Most important, don't make food an issue. When parents come home from work in the evening, family time should emphasize sharing the experiences of the day, not eating. Your relationship is more important than the quantities of food consumed.

Competition with the caregiver: Every important area in child rearing—eating, discipline, toilet training—is likely to be a source of conflict between parents and caregivers. Both must recognize that the child's issues are ones of independence; the caregiver's, ones of control.

℞: Conflict is inevitable. A child can adjust to two or even three different styles of child rearing if each of the adults really cares about him as an individual—and if parents and caregivers are in basic agreement on important issues. Differences in technique don't confuse a child—differences in basic values do.

Supermom and superbaby: People in conflict or under pressure dream about perfectionism. But trying to be perfect creates its own stresses. Any working mother is bound to blame any inadequacy in her own or her child's life on the fact that she's working. Being a perfect parent is not only an impossibility—it would be a disaster. Learning to be a parent is learning from mistakes.

℞ : Understand that there is no perfect way to be a parent. The myth of the supermom serves no real purpose except to increase the parent's guilt. And for children in working families, the pressures are already great. To expect them to be superbabies adds more pressure than they can face. Respect the child by understanding the demands she already faces in the normal stages of growing up. Teaching a child too early deprives her of her childhood. Play is the way a child learns and the way she sorts out what works for her. When she finds it on her own she gains a sense of competence.

Support Systems

We need a cushion for parents who are learning about their new job, to replace the role of the extended family when it is not available. When young parents are under stress—the normal stresses of childbearing and child rearing—they often don't know whom to turn to for help. If possible, I would prefer that grandparents be nearby and available. They can offer their own children a sense of security and support, which comes in handy at each new stress point. But parents often hesitate to turn to grandparents for advice. "They would tell me what to do, and I'd never do it that way" is a refrain I hear. My response is: "But if you know you'd 'never do it their way,' then you'd have a simpler decision to make."

Working men and women can also turn to other parents for support. Childbirth-education classes have been enormously valuable in helping parents face pregnancy and delivery successfully. Peer groups that provide support systems for parents are building on this model. Since its start 10 years ago, for example, The Family Resource Coalition in Chicago has been a drop-in center for single parents trying to raise their children alone in poorer sections of Chicago. There are similar centers across the United States for parents of all circumstances. Memberships in these groups can be counted in the hundreds of thousands. Special peer-support groups have been formed for parents of premature and high-risk babies; others have formed for the parents of almost every kind of impaired child.

What Can Be Done

Why haven't we done more as a nation to help working parents face the stresses of family life? We seem to be dominated by a bias left over from our pioneering ancestors: "Families should be self-sufficient. If they're not, they should suffer for it." Ironically, government help seems to increase families' dependency and insufficiency. As they are now configured, our government programs are available only to those who are willing to label themselves as failures—poor, hungry, uneducated, unmarried, single parents. This labeling produced the effect of giving up one's self-image. Labeled families become a self-fulfilling prophecy. We are reinforcing people not for success, but for failure.

Several of us have just formed a new grass-roots organization in Washington called Parent Action. This is a lobbying organization to demonstrate the energy that parents have. The organization of the American Association of Retired Persons has been successful in lobbying for the elderly. We want to push the concerns of families to the forefront of our nation's conscience.

So far, we in the United States have not even begun to address the burgeoning need for quality care for the children of working parents. We are the only industrialized country (aside from South Africa) that has not faced up to what is happening to young families as they try to cope with working and raising children. Indeed, our disappointing record in supporting families and children suggests that we are one of the least child-oriented societies in the world. The recent failure of the Alliance for Better Child Care, a bill sponsored by the Children's Defense Fund, a Washington-based advocacy group, represents just such an example. It would have provided national funds to increase the salaries of child-care workers so that trained personnel would have an incentive to care for infants and small children.

In order to pay for the kind of care that every child deserves, the cost could be amortized four ways: by federal and state governments, by individual businesses and by the individual family. Business can play a key role. Offering employees parental leave, flexible work schedules and on-site or nearby day care would assure companies of a kind of allegiance that can be seen in European and Asian countries. Businesses that pay attention to the family concerns of their employees are already reaping rewards. Studies demonstrate that employees of such firms display less burnout, less absenteeism, more loyalty to the company and significantly more interest in their jobs.

As a nation, we have two choices. One is to continue to let our biases dominate our behavior as a society. The other is to see that we are a nation in crisis. We are spending billions of dollars to protect our families from outside enemies, imagined and real. But we do not have even 50 percent of the quality child care we need, and what we do have is neither affordable nor available to most families. These conditions exist in the face of all we know about the effects of emotional deprivation in early childhood. The rise in teenage suicide, pregnancies and crime should warn us that we are paying a dreadful price for not facing the needs of families early on. We are endangering both the present and the next generation.

Improving conditions for working parents has a visible payoff. When parents have options and can make their own choices, they feel respected and secure. I can tell when working parents are successfully sharing the day-to-day work of the family. Men walk differently as they enter my office. A father who is participating actively in his child's care walks straighter, has a more jaunty air, and he can't wait to tell me about each of his baby's successes. A working mother who has found a balance between her work and her family speaks more decisively. She handles her baby with assurance, and she is eager to include her solutions in our discussion of her child's progress. These parents are empowered. Helping others to feel the way they do is an investment in the future.

Single-Parent Families: How Bad for the Children?

K. ALISON CLARKE-STEWART

Alison Clarke-Stewart is a professor in the Program in Social Ecology at the University of California, Irvine. She has written extensively about the various environments that influence children's development, including the family and day care. Currently she is doing research on how divorce and child custody affect children. Her books include: Daycare *and* Child Development in the Family.

Researchers know many factors that make divorce harder for children to endure—and the school can't do much about them. But teachers can help keep school from being one more problem.

Six-year-old Nathaniel makes his own lunch before he goes to school. Nine-year-old Katherine comes home to an empty house and spends the afternoon watching television. Twelve-year-old Jason does the shopping, babysits for his younger sister, and sighs a lot. There's no question, children today do not live the protected, dependent existence that most of their parents—and teachers—did as youngsters. Responsibilities are thrust upon children at earlier and earlier ages. Expectations for their independence and achievement are high. Many of them experience daily stress.

One contributing factor in the complex web of contemporary economics and life-styles is the increased frequency with which children are growing up in single-parent families. A high proportion of these families are the result of divorce, and it is specifically on the distinctive situation of such families that this paper will focus.

Today, in the United States, one schoolchild in three has parents who are divorced. Thirty percent of these children live in stepfamilies. The other 70 percent live with their mothers or fathers alone.

What are the consequences of their parents' divorcing for children's lives, development, and achievement? Are these children "at risk"? If so, how much, and for how long? Should unhappy parents have stayed together "for the sake of the children"? Behavior problems observed in children from "broken homes" are often attributed to the parents' divorce, but is this always an accurate assessment? Are

From *NEA Today*, January 1989, pp. 60-64. Reprinted by permission of the National Educational Association of the United States.

there ways that schools and teachers can help children with problems rooted in their parents' divorce?

As divorce has become more and more common in this society, researchers have asked these questions, and the answers they have come up with are both worrying and encouraging. Worrying, because their observations show that children do indeed suffer, and suffer severely, when their parents get divorced. Encouraging, because they also show that negative effects on children's psychological well-being are not inevitably long-lasting. Children can be helped through the painful transition of their parents' divorce to a healthy, happy, and well-adjusted life.

How Divorce Hurts

The effects of divorce begin long before the divorce itself, for both parents and children. In one study, observations of children as long as 11 years before their parents separated showed the effects of predivorce family stress. Boys in families in which the parents subsequently divorced were more impulsive and aggressive than boys in nondivorcing families. For parents, the effects begin to show in the years before the separation, through such symptoms as headaches, fatigue, weight loss, depression, anxiety, and mood swings—and these symptoms intensify after the separation. On a scale of stressful life events, separating from a spouse is second in intensity only to the death of a spouse. Over 40 percent of the adults going through a divorce report suffering from at least five physical or psychological symptoms; one-fifth need psychiatric help or hospitalization.

For children, too, the initial reaction to their parents' separation is traumatic. Children whose parents get divorced are initially distraught, shocked, afraid for their own futures. It doesn't make it any easier that one in three of their friends may be in the same boat. Losing *their* mother or *their* father is devastating. Their world turns upside down. Divorce is most devasting for "innocent victims"—those who have no control over its initiation—and children never initiate divorces.

In one study, interviews with children whose parents were getting divorced showed that none of them were happy about their parents' di-

vorce, even if the parents were often in violent conflict with each other. More than three-quarters of the children opposed the divorce strongly, and even five years later one-third were still disapproving, dissatisfied, and intensely unhappy. The nuclear family is all the child knows, so children inevitably experience a strong feeling of loss—of the family unit, of security, and of their fairy-tale fantasy of "happily ever after."

After the divorce, the losses continue. For some things in life—and parents may be among them—two is always better than one. One parent can be in only one place at a time, and for parents going through a divorce, that place is most often work, therapy, or the lawyer's office. One parent can have only one point of view, and for divorcing parents that point of view is most often their own. One parent can model only one gender role, give only so many hugs, offer so much discipline, and earn so much money.

Parents going through a divorce and the period following it are overwhelmed, overworked, and disorganized. There is not enough time for work or for themselves. They are absorbed in their own problems of survival, in their involvement in work (for many women, for the first time), in dating, in self-improvement, and in the search for support.

The children are often neglected. In the first couple of years after the divorce, children have less regular bedtimes and mealtimes, eat together as a family less, hear fewer bedtime stories, and are more often late for school. Discipline is less consistent, positive, and affectionate. And perhaps most salient of all, the aftermath of divorce brings economic disaster for most mothers and children.

Recent studies in a number of states have shown that after a divorce women suffer a drastic drop in income and

> **Not one child was happy about a family divorce, even if the parents were often in violent conflict with each other.**

standard of living—in California, for example, a drop of 73 percent. Men's standard of living improves—42 percent in the states included in this study. Most women are not prepared to support themselves financially, even if they worked before the divorce. They commonly receive inequitable divorce settlements, no lifetime alimony, and a limited amount of spousal and child support (often not paid). They have few job prospects, no job histories, limited earning potential, and no careers. Because 90 percent of children in divorced families live with their mothers, this economic disaster directly affects the children. No-fault divorce has created a new impoverished class. More than half of poor families are made up of single mothers with children—and a sizable proportion of these mothers are divorced.

But it's not just the poverty that's hard to live with. It's the *drop* in income—and the more affluent the family, the harder that is to handle. Giving up Junior League friends to live on Hamburger Helper and food stamps is not only economically stressful, it's demoralizing as well.

Small wonder that children from divorced families are more likely than others to become juvenile delinquents, psychiatric patients, suicide victims. More than half have trouble in school—the result of depression, anxiety, guilt, loneliness, low self-esteem, low achievement, and bad behavior.

Getting over Divorce

The good news is that these effects are not inevitable and they don't have to be long-lasting. Divorce is a painful, negative experience for everyone involved. But people—children especially—are resilient, and time heals. The first year after the divorce is the worst emotionally, and it gets worse before it gets better. But by two or three years after the divorce, in most families, routines are back to normal, physical symptoms have disappeared, the intense psychological stress is over, and adults and children have improved self-esteem and are functioning competently.

The process of adjusting to divorce and subsequent life in a single-parent family is smoother and easier for some adults and children than for others. Some individuals bounce back within a year or two. Others never really get over the experience. Although children whose parents get divorced are "at risk" for psychological and behavioral problems, these problems are not *inevitable*. Researchers currently are probing into the conditions and personal qualities that determine whether a child makes a quick and complete recovery from divorce and a positive adjustment to life in a single-parent family. They have found a number of factors that seem to be critical.

Age. One important determinant of children's reactions to their parents' divorce is age. The younger a child is, the better the prognosis for a complete adjustment. Preschool children don't know what "divorce" is. They don't understand what's going on, and they react to their parents' separation with bewilderment, fear, and regression. But in the long run, they are the most likely to be emotionally unscathed.

Very young children have spent less time in a conflicted family. Their familiarity with and attachment to the family unit is less. And the parents themselves are younger, which makes their recovery easier.

Children who are 6 to 8 years old when their parents divorce understand what is going on better than younger children, but they hurt more. They yearn for the lost parent, and they feel rejected, torn in two, angry at the custodial parent. They don't have a well-developed sense of time, nor do they understand the nature of blood ties. So when they are with one parent they miss the other. They are afraid that while they're apart, the missing parent will find another son or daughter and forget them.

Over the long run, a bare majority of these children adjust fairly well. In a study of 60 divorced families in California by Judith Wallerstein, for example, 10 years after the divorce, 40 percent of the children who had been in this age range at the time of divorce were still functioning poorly.

Children who are 9 to 12 years old when their parents divorce are more upset than younger children. Their parents tell them more about the reasons for the divorce. They often align with one parent (usually the custodial parent) against the other. They are the most likely of all to suffer psychosomatic symptoms of stress and sup-

pressed anger and to have problems in achievement and conduct at school.

One parent can model only one gender role, give only so many hugs, offer so much discipline, and earn so much money.

An increase in household responsibilities and the need to make money often thrust these children into a precocious independence that may include premature sexual awareness or sexual activity.

Similarly, young adolescents, 13 to 16 years old, may be pushed too fast into independence by their parents' divorce. At the best of times, early adolescence is a vulnerable period of shaky self-esteem and conflicts over autonomy. A divorce may precipitate an adolescent's dropping out of school, getting pregnant, or getting into trouble with the law. Young adolescents react to their parents' divorce with unrealistic anguish, anxiety, and outrage: How could you do this to me? Along with the children who are 9 to 12 at the time of the divorce, they have the bleakest long-term outlook. In Wallerstein's study, slightly over half the children in this age range were doing poorly 10 years later.

Sex. For a variety of reasons, divorce is harder on boys than on girls, and boys are more likely to have problems. Boys are more vulnerable in general, and boys—who, like girls, are usually in a mother's custody—are most likely to lose the parent who is their gender-role model and the stronger authority.

Family competence and confidence. Adults who are more intelligent, assertive, self-assured, well-educated, creative, imaginative, mature, emotionally stable, tolerant of frustration, good at coping, willing to take risks, and socially bold are better able than most to deal with divorce and single parenthood, and so are their children.

Similarly, children with strong personal qualities tend to handle the divorce situation more easily. Ironically, however, the children who are most

likely to need such strong personal qualities, because their parents are getting divorced, are least likely to possess them, because they are more likely to have grown up in an unharmonious family environment.

Economic situation. Perhaps the single best predictor of the long-term consequences of divorce is the family's financial situation. The drastic drop in income and economic insecurity that accompany many divorces present severe challenges for both parents and children. Stories of single-parent families struggling for survival—living on cold cereal for dinner and trying to keep up the mortgage payments or moving from opulent abodes to tiny apartments in impoverished neighborhoods—are common. These changes inevitably lead to depression and resentment. For children, the economic drop packs a triple whammy: they lose material objects and opportunities, they lose status with their peers, and they are victims of their mothers' distraction and depression. Economic factors have a powerful effect on parents' and children's adjustment to divorce.

Parents' caring and availability. Children's relationships with both their parents after the divorce are very important for a healthy adjustment. These relationships, researchers have found, depend in large part on the child's continuing contact with both parents and on the ability of both parents to provide adequate supervision and consistent, authoritative discipline balanced by ample affection.

Because good relations with both parents have been found to be important for children, many states now award joint or shared custody of children to divorcing parents. Such arrangements sound ideal. The children do not "lose" a parent. They receive a more balanced exposure to two adults. Both parents continue to contribute fully to childrearing. And there is a greater likelihood that the expenses of child support will be shared. For the parents, there is regular and reliable relief from child care as well as the opportunity to make important decisions about the child and to offer daily, not Disneyland, care.

Little is known, however, about whether children really do better in joint custodial arrangements. Existing research is based on small, self-selected samples, and the results of different studies are not entirely consistent. There do seem to be some benefits of joint custody in terms of stress, satisfaction, self-esteem, and symptoms—if joint custody was the choice of the parents rather than of the courts. There is also some evidence that parents with joint custody are less likely than parents with sole custody to return for relitigation of the custody arrangement—again, if they themselves originally chose joint custody.

Court-ordered joint custody, however, may not have any of these benefits. Recent evidence, again collected by Judith Wallerstein, suggests that two years after the divorce, children in court-ordered joint custody arrangements are not doing as well as children in families where the court ordered sole custody. A possible reason is that in the families with court-ordered joint custody, the parents retained a rigid (court-ordered) 50-50 custody split, while only half the couples who had chosen joint custody were still following a 50-50 split. The others had slipped into the more conventional weekday/weekend division of time.

Whatever the legal arrangement, what is most important from the children's perspective is the *quality* of their relationship with both parents. If either parent disappears from the family, if either parent is rejecting, the child will suffer. To promote their children's satisfactory adjustment, parents must look out for the children's needs as well as their own, and not become overly self-absorbed—a challenge when they, too, are hurting.

Parents' current relationship. Children also suffer more if their parents are hostile toward each other. Some divorce researchers have gone so far as to suggest that the reason children of divorced parents have problems is not that they are separated from one of their parents but that their parents continue to fight overtly—sometimes violently—in front of them. In numerous studies, parental conflict or cooperation before and after the divorce has been found to predict both parents' and children's psychological well-being. It is most damaging to children when parents go on fighting and neglect the child or use the child as a pawn in their continued battling—

for example, through custody relitigation or child-snatching.

Stability of circumstances. Another factor that makes adjusting to a divorce difficult for children is the number of changes that inevitably accompany divorce. Moving to a new town and leaving old associations behind immediately upon separation may be the best thing for the parent, but it is not usually best for the child. The more changes children experience—moving to a new neighborhood, starting a new school, having mother start a job, going through repeated separations and reconciliations, living with changes in the custody arrangement—

What is most important from the child's perspective is the *quality* of his or her relationships with both parents.

---

the harder it is to adjust. When parents remarry and the child becomes part of a stepfamily—which happens 1,300 times every day in this country—the change may, again, be good for the parent's mental health but not necessarily for the child's, since it adds new relationships, new conflicts, new rivalries, new uncertainties, and new complexities.

Despite the problems of separation and transition to a new family form, in certain limited ways children can benefit from change. Children who move to a new class or a new school a year or two after the divorce, for example, have had a chance to adjust to living in a divorced family. The change gives them the opportunity to shed any bad reputation they may have made for themselves during the time of emotional crisis and go on to more positive relationships and achievements.

Access to outside help. Finally, the parents and children who adjust best to divorce are those who get help. Divorce is a trauma it's hard to go through alone, and adults and children alike benefit from the opportunity to talk about their experiences to sympathetic and supportive listeners. These listeners may be family members,

friends, teachers, counselors, therapists, or other people who are going through divorce. Social support, from either a network of emotionally supportive and accepting friends or participation in social or professional groups, has been found to buffer stress. What's important is that divorcing parents and children be assured that they are worthy, that they are loved, and that things will—eventually—get better. If they can be given advice about how to speed the process of things getting better, or if they are provided with tangible services, from laundry to loans, this also is helpful.

What Can Teachers Do?

In any year, in any class, the odds are high that there will be some children who are going through some phase of a parental divorce or remarriage. Teachers may be puzzled, annoyed, or completely frustrated by the effects of these events on the children's behavior in school. What can they do to assist these children and allay their own frustrations?

For one thing, teachers should try to be well-informed about what to expect from children under these circumstances. They should know that children, especially boys, are likely to act up and act out, to be distracted and withdrawn, to let their schoolwork slide, for as long as two years after their parents separate. During this time, these children, and their parents, need support and sympathy, not judgmental evaluations and criticism.

Teachers can attend workshops, read books, talk to their colleagues about the problems divorce creates and about possible solutions to those problems. Many schools now offer group programs for children whose parents are divorced, and there is growing evidence that these programs are helpful in children's adjustment.

Children whose parents divorce go through a slow and painful process of coming to understand and cope with the divorce and their new lifestyle and often reduced circumstances. This process can be guided—and children's adjustment can be eased—but time and support are necessary.

Children need to acknowledge the reality of their parents' separation, disengage from the parents' conflict, resolve their own feelings of loss and anger, accept the permanence of the divorce, and achieve realistic hopes and dreams for themselves. All this takes time. Classroom teachers can give children whose parents have just split up a break for some period of adjustment and transition, reducing their stress with lighter assignments and extra attention. Being patient and sympathetic is likely to pay off in the end.

Another way teachers can alleviate the problems created by divorce is by raising the consciousness of their other students about what divorce means and about what children whose parents are divorcing might be experiencing. Later on, teachers can help children whose parents are divorced by offering them a fresh start after they have made the initial adjustment to the divorce. In new classes or workgroups, their fellow students won't be biased by any bizarre or disruptive behavior they may have shown in the immediate aftermath of the divorce.

Looking more toward the future, teachers should do as much as they can to prepare their students for adult life in the twenty-first century. Two points are particularly important here. Students need preparation for the difficulties and challenges of marriage and family life, so that they won't take lightly the decisions they'll be making about when and whom to marry and when to have children. Girls need preparation to pursue lucrative careers and to be self-supporting. This is no longer a feminist issue alone. It is an issue of economic survival.

Divorce is a social phenomenon that affects us all. It is up to all of us, then, to help children and their parents cope with it as well as they can.

For Further Reading

Divorce. Sharon J. Rice and Patrick C. McKenry. Sage Publications, 1988. A systematic summary of recent research on the sociological and psychological processes involved in divorce.

Growing Up Divorced. Linda Bird Franke. Linden Press/Simon & Schuster, 1983. This is one of the many books available for parents—to inform, to educate, and to assist in their challenging task of rearing children after divorce. It provides an excellent review of the research demonstrating how divorce presents a series of crises for children, depending on their age and sex.

Interventions for Children of Divorce: Custody, Access, and Psychotherapy. Walter F. Hodges. Wiley, 1986. For those who are interested in the kinds of therapy and support programs currently available for children of divorce, this book offers an introduction. It also gives a thorough review of research showing the effects of divorce on adults and children.

Mothers and Divorce: Legal, Economic, and Social Dilemmas. Terry Arendell. University of California Press, 1986. *The Divorce Revolution.* Lenore Weitzman. Free Press, 1985. The sociologist authors of these books explore the dire economic and social consequences of divorce for modern middle-class single mothers. Both call for drastic reforms to make divorce legislation more equitable for men and women and to provide adequate support for child rearing.

"Single Parent Families: A Bookshelf: 1978-1985." Benjamin Schlesinger. *Family Relations,* vol. 35, pp. 199-204, 1986. This article lists 80 books and special issues of journals on single parents that appeared between 1978 and 1985. A hint of the vast literature available on this subject, this annotated list suggests where to start reading.

"Single Parenting: A Filmography." Lee Kimmons and Judith A. Gaston. *Family Relations,* vol. 35, pp. 205-211, 1986. This annotated listing of films provides teachers with a description of a broad range of available films, filmstrips, and videotapes that deal with the single-parent experience. All would be useful for classes, support groups, or workshops.

Where Are the Parents?

John McCormick

By the 25th spring of her increasing discontent, Marijke Raju was ready to retaliate. She was fed up with indulgent parents who let third graders play baseball or hit the mall rather than finish their homework. And she'd had her fill of nonacademic interruptions—bus-boarding drills today, an assembly to unveil the school's chocolate-sales drive tomorrow—that clutter her third graders' schedule in the middle-class Chicago suburb of Northlake, Ill. "You're the parent, the nurse, the policeman, the social worker and, very last, you are the teacher," she says. To make matters still worse, those children who don't encounter rigor at home resent the discipline Raju imposes at school. So, last May, when someone slashed her tire in the parking lot, Raju decided *someone* should pay—and that someone should be a parent.

As it played out, an administrator reimbursed Raju before she could reach the school's parents' auxiliary. But the incident—and the target of Raju's ire—reflects a new reality. In faculty rooms across America, hypercriticism of the nation's educators is beginning to meet its match. Teachers are losing patience with demanding but unsupportive parents who blame everyone but themselves for Johnny's tepid performance. Judging by what they do rather than the lip service the offer, many of today's parents plainly put their own needs, and especially their careers, ahead of their children. While some of that is understandable, particularly in households where merely keeping food on the table is a dicey proposition, the unpleasant consequence is a void schools cannot fill. Equally frustrating are the worthy but increasing intrusions—lessons in everything from AIDS awareness to self-esteem to handgun safety—that a too busy society now expects its schools to impart. "We've asked schools to do too much," laments Brown University education expert Theodore Sizer. "Teachers aren't parents."

To the schools we consign our most prized possessions: our children and our tax dollars. But many of the nation's 45 million schoolchildren are woefully unprepared for each day's work. Some days it seems that fewer kids come to school hungry because their parents are poor than come tired because parents let them watch television too late. Teachers' efforts to boost achievement must navigate a flood tide of societal changes—high numbers of broken homes and working parents, to name two—that reduce the amount of influence kids get from authority figures at home. "What we used to call 'teaching' is now morning-to-night service to families," says Louise Sundin, president of the Minnesota Federation of Teachers. "Some days it looks like nobody else is helping."

The parents most driven professionally can be the least helpful at school. Many behave as though the school exists for their child alone; a particularly annoying subspecies of the self-absorbed pulls kids out of class for family vacations *and* asks teachers to prepare a week's lessons, presumably to be administered by the ski patrol. Connecticut educator Peter Buttenheim reserves the term "designer parents" for a growing, affluent cadre obsessed by the end product of education rather than the process. Designers typically suspect that *their* children's needs aren't being met, and treat even bright and enthusiastic teachers much as they would an unproven auto mechanic.

"Affluenza," as it is known in the trade, takes many forms. Veteran teachers, faced with a generation of passive learners weaned on television, say too many parents have lost their good sense or their spine. New Haven teacher Wendy Wells says her well-heeled and media-savvy students display plenty of surface sophistication, but lack critical powers of observation and the desire to study things in depth. "We don't teach as much because kids don't come with the same work ethic," she says. "Homework isn't done because the family went to the 'Ice Capades'."

Changes in family life has distanced parents from schools. Parents' lives are so hectic that schools often can't find them when problems arise; one mother informed a suburban Chicago school that she didn't give her unlisted telephone number to *anyone*. With so many parents working, one third of all elementary students return to empty homes. Home life is so closely tied to school performance that 70 percent of elementary principals now keep formal records of each child's family structure. (Fully 97 percent of the National Association of Elementary School Principals think children from single-parent homes pay a price academically.)

For many teachers, the dysfunctional family is more than an abstract term. Some kids reach kindergarten without having been read to or even talked to, and can interact with other children only by hitting them. Schools nationwide try to educate students who disappear for weeks without explanation; of the 26 seventh graders in one Los Angeles music-appreciation class, only four showed up regularly last year. And in drug-education classes, teachers often wonder who's teaching whom. "They say, 'I went to my uncle's house and they were measuring drugs on the scales'," says Helene Sapadin of New Haven, Conn. "Here we are saying that drugs are bad, and we're talking about their *families*."

When parents can't or won't convey

WARD CLEAVER, PHONE HOME

Parents are pressed for time
73% of mothers with school-age children work outside the home. Nearly one fourth of all children under age 18 live with a single parent, and only 7% of school-age children live in a two-parent household where there is only one wage earner.

So schools teach the new facts of life
According to one survey, almost all elementary schools (95%) teach drug education, and more than half start teaching it in kindergarten. Most (72%) teach sex education.

SOURCES: BUREAU OF LABOR STATISTICS; NATIONAL ASSOCIATION OF ELEMENTARY SCHOOL PRINCIPALS

Fathers and mothers blame everyone but themselves for Johnny's tepid academic performance

crucial information to their children, legislatures and school boards rush to the rescue. Allan Vann, author of a book on bloated school curricula, likens the process to pouring water into an already filled glass. "Named *one* subject that's been *dropped* from elementary schools in the 1980s," grumped a recent newsletter from the principals' association. "Now, think about the subjects that have been *added:* AIDS, sex- and drug-abuse education, hygiene, family-life training, nutrition and fitness, environmental education, conflict resolution . . ." The list will never be inclusive. "Who's against bike safety?" asks Bruce Berndt, president of the Chicago Principals' Association. "But how much time should we spend on something like that?"

The most common argument for the swollen nonacademic curriculum is that if schools don't impart these often crucial lessons, no one else will. Consider the burden of teachers at Miami Beach Senior High School, who must acculturate a student body of 2,100 students of 67 nationalities. Principal Daniel Tosado says there is no other institution to help

poor immigrant students and their families. But some educators say that misses the larger point. If south Florida mobilized church groups, nationality associations or elderly volunteers to help families with language training and social-service referrals, couldn't Tosado's staff devote more time to the classwork students will need if they're to achieve their dreams of a better life?

If teachers feel overwhelmed, many parents feel unwelcome. For too long some schools made parents feel like intruders. "We restricted conferences to certain days and we didn't welcome parents into classes," says Bob Chase, vice president of the National Education Association. "The barriers were unspoken but they suggested that we were the professionals." Moreover, the popularity of teacher-bashing during the 1970s and early 1980s made teachers nationwide feel defensive; undoubtedly many deflected their discomfort back at parents. Chase now thinks such barriers are falling. "Teachers are reaching out," he says. "We need the community's help."

Too often, though, both parents are teachers recite the timeworn mantra—"Parents and schools must work together"—and then blunder along separately. If any group should be capable of closing the gap it's the Parent Teacher Association. And PTA national president Ann Lynch is trying to set an agenda for a different demographic age. One example: chapters are urged to divide the old monthly meetings into morning, evening and weekend sessions so every working parent can participate. "We're hoping schools that say, 'We want parental involvement' will back that up with outreach programs," she says. "Too many parents don't have relationships with schools until there's a problem."

Terrel Bell, a former U.S. Education secretary, suggests a more formal approach: he would have every state require annual, written agreements between parents and schools as a precondition for enrollment. Among other things, parents would warrant that each child will get a good night's sleep, arrive at school on time and have a place at home to study. "This would impress on many parents their obligation," says Bell. "You get the service free but you

have to make the commitment." In experiments around the nation, the San Francisco-based Quality Education Project has found that merely asking parents to sign pledges similar to Bell's proposed contract makes them feel far more accountable for their children's schoolwork. Indianapolis educators use a different approach: they search out parents at major employers for lunchtime workshops on such topics as helping a child learn to read. Minneapolis offers Success by 6, an amalgam of business, labor, government, health and education initiatives to help parents nurture the skills their kids will need to flourish in the early grades.

Many educators say there is no tactful way to impress on parents how much impact their priorities have on their children—and how important it is that they get involved at school. When academic or behavior problems arise, teachers routinely rearrange their professional lives to schedule special meetings at times convenient for parents. Not enough parents, they say, ever offer to do the same.

In the end, we've decided as a culture that education is too important to be left just to the educators, and that parenting is too important to be left solely to the parents. Those axioms, as a practical matter, lead to shared power and shared responsibilities. They can be a prescription for resentment and neglect—or an opportunity to raise a child successfully. For the moment, teachers would prefer to emphasize the latter. Heed us, they're crying. Help us. Help us help your children.

With Karen Spinger *in Chicago,* Patrick Rogers *in New York,* Leslie Barnes *in San Francisco and* Peter Katel *in Miami*

Appropriate Educational Practices

Instruction versus guidance, systematic versus emergent, teacher-chosen versus child-initiated. These are some of the ideas around developmentally based education that are currently debated by caregivers, teachers, parents, and school boards. The principles and philosophies behind these discussions are complex. Those involved in the discussions are firm in their views.

Some hold that young children must be prepared for the twenty-first century, which is arriving soon as the post-industrial information technology-based era. They sense the urgency of transformed skills and abilities that will be necessary to function effectively in society. To be next century's adults, today's children require an infusion of powerful instruction and many believe early childhood is the time to begin. Those on this side of the debate believe direct instruction, based on visionary goals, and use of academic tools (such as workbooks, basal readers, sequenced tasks, and paper/pencil) are appropriate practice to prepare young children for entry to the next century.

The other side of the debate, while affirming the necessity of preparation, emphasizes young children's learning in the immediate present rather than the future. To them, the path to effective adult skills and abilities is developmental. Young children learn through exploration of physical objects and their instruction is embedded in the activity itself. The urgency they sense is for children to engage the world and construct their own knowledge. Appropriate practice, to developmentalists, is child-initiated activity, based on emergent goals, using objects of the physical world as tools of learning.

The strength of today's debate over appropriate practice in early childhood indicates another swing of the educational philosophy pendulum. The pendulum has always swung, and this time it involves an early childhood community that is more sure of its knowledge and more mature in its practices. It is also a community more divided over its philosophy than on earlier swings.

As knowledge and practice expand, a seeming paradox may be occurring that causes a rupture in philosophy. When any professional community grows, it divides its tasks. The early childhood education community is no exception: one groups studies children, another designs curriculum, still another teaches. Knowledge of children is built by some, while practice with children is perfected by others. If the two work behind closed doors, they may achieve differing goals, while still using each other's language. Early childhood philosophy is further influenced by opinions from other fields when state or national conditions shift attention to education.

This process is similar to a cottage business that grows into an industry. Concepts once designed and executed locally are now designed in one department to be engineered elsewhere. The product will probably not emerge as it was originally intended. The early childhood profession is currently in danger of the same growth problem. Curricular concepts are being predesigned for children to engineer with little variability. Practices with children become less dependent on the individuals in the groups and more dependent on commercial sourcebooks. The trade-off is a homogenized program, developmental only by the label.

Some early childhood educators may be losing their original intention. The current debates indicate this is true. The reason for a sense of loss is that attention is shifting from the children, whose development they mean to ensure, to the products of education. The search for "how tos" can lead to the assumption that the instant curriculum can truly be developmentally appropriate, or that a prepackaged, sterile environment will automatically result in quality. The press to prove child achievement should be recognized as a short-term educational product. Authentic appropriate practice, based on children's development, has no short cuts and cannot be trivialized.

The early childhood community has no exclusive ownership of the phrase "developmentally appropriate practice," since development does not end at age seven or eight. Any group of educators can use the phrase and apply it to any age learner. By detailing specifics of routines and procedures and materials and resources suitable for young children, however, the early childhood profession strengthens its identity. It is a helpful exercise to ensure the match of practice with childhood. Putting thought and planning and process behind the words involves using knowledge of child development to inform caregiving decisions and curricular choices. This is also an exercise in teacher autonomy; to own and value the work of the profession.

The current debate on developmentally appropriate

practice is a healthy one, calling for knowledge to remain based on young children and practice to resist standardization. Hopefully, the early childhood community will arrive in the twenty-first century with its philosophy intact.

Looking Ahead: Challenge Questions

What does the idea of gearing programs to children's abilities mean in practical terms?

How does developmentally appropriate practice relate to quality caregiving?

Based on your philosophy of education, what is the optimal level of structure appropriate in preschool? How would specific program components reflect optimal structure?

What role does television play in children's learning today? What should television provide for children in the future?

Should young children be retained in kindergarten? If so, for what reasons? How does grade retention relate to developmentally appropriate practice?

What is your view of the importance of developmentally appropriate practice during each of the following stages: infancy and toddler years? preschool? kindergarten? primary grades?

National Association for the Education of Young Children

Position Statement on Developmentally Appropriate Practice in Programs for 4- and 5-Year-Olds

Background information

In the mid 1980s, a great deal of public attention has focused on the quality of our nation's educational system. Early childhood education programs for 4- and 5-year-old children have become the focus of some controversy. Various issues are under debate, including the length of program day for this age group, the effect of various forms of sponsorship, and the nature of the curriculum.

Curriculum issues are of particular concern to early childhood educators in light of the increasingly widespread demand for use of inappropriate formal teaching techniques for young children, over-emphasis on achievement of narrowly defined academic skills, and increased reliance on psychometric tests to determine enrollment and retention in programs.

These trends are primarily the result of misconceptions about how young children learn (Elkind, 1986). In many cases, concerned adults, who want children to succeed, apply adult education standards to the curriculum for young children and pressure early childhood programs to demonstrate that children are "really learning." Many programs respond by emphasizing ac-

ademic skill development with paper-and-pencil activities that are developmentally inappropriate for young children.

The National Association for the Education of Young Children (NAEYC), the nation's largest professional association of early childhood educators, believes that high quality, developmentally appropriate programs should be available for all 4- and 5-year-old children. NAEYC believes that quality is not determined by the length of the program day or by the sponsorship, although these factors can affect quality. NAEYC believes that a major determinant of the quality of an early childhood program is the degree to which the program is developmentally appropriate. This position statement describes both appropriate practices and inappropriate practices in early childhood programs. These beliefs about appropriate practice are supported by a growing body of both laboratory and clinical classroom research and theory. This statement is intended for use by teachers, parents, school administrators, policy makers, and others who provide educational programs for 4- and 5-year-olds.

Position Statement

How young children learn

Young children learn by doing. The work of Piaget (1950, 1972), Montessori (1964), Erikson (1950), and other child development theorists and researchers (Elkind, 1986; Kamii, 1985) has demonstrated that learning

is a complex process that results from the interaction of children's own thinking and their experiences in the external world. Maturation is an important contributor to learning because it provides a framework from

From *Young Children*, Vol. 41, No. 6 (September 1986), pp. 20-29. © 1986 by The National Association for the Education of Young Children, 1834 Connecticut Ave., N.W., Washington, DC 20009.

which children's learning proceeds. As children get older, they acquire new skills and experiences that facilitate the learning process. For example, as children grow physically, they are more able to manipulate and explore their own environment. Also, as children mature, they are more able to understand the point of view of other people.

Knowledge is not something that is given to children as though they were empty vessels to be filled. Children acquire knowledge about the physical and social worlds in which they live through playful interaction with objects and people. Children do not need to be forced to learn; they are motivated by their own desire to make sense of their world.

How to teach young children

How young children learn should determine how teachers of young children teach. The word *teach* tends to imply *telling* or *giving information*. But the correct way to teach young children is not to lecture or verbally instruct them. Teachers of young children are more like guides or facilitators (Forman & Kuschner, 1983; Lay-Dopyera & Dopyera, 1986; Piaget, 1972). They prepare the environment so that it provides stimulating, challenging materials and activities for children. Then, teachers closely observe to see what children understand and pose additional challenges to push their thinking further.

It is possible to drill children until they can correctly recite pieces of information such as the alphabet or the numerals from 1 to 20. However, children's responses to rote tasks do not reflect real understanding of the information. For children to understand fully and remember what they have learned, whether it is related to reading, mathematics, or other subject matter areas, the information must be meaningful to the child in context of the child's experience and development.

Learning information in meaningful context is not only essential for children's understanding and development of concepts, but is also important for stimulating motivation in children. If learning is relevant for children, they are more likely to persist with a task and to be motivated to learn more.

The following example illustrates how young children learn, some appropriate ways to teach young children, and how all aspects of children's development are interrelated in appropriate activities for young children.

A group of 4-, 5-, and 6-year-old kindergarten children is building a road with unit blocks. One child mentions that his mother is in the hospital, and some of the others begin to share their ideas and fears about what happens in a hospital.

Rich Rosenkoetter

For children to fully understand and remember what they have learned, whether it is related to reading, mathematics, or other subject matter areas, the information must be meaningful to the child in context of the child's experience and development.

This activity may develop in one of two basic ways. With either type of direction, however, children will have an opportunity to expand their knowledge and skills in all developmental areas. The children will exchange ideas about, fears of, and ways of coping with hospitals as they talk. They will use their large and small muscles to experiment with balance, weight, and symmetry and other mathematical concepts as they build with the blocks. As they play, the children will practice ways to cooperate and collaborate with others; they may even plan the hospital before they build. While they play, they may need written words, perhaps as labels for *emergency* or road signs. At the conclusion of the activity, they will feel competent about their ability to sustain a complex activity and confront their emotional concerns.

The activity may develop one way if the children are very familiar with hospitals, know each other well, and have adequate play space and access to a variety of props and materials. The activity may be primarily self-motivated and self-directed. The children may design an elaborate hospital, use tables for stretchers, apply bandages, and write out prescriptions on pads of paper. The teacher for this group serves primarily as a resource, to write a sign when the children request it, for instance, or to make arrangements for a field trip or classroom visitor to explore an idea about hospitals or health or construction in greater detail.

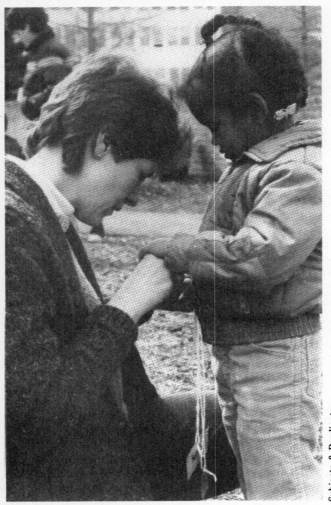

Subjects & Predicates

Interactions and activities are designed to develop children's self-esteem and positive feelings toward learning.

observes the play and makes professional judgments about how to build upon the children's understanding and concerns.

Developmentally appropriate practice for 4- and 5-year-olds

Developmentally appropriate teaching strategies are based on knowledge of how young children learn. Curriculum derives from many sources such as the knowledge base of various disciplines, society, culture, and parents' desires. The degree to which both teaching strategies and the curriculum are developmentally appropriate is a major determinant of program quality. Developmentally appropriate programs are both age appropriate and individually appropriate; that is, the program is designed for the age group served and implemented with attention to the needs and differences of the individual children enrolled.

Because people develop concepts from both positive and negative examples, the components of a program for 4- and 5-year-olds are described here both in terms of what is appropriate and what is *not* appropriate practice. These components overlap considerably and have been identified here for purposes of clarity only.

Marietta Lynch

Outdoor activity is planned daily so children can develop large muscle skills, learn about outdoor environments, and express themselves freely and loudly.

If the children are younger or less experienced, the activity may develop differently. The teacher may need to stimulate and promote the activity more actively to extend it. The teacher may observe that the children's play is limited to driving ambulances on the road and making the sounds of screaming sirens as they enter the emergency area of the hospital. This teacher might ask some open-ended questions about what happens next to the patient in the ambulance, or what items are found in the hospital. If the children express interest, several opportunities can then be offered to stimulate their thinking and ability to expand their play. Perhaps props such as stethoscopes, bandages, or hospital gowns will give the children the tools to explore what happens after the ambulance arrives. If the children's experience is limited, maybe a story with illustrations will prompt more elaborate play later in the day, or a field trip can be taken so children can see some parts of a hospital firsthand. Perhaps the children will carry out the theme in their artwork or by dictating stories about the times when they were sick at home.

Regardless of how the activity develops, the teacher

Integrated Components of
APPROPRIATE and INAPPROPRIATE Practice for
4- and 5-Year-Old Children

Component	APPROPRIATE Practice	INAPPROPRIATE Practice
Curriculum goals	• Experiences are provided that meet children's needs and stimulate learning in all developmental areas—physical, social, emotional, and intellectual.	• Experiences are narrowly focused on the child's intellectual development without recognition that all areas of a child's development are interrelated.
	• Each child is viewed as a unique person with an individual pattern and timing of growth and development. The curriculum and adults' interaction are responsive to individual differences in ability and interests. Different levels of ability, development, and learning styles are expected, accepted, and used to design appropriate activities.	• Children are evaluated only against a predetermined measure, such as a standardized group norm or adult standard of behavior. All are expected to perform the same tasks and achieve the same narrowly defined, easily measured skills.
	• Interactions and activities are designed to develop children's self-esteem and positive feelings toward learning.	• Children's worth is measured by how well they conform to rigid expectations and perform on standardized tests.
Teaching strategies	• Teachers prepare the environment for children to learn through active exploration and interaction with adults, other children, and materials.	• Teachers use highly structured, teacher-directed lessons almost exclusively.
	• Children select many of their own activities from among a variety of learning areas the teacher prepares, including dramatic play, blocks, science, math, games and puzzles, books, recordings, art, and music.	• The teacher directs all the activity, deciding what children will do and when. The teacher does most of the activity for the children, such as cutting shapes, performing steps in an experiment.
	• Children are expected to be physically and mentally active. Children choose from among activities the teacher has set up or the children spontaneously initiate.	• Children are expected to sit down, watch, be quiet, and listen, or do paper-and-pencil tasks for inappropriately long periods of time. A major portion of time is spent passively sitting, listening, and waiting.
	• Children work individually or in small, informal groups most of the time.	• Large group, teacher-directed instruction is used most of the time.
	• Children are provided concrete learning activities with materials and people relevant to their own life experiences.	• Workbooks, ditto sheets, flashcards, and other similarly structured abstract materials dominate the curriculum.
	• Teachers move among groups and individuals to facilitate children's involvement with materials and activities by asking questions, offering suggestions, or adding more complex materials or ideas to a situation.	• Teachers dominate the environment by talking to the whole group most of the time and telling children what to do.

3. APPROPRIATE EDUCATIONAL PRACTICES

Component	APPROPRIATE Practice	INAPPROPRIATE Practice
Teaching strategies cont.	• Teachers accept that there is often more than one right answer. Teachers recognize that children learn from self-directed problem solving and experimentation.	• Children are expected to respond correctly with one right answer. Rote memorization and drill are emphasized.
Guidance of socioemotional development	• Teachers facilitate the development of self-control in children by using positive guidance techniques such as modeling and encouraging expected behavior, redirecting children to a more acceptable activity, and setting clear limits. Teachers' expectations match and respect children's developing capabilities.	• Teachers spend a great deal of time enforcing rules, punishing unacceptable behavior, demeaning children who misbehave, making children sit and be quiet, or refereeing disagreements.
	• Children are provided many opportunities to develop social skills such as cooperating, helping, negotiating, and talking with the person involved to solve interpersonal problems. Teachers facilitate the development of these positive social skills at all times.	• Children work individually at desks or tables most of the time or listen to teacher directions in the total group. Teachers intervene to resolve disputes or enforce classroom rules and schedules.
Language development and literacy	• Children are provided many opportunities to see how reading and writing are useful before they are instructed in letter names, sounds, and word identification. Basic skills develop when they are meaningful to children. An abundance of these types of activities is provided to develop language and literacy through meaningful experience: listening to and reading stories and poems; taking field trips; dictating stories; seeing classroom charts and other print in use; participating in dramatic play and other experiences requiring communication; talking informally with other children and adults; and experimenting with writing by drawing, copying, and inventing their own spelling.	• Reading and writing instruction stresses isolated skill development such as recognizing single letters, reciting the alphabet, singing the alphabet song, coloring within predefined lines, or being instructed in correct formation of letters on a printed line.
Cognitive development	• Children develop understanding of concepts about themselves, others, and the world around them through observation, interacting with people and real objects, and seeking solutions to concrete problems. Learnings about math, science, social studies, health, and other content areas are all integrated through meaningful activities such as those when children build with blocks;	• Instruction stresses isolated skill development through memorization and rote, such as counting, circling an item on a worksheet, memorizing facts, watching demonstrations, drilling with flashcards, or looking at maps. Children's cognitive development is seen as fragmented in content areas such as math, science, or social studies, and times are set aside to concentrate on each area.

Component	APPROPRIATE Practice	INAPPROPRIATE Practice
Cognitive development cont.	measure sand, water, or ingredients for cooking; observe changes in the environment; work with wood and tools; sort objects for a purpose; explore animals, plants, water, wheels and gears; sing and listen to music from various cultures; and draw, paint, and work with clay. Routines are followed that help children keep themselves healthy and safe.	
Physical development	• Children have daily opportunities to use large muscles, including running, jumping, and balancing. Outdoor activity is planned daily so children can develop large muscle skills, learn about outdoor environments, and express themselves freely and loudly. • Children have daily opportunities to develop small muscles skills through play activities such as pegboards, puzzles, painting, cutting, and other similar activities.	• Opportunity for large muscle activity is limited. Outdoor time is limited because it is viewed as interfering with instructional time or, if provided, is viewed as recess (a way to get children to use up excess energy), rather than an integral part of children's learning environment. • Small motor activity is limited to writing with pencils, or coloring predrawn forms, or similar structured lessons.
Aesthetic development	• Children have daily opportunities for aesthetic expression and appreciation through art and music. Children experiment and enjoy various forms of music. A variety of art media are available for creative expression, such as easel and finger painting and clay.	• Art and music are provided only when time permits. Art consists of coloring predrawn forms, copying an adult-made model of a product, or following other adult-prescribed directions.
Motivation	• Children's natural curiosity and desire to make sense of their world are used to motivate them to become involved in learning activities.	• Children are required to participate in all activities to obtain the teacher's approval, to obtain extrinsic rewards like stickers or privileges, or to avoid punishment.
Parent-teacher relations	• Teachers work in partnership with parents, communicating regularly to build mutual understanding and greater consistency for children.	• Teachers communicate with parents only about problems or conflicts. Parents view teachers as experts and feel isolated from their child's experiences.
Assessment of children	• Decisions that have a major impact on children (such as enrollment, retention, assignment to remedial classes) are based primarily on information obtained from observations by teachers and parents, not on the basis of a single test score. Developmental assessment of children's progress and achievement is used to plan curriculum, identify children with special needs,	• Psychometric tests are used as the sole criterion to prohibit entrance to the program or to recommend that children be retained or placed in remedial classrooms.

3. APPROPRIATE EDUCATIONAL PRACTICES

Component	APPROPRIATE Practice	INAPPROPRIATE Practice
Assessment of children cont.	communicate with parents, and evaluate the program's effectiveness.	
Program entry	• In public schools, there is a place for every child of legal entry age, regardless of the developmental level of the child. No public school program should deny access to children on the basis of results of screening or other arbitrary determinations of the child's lack of readiness. The educational system adjusts to the developmental needs and levels of the children it serves; children are not expected to adapt to an inappropriate system.	• Eligible-age children are denied entry to kindergarten or retained in kindergarten because they are judged not ready on the basis of inappropriate and inflexible expectations.
Teacher qualifications	• Teachers are qualified to work with 4- and 5-year-olds through college-level preparation in Early Childhood Education or Child Development and supervised experience with this age group.	• Teachers with no specialized training or supervised experience working with 4- and 5-year-olds are viewed as qualified because they are state certified, regardless of the level of certification.
Staffing	• The group size and ratio of teachers to children is limited to enable individualized and age-appropriate programming. Four- and 5-year-olds are in groups of no more than 20 children with 2 adults.	• Because older children can function reasonably well in large groups, it is assumed that group size and number of adults can be the same for 4- and 5-year-olds as for elementary grades.

Bibliography

These references include both laboratory and clinical classroom research to document the broad-based literature that forms the foundation for sound practice in early childhood education.

Related position statements

International Reading Association. (1985). *Literacy and pre-first grade.* Newark, DE: International Reading Association.
NAEYC. (1984). *Accreditation criteria and procedures of the National Academy of Early Childhood Programs.* Washington, DC: NAEYC.
NAEYC. (1986). *Position statement on developmentally appropriate practice in early childhood programs serving children from birth through age 8.*
Nebraska State Board of Education. (1984). *Position statement on kindergarten.* Lincoln, NE: Nebraska State Department of Education.
Southern Association on Children Under Six. (1984, July). A statement on developmentally appropriate educational experiences for kindergarten. *Dimensions, 12*(4), 25.
Southern Association on Children Under Six. (1986). *Position statement on quality four-year-old programs in public schools. Dimensions, 14*(3), 29.
Southern Association on Children Under Six. (1986). *Position statement on quality child care. Dimensions, 14*(4), p. 28.
State Department of Education, Columbia, South Carolina. (1983, rev. ed.). *Early childhood education in South Carolina. Learning experiences for 3-, 4-, and 5-year-old children.*
Texas Association for the Education of Young Children. (no date). *Developmentally appropriate kindergarten reading programs: A position statement.*

Developmentally appropriate practices and curriculum goals

Biber, B. (1984). *Early education and psychological development.* New Haven: Yale University Press.
Elkind, D. (1986, May). Formal education and early childhood education: An essential difference. *Phi Delta Kappan,* 631–636.
Erikson, E. (1950). *Childhood and society.* New York: Norton.
Kohlberg, L., & Mayer, R. (1972). Development as the arm of education. *Harvard Educational Review, 42,* 449–496.
Montessori, M. (1964). *The Montessori method.* Cambridge, MA: Robert Bentley.
Piaget, J. (1950). *The psychology of intelligence.* London: Routledge & Kegan Paul.
Piaget, J. (1952). *The origins of intelligence in children.* (M. Cook, Trans.) New York: Norton. (Original work published 1936)
Spodek, B. (1985). *Teaching in the early years* (3rd ed.). Englewood Cliffs, NJ: Prentice-Hall.
Weber, E. (1984). *Ideas influencing early childhood education: A theoretical analysis.* New York: Teachers College Press, Columbia University.

Teaching strategies

Fein, G. (1979). Play and the acquisition of symbols. In L. Katz (Ed.), *Current topics in early childhood education, Vol. 2.* Norwood, NJ: Ablex.
Fein, G., & Rivkin, M. (Eds.). (1986). *The young child at play: Reviews of research* (Vol. 4). Washington, DC: NAEYC.
Fromberg, D. (1986). Play. In C. Seefeldt (Ed.), *Early childhood curriculum: A review of current research.* New York: Teachers College Press, Columbia University.
Forman, G., & Kuschner, D. (1983). *The child's construction of knowl-*

edge: Piaget for teaching children. Washington, DC: NAEYC.

Herron, R., & Sutton-Smith, B. (1974). *Child's play.* New York: Wiley.

Kamii, C. (1985). Leading primary education toward excellence: Beyond worksheets and drill. *Young Children, 40*(6), 3–9.

Languis, M., Sanders, T., & Tipps, S. (1980). *Brain and learning: Directions in early childhood education.* Washington, DC: NAEYC.

Lay-Dopyera, M., & Dopyera, J. (1986). Strategies for teaching. In C. Seefeldt (Ed.), *Early childhood curriculum: A review of current research.* New York: Teachers College Press, Columbia University.

Piaget, J. (1972). *Science of education and the psychology of the child* (rev. ed.). New York: Viking. (Original work published 1965)

Souweine, J. K., Crimmins, S., & Mazel, C. (1981). *Mainstreaming: Ideas for teaching young children.* Washington, DC: NAEYC.

Sponseller, D. (1982). Play and early education. In B. Spodek (Ed.), *Handbook of research in early childhood education.* New York: Free Press.

Guidance of socioemotional development

Asher, S. R., Renshaw, P. D., & Hymel, S. (1982). Peer relations and the development of social skills. In S. G. Moore & C. R. Cooper (Eds.), *The young child: Reviews of research* (Vol. 3, pp. 137–158). Washington, DC: NAEYC.

Baker, K. R., Gardner, P., & Mahler, B. (1986). *Early childhood programs: A laboratory for human relationships* (8th ed.). New York: Holt, Rinehart & Winston.

Erikson, E. (1950). *Childhood and society.* New York: Norton.

Honig, A. S. (1985). Research in review. Compliance, control, and discipline (Parts 1 & 2). *Young Children, 40*(2), 50–58; *40*(3), 47–52.

Moore, S. (1982). Prosocial behavior in the early years: Parent and peer influences. In B. Spodek (Ed.), *Handbook of research in early childhood education.* New York: Free Press.

Rubin, K., & Everett, B. (1982). Social perspective-taking in young children. In S. G. Moore & C. R. Cooper (Eds.), *The young child: Reviews of research* (Vol. 3, pp. 97–114). Washington, DC: NAEYC.

Stone, J. (1978). *A guide to discipline* (rev. ed.). Washington, DC: NAEYC.

Language development and literacy

Cazden, C. (Ed.). (1981). *Language in early childhood education* (rev. ed.). Washington, DC: NAEYC.

Ferreiro, E., & Teberosky, A. (1982). *Literacy before schooling.* Exeter, NH: Heinemann.

Genishi, C. (1986). Acquiring language and communicative competence. In C. Seefeldt (Ed.), *Early childhood curriculum: A review of current research.* New York: Teachers College Press, Columbia University.

Schachter, F. F., & Strage, A. A. (1982). Adults' talk and children's language development. In S. G. Moore & C. R. Cooper (Eds.), *The young child: Reviews of research* (Vol. 3, pp. 79–96). Washington, DC: NAEYC.

Schickedanz, J. (1986). *More than the ABCs: The early stages of reading and writing.* Washington, DC: NAEYC.

Smith, F. (1982). *Understanding reading.* New York: Holt, Rinehart & Winston.

Willert, M., & Kamii, C. (1985). Reading in kindergarten: Direct versus indirect teaching. *Young Children, 40*(4), 3–9.

Cognitive development

Forman, G., & Kaden, M. (1986). Research on science education in young children. In C. Seefeldt (Ed.), *Early childhood curriculum: A review of current research.* New York: Teachers College Press, Columbia University.

Goffin, S., & Tull, C. (1985). Problem solving: Encouraging active learning. *Young Children, 40*(3), 28–32.

Kamii, C. (1982). *Number in preschool and kindergarten.* Washington, DC: NAEYC.

Hawkins, D. (1970). Messing about in science. *ESS Reader.* Newton, MA: Education Development Center.

Hirsch, E. (Ed.). (1984). *The block book.* Washington, DC: NAEYC.

Holt, B. (1979). *Science with young children.* Washington, DC: NAEYC.

Sackoff, E., & Hart, R. (1984, Summer). Toys: Research and applications. *Children's Environments Quarterly, 1–2.*

Wellman, H. M. (1982). The foundations of knowledge: Concept development in the young child. In S. G. Moore & C. R. Cooper (Eds.), *The young child: Reviews of research* (Vol. 3, pp. 115–134). Washington, DC: NAEYC.

Physical development

Cratty, B. (1982). Motor development in early childhood: Critical issues for researchers in the 1980's. In B. Spodek (Ed.), *Handbook of research in early childhood education.* New York: Free Press.

Curtis, S. (1986). New views on movement development and implications for curriculum in early childhood education. In C. Seefeldt(Ed.), *Early childhood curriculum: A review of current research.* New York: Teachers College Press, Columbia University.

Aesthetic development

Davidson, L. (1985). Preschool children's tonal knowledge: Antecedents of scale. In J. Boswell (Ed.), *The young child and music: Contemporary principles in child development and music education. Proceedings of the Music in Early Childhood Conference* (pp. 25–40). Reston, VA: Music Educators National Conference.

Evans, E. D. (1984). Children's aesthetics. In L. G. Katz (Ed.), *Current topics in early childhood education* (Vol. 5, pp. 73–104). Norwood, NJ: Ablex.

Gilbert, J. P. (1981). Motoric music skill development in young children: A longitudinal investigation. *Psychology of Music, 9*(1), 21–24.

Greenberg, M. (1976). Music in early childhood education: A survey with recommendations. *Council for Research in Music Education, 45*, 1–20.

Lasky, L., & Mukerji, R. (1980). *Art: Basic for young children.* Washington, DC: NAEYC.

McDonald, D. T. (1979). *Music in our lives: The early years.* Washington, DC: NAEYC.

Seefeldt, C. (1986). The visual arts. In C. Seefeldt (Ed.), *The early childhood curriculum: A review of current research.* New York: Teachers College Press, Columbia University.

Smith, N. (1983). *Experience and art: Teaching children to paint.* New York: Teachers College Press, Columbia University.

Motivation

Elkind, D. (1986). Formal education and early childhood education: An essential difference. *Phi Delta Kappan,* 631–636.

Gottfried, A. (1983). Intrinsic motivation in young children. *Young Children, 39*(1), 64–73.

Parent-teacher relations

Croft, D. J. (1979). *Parents and teachers: A resource book for home, school, and community relations.* Belmont, CA: Wadsworth.

Gazda, G. M. (1973). *Human relations development: A manual for educators.* Boston: Allyn & Bacon.

Honig, A. (1982). Parent involvement in early childhood education. In B. Spodek (Ed.), *Handbook of research in early childhood education.* New York: Free Press.

Katz, L. (1980). Mothering and teaching: Some significant distinctions. In L. Katz (Ed.), *Current topics in early childhood education* (Vol. 3, pp. 47–64). Norwood, NJ: Ablex.

Lightfoot, S. (1978). *Worlds apart: Relationships between families and schools.* New York: Basic.

Assessment of children

Cohen, D. H., Stern, V., & Balaban, N. (1983). *Observing and recording the behavior of young children* (3rd ed.). New York: Teachers College Press, Columbia University.

Goodman, W., & Goodman, L. (1982). Measuring young children. In B. Spodek (Ed.), *Handbook of research in early childhood education.* New York: Free Press.

Meisels, S. (1985). *Developmental screening in early childhood.* Washington, DC: NAEYC.

Standards for educational and psychological testing. (1985). Washington, DC: American Psychological Association, American Educational Research Association, and National Council on Measurement in Education.

Teacher qualifications and staffing

Almy, M. (1982). Day care and early childhood education. In E. Zigler & E. Gordon (Eds.), *Daycare: Scientific and social policy issues* (pp. 476–495). Boston: Auburn House.

Feeney, S., & Chun, R. (1985). Research in review. Effective teachers of young children. *Young Children, 41*(1), 47–52.

NAEYC. (1982). *Early childhood teacher education guidelines for four- and five-year programs.* Washington, DC: NAEYC.

Ruopp, R., Travers, J., Glantz, F., & Coelen, C. (1979). *Children at the center. Final report of the National Day Care Study, Vol. 1.* Cambridge, MA: Abt Associates.

Developmentally Appropriate Practice: Philosophical and Practical Implications

DAVID ELKIND

DAVID ELKIND is a professor of child study at Tufts University, Medford, Mass. He is a past president of the National Association for the Education of Young Children and the author of The Hurried Child *(Addison-Wesley, 1981),* All Grown Up and No Place to Go *(Addison-Wesley, 1984), and* Miseducation: Preschoolers at Risk *(Knopf, 1987).*

True education reform will come about only when we replace the reigning psychometric educational psychology with a developmentally appropriate one, Mr. Elkind asserts. Unfortunately, the prospects for such a shift are not good.

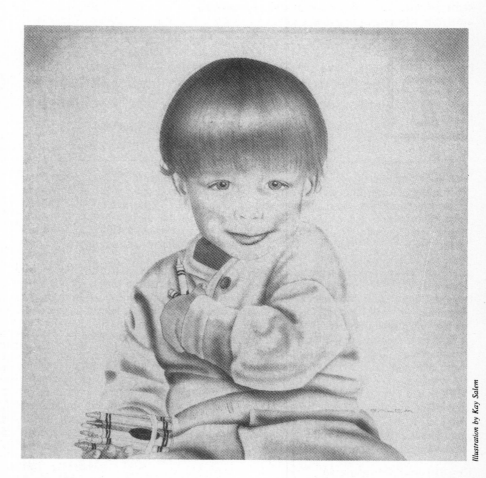

Illustration by Kay Salem

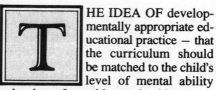HE IDEA OF developmentally appropriate educational practice — that the curriculum should be matched to the child's level of mental ability — has been favorably received in education circles.[1] However, this positive reception is quite extraordinary, for developmentally appropriate practice derives from a philosophy of education that is in total opposition to the "psychometric" educational philosophy that now dictates educational practice in the majority of our public schools. Perhaps for this reason developmental appropriateness has been honored more in word than in deed.

In what follows I highlight some of the differences between these two educational philosophies and contrast a few of their practical implications. My purpose in doing so is to argue that true education reform will come about only when we replace the reigning psychometric educa-

tional psychology with a developmentally appropriate one.

TWO PHILOSOPHIES

Any philosophy of education must include some conception of the learner, of the learning process, of the information to be acquired, and of the goals or aims of education. The developmental philosophy differs from the psychometric philosophy on all four counts. I should mention that the developmental philosophy that I present here derives from the research and theory of Jean Piaget.[2]

Conception of the learner. Within a developmental philosophy of education, the learner is viewed as having *developing* mental abilities. All individuals (with the exception of the retarded) are assumed to be able to attain these abilities, though not necessarily at the same age. For example, we expect that all children will attain the concrete operations that Piaget described as emerging at about age 6 or 7. These operations, which function much like the group of arithmetic operations, enable children who have attained them to learn and to apply rules. However, not all children will attain these

From *Phi Delta Kappan*, October 1989, pp. 113-117. Reprinted by permission of *Phi Delta Kappan* and David Elkind.

The developmental approach implies little or no automatic transfer of learning; the psychometric approach assumes spontaneous transfer.

operations at the same age. Accordingly, a developmental philosophy sees individual differences in ability as differences in *rates* of intellectual growth.

This conception of mental ability contrasts sharply with that of a psychometric philosophy of education. According to the psychometric position, the learner is seen as having *measurable* abilities. This philosophy assumes that any ability that exists must exist in some amount and must, therefore, be quantifiable. For example, intelligence tests — the flagships of the psychometric philosophy — are designed to assess individual differences in the ability to learn and to adapt to new situations. A psychometric perspective regards individual differences in performance as reflecting differences in *amount* of a given ability.

Both of these opposing conceptions of human ability contain some truth. However, they have far different pedagogical implications.

From a developmental perspective, the important task for educators is *matching curricula* to the level of children's emerging mental abilities: hence the principle of developmental appropriateness. Curriculum materials should be introduced only after a child has attained the level of mental ability needed to master them. This in turn means that curricula must be studied and analyzed to determine the level of mental ability that is required to comprehend them.

From a psychometric point of view, the most important task for educators is *matching children* with others of equal ability. Bright children are assumed to be able to learn more in a given time than less bright children. In practice, this philosophy leads to so-called "ability grouping," which in effect allows bright children to go through the material more quickly than slower children. This psychometric orientation also underlies the provision of special classes for the gifted and for the retarded.

Conception of the learning process. Within the developmental philosophy of education, learning is always seen as a *creative* activity. Whenever we learn anything, we engage the world in a way that creates something new, something that reflects both our own mental activity and the material we have dealt with. We never simply copy content; we always stamp it with our unique way of viewing the world. The child from Connecticut who heard the Lord's Prayer as "Our Father, Who art in New Haven, Harold be thy name" is not the exception but the rule. Everything we learn has both a subjective and an objective component.

The conception of learning as a creative or constructive process has a very important practical implication. It means that we cannot talk of learning independently of the content to be learned. The material to be learned will always interact with the learning process in some special way. Long after Piaget discovered the successive stages and organizations of mental operations, he continued to study the ways in which children attained different concepts, such as space, geometry, time, and movement and speed.[3] In so doing he emphasized the fact that merely knowing the stages of mental development does not provide special insight into how children use the operations at any given stage to attain any particular concept. The only way to discover how children go about learning a particular subject is to study children learning.

By contrast, the psychometric philosophy views learning as governed by a set of principles (e.g., intermittent reinforcement) and consisting of the acquisition of a set of skills (e.g., decoding) that are independent of the content to be learned. Early workers in this tradition enunciated such principles as "mass versus distributed" or "whole versus part" learning, which were presumed to operate independently of the content to be learned. Indeed, early studies of memory employed nonsense syllables in order to eliminate the effect of content on the study of memory.

The limitations of this approach were dramatically demonstrated by Jerome Bruner, Jacqueline Goodenough, and George Austin in their seminal work on problem solving.[4] Before the publication of their work, problem solving was spoken of in terms of "trial and error" or "sudden insight" because most of the work had been done with animals. What Bruner and his colleagues demonstrated was that human subjects, when presented with complex problems, employ complex problem-solving activities — in other words, "strategies." Put differently, the content of the problem determines the level of the problem-solving activities that humans employ.

Nonetheless, this insight seems to have been lost. The current interest in teaching young children such things as thinking skills,[5] learning strategies,[6] or computer programming[7] reflects a regression to the idea that thought and content can be treated separately. It is assumed that — once children learn thinking skills or learning strategies or computer programming — these skills will automatically be transferred to different kinds of content. To be sure, transfer of training does occur, but it is far from automatic. Transfer happens when students are active, not passive, learners.[8] But what can we possibly mean by *activity* if not that students are consciously aware of the content they are thinking about or applying strategies to? Mental processes are always content-oriented.

The developmental approach implies that there is little or no automatic transfer from one subject to another, whereas the psychometric approach assumes that the skills and strategies of thinking often transfer spontaneously to new areas.

Conception of knowledge. From a developmental perspective, knowledge is always a construction, inevitably reflecting the joint contributions of the subject and the object. This is far from a new idea, and it harks back to the Kantian resolution of idealist (all knowledge is a mental construction) and empiricist (all knowledge is a copy of an externally existing world) interpretations of how we come to know the world.[9] Kant argued that the mind provides the "categories" of knowing, while the real world provides the content. Knowledge is thus always a construction of the mind's *interaction* with the world and cannot be reduced to one or the other.

What Piaget added to the Kantian solution — and what makes Piaget a neo-Kantian — was the demonstration that the categories of knowing (the mental operations of intelligence) are not constant, as Kant had supposed. Rather, the categories change with age. This idea adds a developmental dimension to the Kantian version of the construction of knowledge. As their mental operations develop, children are required to reconstruct the realities they constructed at the previous developmental level. In effect, a child creates and re-creates reality out of his or her experiences with the environment.

The reality of the young child — his or her knowledge of the world — is thus different from the reality of the older child and adult. For example, young children believe that a quantity changes in amount when it changes in appearance — that, say, the amount of liquid in a low, flat container is greater when it is poured into a tall, narrow one. Older children, whose reality is different, can appreciate the fact that a quantity remains the same in amount despite changes in its appearance. In other words, older children recognize that quantity is conserved. From a developmental perspective, the young child's conception of quantity is not "wrong." It is, in fact, as developmentally appropriate as the older child's grasp of conservation.

From the psychometric point of view, knowledge is something that a child acquires and that can be measured independently from the processes of acquisition. This separation is reflected in the distinction between intelligence tests and achievement tests. One consequence of the separation between learning and content is that knowledge is measured against an external standard that is independent of the learner. When compared to such an external standard, a child's responses can be assessed as being either "right" or "wrong."

Certainly, there is a right and a wrong with respect to some types of knowledge. The Bastille was stormed in 1789, not in 1650; two plus two equals four, not five. We have to distinguish here between what I have elsewhere termed *fundamental* knowledge, which we construct on our own, and *derived* knowledge, which is constructed by others and which we must acquire at second hand.[10] The terms *right* and *wrong* are useful only in connection with derived knowledge.

The developmental approach introduces the idea that there can be differences in knowledge without any reference to "right" or "wrong." The idea of difference, rather than of correctness, is important not only with respect to fundamental knowledge, but also with respect to creative thinking. For example, many bright children come up with ideas that are different from those of their peers and teachers. Unfortunately, these ideas are often regarded as wrong rather than as different and original. One bright child, when asked to write something about the color blue, wrote about Picasso's Blue Period and was teased and jeered. A greater appreciation for such differences would make the life of bright children in our schools a lot easier.

Conception of the aims of education. The aims of developmental education are straightforward. If the learner is seen as a growing individual with developing

The developmental approach seeks to create students who *want to know,* not students who *know what we want.*

abilities, if learning is regarded as a creative activity, and if knowledge is seen as a construction, then the aim of education must surely be to facilitate this development, this creative activity, and this construction of knowledge. Piaget put the aims of education from a developmental perspective this way:

> The principal goal of education is to create men who are capable of doing new things, not simply repeating what other generations have done — men who are creative, inventive, and discoverers. The second goal of education is to form minds which can be critical, can verify, and not accept everything that is offered. The greater danger today is of slogans, collective opinions, ready made trends of thought. We have to be able to resist them individually, to criticize, to distinguish between what is proven and what is not. So we need pupils who are active, who learn early to find out by themselves, partly by their own spontaneous activity and partly through material we set up for them; who learn early to tell what is verifiable and what is simply the first idea to come to them.[11]

The aim of developmental education, then, is to produce thinkers who are creative and critical. This aim will not be achieved, however, by teaching thinking skills to children and adolescents. Rather, the way to pursue this aim is by creating developmentally appropriate learning environments that challenge the child's emerging mental abilities. Creative thinking and critical thinking are not skills to be taught and learned. They reflect basic orientations toward the self and the world that can be acquired only when children are actively engaged in constructing and reconstructing their physical, social, and moral worlds.

The aim of psychometric education is to produce children who score high on tests of achievement. In other words, the aim of education is to maximize the acquisition of quantifiable knowledge and skills. Perhaps former Secretary of Education William Bennett stated this view of the aims of education as well as anyone:

> We should want every student to know how mountains are made, and that for most reactions there is an equal

and opposite reaction. They should know who said "I am the state" and who said "I have a dream." They should know about subjects and predicates, about isosceles triangles and ellipses. They should know where the Amazon flows and what the First Amendment means. They should know about the Donner party and about slavery, and Shylock, Hercules, and Abigail Adams, where Ethiopia is, and why there is a Berlin Wall.[12]

In this statement Bennett echoes a theme that was also sounded in *A Nation at Risk,* which was published three years earlier and decried the poor performance of American students on achievement tests, especially when compared to the performance of children from other nations. Moreover, Bennett's remarks foreshadowed the best-selling critiques of U.S. education by Allan Bloom and E. D. Hirsch, Jr., which charged that American education was failing to provide children with the basic knowledge of western civilization.[13]

Young people should certainly be exposed to Shakespeare, they should know the basics of geography, and they should be familiar with current events. A developmental approach to education does not deny the importance of such knowledge. The difference between the two approaches is a matter of which acquisition comes first. Those who hold a developmental philosophy believe that children who are curious, active learners will acquire much of the knowledge that Bennett, Bloom, and Hirsch call for — and many other things as well. But, from a developmental perspective, the creation of curious, active learners must *precede* the acquisition of particular information. To put the difference more succinctly, the developmental approach seeks to create students who *want to know,* whereas the psychometric approach seeks to produce students who *know what we want.*

IMPLICATIONS OF A DEVELOPMENTAL PHILOSOPHY

Now that we have looked at these two contrasting educational philosophies, we can review a few of the implications for the practice of education of adopting a developmental perspective. Once again, my interpretation is largely based on the

Piagetian idea of the development of intelligence.

Teacher training. Students of most disciplines must learn the basic material of their discipline. A physics student has to learn about the rules that govern the physical world; a chemistry student must learn how the basic chemical elements interact; a biology student must learn about plants and animals. Education is perhaps the only discipline wherein students do not learn the basic material of the discipline at the outset. Students take courses in curriculum, in methods, in educational philosophy, in assessment, and in classroom management. They take only one (or at most two) courses in educational or developmental psychology.

But the basic material of education is not curriculum. Nor is it assessment or methods. The basic material of education is children and youth. A teacher training program that is truly developmentally appropriate would have its students major in child development. Trained in this way, a teacher would be, first and foremost, a child development specialist. Students with a strong foundation in child development can integrate what they learn about curriculum, assessment, and management with what they know about how children of various ages think and learn.

From a developmental point of view, the recommendation of the Holmes Group that we do away with the undergraduate major in education and substitute a year or two of graduate training and internship will not produce better teachers. There *is* a need for teacher training at the undergraduate level — not in traditional education courses, but in child development.

Curriculum. From a developmental point of view, there are several principles that should guide the construction of the curriculum. First, a curriculum must be constructed empirically, not a priori. There is no way to figure out how children learn a subject without studying how they actually go about learning it. Thus it is truly a scandal that curriculum publishers not only fail to do research on the materials they produce, but also fail even to field-test them! In no other profession would we allow a product to be placed on the market without extensive field-testing.

In a truly developmental system of education, teachers would have the opportunity to construct and test their own materials. They could see what works and what doesn't, and they could try out different sequences and methods. The

way curriculum materials work will always depend on the specific group of children in the classroom in any given year. So a curriculum should never be final; it should always be open, flexible, and innovative. Such a curriculum is exciting for the teacher and for the pupils and makes both learning and curriculum innovation cooperative ventures.

Second, I believe that a curriculum should be localized, particularly for elementary schools. I know that this is contrary to trends in other countries, which have uniform curricula for all children. Japan and France are but two of the countries with such uniform national curricula. England, too, will be initiating a uniform national curriculum in 1990. But such national curricula eliminate the possibility of localizing materials to include particulars from the environment in which children actually live and learn.

Such localized curricula hold a great deal of intrinsic interest for children. For example, in learning math, children living in Hawaii might be asked to match coconuts and palm trees, whereas children living in the Northeast might be asked to match acorns and oaks. Likewise, it would add to children's enjoyment if the stories they read took place in their own community or one similar to it. In social studies, too, children are delighted to find a picture of a building that they have actually been in, rather than one that they have never seen. To be sure, children like stories about places and events that are new to them. Nonetheless, they also enjoy reading stories that relate directly to the world they live in. Children, no less than adults, appreciate *both* fantasy and the realism of local reference.

Finally, we need to study curricula to determine their level of developmental difficulty. Developmental difficulty is quite different from psychometric difficulty. The psychometric difficulty of a curriculum or a test item is determined by the number of children of a particular age who successfully learn the material or who get the item correct. A curriculum or test item is generally assigned to the grade or age level at which 75% of the children can succeed.

Developmental difficulty, by contrast, must be determined by examining the actual "errors" children make in attempting to master a problem or task. For example, when young children who have been taught the short *a* sound are asked to learn the long *a* as well, they have great difficulty. The problem is that they are being asked to grasp the fact that the same letter can have two different sounds. Un-

derstanding that the same symbol can stand for two different sounds, however, requires the attainment of the mental abilities that Piaget calls *concrete operations*. A teacher who holds a developmental philosophy would thus avoid teaching phonics until he or she was quite sure that most of the children could handle concrete operations. Because the developmental difficulty of any particular problem or task can be determined only by active investigation, part of the experimental work of teaching would be to explore the developmental difficulty of the available curriculum materials and to try out new materials that might work differently or better.

Instruction. Developmentally speaking, it is as impossible to separate the learning process from the material to be learned as it is to separate learning from instruction. This is authentic teaching. From this perspective, the teacher is also a learner, and the students are also teachers. The teacher who experiments with the curriculum is learning about the curriculum and about the children he or she teaches. And children who work cooperatively and who experiment with curriculum materials are teaching as well as learning.

One way to highlight the difference between authentic teaching and psychometrically oriented teaching is to look at how each type of instruction handles the asking of questions. In psychometrically oriented teaching, the teacher often asks students questions to which the teacher already knows the answers. The purpose is to determine whether the students have the same information as the teacher. But asking questions to which one already has the answers is not authentic behavior. A much more meaningful approach is to ask children questions to which one doesn't have the answers. Finding the answers can then be a learning experience for teacher and students alike. The authentic teacher asks questions to get information and to gain understanding, not to test what students know or understand. Such questioning reflects the fact that the authentic teacher is first and foremost an enthusiastic learner.

Assessment. Developmental assessment involves documenting the work that a child has done over a given period of time. Usually this is done by having a child keep a portfolio that includes all of his or her writing, drawing, math explorations, and so on. In looking through such a portfolio, we can get a good idea of the quality of work that the child is capable of doing and of his or her progress over the given period.

Psychometric assessment involves measuring a child's achievement by means of commercial or teacher-made tests. A child's progress is evaluated according to his or her performance on such tests. Unlike a portfolio of work, the psychometric approach yields a *grade* that symbolizes both the quantity and the quality of the work that the child has done over a given period of time. Although some testing can be useful, it is currently so overused that many children and parents are more concerned about grades and test scores than about what a child has learned. The documentation of a child's work tends to avoid that danger.

I have tried to demonstrate that, while the idea of developmentally appropriate practice has been well received among educators, it really has little chance of being widely implemented. Without a change in underlying philosophy, changes in educational practice will be superficial at best. No classroom or school can truly be developmentally appropriate if its underlying philosophy is psychometric.

How can we change that underlying educational philosophy? It might seem that what is required is a paradigm shift of the sort described by Thomas Kuhn as characterizing major scientific revolutions.[14] Yet neither the developmental thinking of Freud nor that of Piaget has been sufficient to effect such a shift. This may reflect the fact that educational practice is dictated more by social, political, and economic considerations than it is by science. Unfortunately, a major shift in educational philosophy is more likely to come about as a result of economic necessity than as a result of scientific innovation.

1. Sue Bredekamp, *Developmentally Appropriate Practice* (Washington, D.C.: National Association for the Education of Young Children, 1987).

2. Jean Piaget, *The Psychology of Intelligence* (London: Routledge & Kegan Paul, 1950).

3. Jean Piaget and Bärbel Inhelder, *The Child's Conception of Space* (London: Routledge & Kegan Paul, 1956); Jean Piaget, Bärbel Inhelder, and Alina Szeminska, *The Child's Conception of Geometry* (New York: Basic Books, 1960); Jean Piaget, *The Child's Conception of Time* (London: Routledge & Kegan Paul, 1967); and idem, *The Child's Conception of Movement and Speed* (London: Routledge & Kegan Paul, 1970).

4. Jerome S. Bruner, Jacqueline J. Goodenough, and George A. Austin, *A Study in Thinking* (New York: Wiley, 1956).

5. Joan Boykoff Baron and Robert J. Sternberg, *Teaching Thinking Skills: Theory and Practice* (New York: Freeman, 1987).

6. Edwin Weinstein and Richard Edwin Mayer, "The Teaching of Learning Strategies," in Merlin C. Wittrock, ed., *Handbook of Research on Teaching*, 3rd ed. (New York: Macmillan, 1986).

7. Seymour Papert, *Mindstorms* (New York: Basic Books, 1980).

8. David N. Perkins and Gavriel Salomon, "Teaching for Transfer," *Educational Leadership*, vol. 46, 1988, pp. 22-32.

9. Immanuel Kant, *Critique of Pure Reason* (New York: Wiley, 1943).

10. David Elkind, *Miseducation: Preschoolers at Risk* (New York: Knopf, 1987).

11. Quoted in Richard E. Ripple and Verne E. Rockcastle, eds., *Piaget Rediscovered: A Report of the Conference on Cognitive Studies and Curriculum Development* (Ithaca, N.Y.: School of Education, Cornell University, 1964), p. 5.

12. William J. Bennett, *First Lessons: A Report on Elementary Education in America* (Washington, D.C.: U.S. Department of Education, 1986), p. 3.

13. Allan Bloom, *The Closing of the American Mind* (New York: Simon & Schuster, 1987); and E. D. Hirsch, Jr., *Cultural Literacy: What Every American Needs to Know* (Boston: Houghton Mifflin, 1987).

14. Thomas S. Kuhn, *The Structure of Scientific Revolutions*, 2nd ed. (Chicago: University of Chicago Press, 1970).

Quality Infant/Toddler Caregiving:

Are There Magic Recipes?

Alice Sterling Honig

Alice Sterling Honig, Ph.D., is Professor of Child Development at Syracuse University, New York. For the past 13 years, she has been program supervisor of the Syracuse Children's Center, the longest federally funded infant/toddler child care center in the United States.

A magic elixir for helping infants and toddlers grow into successful school achievers, socially adept with parents, peers, and teachers, would fetch a high price from today's parents and other caregivers. Busy with professional commitments, parents hope that child care professionals will know of the programmatic package, the right toys, the exact exercises, and other "cookbook" ingredients to produce that well-adjusted, eager young learner so devoutly desired.

A survey of research findings on environmental and personal variables that can support dreams for children's success provides clues to many of the ingredients required for a high-quality infant/toddler program (Honig, 1985a). Yet most of these ingredients are not specifically or routinely taught in schools; neither can they be easily bought or prescribed uniformly in identical doses as panaceas for childrearing.

Individualized, attentive loving

The primary ingredient to help young children flourish consists of *loving, responsive* caregivers, generously committing *energy, body-loving,* and *tuned-in attentiveness* to their child's well-being. And every ingredient counts! Since infants come into the world with different temperaments and styles of adjusting, this commitment requires much patience and much flexibility as new parents and caregivers tune into and learn about their child's unique qualities. Getting to know a baby takes time and committed interest. The new baby may be impulsive or reflective; adaptable, irritable, or slow to warm up (Thomas, Chess, & Birch, 1968). Adults have to be aware of differences in temperament, lest, for example, they respond to the intense baby's irritability with negative or exasperated tensions. Such responses can create miseries for an infant who already has troubles (Wittmer & Honig, 1988). Perhaps she finds it hard to get a thumb to her mouth to suck for self-comfort and lacks the easy adaptability of a temperamentally calmer child. Each baby needs a caregiver who recognizes and validates his or her special self. Dancing an Eriksonian duet of "giving and getting" in infant nurturing requires the commitment of both partners (Honig, 1987), but the caregivers need to be the skillful initiators. Adults are the driving force in the spiral growth of baby loving and cooperating. It is the adult "expert" partner who imbues the early relationship with somatic certainty (the security babies build through physical closeness) and the predictability of daily rhythms.

Because of the need to create a meaningful harmony in personal interchanges with infants, selecting caregivers of infants poses a different problem from selecting preschoolers' caregivers. Furman (1986), in her perceptive book for nursery teachers, advises that preschool teachers should leave sensuous and intimate relations to parents. But for babies, such relations are integral to their care. The quality infant/toddler caregiver *must* be involved and, of course, needs to be relaxed and to accept the sensuous nature of intimate ministrations such as feeding, burping, cuddling, and diapering.

Respecting tempos and exploration needs

Research has clarified specific qualities caregivers should have that nurture the roots of intellectual competence, cooperative interactions, and resilience in coping with stresses (Honig, 1986). Some of these adult qualities are: tender, careful holding in arms; feedings that respect individual tempos; accurate interpretation of and prompt, comforting attention to distress signals; giving opportunities and freedom to explore toys on floor; and giving babies control over social interactions (Martin, 1981). Feedings should be as lengthy or short as the nursing baby desires. Holding and cuddling on hips and shoulders and laps should be leisurely. The toddler who needs to confirm your presence by piling toys into your lap after brief trips away from you needs to know that you will accept these tokens, these demands for attention. Toddlers often seesaw dramatically between needs for securing adult involvement and needs to defy adults with indifference or disobedience.

Adult generosity promotes babies' cognitive alertness and secure trusting attachment to caregivers (Ainsworth, 1982; Stern, 1985). Such gifts set foundations for an inner sense of safety and of high self-esteem (Honig, 1982a): All is right with the world; grown-ups are predictable and kind; peo-ple can be counted on to care for baby and to fix and soothe troubles, whether a scraped knee, a fearful feeling, or a hunger crankiness. Tender, tuned-in caregiving energizes toddlers' joyous and courageous explorations of strange environments. Courage to cope flows from adult caring and, significantly, also leads to increased compliance and cooperation with caregivers (Honig, 1985b; 1985c).

Language mastery experiences

Rich language interchanges and lengthy sequences of turn-taking talk are further critical ingredients to promote optimal development (Honig, 1984). Caregivers need to read books in a leisurely, involved fashion on a daily basis with young children. This frequent reading correlates with later intellectual zestfulness, rich language skills, and child success at school entry (Swan & Stavros, 1973). Research in family day care and center care as well as in families confirms the importance of language mastery in boosting cognitive competence of infants and toddlers (Clarke-Stewart, 1973; Carew, 1980; Tizard, 1981).

Shared activities

Colorful toys and environments can indeed aid early learning. Yet provision of graded materials needs genuine, insightful thoughtfulness from caregivers using the equipment. Adults need to *understand infant developmental levels and sensorimotor stages* when providing toys to promote understandings of space and causality. Adults need to engage in joint activities as grist for child learnings. Roll a ball back and forth. Watch what interests a baby, and *talk* about what she is pointing to, jabbering at, or exploring with eyes or hands. Otherwise, too many toys in a center may simply result in babies crawling and toddlers wandering aimlessly among scattered playthings or engaging in chaotic, even destructive, behaviors with materials.

The too-difficult toy or learning game urged by a pushy parent or caregiver can turn off a child's interest in learning. Toddlers often show us that we have chosen just the right toy by enthusiastically tackling that activity (such as stacking cups or pushing poker chips through a coffee can slot) over and over again. Thus, young children need both ingredients:

1) responsive adults who ensure children's well-being through innumerable small interchanges of mutually pleasurable caregiving, language-permeated playfulness, and bodily cherishing and

2) a variety of learning opportunities and challenges tailored to children's capabilities and interests.

Such a "prescription" is most likely to lead to young children with ego-resilience, self-control, and the internal motivation to persist positively at difficult problem-solving tasks (Matas, Arend, & Sroufe, 1978).

Feeding finesse and health care

Optimal nutrition and preventive health care measures to boost wellness are important ingredients sometimes given insufficient attention as promoters of intellectual motivation and achievement. For example, iron deficiency, even without anemia, is associated with infant irritability, shortened attention span, solemnity, and lowered IQ. Fortunately, administration of intramuscular iron to such infants produces higher IQ scores and more infant responsive smiling for a caregiving adult within a week (Honig & Oski, 1986). Scrupulously careful handwashing procedures can reduce the frequency of infectious illness, particularly diarrhea, in centers (Lee & Yeager, 1986).

Promoting baby altruism

Another domain sometimes neglected in setting up infant/toddler programs has to do with the nurturing of prosocial, altruistic behaviors. Adults need to be aware of how important they are as early rule-givers and role models for caring, sharing, and helping. Yarrow and colleagues (Pines, 1979) found that when mothers categorically rejected aggression and hurting as a way for their toddlers to resolve social problems, *and* consistently displayed empathic comfort for the toddlers' own hurts and frights, then well before 2 years of age these children showed concern for others' distress. Toddlers offered comforts (such as their own bottle or blanket!) to upset peers and tired family members. Such "baby altruism" was quite stable when the children were studied through teachers' reports 5 years later.

Caregiver expectations about children can lead to self-fulfilling prophecies. Baumrind (1977) describes "authoritative parenting" where families with high involvement and commitment to their young ones *and* high expectations and firm rules with reasons have children most likely to be good learners and reasonable with preschool teachers and peers. Adults who expect toddlers to be terrors may very well see their fears fulfilled. Calm caregivers with a sense of humor and extra supplies of patience and admiration will find toddlers brave (though unsteady) adventurers on the rough trails toward independent, self-actualized functioning. Adjusting one's will and wishes to those of peers and teachers is bound to be a struggle. Adult empathy can ease the toddler's inevitable trials. The no-saying toddler who insists he wants to take a bath with his new shoes on can be exasperating—but also a remarkable little person in stretching a caregiver's coping ingenuity. The hungry, yet defiant, toddler who gleefully runs away calling "No no no" when called for lunchtime will cheerfully charge back to the lunch area if lured with comments such as "Yummy hamburgers, good carrots!"

Continuity of care and cognitive facilitation

One of the concerns child development specialists have is whether "inoculations" such as high-quality, enriched out-of-home care can provide a supplemental boost for infants and toddlers who have otherwise had insufficient loving and language experiences. A further question is whether such enrichment for young children will have lasting effects. Will family and school need to continue to provide optimal supports for children over many years? Longitudinal research suggests that long-range effects of early stimulation do depend crucially on the *stability* and *continuity* of care. For example, early optimal home stimulation scores are more likely to correlate with positive outcomes for children when *later* home scores also show parental facilitation of cognitive development. On the other hand, remedially enriching early education programs as a supplement for disadvantaged infants and preschoolers do indeed seem to prevent a typical downward slide in intelligence test scores for children from low-education families (Honig & Lally, 1982; Ramey & Gowen, 1986). Quality infant/toddler programs have even been found to decrease social delinquency in later adolescent years (Berrueta-Clement, Schweinhart, Barnett, Epstein, & Weikart, 1985; Lally, Mangione, Wittmer, & Honig, 1986).

Conclusions

Lest these various prescriptions for an optimal infant/toddler rearing environment seem too difficult to expect from adults who may not have much training initially in child development knowledge and skills, it is important and cheering to note how many easy-to-read materials are currently available for caregivers. Many journals, such as *Young Children* or *Day Care and Early Education*, frequently provide special articles for infant/toddler teachers with creative curricular ideas and special insights about aspects of early development. Books with homey, easy-to-carry-out learning games with toddlers are available (Honig, 1982b; Miller, 1985).

Directors and trainers of infant/toddler caregivers will also find materials to enhance their continuous in-service efforts to ensure high-quality care (Willis & Ricciuti, 1975; Honig & Lally, 1981; Cataldo, 1983; Greenberg, 1987a, 1987b; Godwin & Schrag, 1988). Such resources can especially help the busy caregiver to restructure daily routines into enriching experiences. Metamorphosed through adult sensibilities, skills, and creativity, daily care situations can be turned into prime opportunities to further the early learning careers of infants and toddlers.

References

Ainsworth, M. D. S. (1982). Early caregiving and later patterns of attachment. In M. H. Klaus & M. O. Robertson (Eds.), *Birth, interaction and attachment*. Skilman, NJ: Johnson & Johnson.

Baumrind, D. (1977). Some thoughts about child rearing. In S. Cohen & T. J. Comiskey (Eds.), *Child development: Contemporary perspective* (pp. 248–258). Itasca, IL: Peacock.

Berrueta-Clement, J., Schweinhart, D. J., Barnett, W. S., Epstein, A. S., & Weikart, D. P. (1985). *Changed lives: The effects of the Perry Preschool Program on youths through age 19*. Ypsilanti, MI: High/Scope Press.

Carew, J. V. (1980). Experience and the development of intelligence in young children at home and in day care. *Monographs of the Society for Research in Child Development, 45*(6–7, Serial No. 187).

Cataldo, C. Z. (1983). *Infant and toddler programs: A guide to very early childhood education*. Reading, MA: Addison-Wesley.

Clarke-Stewart, K. A. (1973). Interactions between mothers and their young children: Characteristics and consequences. *Monographs of the Society for Research in Child Development, 38*(6–7, Serial No. 153).

Furman, E. (Ed.). (1986). *What nursery school teachers ask us about.* Madison, CT: International Universities Press.

Godwin, A., & Schrag, L. (Eds.). (1988). *Setting up for infant care: Guidelines for centers and family day care homes.* Washington, DC: NAEYC.

Greenberg, P. (1987a). Ideas that work with young children: Infants and toddlers away from their mothers? *Young Children, 42*(4), 40–42.

Greenberg, P. (1987b). Ideas that work with young children: What is curriculum for infants in family day care (or elsewhere)? *Young Children, 42(5),* 58–62.

Honig, A. S. (1982a). The gifts of families: Caring, courage, and competence. In N. Stinnett, J. Defrain, K. King, H. Lingren, G. Fowe, S. Van Zandt, & R. Williams (Eds.), *Family strengths 4: Positive support systems* (pp. 331–349). Lincoln, NE: University of Nebraska Press.

Honig, A. S. (1982b). *Playtime learning games for young children.* Syracuse, NY: Syracuse University Press.

Honig, A. S. (1984, Winter). Why talk to babies? *Beginnings,* pp. 3–6.

Honig, A. S. (1985a). High quality infant/toddler care: Issues and dilemmas. *Young Children, 41*(1), 40–46.

Honig, A. S. (1985b). Research in review: Compliance, control and discipline (Part 1). *Young Children, 40*(2), 50–68.

Honig, A. S. (1985c). Research in review:

Compliance, control, and discipline (Part 2). *Young Children, 40*(3), 47–52.

Honig, A. S. (1986). Research in review: Stress and coping in children. In J. B. McCracken (Ed.), *Reducing stress in young children's lives* (pp. 142–167). Washington, DC: NAEYC.

Honig, A. S. (1987). The Eriksonian approach: Infant-toddler education. In J. Roopnarine & J. Johnson (Eds.), *Approaches to early childhood education* (pp. 49–69). Columbus, OH: Merrill.

Honig, A. S., & Lally, J. R. (1981). *Infant caregiving: A design for training.* Syracuse, NY: Syracuse University Press.

Honig, A. S., & Lally, J. R. (1982). The family development research program: Retrospective review. *Early Child Development and Care, 10,* 41–62.

Honig, A. S., & Oski, F. A. (1986). Solemnity: A clinical risk index for iron deficient infants. In A. S. Honig (Ed.), *Risk factors in infancy* (pp. 69–84). New York: Gordon & Breach.

Lally, J. R., Mangione, P., Wittmer, D., & Honig, A. S. (1986, November). *An early intervention program 10 years later: What happened to high risk infants who received quality early childhood education? The Syracuse University study.* Seminar presented at the annual conference of the National Association for the Education of Young Children, Washington, DC.

Lee, C., & Yeager, A. (1986). Infections in day care. *Current Problems in Pediatrics, 16,* 129–184.

Martin, J. A. (1981). A longitudinal study of the consequences of early mother-infant interaction: A microanalytic approach. *Monographs of the Society for Research in Child Development, 46*(3, Serial No. 190).

Matas, L., Arend, R. A., & Sroufe, L. A. (1978). Continuity of adaptation in the second year: The relationship between quality of attachment and later competence. *Child Development, 49,* 547–556.

Miller, K. (1985). *Things to do with toddlers and twos.* Marshfield, MA: Telshare Publishing Co.

Pines, M. (1979). Good samaritans at age two? *Psychology Today, 13*(1), 66–77.

Ramey, C. T., & Gowen, J. W. (1986). A general systems approach to modifying risk for retarded development. In A. S. Honig (Ed.), *Risk factors in infancy* (pp. 9–26). New York: Gordon & Breach.

Stern, D. (1985). *The interpersonal world of the infant: A view from psychoanalysis and developmental psychology.* New York: Basic.

Swan, R. W., & Stavros, H. (1973). Child-rearing practices associated with the development of cognitive skills of children in low socioeconomic areas. *Early Child Development and Care, 2,* 23–38.

Thomas, A. S., Chess, S., & Birch, H. G. (1968). *Temperament and behavior disorders in children.* New York: New York University Press.

Tizard, B. (1981). Language at home and at school. In C. B. Cazden (Ed.), *Language in early childhood education* (rev. ed., pp. 17–27). Washington, DC: NAEYC.

Willis, A., & Ricciuti, H. A. (1975). *A good beginning for babies: Guidelines for group care.* Washington, DC: NAEYC.

Wittmer, D. S., & Honig, A. S. (1988). Teacher recreation of negative interactions with toddlers. In A. S. Honig (Ed.), Optimizing early child care and education [Special issue]. *Early Child Development and Care, 31,* 77–88.

Why Not Academic Preschool?   (Part 1)*

Ideas That Work With Young Children

Polly Greenberg

Polly Greenberg has been an early childhood educator for many decades. On a continuum of one-to-ten, ten being a perfectly developmentally appropriate teacher, colleagues (playfully) rate Polly 8-1/2.

? I am a preschool director. I have looked into NAEYC's accreditation system to see whether I want to discuss getting into it with our board and staff. I see the obvious advantages—it would look good to parents and prospective parents, be a morale booster to staff, and be a vehicle for improving our program. Of course we seek educational excellence. We want to be the best.

This is where I balk at accreditation. *We* believe that 3- and 4-year-olds can *learn*, and *expect* them too. Our parents are educated and would never put up with an inferior program where children just play. Yet reading NAEYC's materials, and other current publications, I sense that it is the *academic* approach that may be "inferior." We also believe in strong discipline. Life requires it. Truth to tell, I do feel in a quandary. Can you clarify this?

On the most important point you raise, all leaders of early childhood education (whether expert practitioners, or teacher educators,

or specialists like researchers or theoreticians, or teachers who specialize in the needs of children with unusual disabilities or in areas such as language, literacy, one or two of the arts) would agree: **We all believe that 3- and 4-year-olds can learn; we all expect them to learn.** We all agree that self-esteem is an *essential* for optimal development to take place; and we all are quick to state that **a big part of a child's self-esteem comes from feeling competent—from becoming increasingly competent in "things that count in the child's world."** (This is why children from corners of our culture where adults believe—because their lives have taught them so—that children should learn to protect themselves physically feel *good*, not *bad*, if they're daring fighters. In *their* world, being a good fighter is a "thing that counts.") Like you, we also believe strongly in discipline—**self**-discipline.

Two major sharply contrasting approaches to early childhood education

There are two major, sharply contrasting approaches to these shared goals, two sharply contrasting philosophies (models) of education for 3-, 4-, and 5-year-olds—and many carefully conceptualized (or carelessly occur-

ring) variations at all points along a continuum within both of these very broad categories. Seldom do we see *excellent* examples of *either* philosophy. The majority of excellent programs mix aspects of each model. Because understanding the differences between the models is so important, this article will be in two parts, in order to explore the subject.

The first early childhood education philosophy is exemplified in traditional American nursery/kindergarten/ first grade education (1920/present)

The child is believed to be an active learner who learns best when she

● moves at will, becomes involved in something, usually with other children (purposefulness and creative thinking are encouraged)

● makes *major* choices—chooses among a variety of worthwhile "live" activities ("live" meaning that the child is not choosing only among worksheets)

● initiates and "does" within a richly prepared indoor and outdoor environment (initiative is encouraged)

● discovers, dismantles, reassembles

● discusses with friends and grown-ups

● grapples with challenges (some of which she inadvertently stumbles into,

*Future editions will address other major goals, which program serves them best, and the repercussions of these programs in later life.

From *Young Children*, Vol. 45, No. 2, January 1990, pp. 70-80. Copyright © 1990 by Polly Greenberg, NAEYC, 1834 Connecticut Avenue, N.W., Washington, DC 20009.

and some of which she consciously sets out to conquer)

• constructs understandings, each at her own rate of intellectual development

• plans and collaborates with friends and adults

• solves problems she runs into (not problems that are concocted out of context and set before her in bite-sized portions of "a problem-solving curriculum")

• *creates* concepts and *recreates* or elaborates upon them as she learns something new that seems true but doesn't mesh with what she thought she knew

• works with an interesting, intuitive, endorsing adult who mingles with children as they play and work, and in informal interest groups, skill groups, and social groups—all of them often minigroups

• evaluates her own work and behavior with peer and adult participation

• feels rewarded by the satisfaction of a job well done (intrinsic reward)

• experiences spontaneous encounters with learning as her mind meets interesting or puzzling things that capture her attention and intrigue her, **which always include things related to what adults and older children do, hence generally include pretending to read books by 2 or 3 years of age; writing letters and numerals while playing and drawing somewhere between ages 3 and 7 (typically beginning by 4 or 5 years old); and guess-spelling, asking how to spell words, and real reading at 5, 6, or 7, if not sooner.**

All of this is believed to be best learned through enriched free play and teacher-designed, teacher-guided projects usually planned so they expand upon what the child has freely elected to do. Sophisticated guidance and enrichment intended to ensure that opportunities to develop creativity, imagination, generous amounts of math, science concepts, social studies concepts, language, and literacy, as well as opportunities to learn in all the arts, grow out of or are interplanted in a **naturalized** manner throughout what the child has become absorbed in. Teachers, parents, the community; and supervisors, consultants, and teacher educators connected in one way or another with the program determine what should be included in the curriculum, but it isn't believed that

As they learn a vast amount in all areas through their play and projects, children develop positive self-esteem with regard to their competence in using language and math adeptly, and in thinking in a scientific, self-disciplined, problem-solving mode.

there is a fixed body of knowledge that children should "master."

Teachers assess children's progress by

• *observing* them;

• *recording and keeping* anecdotal notes about anything of particular interest or very typical emotionally, socially, physically, intellectually, academically, aesthetically, or otherwise;

• *identifying* special needs in any of these areas, and following up or referring as needed;

• *collecting and keeping* samples and photos of their activities; and

• *sharing* extensively in the information- and opinion-gathering process with the child's parent(s) and other staff. (This is how those of us who were trained as nursery educators before the advent of the achievement testing craze that started sweeping into our schools in the '60s were taught to assess young children's progress. Mercifully, "test mania" and related atrocities—such as omitting, deleting, or putting in parentheses children who, for whatever reason, are not in that magical and mythical place called Average—are beginning to be attacked from all sides. See, for example, Kamii, 1990.)

This philosophy of education assumes that what children learn casually and naturally as they live their lives and play their days away is valuable learning, nature's way of educating children, God's way, if you will; and that though it can be improved upon by the careful craftswomen that expert early childhood practitioners are, adults should not *deprive* children of natural learning by making them sit down and be taught at. This philosophy believes not *only* in preparing the environment for excellent play, but *also* that for the child to have **optimal** learning opportunities, adults

(parents or teachers) need to **enrich** the play, **plan** projects, and **teach** children many things somewhat in the same way that one **naturalizes** plants. You carefully arrange your purposeful additions to the landscape here and there and all around in the midst of what's happening there naturally so that to a person stumbling into it, all seems relaxed and natural. We **naturalize** "subjects" and "skills" and the conventional knowledge that we expect children to learn, throughout the children's learning environments (home, school, community).

This naturalizing means that "subjects" are integrated, but more than this: It means that children learn "subject" area "skills" and "subskills" and facts in meaningful contexts, sometimes in thematic, teacher guided projects— **as a need for these skills crops up in activities a child has eagerly elected to involve himself in**. For a long time, there have been as wide a variety of OK ways to do this as there have been first-rate teachers. There have also, for a long time, been published curricula featuring this philosophy. Emphasis is equally on all aspects of each child's development: **Intellectual learning is fostered,** but is not given priority over physical, social, and emotional learning. Various theoretical frameworks are adhered to, but not given priority over children's individual needs. Academics may be informally included in the array of learnings occurring, **but learning is never narrowed to "mere" academics.** You say you believe that children are capable of learning and should learn when 3, 4, and 5 years of age. Developmentally appropriate program people believe this strongly, but resist the idea of *limiting* learning to academics only.

Children have opportunities at school (as they do at home in moderately literate families) to learn letters and sounds and a great deal more that goes into easy early reading, but they learn most of it one child at a time during sociable playing, drawing, and talking times with friends. Children learn

- as they experiment and discover, or
- as a need for the new knowledge comes up **for an individual** in his play and projects, or
- as children's observant teachers purposefully expand upon what a child (or small group) is doing to include literacy experiences, or
- when adults are reading stories to children and conversing about them, or
- when an adult is engaged in an activity and children are invited to join in if they wish.

In the 1940s, '50s, and '60s, when it was the predominant approach to learning in nursery schools, and especially in public kindergartens and first grades, this was called *the language experience approach*; now we know it as *the whole language approach* or *emerging literacy*. There are small differences between language experience and whole language, but from the expert classroom teacher's perspective, they're insignificant.

(It must be admitted that within this broad category of educators who believe in learning through play and projects is a contingent that finds the alphabet anathema and shies away from the sounds of letters as if they would infect children with a fearful anti-education virus. But although some theoreticians "freak at the thought," as one literacy specialist phrased it, many ordinary, very child-development-oriented classroom teachers, and probably *most* parents, certainly most middle-class parents, include exposure to letters and sounds, and friendly explanations, in with everything else they expose 2-, 3-, 4-, and 5-year-old children to at school or at home. Therefore, without "instruction," many children learn about them. As the pendulum now swings away from academic preschool, we are likely to see a return of the 1950s extremists, who shuddered at the thought of phonics—*even if offered in a playful, natural manner*—before children reached first grade.)

The same is true of math. Children have opportunities to figure out numerical relationships as they play and work with objects and people, to count, to make graphs, to classify things, to weigh things, to learn liquid and linear measurement, more and less, bigger and smaller, adding on and taking away, how to recognize numerals—**but all as it comes up in their play and projects,** or as their teachers **extend these play and project activities to include such experiences.** In math learning, understanding (mastering) the basics (the principles involved) should precede memorizing the details (skills and facts).

→ For children to learn optimally this way, teachers must be given

- **training in**
  — child development, including, some of us believe, the depth, interpersonal, and humanistic psychologies,
  — observing individual children, including the art and science of taking pertinent notes,
  — working informally as equal people with all parents,
  — working with specialists as needed in assessing and assisting children and families with special needs,
  — recognizing moments when one can connect with a child to develop trust and friendship, from which learning grows (a sophisticated skill),
  — creating a complex, stimulating, ever-fresh yet predictable and manageable learning environment including a variety of interlinked learning centers,
  — recognizing moments when a child or group of children could learn something new—a new idea, an approach to solving a problem, a new fact, a new skill,
  — interjecting thought-provoking comments and queries without interrupting or interfering (a skill that many expert teachers believe intuitive teachers do better than non-intuitive teachers, no matter how well trained),
  — helping children with the intricacies and nuances of having and being friends,
  — helping children discipline **themselves** (develop inner controls); and
  — helping each child feel good about himself or herself throughout all this.
- **authority to use their**
  — intuition,
  — judgment,
  — knowledge,

— materials, and
— resources

in making the moment into a learning encounter—possibly one that can be expanded into a week-long or six-week-long project with depth, dimensions, aspects, and angles "covering" in a web-like way learning in many "subject" areas, totaling educational excellence. (In all honesty, we need to note that a great number of teacher education programs purporting to believe in this general approach to early education do *not* give students a thorough grounding in these things, nor do many work places give teachers the freedoms and support necessary for them to fully use their sensitivities and skills.)

Nature has made the human mind so it seeks stimuli to pique it, thus rapidly expanding thinking processes and knowledge.

Said a very good teacher of 3s (who has taught in academic preschools, and now does staff development work in developmentally appropriate programs) when she read this list:

A really good teacher using *any* philosophy should be trained in all this. The problem is, if the principal or director is big on the academic approach to preschool, you never get time to use all this. Your teaching isn't evaluated on these kinds of things. You are evaluated on how orderly and quiet the children are, how well you write up and present each step of your lesson plan, and the children's standardized test scores. It's appreciated if you do all this other too, but it isn't relevant in evaluating you, so you don't spend time doing it and becoming better at it all. You need all this training *and* a chance to perfect your ability to do it in a real, live, three-ring circus classroom, *and* to be evaluated (valued) for these skills. Besides, an academic preschool conditions *parents* to value the wrong approach, too, so your parents are *against* your good teaching, instead of supportive of it.

This general category—currently called **developmentally appropriate practice**—includes approaches, theories, and emphases associated with people such as John Dewey, Patty Hill,

3. APPROPRIATE EDUCATIONAL PRACTICES

Arnold Gesell, Lucy Sprague Mitchell, Harriet Johnson, Carolyn Pratt, Barbara Biber, Margaret Naumburg, Cornelia Goldsmith, Erik Erikson, Jean Piaget, David Weikart, and David Elkind.

Disparate, far from monolithic, ranging from the original Progressive Educators to the contemporary Piagetian constructivists, this group nonetheless has been characterized by general consensus. This consensus is most recently displayed by the publication of *Developmentally Appropriate Practice* (Bredekamp, 1987) by NAEYC. As one contemporary educator described the process behind that document:

We thrash out all our viewpoints and convictions and produce a broad set of statements we can *all* accept, even though we also cherish our differences.

This general approach is advocated by NAEYC now, and has been—with varying emphases over the years—consistently ever since it originated in 1926 as the National Association for Nursery Education. The approach is currently called "developmentally appropriate" early childhood education (with or without the literal numerals or alphabet letters, depending upon which subgroup you're listening to). It's the approach to young children's development and learning taught throughout much of this century by Columbia Teachers College, Bank Street College of Education, Vassar College, Wheelock, Peabody, Sarah Lawrence, the University of Maryland, the Merrill-Palmer Institute, newer programs such as Pacific Oaks and Erikson Institute, and other institutions *specializing* in education for children younger than 6. Mid-century British Infant Schools have used this general approach. Traditional nursery/kindergarten education was developed in tandem with the child study and psychoanalytic psychology movements, and it has absorbed a lot of basics from both. (Since the '60s, it has taken on some basics from other psychologies, too.)

Currently, this "developmentally appropriate" philosophy is being strongly promoted by all national education associations that have published position statements on early childhood education. Among them are the National Association of Elementary School Principals, the Association for Supervision and Curriculum Development, and the National Association of

State Boards of Education; **so if you choose to move your school in this direction, you're in good company.** The reason all those leaders are forcefully advocating this kind of educational experience for 3-, 4-, and 5-year-olds— and even for 6- and 7-year-olds—is that a wealth of recent research confirms and corroborates what most expert practitioners have been explaining, writing, and teaching for 100 years: **This is the most effective way to educate young children. It works best in the long run, and with any luck, life *is* longer than 5 or 6 years, so there's no need for 5-year-olds to know everything they will need to know throughout their school and later years.**

The second early childhood education philosophy is represented by the recently introduced (1960s), basically academic preschool/ kindergarten/first grade

The child is believed to learn best when he

- sits still, pays attention to the teacher who is "instructing," or does assigned, often paper-and-pencil, seatwork (receptivity is praised)
- makes *minor* choices—which color paper he wants for making a patterned craft item (it's expected that he *will* make the craft item; not to do so usually isn't an option)
- obeys and follows directions in the classroom (compliance is rewarded with compliments)
- initiates and "does" only during a brief free play period, at recess, and on his own time at home in a home environment (that *may* be loaded with learning opportunities, and *may* offer an adult to assist the child in interpreting and expanding the learning his mind comes upon; or *may* be an environment in which learning opportunities are starkly limited and in which an adult is not available to promote spontaneous learning)
- discovers, but on a narrowly restricted scale—discovers the right answer from among several possible answers on a workbook page
- discusses, but in a formal, teacher-led, tightly topic-related format; children have little chance to learn through informal conversation with one another while in the classroom
- experiences few intellectual chal-

lenges to grapple with and construct understandings from—his own rate of intellectual development may or may not be recognized, but is seldom honored and responded to in the curriculum that confronts him
- goes along with plans his teacher has made—teachers and children do very little planning *together;* children are expected to tolerate their circumstances good-naturedly
- solves only prefabricated, packaged problems out of a purchased curriculum, if (officially) any; even social problems are usually "solved" for him because the teacher, focused as she is on the academic curriculum she must "cover," doesn't have time to help the child see and test behavioral alternatives, so she tells him the rule and possibly puts him in "the time-out chair to think about it"; very little assertiveness and stridency is "allowed"
- memorizes facts (may create some concepts), waits to be told whether he has gotten them "right" or "wrong," tries again (often guessing, because if that answer was wrong, maybe this answer will be right), doesn't develop *evidence* that he's right or wrong
- works with an almost-always-right adult who approves of him when he's right and disapproves when he is wrong, usually in "instructional" settings, rarely in small interest or social groupings
- awaits, passively, adult evaluation and praise (extrinsic reward) rather than judging for himself whether or not his work is good and his behavior helpful
- experiences reprimands and restraining procedures when he spontaneously encounters something that captures his attention and intrigues him but does not happen to be on the worksheets he has been assigned or in the lesson he's supposed to be attending to

After reading this description of the academic "preschool," an excellent teacher of 3s said:

I used to teach this way. I strolled around my classroom distributing sheets of paper and bundles of brisk directives. I taught like this because that's how my teachers taught *me* all through school. I didn't go to preschool, so I knew no other way.

I went through a teacher education program, but even though what I wanted was kindergarten, or even younger, what I learned was mostly all meant for upper elementary teachers, with some special stuff and caveats tacked on for kindergarten teachers. (I didn't know at the time that there was a special field, at *that* time known as "nursery education," or I would've looked for a school specializing in it, instead of dabbling in it as my elementary-oriented college did.) This was the heyday of cognitive, cognitive, cognitive, too, so they didn't emphasize all the rest of the child. I was flimflammed into skill-by-skill teaching.

When I started work, it was in a preschool I later learned would be called an academic preschool, but until all the debate began in the mid-1980s, I thought it was the way *all* preschools were. It was a top-of-the-line private school. So all the wrong ideas and strategies I had learned were reinforced. I spent my days chiding children. If my aide and I had a child who refused to "perform," we pursued him like furies. I remember the frightened little faces of those who never did well. If tears troubled their eyes, I felt I was reaching them, motivating them. I look back now and feel it was an affront to childhood, just pure intimidation and pretension (which cynics say is the aim of most human behavior anyway). I worry now, praying I didn't char any little hearts with my predictions about how they would never amount to anything if they didn't work harder. They were only 3 years old!

I didn't realize the extent to which young children are motivated to be like grown-ups and older children, which, in a literate society, includes using the 3Rs. I didn't trust children to evolve a "mastery" in their own way, each in his own time, if given encouragement and assistance.

In this broad category and philosophy of education, which could be described as a **behavior modification** approach, the schedule includes play periods, but they're brief and are seen as a break for "rest and recreation." Projects and some of the arts are scheduled, but are offered as "enrichment": play and projects are important but peripheral activities, not the core curriculum. The core curriculum is a tightly structured sequence of splinter skills, presented to the child through a strictly structured sequence of instructional steps. These educators believe that all of this is best learned through short periods of separated subject instruction, intended to give the child the necessities for *later* learning *earlier*. This minimizes the importance of the child's *present* age and stage, causing a commentator to remark:

If there were no need for a certain set of years, nature, which is ultra-efficient, would telescope childhood and jump from one to six without all the years in between. They are all there for a *reason*.

It's believed that there is a fixed body of knowledge that 4-year-olds need to

master. Adults either

● don't realize how much more easily children learn abstract academic subskills *later*, say at 6 or 7, or

● believe that learning must be unpleasant to be effective, or

● are unaware that *the same abstract academic* subskills can be taught as the need arises in contexts meaningful to this age group.

Here, the former academic preschool teacher exclaimed:

That's it! That's exactly it! The fact that children need to learn these things doesn't translate to mean they need to learn them *now*, when they're just 3 and 4 years old. It *is* true that I used to think learning was a sort of grim business. I used to envision children huddled around their squadrons of clumped-together school desks, slumped over their work; that was "learning." How funny it seems now! I used to think I was doing a good job when I saw all my docile little children chastened and conforming. Now I look for *joy*—love of learning.

Children's progress is assessed with tests, so there's heavy emphasis on mastery. The degree of children's measurable "performance" in academic tasks is what's valued. Children are positively "reinforced" (given stars, smiles, etc.) for absorbing, at least for the moment, as much memorized information in the form of abstract symbols (letters, shapes) as they reasonably can. Adults control most of the use of space, time, and materials in all early childhood programs in that they arrange and manage all of it, set behavioral standards, and so on. But in the academic preschool there is little if any emphasis on children using most of the space most of the time *in their way*.

This broad category of programs and philosophies features

● direct instruction;
● teacher as minute-by-minute schedule planner;
● emphasis on
  —the subskills involved in reading and math,
  —symbols representing things (letters, numerals) instead of on examining and exploring the things themselves, and
  —conventional knowledge such as days of the week, colors, courtesies, and so on;
● curriculum **prepared outside the classroom—purchased by the pro-**

gram and "covered" by the "teacher" (in contrast to curriculum created by the teacher, or purchased curricular materials that provide a sound philosophy, a framework to preclude a piecemeal, mishmash bunch of activities, and many time-saving specifics, but also encourage and enhance teacher creativity and familiarity with the local community);
● "child as the recipient of lessons";
● "sooner is better";
● "learning through a limitless supply of paper-and-pencil worksheets";
● emphasis on mastery and testing;
● "operant conditioning";
● "rewards" as "reinforcement" for "right answers"; and
● authoritarian management.

Here, a child care center head teacher murmurs:

Authoritarian management . . . Before I took a graduate school course in early childhood classroom management, I believed in very strong and stern discipline. But my children had very little **self**-discipline. The minute I'd step away, it would all fall apart. Now I lay it on *less*, so the children have developed *more*, more inner controls. Of course I help them with a great deal of guidance.

This loose group of programs descends from Pavlovian and Skinnerian theory. When these programs were first developed in the 1960s, several of the names we heard most were Carl Bereiter and Seigfried Englemann (later a program that grew out of Bereiter and Englemann's work, DISTAR, was published), and Susan Gray from Peabody College, whose project was known as DARCEE. Today's academic preschools and kindergartens are close cousins of the models launched in the '60s. They also represent "moving down" the behaviorist-based curriculum that, in the 1960s, became so popular in elementary schools. The theory behind behaviorist programs is that positive reinforcement *beyond the satisfaction of accomplishing a personally meaningful task* is essential in shaping behavior—in this case, behavior that will help children "achieve" in school.

The traditional Montessori method, though it places great emphasis on respecting children, on children *doing*, learning through a self-paced discovery process, and on *intrinsic reward* (learning materials are self-correcting), and could not be called "academic," would still, many early childhood educational leaders think, fall into this broad behavior modification group because

- the choices are not the child's (there is a strictly sequenced series of activities, and though each child progresses on her own timetable, teachers maintain tight control of how space, time, and materials are used);
- cooperative and collegial planning on the part of the children, *pretend*-type play, playing, and conversation are strongly discouraged;
- play (spontaneous) and projects (group) are not as important a part of the program as are using the special (excellent) Montessori materials;
- there is a right answer to everything, including the correct way to use each clever and useful piece of Montessori equipment, which appears to be a reasonable idea, but does mean that creativity is not central to the program (for example, children are not usually free to use the materials in their *own* ways *in addition to* the correct way; to some "mainstream" early childhood people, this seems restrictive).

Teachers in both developmentally appropriate and academic programs need to be good at classroom management, but the former need to be good at guiding the group through participatory democracy, whereas the latter need to be good at managing in a more didactic and dictatorial manner (though sugarcoated and delivered tactfully). However, many child management techniques used by teachers are shared across the board. Both kinds of teachers manage their classrooms with small gasps of appreciative pleasure; encouraging comments; eyebrow Olympics; little smiles that wilt like cut flowers when a child's work or behavior is disappointing, followed by sad, censorious faces, and gentle blandishments; and, when necessary, looks that pin children to their repeated indiscretions and errors.

Moreover, because in the real world we rarely see either the developmentally appropriate or the academic preschool model in its pure form and at its best, and instead see the two models on a continuum from marvelous to mediocre or worse, the differences are not always as clearcut as they may appear here.

Main areas of disagreement

There seem to be three major areas of disagreement between people who

prefer the academic preschool and people who prefer the so-called "developmentally appropriate." The disagreements center on:

1. How do children most effectively learn *at this age*? We've probably talked about this enough for now.

2. What is most important for children to learn at *this* age, whether they are in a program of one sort or another or at home?

3. What are the repercussions later in the child's school years, adolescence, and adult life of the academic preschool experience versus experience in a developmentally appropriate program? What is the purpose and point of what we unfortunately call "preschool"? (These years aren't pre-*anything* and shouldn't be considered as so, any more than college should be called "pregraduate school," or one's 35-year career should be termed the "preretirement period.")

Another intriguing topic is **why** so many teachers, parents, and others prefer the academic-style preschool, but we will have to defer this discussion till another time.

What is most important for children to learn at this age regardless of the setting they're in?

Let's tackle this giant topic next, and touch upon some highlights.

The presence of high **self-esteem** correlates with school success, therefore it's a very important thing for children to learn at this age. (Moreover, *low* self-esteem correlates with all sorts of serious problems, such as dropping out of school, teen-age pregnancy, alcohol and drug abuse, teen-age depression, and teen-age suicide. If she thought about it, no educator would want to risk contributing to any child's low self-esteem.)

Self-esteem

Self-esteem is generated in children in large part through the process of frequently meeting and mastering **meaningful** new challenges. (This, by the way, is a core concept of the Montessori method, which stresses positive regard for self as an autonomous learner.) A key concept here is **meaningful.** If we expect a young child to master tasks that are meaningless to her *as an individual*, she has little satisfaction or feeling of self-worth in doing the chore, even if she succeeds. Hence we are not fostering maximum feasible positive self-esteem, which *should* be one of our chief goals. (Nor, of course, are we achieving academic excellence with *this* individual child; she "succeeded" because the task was too easy for her! "Performing" that which is personally meaningless and poses no personal challenge produces neither a boost to self-esteem nor educational excellence. Why would good teachers give boringly too easy, meaningless work unless they had never reflected upon it, or believed that they had to, to keep their jobs?)

For intellectually gifted children, meaningless work can be quite destructive, as it tends to *lower* their self-esteem; they feel awkwardly out of place with their peers, who seem to be struggling, and wonder if there's something wrong with *themselves* because everything is such a breeze. For children gifted in other areas than the intellectual (e.g., music, art, athletics), the message of all these academic "activities" may be that *their* specialties are irrelevant. This isn't likely to boost children's self-esteem regarding their specialness. Teaching children to sing, "I'm Special," while ignoring (devaluing) their specialness, seems at best absurd, but it happens everyday. Though it may cause a flurry of controversy to say, it probably happens more commonly in academic programs because teachers aren't given time and a green

> # If a child doesn't desire the goal, the activity isn't motivational. If the child isn't motivated, she will probably not develop the habit of aiming at excellence.

light to explore individual children's *real* specialnesses with them.

It's possible that doing meaningless paperwork makes some children feel good *because they are pleasing an adult who believes the work is meaningful.* The child feels good because she is *being* good, not because it felt good to do the work itself. Being good, that is, pleasing someone you strive to please, can build self-esteem to a point. Being a pleasing, approved-of person surely must be a boost to self-esteem. But we've all heard tales about the son who became a physician only to please his father, or the daughter who married a certain man only to please her parents, and how hollow their lives became unless and until they collapsed and changed them so they were living in ways *they* found meaningful.

In later life—on the job—employed people do have to do certain things to please the boss, to get promoted, to keep the job, to earn the paycheck. But research tells us that *the most successful employees, managers, and CEOs claim to feel more rewarded by feeling they've done an excellent job at something they find meaningful than by any other kinds of "rewards,"* assuming that supervisors provide satisfying inclusion, reasonable recognition for successes, and supportive work climates in all senses of the word *supportive.*

As has many times been pointed out in *Young Children,* self-esteem is generated in children in large part through a process of frequently meeting and **mastering** meaningful new challenges. A key part of this concept is **mastering.** If we expect a young child to master tasks that are impossible for her *as an individual,* there is no satisfaction or feeling of self-worth in slugging away and slogging through the chore—because she's *failing.* Hence, again, with this child as with the child for whom the task is far too easy, we're not fostering maximum feasible positive self-esteem. (In less technological cultures, children are expected gradually to master all aspects of becoming adults of their gender in the community. All of it feels meaningful. All of it can be mastered. Developing *low* self-esteem and all the concomitant problems isn't as dire a likelihood lurking over children's shoulders as it is in complex contemporary America.)

Jerome Kagan, a professor of developmental psychology at Harvard, writes in

Self-esteem is not taught. It's learned, largely through the way adults live with young children.

his fascinating book *The Nature of the Child*:

[A]s the child approaches her second birthday, she shows behavioral signs of anxiety if she cannot implement a behavior she feels obliged to display. The recognition that one cannot meet a standard regarded as appropriate provokes distress . . . . The child cannot ignore parental [and teacher/caregiver] standards because she is in a "closed" situation, dependent upon the care and instrumental help of [these adults]. The child accepts these standards as reasonable demands to be met [**whether or not they are**]. Additionally, the child recognizes that the parents, and many other children, have met these standards, and thus that they are within human capacity. It is not possible for the child to rationalize the standards away.

But if a particular child finds the standards too difficult to attain, she becomes vulnerable to distress. Some people may call this emotion shame; others, guilt; others, a sense of unworthiness. This emotion can generate a feeling of impotence either to cope with problems or to attract the approval and affection of others. The child believes that the self is not worthy of positive regard. . . .

A central fact of modern, middle-class Western society is that standards of academic accomplishment are so high that many children fail to meet them. More important, there is no easy way for a child to do penance for this failure. There are no useful instrumental activities that the American child can engage in to prove his effectiveness, utility, or value. The average middle-class child is an object of sentiment with no useful economic role in the household. The situation contrasts sharply with the child in a rural village in a less developed community, who is aware that his work is of value to the family. . . .

In Third World villages, where the standards set for children are relatively easy to meet (to cook, clean, gather wood, or take care of babies), children less often experience the distress of failure. (1984, pp. 266–268)

If a child is failing at most of the tasks we assign him, we aren't achieving academic excellence, either, because the beleaguered child is learning nothing

except that he "isn't a good student"; which he may, depending upon how many other areas he feels a failure in, interpret to mean that he "isn't a good *person.*" If schoolwork is one of the *few* areas in which the child sees that he continually can't do what he's expected to do (in other words, if he feels successful in most other parts of his life), the discouraging experience will probably only sour him on *school,* not on himself in every dimension.

But if the child is being burdened and blocked by other things of major importance going against him as well (for example, if he's the least liked, most parentally disparaged sibling, or if he's seriously disabled and from a very low-income family, yet in a predominantly middle-class school where there are few mainstreamed children with atypical needs), ***another* low blow to his self-respect may simply add up to too much to bear, resulting in the crushing of any budding self-esteem he may have had.** Furthermore, many children misperceive what their parents mean: A child whose parents push for his academic success in preschool may think that the parents love *achievement* rather than *him.* Not knowing all the skeletons in every child's family closet or psyche, why would good teachers take a risk like this? Programs for 3-, 4-, and 5-year-olds include many children from low-income minority families. Exposure to the kinds of experiences school systems base later education upon is essential before the question of **mastery** ever arises. Whether or not academic preschools are best for this group of children has been extensively investigated; see, for example, the work of David Weikart. It seems paradoxical, but academic preschools are not the most helpful way for low-income children to achieve later academic success. The explanation lies, of course, in the maturation theories of Gesell (physical) and Piaget (mental).

A very important difference between *academic* preschools and kindergartens, and *developmentally appropriate* early childhood programs, revolves around the idea of **mastery:**

● The academic program places a great deal of emphasis on the necessity for each child to **master** predetermined subskills of reading, pre-spelling, and math. There is a corresponding emphasis on **testing.** Because of the extreme focus on mastering a set of adult-selected skills, all in one narrowly defined "academic" dimension of the child's total experience, **the child gets the unequivocal message that self-initiated "mastery" in all other areas (physical agilities, abilities, and feats including those involved in dancing; knowledge and talents in each of the arts including careful observation, reproduction, and appreciation; prowess in appreciating literature; delight and expertise in using mathematical ideas; "street wisdom"; being an exceptionally nurturing person) is unimportant,** of little value.

This may lower the amount of positive self-esteem the child derives from mastery in all nonacademic areas of his life. As previously mentioned, this is not uncommonly magnified in the minds of *gifted* children. In contrast,

• The so-called developmentally appropriate program places heavy emphasis on the necessity for each child of **choosing what he will "master";** and encouraging exploration—as well as mastery—in a wide variety of areas. When the child examines, investigates, messes around, tries out, tries on, develops interest in, develops enthusiasm for, he wins as many brownie points as when he "masters." In many programs, especially programs attended by children from low literacy, non-print-rich, low socioeconomic homes, teachers make sure that many materials and learning encounters involving conversation (language), good books (reading), drawing/talking/dictating stories as accompaniments, captions/labels/signs (writing, spelling, reading), letters, sounds, mathematical concepts, measurements, numerals, and so on are included in the daily free choice program. Teachers engage in activities featuring all this as helpful friends.

Though there may be developmental screening and assessment "tests," there are no norm-referenced, standardized achievement tests. Exposure and comfortable familiarity are valued as much as "mastery"; digging deeply into a topic of interest with an enthusiastic teacher's help—pursuing educational excellence—is also valued as much as is "mastering" a specific body of knowledge (shallowly).

In the developmentally appropriate program, it's assumed that mastery in

all areas of living, using *all* kinds of intelligences (musical intelligence, aesthetic intelligence, interpersonal intelligence, etc.), is valid and worthwhile. The child has many more arenas in which to develop positive self-esteem. It is not assumed, as it is in the academic program, that only academic mastery matters. Nor is it assumed, as it is in the academic program, that each child should be ready to master each academic item on more or less the same day of his life. Children are perennially exposed to the ingredients of academic life: They learn letters, sounds, numbers, shapes, and so on, each in his own way and each in his own time.

Self-discipline

The existence of **self-discipline** in an individual is essential if educational excellence is to be a reality. **Healthy self-discipline** gradually grows as young children strive and struggle

• to manage the plethora of **age- and stage-appropriate tasks** encountered
— in play,
— in adult-started and -guided projects, and
— in the complicated social situations that continually crowd in upon our natural wish to do whatever we want whenever we want to; and

• to internalize the firm, fair guidance grown-ups and older children give. Out of all this each child develops personal standards and aspires to live up to them. If the young child is expected to manage a great many tasks which to a person of *this* age (3, 4, 5) and *this* stage (preoperational, possessed by magical thinking and an innate urgent need to move around, requiring opportunities to initiate, explore, discover, and individuate rather than always to capitulate) seem arbitrary, uninteresting, and very difficult (it's even very difficult for

young children to sit still!), *a great deal of stress comes along with the self-discipline.* This is **unhealthy self-discipline**, self-discipline achieved at much too high a health and mental health price. Of course, another reaction to mission impossible, familiar to us all, is to quit trying, a reaction resulting in "bad" behavior and poor report cards.

Anybody, a child too, can *occasionally* benefit from doing things that seem arbitrary, uninteresting, and very difficult. A little of this is "character building." It builds ability to adjust to what others want, creative coping skills, forbearance, capacity to tolerate frustration—in short, **self-discipline**. But more than just an occasional dose of expectations that are arbitrary, uninteresting, and too difficult **doesn't lead to self-discipline**, it leads to trouble. (We really should digress here to discuss all the things that children learn, not *in spite of* their tendency to move a great deal, but *through the medium of movement*. Oh me, oh my, there's so much to talk about that that will have wait till a later date!)

Lest anyone misunderstand, we hasten to state that all leading early childhood educators believe in discipline, because it's in a context of discipline that each child develops **self**-discipline. On this, as on many things, teachers in academic and developmentally appropriate programs for young children agree. Children need routines, rules, boundaries, behavioral expectations and standards, procedures, policies, limits ... children need control. They need reasonable, age-appropriate control, and of course understanding. They need fair, firm discipline at home (both homes if the parents are divorced). They need it in child care settings. They need it everywhere else they spend significant amounts of time. As any child psychologist, child psychiatrist, psychiatric social worker specializing in family counseling, well-trained traditional nursery school/kindergarten ed-

---

The goal is much more than for children to learn mere academics. We want each child to explore something of interest in considerable depth. This is learning how to learn with excellence.

---

ucator, parent or caregiver whose credential is good success in rearing happy, emotionally well-balanced, productive children will tell us, *as Freud himself told us in book after book,* children left largely undisciplined, lacking guidance in slowly but steadily growing up, indulge their most primitive impulses greedily, devour the time and attention of beloved adults, whiningly demand the first turn, the longest turn, and the most turns, struggle for the best possessions, bite, sulk, howl, and throw half-hour raging tantrums. Many child development specialists are opposed to pressing and stressing children beyond their capacity to cope, but these specialists still strongly believe in child-guidance-style discipline. David Elkind, for example, professor of Child Study at Tufts University and one of the nation's best known proponents of today's "Don't Rush Them" school of thought, writes,

Children need and want help in controlling their impulses; if they are not called upon to control themselves, they use their behavior to control adults. Yet in fact it is scary to a child to have power over adults. Consequently, handed a power they did not want, did not need, and could not handle, such children [are] willful, domineering, given to temper tantrums, and on the whole abominable. (1981, p. xi)

Two things that are extremely important for children to learn at this age are positive self-esteem and healthy self-discipline, and neither is learned through gimmicks and techniques, or through alienating lectures. Whether these characteristics are better learned in academic or developmentally appropriate programs is a question worth pondering. One might guess the latter, because in the former, teachers are so distracted and driven by other objectives and directives that they may not be able to focus as fully on these two great big goals.

For further reading

Bauch, J.P. (Ed.). (1988). *Early childhood education in the schools.* Washington, DC: National Education Association.

Biber, B. (1984). *Early education and psychological development.* New Haven, CT: Yale University Press.

Calkins, L.M. (1986). *The art of teaching writing.* Portsmouth, NH: Heinemann.

Council of Chief State School Officers. (1988). *Early childhood and family education: Foundations for success.* Washington, DC: Author.

DeVries, R., & Kohlberg, L. (in press). *Programs of early education: The constructivist view.* Washington, DC: NAEYC. (Original work published in 1987)

Elkind, D. (1988). The resistance to developmentally appropriate educational practice with young children: The real issue. In C. Warger (Ed.), *A resource guide to public school early childhood programs* (pp. 53–62). Alexandria, VA: Association for Supervision and Curriculum Development.

Gardner, H. (1983). *Frames of mind: Theory of multiple intelligence.* New York: Basic.

Glickman, C.D. (1981). Play and the school curriculum: The historical context. *Journal of Research and Development in Education, 14*(3), 1–10.

Hendrick, J. (1988). *The whole child: Developmental education for the early years* (4th ed.). Columbus, OH: Merrill.

Hill, P.S. (1987). The function of the kindergarten. *Young Children, 42*(5), 12–19. (Originally published in 1926)

Johnson, R. (1987). *Approaches to early childhood education.* Columbus, OH: Merrill.

Jones, E. (1989). *Emergent curriculum: Planning and letting go.* Unpublished manuscript, Pacific Oaks College, Pasadena, CA.

Kamii, C. (1982). *Number in preschool and kindergarten: Educational implications of Piaget's theory.* Washington, DC: NAEYC.

Kamii, C., & Joseph, L. L. (1989). *Young children continue to reinvent arithmetic—2nd grade: Implications of Piaget's theory.* New York: Teachers College Press, Columbia University.

Kamii, C., & DeVries, R. (1978). *Physical knowledge in preschool education: Implications of Piaget's theory.* Englewood Cliffs, NJ: Prentice-Hall.

Karnes, M.B., & Johnson, L.J. (1989). Training staff, parents, and volunteers working with gifted young children, especially those with disabilities and from low-income homes. *Young Children, 44*(3), 49–56.

Katz, L., & Chard, S. (1989). *Engaging children's minds: The project approach.* Norwood, NJ: Ablex.

McCracken, J.B. (Ed.). (1986). *Reducing stress in young children's lives.* Washington, DC: NAEYC.

National Association for the Education of Young Children. (1984). *Accreditation criteria & procedures of the National Academy of Early Childhood Programs.* Washington, DC: Author.

National Association for the Education of Young Children. (1985). *Guide to accreditation by the National Academy of Early Childhood Programs.* Washington, DC: Author.

National Association of State Boards of Education. (1988). *Right from the start.* Alexandria, VA: Author.

National Council for the Social Studies. (1989). Social studies for early childhood education and elementary school children preparing for the 21st Century: A report from NCSS task force on early childhood/elementary social studies. *Social Education, 53*(1), 14–24.

Nebraska State Board of Education. (1984). *Position statement on kindergarten.* Lincoln, NE: Author.

Oken-Wright, P. (1988). Show and tell grows up. *Young Children, 43*(2), 52–58.

Paasche, C.L., Gorrill, L., & Strom, B. (1989). *Children with special needs in early childhood settings.* Menlo Park, CA: Addison-Wesley.

Sawyers, J. K., & Rogers, C. S. (1988). *Helping young children develop through play: A practical guide for parents, caregivers, and teachers.* Washington, DC: NAEYC.

Southern Association on Children Under Six. (1986). *Position statement on quality four-year-old programs in public schools.* Little Rock, AR: Author.

Strickland, D.S., & Morrow, L.M. (Eds.). (1989). *Emerging literacy: Young children learn to read and write.* Newark, DE: International Reading Association.

References

Bredekamp, S. (Ed.). (1987). *Developmentally appropriate practice in early childhood programs serving children from birth through age 8* (expanded ed.). Washington, DC: NAEYC.

Elkind, D. (1981). *The hurried child: Growing up too fast too soon.* Reading, MA: Addison-Wesley.

Kagan, J. (1984). *The nature of the child.* New York: Basic.

Kamii, C. (Ed.). (1990). *Achievement testing in the early grades: The games grown-ups play.* Washington, DC: NAEYC.

NOW, WHICH KIND OF PRESCHOOL ?

Ellen Ruppel Shell

Ellen Ruppel Shell, a Boston-based free-lance writer, is writing a book on day care for Little, Brown & Co.

It's 9:30 a.m. and the 3- and 4-year-old room at Busy Bee Preschool is buzzing with morning activity. Teachers distribute circles cut from stiff white paper and a single black crayon to every child, then instruct them in the fine art of constructing paper snowmen. Task completed, the class cleans up, then gathers in a circle to sing a rousing rendition of the ABC song.

There's just enough time before lunch for a game of "name that number," in which kids shout out the correct answers to simple math problems posed by the teachers. By age 3, all the children at Busy Bee know their alphabet and colors, and by 4, most can recognize geometric shapes and do simple addition as well.

Across town, kids at Simple Simon Children's Center (the schools' names have been changed) gather for an informal chat about the winter solstice. They then mill around the room, settling at activity stations to do puzzles, play with dolls, draw, or join the teacher in arts and crafts loosely based on the earlier discussion. Teachers circulate among the children, offering help and support when needed but otherwise keeping a low profile. Many of Simple Simon's younger charges don't know the alphabet, and few could even begin to add.

Which school is best for your child? Is it the academically-oriented Busy Bee, where children are taught to recognize shapes and colors, recite the alphabet, sound out words and perhaps even read? Or is it Simple Simon, where children direct much of their own learning?

A Century-Old Debate

The question is not a new one. According to University of Illinois education professor Lilian Katz, one of the country's most respected authorities on early childhood education, "The debate is nearly 100 years old and it rages on. Everyone demands certainty, but they probably are not going to get it. Both systematic instruction and child-oriented activities, if done properly, can benefit preschool-age children."

Not surprisingly, many parents favor schools with clearly structured curricula. Places with little direct teaching make some people nervous. After all, what does mucking around in a sandbox or playing with other kids have to do with doing well in school later on or (you've got to think ahead) getting into college? But most experts in early childhood agree that the Simple Simon curriculum is far better suited to the needs and talents of young children.

"We can train pigeons to recognize letters," says Marian Blum, educational director of the Child Study Center at Wellesley College in Wellesley, Mass. "This doesn't mean that we are preparing them to read. Young children have a number of developmental tasks, the most important of which is to come to understand themselves and to see themselves in relation to peers and parents. They can pick up the reading or math along the way, but learning to read or add in a formal manner is not an appropriate activity for preschoolers."

What is appropriate, Blum and other experts contend, is a child-initiated approach, in which children choose from a smorgasbord of hands-on activities — pummeling play dough, piecing together puzzles, engaging in dramatic play, drawing — classic nursery-school activities. The cognitive development of preschoolers, these educators believe, centers on thinking about and manipulating physical objects, not symbols such as letters and numbers.

In many school districts, however, workbooks and readers have replaced finger paint and modeling clay as core kindergarten supplies. And many parents, eager to make sure their kid makes the grade, search out preschools and day-care centers that focus on academic skills. As one mother, who transferred her 4-year-old into a more structured preschool for her pre-kindergarten year, told me: "I'm not convinced that one more year of building with blocks, playing games and working on art projects would benefit my daughter much. A lot of kids in our neighborhood learn to read before kindergarten, so I thought Sarah should too."

Early Learning, Early Failure

What we're seeing, says Sue Bredekamp of the National Association for the Education of Young Children, "is a 'downward escalation' of curriculum, of kindergartners doing worksheets, of first graders learning to spell words they don't even know the meaning of . . . . The inappropriate expectations of this curriculum are causing many kids to struggle and, often, fail."

Bredekamp says that the number of children being held back a year in the first three grades has increased dramatically in the past decade, from roughly 5% to an estimated 20% nationwide. Today, first graders who can't read are commonly held back, Bredekamp says, a sign of failure that can damage the child's ego and lead to future difficulties in school.

She also argues that no child should be refused admission to a kindergarten because of failure to pass an entrance examination. "I have no problem with screening children to make sure they get any special services they might need. But keeping a 5-year-old out of school because he can't sit still and do paperwork is crazy."

Bredekamp and other educators agree that the best way to prepare preschoolers for school is with programs geared to their abilities. For example, since 3- and 4-year-olds have trouble with abstractions, they need concepts served up in a concrete way — counting a jacket's buttons, or the number of table settings at a play party. "If a 4- or 5-year-old is forced to sit through a 45-minute drill on numbers," Bredekamp warns, "the primary thing on his mind is escape, not learning."

Convincing parents that what appears to be play is actually learning is not easy. Demands for a more structured "back to basics" approach increased markedly in the early 1980s, particularly after the publication of *A Nation at Risk* — a report by the Department of Education suggesting that the way to fix the nation's ailing educational system was to demand accountability from educators. Since self-confidence and intellectual curiosity can't be measured on any objective scale, promoting such qualities has taken a back seat in many preschool programs to the teaching of testable skills, such as counting and letter recognition.

Head Start for the Disadvantaged

In support of the basics approach, some educators argue that drilling young children in language and number skills is particularly useful — in fact, essential — for underprivileged children. According to Douglas Carnine, a professor of education at the University of Oregon; "The child-centered people advocate waiting until a child is ready before providing academics. But some kids, particularly disadvantaged kids, may come from unstimulating homes — they may never be ready. If they don't get an academic orientation in kindergarten, they may never grow into successful students."

Carnine directs the Follow Through Project, which combines academic drills with child-initiated learning. The project uses a direct-instruction program called DISTAR — prepackaged teaching material for kindergarten and preschool teachers. Children learn to read using phonics: They practice the sound of each letter until everyone has mastered it. Then they string the sounds together to read words. Math is taught using counting drills, number writing and simple equations.

The DISTAR curriculum takes up at most an hour and a half a day, Carnine says, and children are encouraged to choose their own activities before and after the formal lessons. He admits the program may appear dry and didactic to an outsider. But children, he says, see it as fun.

Tufts University psychologist David Elkind disagrees, contending that the DISTAR approach is inappropriate for most young children of all socioeconomic backgrounds. "In fact, my sense is that DISTAR is even worse for young disadvantaged children, because it imprints them with a rote-learning style that could be damaging later on. As Piaget pointed out, children learn by manipulating their environment, and a healthy early education program structures the child's environment to make the most of that fact. DISTAR, on the other hand, structures the child and constrains his learning style."

"The kind of learning DISTAR tries to promote can be more solidly elicited by the child doing things," says Harriet Egertson, an early childhood specialist at the Nebraska Department of Education. "The adult's responsibility is to engage the child in what he or she is doing, to take every opportunity to make their experience meaningful. DISTAR isn't connected to anything. If you use mathematics in context, such as measuring out spoons of sugar in a cooking class, the notion of addition comes alive for the child. The concept becomes embedded in the action and it sticks."

An Ideal Learning Experience

While it is clear that most educators and developmental psychologists strongly support the less-academic approach, there is surprisingly little data to support their contentions — or for that matter, those of the opposition. Katz, of the University of Illinois, believes that in its pure form neither approach — completely spontaneous play nor structured teacher-directed work — gives preschoolers all they need. The teacher's job, she says, is to set the stage, to bring materials to the classroom and help children pursue projects they choose — not lecturing but, upon occasion, offering instruction.

As an example of what she means, Katz describes a preschool class that got interested in the goings-on at a nearby construction site. The class visited the site every week, learned about the machines and tools, and got to know the construction workers. After each visit they returned to the classroom to draw pictures and make models of what they had seen. The project, which went on for eight weeks, was neither entirely spontaneous nor teacher directed. It was, Katz says, "an ideal educational experience."

So, what method *is* best for a child? That depends on the child. Some are over-

Some push the ABCs, simple math and carefully structured play. Others feature arts and crafts, games, and mucking around in the sandbox. An old war heats up.

whelmed by a school that offers a large number of choices, while others do best when challenged by a number of options. Some children relish solving complex problems, others are bored or intimidated by them. Ultimately, parents must decide for themselves which educational approach is best for their children. Many will undoubtedly opt for schools that offer teacher-directed drills and paperwork, hoping to give their kids an early edge. But as Bredekamp points out, too much structure at an early age can backfire later on.

"Many teens today were taught to read at age 5 and now wouldn't dream of cracking a book," she says. "They're burned out. The job of early educators is to excite children about learning, not to cram it down their throats. Let's face it, you've got your entire life to read *The New York Times*, but only a few years to be a child."

6 STEPS TO CHOOSING A PRESCHOOL

Experts agree that the most important question parents can ask themselves about prospective preschools is, "Would I enjoy spending my time here?" If the place just doesn't feel comfortable to you, it's probably not the school for your child. Check out the schools you are considering with an appropriate local social service agency to see if any complaints have been filed against them. But ultimately, it's up to you whether a school is a safe, healthy environment for your child.

Once you've narrowed your list, spend a morning or afternoon at each school without your child. Any place that won't allow you to do this isn't worth your time. Here are some things to look for:

1 **The student-teacher ratio:** There should be at least one teacher for every eight 3- to 5-year-olds and no more than 16 children in the entire group. But don't be impressed by teacher overload.

2 **Physical layout:** While you may prefer matching furniture, soft lighting and pastel wall coverings, your child could be better off with a decor of paint splatters and crayon scribbles. The place should be neat, clean and fairly well organized, but any attempt to impress parents rather than inspire kids is suspect.

The school should have a quiet corner where children can look at books or daydream, as well as a well-equipped playground. It should have space for your child to store his personal belongings — extra clothes, a sleep toy or blanket — and enough art supplies, appropriate toys, and ongoing projects to keep children engaged.

3 **The staff:** In general, if you see teachers spending much of their time drinking coffee and chatting, it's clear they're not too interested in children. More specifically, do they really listen when children ask questions, or brush them off with general responses? Do they show real sympathy when a child falls and bruises her knee, or mindlessly slap on a bandage? Do they take advantage of spontaneous learning opportunities, or doggedly stick with the curriculum?

While not every whim should be catered to, children should be allowed to participate in an independent activity, such as doing a puzzle, coloring or looking at picture books, if they choose not to join in during group time. Also, beware of teachers who too forcefully attempt to draw out naturally quiet children, or who tirelessly entertain kids with a steady stream of stories, puppet shows and other activities. Children are at school to learn for themselves, not to be entertained.

4 **The school philosophy:** Ask the school director to describe his or her personal child-care philosophy (if the director doesn't understand what you mean, you're in the wrong school). Then, if you're still interested, ask if it's OK to pay a short, unannounced visit in the near future. Again, if there are objections, go elsewhere. The best times to visit without disrupting routine are usually early morning, just after drop-off time, or late afternoon.

5 **Your child's reaction:** Once you've decided on a school, bring your child in for a visit and get his or her reaction. If it's favorable, count on spending at least a few hours at the school during the first week to help your child get used to the place. It's natural for children to cry a bit before their parents leave for the day, but if the crying continues after the first two weeks, or if your child is tearful and clingy when picked up after school, there's something wrong. Discuss the problem with your child's teachers and, if necessary, take a bit more time to make sure you've made the right choice. It's better to take your child out quickly than to leave him or her in an uncomfortable situation.

6 **Give yourself enough time:** Finding the right school requires patience, persistence and assertiveness. What appears to be an excellent school by most standards may be inappropriate for your child. The only way to know is to get out there and look.

—E.R.S.

WHAT'S MISSING IN CHILDREN'S TV

A powerful medium of persuasion is failing its promise. The US Congress demands reform. Other nations watch in suspense. Cast your vote for the programs TV should show.

Peggy Charren

Peggy Charren is founder and president of Action for Children's Television (ACT) and a Visiting Scholar in Education at Harvard University's Graduate School of Education. As former director of the Creative Arts Council of Newton, Massachusetts, she worked with theater and dance groups, artists, musicians, poets, and writers to develop programs for classroom enrichment.

I LIKE CHILDREN'S TELEVISION.

It can offer our youngest viewers the opportunity to learn about a wide variety of places, people, occupations, ideas, life styles, and value systems, many of which will affect the way they will live the rest of their lives. It can help children to think, to question, to imagine, to create. It can introduce them to the stories of Anansi the Spider Man and Coyote the Trickster...the legong and bari dance of the children of Bali. It can teach them to value poetry and music, freedom of expression and peace. It can empower them to act to make their world a better place.

It *can* do all this...but is it *doing* it? I'm convinced that it's not doing nearly enough.

Children in the US today spend four hours a day watching TV, more time than they spend in the classroom, or in any activity except sleep. Many people worry about the effects of television on children.

They worry about incessant exposure to violence. Are children learning that aggressive behavior is an acceptable solution to problems?

What are the effects of TV's racial and sexual stereotypes?

How has TV's rapid-fire delivery affected children's ability to learn?

Some feel that TV is a plug-in drug and the only way to deal with it is to get rid of the set. I disagree. I like television.

People around the world feel the same way, as I heard repeatedly in a small town outside of Paris this fall at FIMAJ, the first international market for children's TV programming. It's interesting to note that many people in countries like France and Britain have not been concerned in the past about children's TV. Now, however, as their networks become more commercialized, these nations are beginning to understand what some of us in the US have been decrying for decades. And, although other countries have not developed the quantity of children's programming the US has, all of us gathered in France shared one problem—how to get the good stuff on the air.

I met people from several continents waiting with suspense for the outcome of US legislation intended to assure a certain amount of high-quality television for children. I have pushed this legislation for the same reason I started Action for Children's Television (ACT)—because TV is one of the most powerful, cost-effective instruments of education the world has ever known.

Unfortunately, it's often used to showcase violence, raunchy rock rhymes, dirty words, and sexual innuendo. Many adults, frustrated and angry with this television fare that children watch, want to censor it. But censorship is not the way to protect children's rights to entertainment and education on the TV screen. The right to express what some consider offensive speech is the price Ameri-

From *World Monitor*, December 1990, pp. 28-30, 32-34. Copyright © 1990 by Peggy Charren. Reprinted with permission of Peggy Charren and Action for Children's Television (ACT).

cans pay for freedom of political speech. And we cannot afford to risk losing that freedom.

ACT is proud of the fact that it has never once in its 20-year history told a broadcaster to "take this program off the air because we don't like it." ACT supports a broadening, not narrowing, of television viewing options, and we believe that children and young adolescents are best served by programming designed especially for them, not by cleaned-up adult TV fare.

ACT wants each American child to grow up with the ability to thoughtfully determine his or her own individual understanding of right and wrong, based on the widest possible amount of information that parents, schools, and television can provide.

It's obvious that TV could be doing a lot more, but, as we'll see, the present profit-oriented environment of the television industry makes that especially difficult. That's why we're interested in hearing from you, the home or school viewer: What do *you* as a parent, teacher, or other adult TV watcher think is missing from children's TV? What type of educational programming do you feel is needed to balance the current fare?

The main link between the needs of American children and broadcasters' responsibility to the American public as a whole is the legal obligation imposed upon each American broadcaster to serve the public interest as defined in the US Communications Act of 1934. (See box, Why a New Bill.)

It is the responsibility of the broadcasting media to provide as broad a range of opinions as possible and to keep the public informed about all sides of a controversial issue. Of course, not all controversial topics are appropriate subjects for children's television. But a surprising number are, if they are handled in a manner suited to the age of viewers.

Playing against this opportunity is economic reality. American commercial cable companies, local stations, and national networks are corporations, with a responsibility to their shareholders to maximize profits. Maximum diversity of service to the television public does not usually go hand in hand with maximum profits. And the necessary compromise between diversity and profits is not easy to achieve; nor does it tend to favor the public interest.

Instead, with certain significant exceptions, commercial TV is used to educate children to behave as a market segment, to lobby for products they don't need, to consume instead of to save. Children are persuaded to buy what they want before they can know what they need.

Unlike adults, children do not zap the ads when they use a remote control device. The ads feature more children and better animation than the programs they interrupt. Children like commercials, and corporations know how to take advantage of this sad fact of TV life.

Research and common sense indicate that advertising to children is inherently unfair and deceptive. In fact a number of countries—including Belgium, Denmark, and Sweden—ban TV selling to children. Others—including Finland, France, and the Netherlands—have restrictions.

For-profit corporations try to make their trade names and products an integral part of the everyday life of consumers. They are particularly determined to reach young children, not just to increase current profits but to build brand identity for future sales. Brand-name preference persists over very long periods of time and adds enormous value to any consumer product. That's why the vice-president of Grey Advertising says: "It isn't enough to just advertise on television....You've got to reach kids throughout their day—in school, as they're shopping in the mall...or at the movies. You've got to become part of the fabric of their lives."

ACT has filed formal complaints against deceptive advertising practices with the Federal Trade Commission and the Federal Communications Commission, but as yet no action has been taken.

HALF-HOUR COMMERCIALS

In an insidious variation some advertisers, toy manufacturers, and television producers have turned children's shows into half-hour ads for toys—GI Joe, ThunderCats, and other war-related product lines for boys; Day-Glo colored stuffed animals for girls. Hasbro even turned a plastic necklace, Charmkins, into a series.

During the 1980s, toy manufacturers turned more than 70 toys into TV series, blurring the distinction between editorial and commercial speech and creating a toy promotion bonanza for the advertiser.

Perhaps the most dangerous example of willingness to commercialize the environment of childhood is Whittle Communications' "Channel One," a daily 12-minute classroom newscast interrupted by four 30-second commercials. In return for guaranteeing that at least 92% of its students will watch these ads every day, each school that accepts the program receives free TV monitors for most of its classrooms.

The 4,700 schools that have said "yes" to this Trojan horse of a deal are ignoring some basic educational, moral, and legal tenets. Learning works best when you feel good about yourself. Teen counselors call it self-esteem. But advertising works when a felt need is created that only a product will satisfy. Advertising in a classroom emphasizes economic differences. It is outrageous to tell students to spend money on anything when so many live in poverty.

It is worth noting that some states, including California and New York, have banned "Channel One" in the classroom and more than 12,000 schools across the country have signed up for "CNN Newsroom," a daily, 15-minute, commercial-free newscast, applauded by educators and available without charge from Ted Turner's Cable News Network. The Discovery Channel's "Assignment Discovery" and The Christian Science Monitor's "World Classroom" are two other ad-free services.

But, despite the depressing picture I have painted, it is possible for American families to find terrific children's television, uninterrupted by sales pitches, on our TV screens.

One broadcasting entity that does make an effort to meet the needs of children is, of course, the Public Broadcasting Service. PBS, since its inception more than 20 years ago, has been a constructive noncommercial alternative to commercial television and has had a profound and positive impact on children's lives. PBS has pioneered much creative programming for young people—"Mister Rogers' Neighborhood," "Sesame Street," "3-2-1 Contact," "WonderWorks," and "Long Ago and Far Away"—and has made TV learning both in school and at home a high adventure. However, public television's limited resources must be used to serve adult audiences as well. We cannot rely solely on the public system to fill the children's programming gaps left open by commercial TV.

That's why people like Gerald Lesser, Harvard University professor of education and developmental psychology, are pursuing other avenues. Dr. Lesser recently met with producers, educators, and researchers from several nations looking for ways to cooperate in creating original news programming for children.

In the past Japan, Norway, Canada, and Britain, among others, have achieved varying degrees of success with children's news shows, while countries like Hungary and Yugoslavia are entering the field for the first time. Their hope is that international cooperation—sharing ideas and perhaps resources—will result in news shows that will appeal to children and hold their interest.

CABLE AND CASSETTES
Educational and pay cable channels provide some engaging options without commercials for families that can afford the extra expense. In addition to the

Action for Children's Television

Twenty years ago, I found that the children's TV programming available to my two young children did not offer them enough choice. I decided to do something about it. I started Action for Children's Television.

Although concern about television and children was widespread in 1968, there was no organized advocacy for change. I wasn't sure *how* to become a child advocate. I knew that I didn't want to use censorship tactics as a way to change television. Censorship meant fewer choices. We needed more choice, not less. I knew that many of my friends felt the same way.

So we took the first step. We began in a manner commonly referred to as grass roots—and it doesn't get much grassier than Newton, Massachusetts, a suburb of Boston. Meetings in my sitting room progressed to discussions in New York and Washington with TV executives and government representatives.

Today ACT is a public charity, with a paid staff of four, more than 100 volunteer representatives across the country, more than 10,000 contributing members, and the support of 150 major national associations, including health, education, and parent organizations and trade unions. We conduct business as a public company, with an outside board of directors, an annual audit, and an annual report. Our yearly budget is approximately $175,000.

Instead of censorship, ACT looks to the laws that regulate broadcasting as the vehicle for change. ACT's goal has been to increase viewing options for children and young teens, to get on that small screen the kind of choices one finds in a good children's library. Traditionally, ACT's program has involved two parallel sets of activities: (1) legal argument before regulatory agencies and (2) education of the public through the print and electronic press, outreach programs, publications, and private-sector advocacy.

ACT's strategies to broaden children's viewing options

within the existing system are carried out simultaneously on several fronts:

1. Petition the FCC (Federal Communications Commission) to increase the amount of service that broadcasters are required to provide for young audiences, so that children and young adolescents will have more choice.

2. Work in support of affirmative action to bring more minorities and women into positions of power in the television industry, because this will help to eliminate racism and sexism from television programming.

3. Encourage increased funding of public television, which provides impressive noncommercial alternatives for children.

4. Educate broadcasters and cablecasters about the diverse needs of young audiences.

5. Encourage the development of alternative technologies, such as cable television and home video, which increase program choice for young people.

6. Educate parents to take responsibility for their children's television viewing experiences by carefully consulting the television schedule, by turning the TV set off more often, and by talking to children about what they watch.

7. Help teachers, school principals, pediatricians, dentists, and other professionals concerned with the welfare of children pay attention to the influence of television on young audiences.

8. Petition the Federal Trade Commission to eliminate deceptive advertising targeted to children, because America's free speech guarantees do not protect deceptive commercial speech.

These eight strategies do not encompass ACT's entire program. But they demonstrate that television reform does not have to mean censorship. It does not have to mean interference with program content. Instead, TV policymaking should focus on issues of choice, access, and education.—*P.C.*

Why a New Bill

The public interest standard is defined by only a few words in the US Communications Act of 1934, a piece of legislation that charges the Federal Communications Commission to license each broadcaster to operate "in the public interest, convenience and necessity." These seven words are the hook upon which Action for Children's Television hangs its entire program for change. Without the public interest standard, Americans would lose their best legal argument for responsible television service.

More people want to broadcast than there are available frequencies; for each frequency the government selects the broadcaster who will best serve the public interest and gives that person only a short-term license, with the government keeping everyone else off the frequency. In exchange for this scarce privilege bestowed without charge, the broadcaster pledges to act as a trustee for all those kept off—to serve the public interest and show a government agency, the FCC, that it has done so in order to get its license renewed for another term.

Then in 1984 came deregulation.

Deregulation of broadcasting under the Reagan administration seriously hurt children and badly damaged the industry's capacity to serve their needs. TV rules were relaxed or eliminated. For example:

1. The number of stations or channels a single entity could own increased, resulting in giant megasystems with little community affiliation.

2. The length of time a channel must operate before it could be sold went from three years to zero, resulting in rapid turnover, with some stations up for sale twice within one year.

3. Limits on the amount of commercial time per hour were removed.

4. Stations were permitted to replace informative filings in the FCC at renewal time with a post card saying that they had served the public.

5. Stations were freed from the obligation to serve children with a "let 'em eat cable" attitude implied by the then FCC chairman, Mark Fowler.

These deregulatory policies caused stations to be perceived not as public trustees but as economic opportunities.

The Children's Television Act of 1990, recently passed by Congress and allowed to become law by President Bush, puts a limit on the number of minutes of ads per hour in children's programs and requires stations to air educational shows for children as a condition of license renewal. It also provides for a stable funding source for children's programming through a national endowment, although at this time specific funds have not been appropriated.

Admittedly, the number of ads permitted is too high and the program requirement is not very specific, but I believe that, with this law on the books, caring parents will find it easier to guide their children to a more nutritious TV diet.—*P.C.*

Disney Channel and Nickelodeon, there are children's programs worth watching on Showtime, HBO, the Discovery Channel, and the Learning Channel.

Home videocassettes solve the TV problem for many parents, providing for the first time easy access to music shows and TV versions of stories designed for young audiences.

But there is already a cloud on this promising horizon. Some children's videos contain commercials at the beginning, the end, and even in the middle of the tape.

If knowledge is power, what do we do about the fact that the new communications technology boom may work against the interest of the many US citizens who are poor? In a world where information is the prerequisite to responsible action, we cannot afford to divide the TV audience into informational haves and have-nots.

To increase choice for those who cannot afford costly new technologies, ACT recommends cable and satellite policies that reflect this concern. We are working with the American library system to encourage libraries to lend videos as they do books.

Another of ACT's current priorities (see box, **page 111**) is to promote a much higher level of television awareness in the home. Because most of children's TV viewing is done at home, helping young people make sensible viewing choices is ultimately up to parents. We try to encourage parents and children to take a second look at family TV habits: to talk together about the role television plays in children's lives and to find new ways to solve TV-related problems.

The role of television is not to replace families and teachers as the chief influence on children in our society. But television, viewed selectively and in moderation, can encourage children to discuss, wonder about, and even read about new things. Above all, it can lead them to ask questions.

As we set policies that will open the marketplace to new ideas and to the kinds of shows that are missing, we should keep in mind the section on mass media adopted by the General Assembly of the United Nations at the December 1989 Convention on the Rights of the Child. It says in part that mass media education should be directed to "the preparation of the child for responsible life in a free society, in the spirit of understanding, peace, tolerance, equality of sexes, and friendship among all peoples, ethnic, national and religious groups..." That's a meaningful prescription for the future of children's television.

Synthesis of Research on Grade Retention

Although grade retention is widely practiced, it does not help children to "catch up." Retained children may appear to do better in the short term, but they are at much greater risk for future failure then their equally achieving, non-retained peers.

LORRIE A. SHEPARD
AND MARY LEE SMITH

Lorrie A. Shepard is Professor of Research and Evaluation Methodology, University of Colorado School of Education, Campus Box 249, Boulder, CO 80309.
Mary Lee Smith is Professor of Educational Psychology, Arizona State University College of Education, Tempe, AZ 85287. They are the authors of the 1989 book, *Flunking Grades: Research and Policies on Retention*, published by the Falmer Press in London.

Retaining students in grade is often used as a means to raise educatonal standards. The assumption is that by catching up on prerequisite skills, students should be less at risk for failure when they go on to the next grade. Strict enforcement of promotion standards at every grade is expected both to ensure the competence of high school graduates and lower the dropout rate because learning deficiencies would never be allowed to accumulate. Despite the popular belief that repeating a grade is an effective remedy for students who have failed to master basic skills, however, the large body of research on grade retention is almost uniformly negative.

Research Evidence

The purpose of this article is to summarize research-based conclusions regarding the effects of grade retention. We then address the discrepancy between research and practice and consider alternatives to retention.

How many students repeat a grade in school? Although no national statistics have been collected on grade retention, we recently (1989a) analyzed data from 13 states and the District of Columbia. Our estimate is that 5 to 7 percent of public school children (about 2 children in every classroom of 30) are retained in the U.S. annually. However, annual statistics are not the whole story. A 6 percent annual rate year after year produces a cumulative rate of nonpromotion greater than 50 percent. Even allowing for students who repeat more than one grade, we estimate that by 9th grade approximately half of all students in the U.S. have flunked at least one grade (or are no longer in school). This means that, contrary to public perceptions, current grade failure rates are as high as they were in the 19th century, before the days of social promotion.

Does repeating a grade improve stu-

dent achievement? In a recent meta-analysis of research, Holmes (1989) located 63 controlled studies where retained students were followed up and compared to equally poor-achieving students who went directly on to the next grade. Fifty-four studies showed overall negative effects from retention, even on measures of academic achievement. This means that when retained children went on to the next grade they actually performed more poorly on average than if they had gone on without repeating. Suppose, for example, that retained and control groups both started out at the 10th percentile on standardized achievement tests at the end of 1st grade. The retained group was made to repeat 1st grade while the control group was promoted to 2nd grade. Two years later when the retained children completed 2nd grade, they might be (on average) at the 20th percentile. However, the control children, who started out equally deficient, would finish 2nd grade achieving ahead of their retained counterparts by 0.31 standard deviation units, or at roughly the 30th percentile on average.

When Holmes selected only the 25

113

studies with the greatest degree of statistical control, the negative effect of retention was again confirmed. In the 9 positive studies (out of 63), the apparent benefit of retention tended to diminish over time so that differences in performance between retained and control children disappeared in later grades.

Does nonpromotion prevent school dropouts? In a typical end-of-year news story, *USA Today* (Johnson 1988) reported that one-quarter of the 1st graders in a Mississippi community would be held back because they "can't read at a 1st-grade level." Consistent with the view that retention will repair deficient skills and improve students' life chances, the principal explained her decision: "In years past, those students would have been promoted to 2nd grade. Then they might have dropped out in five, six, or seven years."

Researchers of the dropout phenomenon have consistently found a significant relationship between grade retention and dropping out—in the opposite direction, however, from the one imagined by the Mississippi principal. Dropouts are five times more likely to have repeated a grade than are high school graduates. Students who repeat two grades have a probability of dropping out of nearly 100 percent (Association of California Urban School Districts 1985). In the past, these findings were ignored because poor achievement could be the explanation for both grade retention and dropping out. More recently, Grissom and Shepard (1989) conducted three large-scale studies, involving from 20,000 to 80,000 students each. They examined the retention-dropout relation after controlling for achievement and found that with equally poor achievement (and controlling for other background characteristics associated with dropping out), students who repeated a year were 20 to 30 percent more likely to drop out of school. For example, in Austin, Texas, African-American males with below average achievement have a 45 percent chance of dropping out of school; but African-American males with identical achievement scores who have repeated a year of school have a 75 percent chance of leaving school before graduation. A substantially increased risk for dropping out after

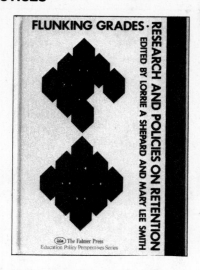

repeating a grade was found even in a large affluent suburban school district with only a 4 percent dropout rate.

What are the emotional effects of retention? In a much-quoted study of childhood stressors by Yamamoto (1980), children rated the prospect of repeating a grade as more stressful than "wetting in class" or being caught stealing. Going blind or losing a parent were the only two life events that children said would be more stressful than being retained. The negative connotations of being held back pervade the American school culture. When Byrnes (1989) interviewed children and used euphemisms to refer to spending two years in the same grade, even 1st graders said, "Oh, you mean flunking." Eighty-seven percent of the children interviewed said that being retained made them feel "sad," "bad," "upset," or "embarrassed." Only 6 percent of retained children gave positive answers about how retention made them feel, like, "you learn more," or "it lets you catch up." Interview transcripts from both high-achieving students and retained students revealed a widely shared perception that retention is a necessary punishment for being bad in class or failing to learn.

Holmes' (1989) synthesis of controlled studies included nearly 50 studies with some social or emotional outcome measures. On average, Holmes found that retained students do more poorly than matched controls on follow-up measures of social adjustment, attitudes toward school, behavioral outcomes, and attendance.

The above research findings indicate, then, that contrary to popular belief,

repeating a grade actually worsens achievement levels in subsequent years. The evidence contradicts commonsense reasoning that retention will reduce school dropout rates; it seems more likely that school policies meant to increase the number of grade retentions will exacerbate dropout rates. The negative social-emotional consequences of repeating represents the only area where conventional wisdom is consistent with research findings: kids have always hated being retained, and the studies bear that out.

Reconciling Research and Practice

Policies of grade retention persist in the face of negative evidence because teachers and parents cannot conduct controlled experiments. Without controlled comparisons, retention looks as if it works, especially if you believe that it does. Consider how the performance of individual retained and control children is interpreted by teachers. A control child does very poorly academically, is considered for retention, but is socially promoted. Consistent with the 30th percentile figure quoted from the Holmes (1989) study above, the control child ends up in the bottom half of the class, still struggling. Teachers then say, "If only we had retained him, his performance would have improved." Meanwhile, a comparable child does repeat, shows improvement during the repeat year on some skills, but in the next grade does even more poorly than the control child. Believing that retention helps, however, and without being able to see the controlled comparison, teachers accept any improvement during the repeat year itself as proof that retention works; and about poor performance in the next grade they say, "He would have done even more poorly without the extra year," or "At least we tried."

Schools are also under considerable political pressure to maintain acceptably high levels of grade retention as proof of high standards. Public belief in the efficacy of retention creates a powerful mandate: Flunk poor-achieving students for their own good as well as society's good. Without a simple way to explain to the public that at-risk students are more likely to learn and stay in school if not retained, schools may sacrifice the best interests of individual children to appease popular demands.

What alternatives are there to retention? There are numerous ways to provide extra instructional help focussed on a student's specific learning needs within the context of normal-grade promotion. Remedial help, before- and after-school programs, summer school, instructional aides to work with target children in the regular classroom, and no-cost peer tutoring are all more effective than retention. Unlike retention, each of these solutions has a research base showing positive achievement gains for participating children over controls. Cross-age peer tutoring, for example, where an average 5th grade student might tutor a 2nd grader who is behind in math, shows learning gains for both the target students and the tutors (Hartley 1977).

One of the fears about social promotion is that teachers will pass on deficient students endlessly as if no one had noticed their problem. Rather than ban retention but do nothing else, creative groups of teachers in a few schools have developed staffing

teams (of regular teachers) to work out plans with the next-grade receiving teachers about how to address the learning difficulties for students who otherwise would have been retention candidates. Similarly, some schools "place" poorly performing students in the next grade with a formally agreed upon Individualized Educational Plan (IEP), akin to the special education model of intervention. The decision to allow a deficient student to advance to the next grade with a plan for special help is analogous to prevalent school policies for gifted students. Instead of double promoting academically gifted students, schools keep them in their normal grade and provide them with enriched instruction. There are two reasons enrichment is preferred over skipping grades. First, normal grade placement is better socially for academically able students. Second, these able children are not equally advanced in every subject, and the amount they are ahead does not come in convenient nine-month units. Parallel arguments can be used to explain why retention does not improve achievement but

promotion plus remediation does. Finally, there is reason to believe that struggling students need a more inspired and engaging curriculum, one that involves them in solving meaningful problems, rather than repetitive, by-rote drills on basic skills. Outmoded learning theories (e.g., Thorndike's [1972] S-R bonds and behaviorism's programmed instruction [Mager 1962]) require children to master component skills before they are allowed to go on to comprehension and problem solving; this theory consigns slow learners to school work that is not only boring but devoid of any connection to the kinds of problems they encounter in the real world.

The second wave of educational reform, exemplified by curricular changes in California and the new standards of the National Council of Teachers of Mathematics, is based on more current learning theory from cognitive and constructivist psychology (Resnick 1987, Wertsch 1985), which holds that skills cannot be learned effectively nor applied to new problems unless the skills are learned in context. For example, students who are given lots and lots of problems to solve about how much tile to buy to floor a room with irregular dimensions and how much paint to buy are more likely to be better at both multiplication facts and problem solving than students who must memorize all

---

Highlights of Research on Grade Retention

A synthesis of the research on grade retention shows that:

● Grade failure rates are as high as they were in the 19th century, before the days of social promotion: Although annual statistics show only about a 6 percent annual rate for retention, year after year that produces a cumulative rate of nonpromotion greater than 50 percent. By 9th grade approximately half of all students in the U.S. have flunked at least one grade (or are no longer in school).

● Retained children actually perform more poorly on average when they go on to the next grade then if they had been promoted without repeating a grade.

● Dropouts are five times more likely to have repeated a grade than are high school graduates. Students who repeat two grades have a probability of dropping out of nearly 100 percent.

● Children in Yamamoto's (1980) study of childhood stressors rated the prospect of repeating a grade as more stressful than "wetting in class" or being caught stealing. The only two life events they felt would be more stressful than being retained were going blind or losing a parent. Both high-achieving and retained students interviewed by Byrnes (1989) viewed retention as a necessary punishment for being bad in class or failing to learn.

● There are many alternatives to retention that are more effective in helping low achievers. These include remedial help, before- and after-school programs, summer school, instructional aides to work with target children in the regular classroom, and no-cost peer tutoring. Groups of teachers in some schools have developed staffing teams to work out plans with the next-grade receiving teachers about how to address the learning difficulties for students who otherwise would have been retention candidates. Some schools "place" poor performing students in the next grade with a formally agreed upon Individualized Educational Plan (IEP), akin to the special education model of intervention.

● The annual cost to school districts of retaining 2.4 million students per year is nearly $10 billion. Summer school costs only approximately $1,300 per student compared to $4,051 for a repeated grade. At a wage of $6 an hour for an aide, it would take the savings from only 1.6 retained students to have an extra adult in every classroom full time to give extra attention to low achieving students.

Remedial help, before- and after-school programs, summer school, instructional aides to work with target children in the regular classroom, and no-cost peer tutoring are all more effective than retention.

Children rated the prospect of repeating a grade as more stressful than "wetting in class" or being caught stealing.

retained to more effective instructional programs.

The Futility of Flunking

Researchers have not been able to tell why retention doesn't work as intended. Some speculate that the negative emotional effects of repeating harm subsequent learning. Others suggest that going through the same material again is a crude and ineffective way to individualize instruction since a child may be more than one year behind in some subjects and only a few months behind in others. Because retention itself is considered to be the treatment, there is usually no additional effort to correct the poor quality of teaching and learning that occurred the first time through. In other words, the child may have failed to achieve grade-level standards because the programs or teachers he had were ineffective. Merely repeating the same curriculum or instruction is not likely to fix the problem. If extra money exists to support remediation along with retention, then educators

their multiplication tables before confronting even one such problem.

How much does retention cost? Can the dollars saved by not retaining students be reallocated to more effective alternatives? Based on an annual retention rate of 6 percent and a per pupil cost of $4,051 (U.S. Department of Education, Center for Education Statistics), we estimated that U.S. school districts spend nearly $10 billion a year to pay for the extra year of schooling necessitated by retaining 2.4 million students (see study cited in author's note at end of article).

Ten billion dollars would go a long way to pay for remedial programs, summer school, classroom aides, or reduced class size to help at-risk students learn. For example, summer school costs only approximately $1,300 per student compared to $4,051 for a repeated grade. Even special education help for a learning disabled child costs on average only $1,600 (half of which is spent on testing and staffing instead of instruction). At a wage of $6 an hour for an aide, it would take the savings from only 1.6 retained students to have an extra adult in every classroom full time.

Ironically, however, retention does not appear as a line item in any educational budget. No jurisdiction appears to bear the cost of the extra year. Because most students do not stay in the same district for 13 years of school, it does not matter to local districts that some students take 14 years. If a student stays in a district only 4 years, then the cost of grades 1–2–3–4 is the same as grades 1–2–3–3. Even states are not aware that they are paying for an extra year. Because the real cost of retention is never explicitly acknowledged, local educators find it difficult to redirect savings from students not

No Benefits from Kindergarten Retention

The decade of the 1980s saw a dramatic rise in the number of children asked to repeat kindergarten. In districts with special programs for "unready" kindergartners, as many as 50 percent were held back (California Department of Education 1988). An extra year before 1st grade is now offered in a variety of different forms: transition classrooms before 1st grade, developmental kindergarten before kindergarten, and straight repeating of kindergarten. According to its advocates, kindergarten retention, because it is intended to prevent school failure caused by immaturity, is different from retention in later grades.

Controlled studies do not support the benefits claimed for extra-year programs, however, and negative side effects occur just as they do for retention in later grades. In a review of 16 controlled studies on the effects of extra-year programs, the predominant finding is one of no difference (Shepard 1989). For example, when researchers followed extra-year children to the end of 1st grade or as far as 5th grade and compared their performance to unready children whose parents refused the extra year, the extra-year children performed no better academically despite being a year older for their grade. The conclusion of "no benefit" holds true even for studies where children were selected on the basis of immaturity rather than for academic risk, and even where a special transition curriculum was offered rather than repeating regular kindergarten.

Although the majority of teachers believe that retention in kindergarten does not carry a social stigma "if handled properly," extra-year children are more likely to have lower self-concepts and poorer attitudes toward school compared to controls (Shepard 1989). Parent interviews reveal both short-term and long-term distress associated with the retention decision such as teasing by peers, tears because friends are going on, and references years later like, "If I had only been able . . . , I would be in 3rd grade now." (Shepard and Smith 1989b).

Various analysts have suggested that kindergarten retention is an educational fad, gaining popularity because of the apparent need to remove unready children from increasingly narrow academic demands in kindergarten and 1st grade. Long periods of seat work, worksheets, and "staying in the lines" are required of children, inconsistent with the normal development of 5- and 6-year-olds. Ironically, retention and holding children out of school, intended to protect them from inappropriate expectations, actually contribute to the escalation of demands, thereby placing more and more children at risk. As kindergartens become populated with 6-year-olds who have had 3 years of preschool, teachers find it difficult to teach to the normal 5-year-olds in the class. The problem can only be solved with more developmentally appropriate curriculum in the early grades and reform of harmful instructional practices, something that many national associations have called for, including the National Association for the Education of Young Children, the National Association of State Boards of Education, the Association for Childhood Education International, the Association for Supervision and Curriculum Development, the International Reading Association, the National Association of Elementary School Principals, and the National Council of Teachers of English. Until this problem of kindergarten retention is addressed on a national scale, educators must deal with its consequences—which will negatively affect the quality of education at every level of schooling.

—Lorrie A. Shepard and Mary Lee Smith

should ask why students can't receive the extra help in the context of their normal grade placement.

The public and many educators find it difficult to give up on retention. To do so seems to mean accepting or condoning shamefully deficient skills for many high school graduates. It is easier for the public to credit research findings that retention harms self-esteem and increases the likelihood of dropping out than to believe the most critical finding—that retention worsens rather than improves the level of student achievement in years following the repeat year. Only with this fact firmly in mind, verified in over 50 controlled studies, does it make sense to subscribe to remediation and other within-grade instructional efforts which have modest but positive evidence of success. Perhaps the futility of flunking students to make them learn would be more obvious if it were recognized that statistically, social promotion has been dead for at least 10 years (i.e., cumulative retention rates are very high). Today's graduates and dropouts are emerging from a system that has imposed fierce non-promotion rates, flunking between 30 and 50 percent of all entering students at least once in their school careers. Strict promotion standards have been enforced for a decade and, as would have been predictable from the retention research findings on achievement, have not appreciably improved the performance of current graduates. Ultimately, hopes for more dramatic improvements in student learning (than can be expected from promotion plus remediation) will only come from thoroughgoing school changes —more support and opportunities for teachers to work together in addressing the problems of hard-to-teach children (Martin 1988), and curricular reforms designed to engage all children

U.S. school districts spend nearly $10 billion a year to pay for the extra year of schooling necessitated by retaining 2.4 million students.

in meaningful learning tasks that provide both the context and the purpose for acquiring basic skills (Resnick 1987).□

References

Association of California Urban School Districts (ACUSD). (1985). *Dropouts from California's Urban School Districts: Who Are They? How Do We Count Them? How Can We Hold Them (or at Least Educate Them)?* Los Angeles: ACUSD.
Byrnes, D. A. (1989). "Attitudes of Students, Parents, and Educators Toward Repeating a Grade." In *Flunking Grades: Research and Policies on Retention*, edited by L.A. Shepard and M.L.. Smith. London: The Falmer Press.
California Department of Education. (1988). *Here They Come: Ready or Not! Report of the School Readiness Task Force.* Sacramento: CDE.
Grissom, J.B., and Shepard, L.A. (1989). "Repeating and Dropping Out of School." In *Flunking Grades: Research and Policies on Retention*, edited by L.A. Shepard and M.L.. Smith. London: The Falmer Press.
Hartley, S.S. (1977). "Meta-Analysis of the Effects of Individually Paced Instruction in Mathematics." Unpublished doctoral dissertation, University of Colorado at Boulder.
Holmes, C.T. (1989). "Grade-Level Retention Effects: A Meta-Analysis of Research Studies." In *Flunking Grades: Research and Policies on Retention*, edited by L.A. Shepard and M.L.. Smith. London: The Falmer Press.
Johnson, H. (April 15–17, 1988). "Reforms Stem a 'Rising Tide' of Mediocrity," *USA Today*: 1–2.
Mager, R.F. (1962). *Preparing Instructional Objectives.* Fearon Publishers.
Martin, A. (1988). "Screening, Early Intervention, and Remediation: Obscuring Children's Potential." *Harvard Educational Review* 58: 488–501.
Resnick, L.B. (1987). *Education and Learning to Think.* Washington, D.C.: National Academy Press.
Shepard, L.A. (1989). "A Review of Research on Kindergarten Retention." In *Flunking Grades: Research and Policies on Retention*, edited by L.A. Shepard and M.L.. Smith. London: The Falmer Press.
Shepard, L.A., and M.L. Smith, eds. (1989a). *Flunking Grades: Research and Policies on Retention.* London: The Falmer Press.
Shepard, L.A., and M.L. Smith. (1989b). "Academic and Emotional Effects of Kindergarten Retention in One School District." In *Flunking Grades: Research and Policies on Retention*, edited by L.A. Shepard and M.L.. Smith. London: The Falmer Press.
Thorndike, E.L. (1922). *The Psychology of Arithmetic.* New York: Macmillan.
Wertsch, J.V., ed. (1985). *Culture, Communications, and Cognition: Vygotskian Perspectives*, 1985 vol. New York: Cambridge University Press.
Yamamoto, K. (1980). "Children Under Stress: The Causes and Cures." *Family Weekly, Ogden Standard Examiner*: 6–8.

Authors' note: Portions of this article were developed for the Center for Policy Research in Education Policy Briefs. (1990, January). "Repeating Grades in School: Current Practice and Research Evidence." New Jersey: Rutgers, The State University of New Jersey.

Guiding Behavior

- Self-Esteem (Articles 22-24)
- Behavior (Articles 25-26)

Adults who live and work with young children on a daily basis often report great satisfaction and fulfillment when developmental progress is observed. There is also considerable ambivalence and strain when children act differently than adults would like or expect. Certainly, children's behavior is not always easy or pleasant to deal with due to their fundamental immaturity, inexperience, and childlike ways of perceiving the world. Coupled with these realities, many people feel there has been a widespread societal breakdown in disciplined behavior in both children and adults. Accordingly, discipline and guidance are common discussion topics for adults who share young children's environments.

Heated, unproductive arguments may occur if adults do not realize that the broad concept of discipline suggests varied meanings and strategies for different people. For some adults, discipline means punishment—swift, painful, and involving fear, coercion, or isolation from peers. But researchers and observers of young children have clearly shown that punished, coerced, and isolated children feel humiliated, lose self-esteem, and fail to develop coping strategies to handle future problems.

For early childhood educators, discipline means guidance. It involves the following steps: first, understanding typical child development and examining one's attitudes about children; second, preventing certain behaviors through monitoring the daily schedule and room arrangement; third, redirecting and modifying undesirable behavior; fourth, modeling and explaining more acceptable, appropriate, or mature behavior; and fifth, using reasoning with children and teaching them verbal skills for peer interaction. Discipline, in this connotation, means steadily building self-control so children can develop positive self-esteem, respect for the needs of others, and gradually move toward healthy independence and problems-solving skills that they may draw upon in future situations.

Any program or plan for guiding behavior must focus on young children. So an appropriate beginning of guidance and discipline is an understanding of the concept of self-esteem. What was once thought of as a singular element of children's development that could be enhanced through use of catch phrases, praise, or stickers is now considered quite complex. Self-esteem involves an inner sense of acceptance and value as well as outer-directed self-regulation and evaluation. Early in life, children begin developing an actual self along with their conception of self. These two dynamics are shaped by others and can at times be in conflict. This is why an attempt to address a child's low self-esteem with words of praise may prove ineffective.

When self-esteem is viewed as both a personal and social interaction, the role of early childhood educators becomes significantly more important than artificially bolstering a child through a particular situation with a smiley-face sticker. It is a process of leading the child to a valued and realistic identity. This process begins with showing respect for children's well-being. In day-to-day transactions, it means acknowledging that children deserve the space to be themselves, make their own decisions, do their own work. At the same time, since children are dependent, respect includes assuming responsibility for nurturing their growth and development. The long-term goal is to foster confidence, initiative, and sociability in children. These can best be accomplished when discipline is regarded as a learning experience and respect is maintained even in difficult circumstances.

The following are practical considerations in devising a plan for guiding behavior—when to intervene in a situation; when to observe from afar; when to curb behavior immediately or wait and discuss it later; when to establish an inviolable rule; and when to encourage cooperative establishment of rules. When assessing behavior, educators should consider what individual children are capable of doing and knowing, what special needs and skills they

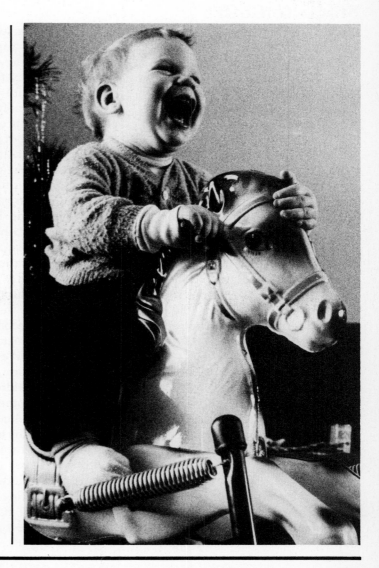

possess, and what opportunities could be provided to promote emotional growth and social and communicative competence. If they understand the causes of frustration and aggression in children, such as unnecessary waiting, crowding, insufficient play materials, or poor curricular planning, educators can make changes so that children's self-esteem and control are supported in healthy ways.

As with all areas of early childhood education, a high-quality, effective plan for guiding behavior does not arrive prepackaged for the teacher's immediate use. Guiding and disciplining is hard work, requiring careful attention to individual children and differing situations. Mastery of authentic and humane guidance techniques takes time reflecting on ethical principles, refining strategies, and seeking the best emotional climate. The early childhood community is fortunate to have excellent sources on guidance and discipline to assist in this process.

Looking Ahead: Challenge Questions

Why is it important to establish an atmosphere of respect during the early childhood years?

What are ways teachers can demonstrate their respect for young children?

How does affective development relate to cognitive development?

How do teachers promote self-esteem during preschool years when children test and challenge the self?

What are the signals of positive or negative verbal environments for young children?

How can adults knowingly act to establish and monitor a helpful verbal environment?

In what ways are approaches to disciplining young children good or bad? What disciplinary methods are especially harmful to children's development?

What are possible causes of young children's aggression? What approaches can teachers use to help children deal with aggressive behavior?

How Well Do We Respect the Children in Our Care?

Stacie G. Goffin

Stacie G. Goffin is Assistant Professor, Early Childhood Education, University of Missouri - Kansas City.

Children are spending increasingly larger proportions of their early years in group settings outside their homes. Statistics abound describing the quantity of mothers currently in the workforce. Interest in early childhood education, however, is more than just the result of increasing maternal employment. There are other crucial statistics.

• Twenty-five percent of all children—47% of black children, 40% of Hispanic children and 10% of white children—are born into and spend their lives in poverty (Halpern, 1987).

• One in five children who entered 1st grade this past fall is at risk of becoming a teen parent, and one in seven is at risk of dropping out of school (Children's Defense Fund, 1988).

• The decreasing number of future workers means every potential employee needs to be competent and skilled.

In combination, these changing demographics and social circumstances have focused attention on early childhood care and education as a solution to welfare reform, teenage pregnancy, female employment and future labor needs. Noticeably absent from this list of public policy concerns, however, is the well-being of children. This omission points to the low priority the general public gives to issues associated with quality. Quality issues argue the validity of children's well-being in the present and contrast with the current focus of arguments supporting early childhood education in terms of future returns.

As early educators, however, we cannot side-step the issue of quality; we need to become more reflective about the "treatment" children are receiving. We can begin by asking the question, "How well do we respect the children in our care?"

As defined by the *New Scholastic Dictionary of American English* (Kessen, 1981), the term *respect* has the following meanings: to be mindful of; to pay attention to; to show consideration and esteem for; to avoid intruding upon; and to avoid violating. Based upon this definition, respect can be both a noun and a verb. As a noun, respect can be a result or outcome of our interactions with children; it can also be a description of our behavior, as in "respectful." The major focus of this discussion, however, is on respect as a verb—as an action word. As early educators, we show our respect *for* children by what we do *with* children.

To answer the question just posed, the various meanings of respect have been amplified in relation to daily interactions with children and their families. They have been used repeatedly to describe 12 active (and knowingly overlapping) categories that frame the ways early childhood educators can display their respect, or disrespect, to children. The intent is to provoke thinking about the meaning and impact of our actions with and for children.

TWELVE ACTIVE WAYS TO RESPECT CHILDREN

Action #1: Showing respect for childhood

The idea of childhood as a separate, developmental period is a relatively recent cultural invention; in fact, it is only several hundred years old (Kessen, 1979; Postman,

1982). Yet, many recent writers have expressed concern that the idea of childhood as a separate developmental period is disappearing (see, for example, Postman, 1982). This implies we have been guilty of intruding into and violating this unique period of growth.

In early childhood settings, examples of this kind of disrespect include ignoring the ways children learn through play and expecting them to learn in ways similar to older children. In addition to being inappropriate, when the curriculum focuses on skills and knowledge children supposedly need for later schooling (e.g., lining up, coloring within the lines, learning pre-skills), children's future development is being emphasized as more important than their current well-being. As a result, childhood becomes merely a stepping-stone to future stages of growth rather than a meaningful time for development in its own right.

Disrespect for childhood is also expressed in the frustration and outbursts of anger many adults display when children "act their age," instead of conforming to adult standards. The term *childish* has acquired a negative, rather than positive, connotation.

Early childhood teachers and caregivers are frequently praised for their patience. When they display their patience because children have failed to meet inappropriate expectations, however, they reveal misunderstandings about child growth and development (Weber-Schwartz, 1987). Those who understand children accept "childish" behavior like negativism, for example ("No! Me do it!"), as developmentally appropriate behavior for 2-year-olds. Even though respectful adults will want to help 2-year-olds learn other ways of expressing their feelings, they also recognize that children behave differently from adults because of their maturational level and inexperience.

Consequently, respect for childhood requires paying attention to and showing esteem for the characteristics of childhood—such as activity, impulsiveness, curiosity, learning through exploration—and then organizing teaching and learning to reflect these understandings. To quote Weber-Schwartz (1987), "Because I accept what *is*, I put energy into effective teaching, not into struggling against the reality that children are children" (p. 53, italics in original).

Action #2: Responding with sensitivity to children's individuality

Respectful actions in this category go beyond respect for childhood. They acknowledge the unique characteristics of individual children and the ways their uniqueness is revealed in decisions, choices, preferences and styles of responding to and interacting with objects and people. To show consideration for these qualities requires we support and encourage these characteristics as worth nurturing. Too often, children's personal ways of responding are viewed as interference with an adult's prepared plans or as misbehavior, rather than as evidence of a child's individuality or personal perceptions of the situation.

Commitment to children's individuality requires accepting and supporting children's personal goals and values as worthwhile. Early childhood settings that primarily function in whole groups and emphasize adult-prescribed learning offer limited opportunities for children to personalize learning through making their own decisions, acting as initiators of their own learning or pursuing their own interests. Yet, it is these flexible opportunities that encourage and support individuality and personal growth. In contrast, heavy doses of group instruction and standardized curriculum encourage and support conformity.

Being mindful of children's in-dividuality also occurs when adults actively listen to children even though their comments may seem trivial. It is reflected in greetings and dismissals recognizing children's arrival and departure, in interesting alternative activities for children who are not interested in the adult-chosen activity and, most important, in consideration of children's individual ways of acting their age.

Admittedly, we cannot always be flexible in response to children's individuality, but we can give more consideration to how well we are accommodating children's needs and interests. Because we adults have more authority than children, it is easy to expect children to adjust to adult preferences; it is less easy to remind ourselves that it is often more supportive and growth-enhancing if we adjust to the individuality of children.

Action #3: Developing nurturing relationships with children
Action #4: Using adult authority with wisdom to facilitate children's growth into caring adults

Adults are bigger and stronger than children. They have more experiences and greater skills. Consequently, the power relationship between children and adults is unequal and unbalanced in favor of adults. The critical issue for children is how adults choose to use their authority. Dreikurs and Solz (1964) use the term *social equality* to describe an optimum relationship between children and adults. In this type of relationship, adults recognize that even though children are dependent upon them and have less knowledge and fewer skills, they are still entitled to respect as human beings.

This respect, however, does not suggest that adults should abdicate their responsibilities toward children. Because children are dependent upon us and are less knowledgeable and skillful, we must assume responsibility for nurturing and fostering their

Table 1
Early Educator Responses to the Question:
"How Well Do We Respect the Children in Our Care?"

I show my respect when:
- I listen to what a child has to say.
- I take time for a child when I'm very busy.
- I play with children.
- I color a picture with children.
- I recognize accomplishments.
- I allow children to settle disputes between themselves.
- I listen to a special song.
- I show interest in a child's project.
- I make eye contact.
- I encourage their viewpoints.
- I allow them to make choices.
- I try to arrange a schedule to be accommodating to a parent.
- I allow for privacy.
- I try to respond with words and actions to a child's uniqueness.
- I call children by their names.
- I know how to say "no."
- I encourage independence.
- I respond to their questions.
- I allow a child to talk uninterrupted.
- I respect a child's choice of friend and play equipment.
- I allow children to make mistakes.
- I realize their individuality.
- I am flexible.
- I allow them to disagree.
- I care for their property.
- I allow transition time.
- I listen to a child's problem and realize how upsetting the situation can be to a child.
- I talk to children as people.
- I give each child a chance to communicate.
- I ask a child for his/her solution to a problem.
- I value their opinions.
- I remember that play is of great importance in each child's life.
- I prepare myself well for class so I don't have to "waste" children's time.

I am somewhat disrespectful when:
- I do not take a child's opinion seriously.
- I avoid an issue a child felt needed immediate attention.
- I use time out.
- I leave the children alone.
- I walk away from a child while he/she is crying.
- I don't stop to listen.
- I respond with "uh-huh."
- I use a "baby-talk" tone of voice with younger children.
- I use angry words under stress.
- I cut their conversations close.
- I finish a task for them to hasten time.
- I forget to follow through on something I promised.
- I answer a question for them with a strange adult present so they are more articulate or seemingly more socially acceptable.
- I spend physical time with a child but am emotionally distant from the situation.
- I behave impatiently.
- I use sarcasm.
- I shout.
- I physically force a child into a situation in which he's uncomfortable.
- My expectations are too high.
- I rush children.
- I don't take care of myself physically or emotionally.
- I call them names; e.g., dumbbell.
- I show frustration because their needs interfere with my schedule.
- I focus on children's bad behaviors.
- I belittle their feelings.
- I sneak up on a child doing wrong.
- I ignore them.
- I stop a child who is really interested in a project.
- I don't allow a child to explain why or how a friend got hurt, or how an accident occurred.

Note: Thanks to all the early educators who shared their thoughts; their own wording has been used as much as possible.

---

growth. This is where wisdom comes in! Nurturing children's development into caring adults requires not only respect for childhood and a child's individuality, but also knowledge and understanding about child growth and development.

Furthermore, despite our frequent acknowledgment of the importance of children's emotional development, since the 1960s this aspect of growth has become a stepchild to cognitive (which often means academic) development. Yet, a nurturing relationship is the basis for child development. It is a necessary foundation for children's growth into caring human beings, as well as their relationships with peers and adults.

In fact, intellectual development and socio-emotional development are inseparable. They can be separated only for purposes of theory, pedagogy and research. This understanding requires adults to be as responsive to children's social-emotional needs as to their intellectual demands.

Action #5: Considering how day-to-day practices influence children
Children learn not only from *what* they are taught, but also from *how* they are taught. They learn from how the day is arranged, how the environment is organized and how others try to teach them. As early childhood educators, we need to become more sensitive to

the cumulative impact of our daily interactions with children, including intrusions into their play and activity, usurpation of their decision-making abilities and lack of attention to their feelings. Table 1 lists a sampling of responses to the title question from early childhood practitioners. Their answers highlight the day-in, day-out interactions that reveal respect, and unintended disrespect, for children.

We need to facilitate children's involvement in personally meaningful activities and experiences. The demands of group living can be softened by allowing children to make meaningful decisions and providing more opportunities for them to pursue their individual interests. We want to minimize the times we unnecessarily or unthinkingly forget to pay attention to children's interests and preferences.

One of the most challenging aspects of early childhood education is trying to understand a child's perspective about an experience. Lack of sensitivity to children's individual ways of making sense of their experiences often leads adults to impose their own ways of organizing and interpreting experiences (see, for example, Paley, 1986; Suransky, 1982).

For example, in one early childhood setting, a group of 4-year-olds sat cross-legged on the floor in a circle, watching as their teacher lifted a pencil, a beanbag and three baby-food jars out of a bowl and then set them on a mat. The teacher announced, "Many of these things have been on the earth for a long time." She held up a baby-food jar of soil and said, "LAND has always been here as far as we know." She returned the jar to the mat and lifted up another jar filled with water, saying, "WATER has always been here as far as we know." She set the jar back on the mat and held up the last jar (which appeared empty) and said, "AIR has always been here as far as we know." She placed the jar back on the mat and asked, "Can you see anything else that has always been here?" Antoine called out excitedly, "The bowl!!"

The teacher answered, "No. MAN made the bowl. Someone INVENTED the bowl. Can anyone think of something in our room that someone made?" Antoine raised his hand and shouted, "Horses on the wall!" The teacher pointed to the teacher-prepared horses decorating the wall above the blackboard. She asked, "What about the horse on the farm? Where did it come from?" Antoine announced excitedly, "Horses!!" The teacher smiled at Antoine and asked again, "Where did they *come*

from—did man make them or did God make them?"

This teacher appeared unaware that her way of thinking about these concepts differed from Antoine's. From Antoine's point of view, the experience probably helped him to learn self-doubt and how to "play the circle-time game." It is likely he also learned that right answers are arbitrary, since his reasoned thinking was consistently corrected. It is unlikely, however, that he learned much about the distinctions between natural and man-made materials, which appears to have been the teacher's objective.

It is equally important to pay attention to children's needs in our scheduling and organizing. Too often we feel that responding to children's needs (e.g., to receive affection, to be first in line, to take more time) interferes with classroom routines or that being tough while children are young, better prepares them for a harsh world later on. In reality, it is just the opposite. By responding to children's needs, we strengthen their abilities to accept themselves and to cope with difficult circumstances.

Sensitivity to children's perspectives is seen when adults try to understand children's thinking, their needs, preferences and reactions. Failure to consider the impact of our day-in, day-out living arrangements with children underestimates the daily impact of teacher-child interactions and can undermine children's opportunities to develop their individuality.

Action #6: Recognizing discipline as a learning experience for children and viewing mistakes as potential learning opportunities
Discipline is frequently confused with punishment; its purpose is often mistakenly limited to stopping inappropriate behavior. Discipline, however, describes the guidance provided to help children understand adult expectations and develop control from within. It is

an ongoing process of guiding children's development.

When children and adults cooperate with each other, classroom life proceeds smoothly. When children do not comply with a teacher's request, the result is usually a discipline encounter. The term *encounter* highlights that the outcome desired by the teacher is not shared by the child, reminding us that children are active decision-makers (Goffin, 1987). These disagreements often result in conflict between teachers and children.

It is this aspect of discipline that has received the most discussion and unfairly earned discipline the one-sided reputation of being negative and unpleasant. Still, the important point is that discipline in general, and discipline encounters in particular, are both learning experiences for children. The ways teachers and caregivers structure these daily experiences clearly reveal their consideration and esteem for children.

A major characteristic of adult-child relationships is the discrepancy between the power and authority of children and adults. We intrude upon children when we use our authority and power to coerce them (most easily characterized by the phrase "Because I said so, that's why!") to fulfill our needs (for order or schedule, for example) without being mindful of their needs, interests and individuality. Respectful adults carefully use their power and authority to help children learn appropriate behaviors and inner controls in ways that show consideration for their feelings and developing capabilities; for example, by acknowledging feelings, providing explanations and linking behavior with rational consequences.

Action #7: Acknowledging children's competencies
Action #8: Organizing a curriculum that provides children with interesting things to think about
We often fail to be mindful of what

children are capable of doing. There is a tendency to narrowly focus on skills and information children do not yet possess. As a result, some early childhood educators see their major responsibility as teaching children the next item in a series of learnings. This emphasis, however, fails to show esteem for children's capabilities. Learning experiences should be organized as extensions and elaborations of children's current interests and understandings—the basis for meaningful learning.

Research reveals that children are much more capable than we have credited them (Bruner & Harste, 1987; Donaldson, 1978; Gelman, 1979). It is demeaning, as well as boring, to have weekly units on fragmented skills or topics such as the color *blue*, the shape of a circle or the letter *C*. It is also frequently meaningless. A 4-year-old, working to create an octopus by gluing precut construction paper tentacles on a yellow circle of paper, turned to his teacher standing nearby and asked, "What am I making?" "Octopuses," the teacher responded. "Why?" he followed up. "Because," the teacher replied, "the letter we're learning about is *O* and octopus begins with it." "Oh," he said as he returned to his gluing.

Children are entitled to activities and experiences that are engrossing and that permit the teacher to challenge their thinking. Learning is more than memorizing labels and making associations between objects. Esteem for children demands we pay attention to their abilities and provide meaningful, relevant and interesting ways for them to expand their understandings. It also requires talking *with* children (instead of *at* them) by attending to what they are doing and asking questions related to their actions.

As the following anecdote clearly reveals, we dominate the learning process when our teaching primarily focuses on what *we*

think children ought to know, regardless of its relationship to their current interests and activities.

During a circle-time activity, the teacher flashed picture cards to the seated children. "And, what is this?" she asked. "A boat," children shouted. "Where does it go?" A child interjected, "Teacher, I rode a boat on my vacation." Another child yelled, "I did, too." "I have a boat at my house," a third child contributed. The children then began talking with each other, sharing comments like: "We went to Disney World on our vacation … We went to Colorado." "Quiet!" the teacher shouted. "Now, I said quiet. That's enough about vacations; you can talk about that at free time. We have to get through this."

> **Research reveals that children are much more capable than we have credited them.**

Action #9: Supporting and strengthening parents in their childrearing responsibilities
Many children spend the majority of their waking hours with their teachers and caregivers. It is easy, therefore, for early childhood educators to lapse into a possessive attitude about the children in their care. This feeling is often heightened by tensions between parents and teachers/caregivers surrounding differing views on issues such as values, discipline, the importance of play and a child-centered curriculum (see Galinsky, 1988). These tensions are perhaps inescapable in any relationship where two unrelated adults care about the well-being of the same child. Still, it must be remembered that it

is parents who have made an unending commitment to their child, and it is with their parents that children are most emotionally intertwined.

Parenting is becoming respected as a challenging as well as highly personalized family enterprise. Parent programs based upon these premises are being called family support programs (Weissbourd, 1983). These programs strive to strengthen parenting by being responsive to parents' individuality and respecting the responsibilities they have assumed as parents.

We can show our support to parents in four ways: 1) by acknowledging the challenge of parenting, 2) by coming to know parents as individuals with their own personalities and family circumstances that help define their parenting, 3) by using these understandings to avoid judgmental interpretations of parents and their decisions, and 4) by acting as advocates for the parent-child relationship (Goffin & Caccamo, 1986). By strengthening and supporting parents in their parenting role, we show consideration for the importance of family in a child's life and express esteem for the challenge of parenthood.

Action #10: Acknowledging the expertise needed to be a professional in early childhood education
Action #11: Speaking out on behalf of early childhood education as a profession
The status of those who care for children is a leading indicator of how society views childhood and shows esteem for children. In general, society expresses limited interest in other people's children and therefore has little regard for those who do (Grubb & Lazerson, 1988). Society's attitude toward child care and caregivers, in particular, reveals the still dominant assumption that parents—mothers in particular—should be held totally responsible for the daily care

and education of their own children. This viewpoint encourages a custodial approach to child care outside the home.

As the number of women in the workforce and concerns for quality education increase, however, the importance of supplementing parents' responsibilities is gaining greater acceptance. We know the importance of our jobs and the contributions we make to children and their families. We know we are both underpaid and undervalued. But too many of us are also uninformed and undereducated about how to fulfill our responsibilities as early childhood educators.

For example, after beginning an afternoon kindergarten session with a 20-minute whole group handwriting exercise, a teacher announced, "Every day, after we have writing, we will have Center Time. Who knows what Center Time is?" "Well," the teacher answered, "if you went to preschool, they probably called it Play Time. And what is the difference between preschool and kindergarten? One is like babysitting and one is real school. And we are in real school here and we do real work, but sometimes we think play is learning, too."

This is a significant time in the history of early childhood education. The field is rapidly expanding. Simultaneously, early childhood educators are attempting to upgrade their status and compensation. Yet, at the same time, we are trying to convince many of the "outsiders" entering the field, as well as those already within our ranks, that early childhood education has a distinctive, professional knowledge base.

Knowledge of child development and early childhood education informs our practice and assures young children of programming specific to their needs and interests. It also provides a rationale for fending off the inappropriate expectations held by those

unfamiliar with the issues unique to early childhood education (Goffin, 1989). More clearly articulating our purposes and convincing educational decision-makers and others about the unique characteristics of early childhood education remain two of our major professional challenges.

Action #12: Speaking out on behalf of children's needs to parents, school administrators, business and community representatives, and policymakers

Recent political and economic events have sensitized us to the realization that children's issues are not above politics. Policies made by business and government structure many of the decisions early childhood educators make for children and the kinds of experiences children live.

As early educators, we experience, either directly or indirectly, the personal stories behind the statistics. Our relationships with parents create the opportunity to release parents' power on behalf of their own as well as other children (Goffin, 1988). Our relationships with the community place us in a unique position to inform others about the needs of children and families. Our knowledge and experiences enable us to help policymakers better understand the lives of their youngest constituents. Therefore, we are violating our responsibility to children when we fail to act on our beliefs and to share our knowledge with others.

Advocacy on behalf of children is a critical vehicle for actualizing our commitment to children. It is a necessary component of an expanded vision of the role of the early childhood educator.

It is important to recognize that advocacy includes, but is not limited to, political activity. Everyone can participate in personal advocacy (Goffin, 1988). When we personally reach out or speak out to others and, by our interpersonal actions, try to help children and

their families achieve needed or desired outcomes, we are performing personal advocacy. Personal advocacy takes advantage of opportunities to use our expertise on behalf of children and families.

A child care director's presentation to architects and a church committee about the importance of low windows in children's classrooms—despite her uncomfortable feelings of "exceeding her proper limits"—demonstrates personal advocacy. This director spoke out on behalf of children's needs for light and an aesthetically pleasing environment, despite her discomfort and anxiety. Her personal advocacy efforts resulted in differently designed, more appropriate classrooms for children.

Early childhood educators are among those who speak on behalf of others' children, not just their own. Our caring cannot be restricted to classrooms if we truly want to improve the lives of children.

Conclusion

This article began by emphasizing respect as an action word. It was suggested that educators show their respect *for* children by what they do *with* children. The 12 categories just described, however, reveal that showing our respect requires we go beyond our interactions with children. Esteem for childhood requires not only respectful actions with children but respectful actions on their behalf.

References

Bruner, J., & Harste, H. (1987). Introduction. In J. Bruner & H. Harste (Eds.), *Making sense: The child's construction of the world* (pp. 1-25). New York: Methuen.

Children's Defense Fund. (1988). *A children's defense budget FY89: An analysis of our nation's investment in children.* Washington, DC: Author.

Donaldson, M. (1978). *Children's minds.* New York: W. W. Norton & Company.

4. GUIDING BEHAVIOR: Self-Esteem

Dreikurs, R., & Solz, V. (1964). *Children: The challenge*. New York: Dutton.

Galinsky, E. (1988). Parents and teacher-caregivers: Sources of tension, sources of support. *Young Children, 43*(3), 4-12.

Gelman, R. (1979). Preschool thought. *American Psychologist, 34*, 900-905.

Goffin, S. G. (1987). Introduction. In S. G. Goffin & S. Vartuli (Eds.), Classroom management in new context: Teacher as decision-maker [special issue]. *Dimensions, 15*(4).

Goffin, S. G. (1988). Putting our advocacy efforts into a new context. *Young Children, 3*(3), 52-56.

Goffin, S. G. (1989). Developing an early childhood research agenda: What can we learn from the research on teaching? *Early Childhood Research Quarterly, 4*, 187-204.

Goffin, S. G., with Caccamo, J. (1986). *In partnership with parents*. Jefferson City, MO: State Department of Elementary and Secondary Education, Division of Special Education.

Grubb, N. W., & Lazerson, M. (1988). *Broken promises: How Americans fail their children*. Chicago: University of Chicago Press.

Halpern, R. (1987). Major social and demographic trends affecting young families: Implications for early childhood care and education. *Young Children, 42*(6), 34-40.

Kessen, W. (1979). The American child and other cultural inventions. *American Psychologist, 34*, 815-820.

Kessen, W. (1981). (Ed.). *New scholastic dictionary of American English*. New York: Scholastic, Inc.

Paley, V. G. (1989). On listening to what children say. *Harvard Education Review, 56*(2), 122-131.

Postman, N. (1982). *The disappearance of childhood*. New York: Delacorte.

Suransky, V. P. (1982). *The erosion of childhood*. Chicago: The University of Chicago Press.

Weber-Schwartz, N. (1987). Food for thought: Patience or understanding? *Young Children, 42*(3), 52-54.

Weissbourd, B. (1983). The family support movement: Greater than the sum of its parts. *Zero to Three, 4*(1), 8-10.

Nurturing Success

Positive ways to build self-esteem in your children

PATRICIA H. BERNE
WITH EVE BERNE

Dr. Patricia H. Berne, a former nursery school teacher, is now a practicing clinical psychologist in Washington, D.C. Her book, Building Self-Esteem in Children, *and her work with the National Council for Self-Esteem have nurtured and encouraged teachers, parents, and children across the country.*

Eve Berne, Patricia Berne's daughter, is a former day-care teacher and assistant director. She is currently special projects consultant for a child-care resource and referral center in Cambridge, MA.

I remember talking with a friend of mine, Sally, the mother of five children. One day as we sat together on the beach and watched our children play, Sally told me she had a very wise uncle. She thought he was wise because he had given her the most important piece of advice about raising children. Naturally, I asked her what that advice was. She said her uncle's words were: "The most important thing you can give children, more important than any material thing you might be concerned about, is a sense of self-confidence." Furthermore, he had told her, if she could give her children confidence in themselves, they would be able to get all the other things they needed for themselves.

As we sat on the beach and thought about Sally's uncle's words and our children played together in front of us, I know we wished very much, as most parents do, to give our children self-confidence.

As a mother, teacher, and counselor, I have spent much of my effort and thought building self-esteem in children, because self-esteem seems to be the foundation of self-confidence. Perhaps both words describe the same quality.

Self-esteem doesn't mean overconfidence. When you have self-esteem, you know yourself and accept yourself with your limitations; you are not ashamed of your limitations but simply see them as part of the person you are, perhaps as a boundary you're challenged to expand.

Children's self-esteem grows when they know you care enough to be with them.

In the first years of a child's life personal feelings of esteem are directly related to the people closest to him or her. When the people are nurturing and the environment they create offers opportunities for success, the child is well on his way to a healthy self-image.

Children who feel good about themselves take part in healthy relationships. They are open to new ideas and eager to share their own. Their confidence enables them to face challenges, cope with disappointments, and enjoy successes. These are children who are anxious to discover and share the wonder of life.

Success nourishes self-esteem. As children grow, they expand their perception of the people who influence them from family members to other caregivers. This gives special meaning to the people in an early childhood environment. In this setting children can experience success in their relationships with others (feeling loved and lovable, giving and receiving affection, building friendships); and in their abilities to relate as skillful, competent, and capable people.

In contrast, low self-esteem interferes with a child's ability to learn and to relate well to others. In some children, feelings of inadequacy surface in bossy and aggressive behavior. This may cause other children to become submissive and unsure.

These feelings show how a negative self-image affects a child and those around him. If he is perceived as a "difficult child," his behavior can start a cycle in which everyone involved shares a loss of esteem because each person shares a part of the frustration.

The nurturing environment you create and the supportive, caring relationships you build with your children will provide them with a strong foundation for future success. Here are some ways to reinforce and build self-esteem in your children throughout the year.

Building Positive Relationships

One of the first steps in developing children's self-esteem is to establish good relationships with them. Relationships that are mutually loving and caring, honest, and supportive create an atmosphere for healthy human growth. Here are some principles that focus on building such relationships with children.

■ **Create an atmosphere of trust.** The tone of your voice, your belief that each child is worthwhile and unique, and the care you take to kneel and speak to each child at eye level are immediate indicators to children that you are someone they can trust. In addition to using words and gestures to affirm that you care and value children, make sure your physical setting supports this attitude.

Some children feel valued when they can accomplish certain things by themselves, such as choosing between activities, returning toys to low-level shelves, and reaching for an intriguing book. Others feel important when they can be assured of structured activity. A teacher-directed collage project with a lot of materials to choose from can fulfill the needs of a child who is hesitant to make choices, while still enabling him to grow.

For some youngsters, noise, activity, and large numbers of people can be overwhelming. A quiet corner with a soft couch and fluffy pillows offers a welcome and safe retreat.

■ **Help children say goodbye.** Often at the beginning of the year, children create dropping-off rituals as a way to say goodbye to their parents. One youngster used the mail slot in the classroom door as a special, final place to touch his father's hand. Other children may run to the window to say goodbye. Respecting and supporting these goodbye routines communicates to children that you understand and value their relationships with family members.

■ **Keep children informed of the day's activities.** Let children know what their choices are when they arrive in the morning. Prior to transitions, keep them informed as to what will happen next. Notify them when cleanup time approaches so they will have ample time to complete the activities in which they are involved. Each day take advantage of snacktime to talk about what is scheduled for the rest of the day. There is comfort in predictability, and predictability helps children feel in control and capable.

■ **Be available to children.** When you agree to be available to a child, let the child know you are available specifically for him for this period of time. This

10 Principles of Self-Esteem

1. Children feel more confident in a setting that is conducive to their feeling cared for and valued.

2. Children's self-esteem grows when they know you care enough to be with them.

3. A moment's reflection about the wording of a question can make a significant difference in a child's self-esteem.

4. Children are enhanced by the network of people, things, and events that make up their lives. When you accept children in their network, you accept them completely.

5. Growth in self-esteem is connected with children's acceptance of their right to have strong feelings.

6. In a trusting and nonjudgmental atmosphere, self-esteem can grow.

means giving that child your *full* attention. Children appreciate not only your availability but also your undivided attention. When you spend time alone with a child, whether it's for five minutes or five hours, you're giving that child quality time. That helps build self-esteem because your attention to him affirms his value to you.

■ **Keep questions open-ended.** Keep your requests open-ended and invitational, for example, "Would you like to join us in playing this game? If you're not sure, I can ask you again in a few minutes." Always give children another chance to choose. They are still learning the art of making choices.

Instead of speaking to a child in an accusing tone ("You forgot to put the blocks away," which translates to "You betrayed my trust"), use an invitational approach ("Did you forget to put the blocks away? It's easy to forget things like that. Would you like some help?").

Try to put yourself in the child's position as you pose questions and suggestions. Avoid setting up a situation where a child is forced to express judgment about a fellow pupil. By asking, "Do you want to play with Darlene?" you may be putting the child in a position where he feels an obligation to please you — the acceptable answer in this case being, "Yes." Or, it may be that the child doesn't mind playing with Darlene but has no interest in what she is doing. Instead, phrase questions with a focus on the task or the toy, for exam-

ple, "Darlene's using the blocks. Would you like to use them, too?" You're now giving the child a free choice — no strings attached for the child or the teacher.

■ **Remember names and details about children.** Especially at the beginning of the year, it builds self-esteem in children when you care enough to remember not only *their* names, but the names of their pets, their family members, places they told you about, and other significant details about them. Familiarity with concrete names shows you were really listening and you really understood. When I work with children, I like to remember stories they tell me, including some of the details. I like to mention these stories to them at a later date when some statement comes up that triggers my memory. Remembering such details indicates to children that their lives were real to me and that I found these details important.

■ **Be nonjudgmental.** To a child, embarrassment translates into humiliation — picturing oneself as worthless, incompetent, and unlovable. Suppose a child accidentally spills something at snacktime. Ease any embarrassment the child might feel and help maintain self-esteem by being casual and matter-of-fact. "Oh, I have problems pouring, too. Let's clean it up together."

The goal is to remedy mistakes and accidents inconspicuously. If you notice a child has wet his pants, take him aside quietly and say, "Let's change your pants. We keep extras here because this happens to other children, too." Your acceptance, along with a smile and gentle voice, conveys nonjudgmental acceptance. The more sensitive you are to each child's feelings the safer he will feel.

■ **Find ways to share laughter.** Relationships are usually more inviting if children expect they're going to be fun, and maybe even funny. But using humor effectively requires special sensitivity toward each child.

For example, reaching a withdrawn child through humor means understanding what he may be sensitive to and what he might think is funny. Then, telling an appropriate story from the mouth of a friendly, funny puppet can establish the beginnings of a positive and enjoyable relationship.

Laughter can also be a healing force.

For some children, exaggerating a situation until it can be laughed at helps heal the wounds of embarrassment. Help children to understand that everyone makes mistakes and laughter can be healthy, helpful, and healing.

Remember, too, when you enable a child to see himself as an entertaining person, someone people enjoy being with, you contribute to his healthy self-esteem. Acknowledge a child's sense of humor and help him feel good about himself for making you and others laugh and smile.

> **"The most important thing you can give children, more important than anything material, is a sense of self-confidence."**

Dealing with Strong Emotions

Many children don't express strong emotions such as fear, sadness, anger, or loss, for fear of being overwhelmed by their emotions. These feelings are then repressed but don't go away unless they are dealt with. Other children express these feelings through emotional outbursts. They do not always know why these outbursts happened and are often embarrassed afterwards. It is important for children to have appropriate outlets for these sometimes overwhelming feelings. Here are some ways to help your children express them in healthy ways.

■ **Acknowledge a child's right to strong emotions.** Feelings are real experiences. When adults deny that children have a legitimate right to strong feelings, they are denying the children's sense of themselves as capable of being thinking, discriminating, evaluating, and honest persons. I remember one child who had been bitten by another in a nursery school. Although the skin was not broken by the bite, the teeth marks

---

7. Success comes from acknowledging the positive in a nonevaluative way.

8. Humor can be a great antidote for low self-esteem, especially when children want to get out of their depressed state quickly.

9. Children's self-esteem grows when they know that you want to share something you value with them.

10. Self-esteem thrives on success. The bridge you build for the child can provide a successful "crossing."

were clearly visible, and the child was crying. The teacher said to the child, "You're not hurt." As the child continued to cry, the teacher kept on insisting the child was not hurt.

My concern here was that the child's sense of reality was being denied. Of course the child wanted the teacher's attention, and in fact may have been more scared or angry about the bite than hurt. Instead of simply insisting, "You're not hurt," the teacher could have reflected on some of the possible feelings that were present, for example, "Maybe you're scared. Maybe you're angry. Maybe you'd like me to comfort you." Instead, the child was told *what he wasn't feeling,* which left a kind of vacuum in his sense of reality. He was being told he had no right to cry. As adults, we don't have to agree with a child's view of a situation, but we can still acknowledge the child's right to his feelings.

■ **Provide appropriate outlets for children's strong feelings.** Some children hear phrases such as, "Don't be afraid," or "Don't be sad," so often that they perceive experiencing these strong emotions, especially anger, as something akin to being bad. Others become champions of denial, not even recognizing that they are angry.

■ **Reassure frightened children with concrete facts.** When a child is very frightened about an event, your calm

"Nothing is as effective in building self-esteem as success. It even has the power to reverse a child's negative self-image."

tone, informational statements about what is predictable, and any reference you can make to what he knows to be true will be reassuring. One teacher slowly brought a sobbing child close to her and quietly asked him to breathe along with her. As children learn patterns to help them calm down, they feel more in control of their lives, strong emotions don't seem so frightening, and their esteem is enhanced.

Inviting Success

Nothing is as effective in building children's self-esteem as success. It even helps to reverse a child's negative self-image. The suggestions that follow offer ways for you to build success into children's lives by finding their existing interests and capitalizing on previous successes.

■ **Acknowledge children's accomplishments.** It's easy to forget to notice when a child does something well after the first time, for example, "Kim, you were able to put all those cans back on the shelf by yourself again today. You know, that's really great."

Giving children concrete examples of past successes is another way to build their feelings of confidence. When inviting children to learn a new skill, base your interaction on a skill that was already learned. For instance, when a child seems reluctant to use a new addition to the art table — a big container of glue — the teacher can remind the child of something he already knows about: "Do you want to try using this glue with me? Yesterday you painted at the easel, so you already know how to use a brush. The pot of glue is like a pot of paint and you can use this brush to spread it on the paper. Let's try it together."

■ **State the positive without evaluating.** Recognize what is positive and successful in a child's work or behavior, then acknowledge it by describing what you see and how you feel. Whenever possible, avoid evaluating children, their behavior, or what they do, even if your evaluation is favorable. Most typical evaluations include "right," "wrong," "good," "bad," "better," and "worse." Instead of evaluating children or their work, I have found it more success-

ful to *describe.* For instance, when children draw pictures and show them to me, instead of saying, "It's a good picture," I talk about the details of the picture. In this way the child knows that I am looking at the picture in depth. Sharing reactions to the picture encourages an interaction in the relationship, which enhances self-esteem. The same applies when children show me other things they've accomplished or made. I talk about the effort they put into the work, the choice of materials, colors, and shapes. All this is a validation and affirmation of them, not merely an evaluation of their product.

■ **Share something that belongs to you.** By allowing children to hold and touch something you have worn, you are sharing with them something you have chosen for yourself. A favored item of mine was a necklace, the pendant of which was a magnifying glass. I'd take it off and hand it to a child. He could use it to examine his skin, fingernails, clothing, or anything else that occurred to him. This magnifying glass often bridged difficult beginnings with a new child. Sometimes it even went overnight to some child's home.

Lighting the Spark

Be aware that whatever you do, you are modeling certain behaviors. Children imitate as well as draw conclusions from what they observe. As a teacher and caregiver of young children, one of your most important privileges is to invite into the world the miracle of human growth and the unique spark that is a part of every child. Within this spark lives the hidden potential in a child, waiting to be realized over a lifetime — the abilities to relate; to love and be loved; to feel alive and powerful; to be able to trust and feel compassion; to be playful and curious; to forgive mistakes and take risks; and to live a full, emotional life.

What you do to build self-esteem in each child this year not only affects that child today, but builds a foundation to nurture a person who can one day have a positive influence in the world. You *can* make a difference in a child's world.

Portions of this article were excerpted from Building Self-Esteem in Children *by Patricia H. Berne and Louis M. Savary (The Continuum Publishing Co., 1981).*

Children's Self-Esteem

The Verbal Environment

Marjorie J. Kostelnik, Laura C. Stein and Alice P. Whiren

Marjorie J. Kostelnik, Laura C. Stein and Alice P. Whiren are faculty members in the Department of Family and Child Ecology, Michigan State University, East Lansing.

Young children continually gather information about their value as persons through interactions with the significant adults in their lives (Coopersmith, 1967; Swayze, 1980). This process begins in the home but very quickly extends to the educational settings in which children participate. Thus family members, caregivers and teachers serve as the mirror through which children see themselves and then judge what they see (Maccoby, 1980). If what is reflected is good, children will make a positive evaluation of self. If the image is negative, children will deduce that they have little worth; they are sensitive to the opinions adults have of them and often adopt these as their own.

In the classroom, teachers convey either enhancing or damaging attitudes that frequently are manifested in what they say to children and how they say it. Such manifestations may or may not be the result of conscious decisions on their part. Yet teacher verbalizations are a key factor in the degree to which children perceive themselves as worthy and competent or the opposite (Kostelnik, Stein, Whiren & Soderman, 1988). Consider the following scenario:

Imagine that you are invited to visit an early childhood program in your community. You arrive early and are asked to wait in the classroom until the youngsters return from a field trip. Surveying your surroundings, you notice brightly colored furniture comfortably arranged, sunlight softly streaming through the windows, children's art work pleasingly displayed and a large, well-stocked aquarium bubbling in a corner. You think to yourself, "What a pleasant environment for children."

Just then, a child bursts into the room sobbing. She is followed by an adult who scolds, "Maria, stop that bawling." As the other youngsters file in, you hear another child exclaim, "When do we get to take our projects home?" An adult snaps, "Why can't you listen. I just said they stay here until tomorrow."

Your favorable impression is ruined. Despite the lovely physical surroundings, the way in which adults are talking to children has made the setting uninviting. You wonder whether children could ever feel good about themselves under such circumstances. What you have overheard has made you privy to an invisible but keenly felt component of every program—the verbal environment.

THE VERBAL ENVIRONMENT

Adult participants in the early childhood setting create the verbal environment. Its components include words and silence—how much adults say, what they say, how they speak, to whom they talk and how well they listen. The manner in which these elements are enacted dictates children's estimations of self-worth. Thus verbal environments can be characterized as either positive or negative.

From *Childhood Education*, Fall 1988, pp. 29-32. Reprinted by permission of Marjorie J. Kostelnik, Laura C. Stein, Alice P. Whiren and the Association for Childhood Education International, 1141 Georgia Avenue, Suite 200, Wheaton, MD. Copyright © 1988 by the Association.

Characteristics of the Negative Verbal Environment

Negative verbal environments are ones in which children are made to feel unworthy, incompetent, unlovable or insignificant as a result of what adults say or do not say to them. Most practitioners can readily identify the most extreme illustrations: adults screaming at children, making fun of them, swearing at them or making them the target of ethnic slurs. Yet there are less obvious, more common adult behaviors that also contribute to negative verbal environments:

1) *Adults show little or no interest in children's activities because they are in a hurry, busy, engrossed in their own thoughts and endeavors, or tired.* Whatever the reason, they walk by children without comment and fail to acknowledge their presence. When standing near children, they do not talk with them and respond only grudgingly to children's attempts to initiate an interaction. In addition, grownups misuse time designated for interaction with children by talking more with their colleagues than the youngsters. Rather than paying attention to children, most of the adult's time is spent chatting with other adults. Children interpret these behaviors as obvious signs of disinterest.

2) *Teachers pay superficial attention to what children have to say.* Instead of listening attentively, they ask irrelevant questions, respond inappropriately, fail to maintain eye contact or cut children off. Occasionally they simply ignore the communication altogether, saying nothing, thus treating the children as if they were not present.

3) *Adults speak discourteously to children.* They interrupt children who are speaking to them, as well as youngsters who are talking to one another. They expect children to respond to their own requests immediately, not allowing them to finish what they are doing or saying. Their voice tone is demanding, impatient or belligerent; they

neglect such social courtesies as "Excuse me," "Please" and "Thank you." In addition, their remarks often make children the butt of a group joke. Young children attend as much to the sarcastic tone of voice as to the meaning of words and are not able to appreciate the intended humor.

4) *Teachers use judgmental vocabulary in describing children to themselves and others.* Typical demeaning labels include "hyper," "selfish," "greedy," "uncooperative," "motor mouth," "stubborn," "grabby" and "klutsy." Adults say these words directly to children or to another person within the child's hearing. In either case, youngsters are treated as though they have no feelings or are invisible or deaf.

5) *Staff members actively discourage children from talking to them.* They tell children that what they are doing or saying is uninteresting or unimportant and that they should be doing or talking about something else. Thus youngsters hear admonishments like: "All right, already! I'm sick of hearing about your troubles with Rhonda; find something else to talk about." Or, "I don't want to hear one more word about it. Not one peep!" Sometimes adults put children off by saying, "Hush," "Not now" or "Tell me about it later." The "later" seldom comes.

6) *Grownups rely on giving orders and making demands as their number-one means of relating to children.* Their verbalizations consist of directions ("Sit in your chair") and admonishments ("No fighting," "Everybody get your coats off and settle down for lunch," "Stop fooling around"). Other comments that are positive in tone or content are relatively scarce.

7) *Adults ask questions for which no real answer is expected or desired.* Typical queries might include: "What do you think you're doing?" "Didn't I tell you not to stomp in the mud?" "When will you ever learn?" Regardless of how chil-

dren respond, their answers are viewed as disrespectful or unwelcome. Children soon learn that these remarks are not a real invitation to relate to the adult.

8) *Caregivers use children's names as synonyms for the words "no," "stop" or "don't."* By barking out "Tony" or "Allison" as a reprimand, adults attack the essence of the child's being, thereby causing children to associate the most personal part of themselves with disapproval and rejection. When using this tactic adults fail to describe the objectionable behavior or to clarify the reason for the negative tone of voice, thus leaving children with the notion that something is inherently wrong with them as persons.

9) *Teachers use baby talk in giving information or directions.* Instead of clearly stating, "Ruth and Toby, please put the puzzles in the puzzle rack," adults confuse and demean children by saying, "We need to put the puzzles in the puzzle rack," when they have no intention of assisting. Other kinds of baby talk involve using the diminutive form of a name (*Jackie* instead of *Jack*), even though the child and the parents prefer the other. These may be combined in particularly exaggerated ways, as when one caregiver pursed her lips and squealed in a high pitch, "How are we today, Jackie? Shall we quit crying and ride the horsie?" Such messages define children as powerless and subservient; these statements are never used between persons of equal status.

10) *Adults dominate the verbal exchanges that take place each day.* They do all the talking and allow children little time to respond either to them or their peers. Feeling compelled constantly to query, inform or instruct, they bombard children with so much talk that youngsters have few opportunities to initiate conversations on topics of their own choosing. This leaves children feeling rushed and unsatisfied.

All of the preceding verbal behaviors convey to children adult attitudes of aloofness, disrespect, lack of acceptance and insensitivity. Such encounters tend to make children feel inadequate, confused or angry (Hoffman, 1963). A different set of circumstances exists in programs characterized by a positive verbal environment.

Characteristics of the Positive Verbal Environment

In a positive verbal environment, adult words are aimed at satisfying children's needs and making children feel valued. When speaking to children, adults focus not only on content but also on the affective impact their words will have. Adults create a positive verbal environment when their verbal exchanges with children have the following attributes:

1) *Adults use words to show affection for children and sincere interest in them.* They greet children when they arrive, take the time to become engaged in children's activities and also respond to their queries. In addition, they make remarks showing children they care about them and are aware of what they are doing: "You've been really working hard to get the dinosaur puzzle together." "You seem to be enjoying that game." They laugh with children, respond to their humor and tell chidlren they enjoy being with them.

2) *Adults send congruent verbal and nonverbal messages.* When they are showing interest verbally, they position themselves near the child at a similar height from the floor, maintain eye contact and thoroughly pay attention. Other actions, such as smiling or giving a pat, reinforce praise and words of positive regard. Incongruent messages, such as following through on a limit while smiling or pinching a child's cheek hard while giving praise, are avoided.

3) *Adults extend invitations to children to interact with them.* They may say, "Here's a place for you right next to Sylvia" or "Let's take a minute to talk. I want to find out more about your day." When children seek them out, grownups accept the invitation enthusiastically: "That sounds like fun." "Oh good, now I'll have a chance to work with you."

4) *Teachers listen attentively to what children have to say.* They show their interest through eye contact, smiling and nodding. They encourage children to elaborate on what they are saying by using such statements as "Tell me more about that" or "Then what happened?" Moreover, adults pause long enough after making a comment or asking a question for children to reply, giving them time to gather their thoughts before responding. Such reactions make children feel valued and interesting.

5) *Adults speak courteously to children.* They refrain from interrupting children and allow them to finish what they are saying, either to the adult or another child. The voice tone used by adults is patient and friendly, and social amenities such as "Please," "Thank you" and "Excuse me" are part of the verbal interchange.

6) *Adults use children's interests as a basis for conversation.* They speak with them about the things youngsters want to talk about. This is manifested in two ways. First, they follow the child's lead in conversations. Second, they bring up subjects known to be of interest to a particular child based on past experience.

7) *Adults plan or take advantage of spontaneous opportunities to talk with each child informally.* In the course of a day, children have many chances to talk with adults about matters that interest or concern them. Eating, toileting, dressing, waiting for the bus, settling down for a nap and just waiting until the group is called to order are treated as occasions for adult-child conversation. Adults do not wait for special, planned time to talk with youngsters.

8) *Teachers avoid making judgmental comments about children either to them or within their hearing.* Children are treated as sensitive, aware human beings whose feelings are respected. Discussions about children's problems or family situations are held in private between the appropriate parties.

9) *Adults refrain from speaking when talk would destroy the mood of the interaction.* When they see children deeply absorbed in activity or engrossed in conversation with one another, staff members allow the natural course of the interaction to continue. In these situations they treat silence as a sign of warmth and respect and refrain from too much talk at the wrong time.

10) *Grownups focus their attention on children when they professionally engage with them.* They put off housekeeping tasks and personal socializing so that they are fully available for interaction with children. When possible, adults involve children in maintenance tasks and interact with them. In a positive environment, adults are available, alert and prepared to respond to children.

Importance of a Positive Verbal Environment

Positive verbal environments are beneficial both to the children and the adults who participate in them. In such an atmosphere, children get the message that they are important. This enhances their self-perceptions of competence and worth (Openshaw, 1978). Additionally, children's self-awareness increases as they have opportunities to express themselves, explore ideas and interact spontaneously with other children and adults (Kostelnik et al., 1988). These conditions also increase the likelihood that youngsters will view the adults in the program as sources of comfort and support. As a result, adults find it easier to establish and maintain rapport with the children. This in turn makes youngsters more receptive to the social learnings adults wish to impart to them (Baumrind, 1977; Katz, 1977). These include rules, customs and how to get along with other people.

In sum, adult behaviors that characterize a positive verbal environment are synonymous with those commonly cited as representing warmth, acceptance, respect and empathy (Coletta, 1977; Gazda, 1977; Rogers, 1961). All four of these components contribute to the relationship-building process and provide the foundation for constructive child growth and development.

Establishing a Positive Verbal Environment

Few helping professionals would knowingly act in ways that damage children's self-esteem. Observations of early childhood settings, however, show that frequently adults unintentionally slip into verbal patterns that produce the negative verbal environment described here (Kostelnik, 1978, 1987). Recent interviews with day care, Head Start, preprimary and elementary school teachers point to three common reasons why this occurs (Kostelnik, 1987):

• Adults fail to consciously consider the impact their words have on children.

• Adults get caught up in the hurried pace of the job and think they cannot take the time to have more positive verbal interactions with the children.

• Adults are not used to thinking before speaking and, as a result, say things they do not really mean and talk in ways they do not intend.

Over the years it has become increasingly clear that positive verbal environments do not happen by chance. Rather, their crea-

tion is the result of purposeful planning and implementation. Those who are successful in their efforts first recognize the characteristics of the positive verbal environment and then incorporate the corresponding behaviors into their interactions with children. The steps for achieving these results are listed below:

1) *Familiarize yourself with the features of both positive and negative verbal environments.* Reread the guidelines presented here. Think about situations from your experience that illustrate each one.

2) *Listen carefully to what you say and how you say it.* Consider how children may interpret your message. If you catch yourself using habits that are poor, correct them on the spot. Ask colleagues to give you feedback about how you sound, or carry a tape recorder with you for a short period of time as a means of self-observation.

3) *Make a deliberate decision to create a positive verbal environment.* Select one characteristic and think of how to integrate it into your daily routine. Practice such simple strategies as using children's names in positive situations, showing your pleasure in their company or inviting children to elaborate on what they say. Try these techniques one at a time, until they become second nature to you. As you become more proficient, gradually increase the number of techniques you use.

4) *Keep track of the positive verbal behaviors that you use.* Ask a colleague to help you identify positive verbal characteristics and determine how often you use them. As you substitute more positive approaches to verbal interaction for the negative ones, you will have a record of your success. Self-improvement is easier to recognize when short evaluations are carried out periodically.

5) *Give recognition to other staff members who are attempting to improve the verbal environment for children.* Words of approval and en-

couragement are as important to adults as they are to children. Progress toward any goal is made easier when others recognize both effort and achievement.

What adults say to children conveys to them messages of competence or inadequacy. Through their verbalizations teachers create a climate in their classroom that is called the verbal environment, a key factor in the degree to which children develop high or low self-esteem. Such environments are characterized as either positive or negative. Continual exposure to a negative verbal environment diminishes children's self-esteem, whereas exposure to a positive verbal environment enhances children's self-awareness and perceptions of self-worth. To ensure that the verbal environment is a positive one, teachers should consider carefully what they say to children and make purposeful attempts to follow the guidelines cited in this article. The outcome of these efforts is a classroom in which children feel good about themselves and see the teacher as a positive presence in their lives.

References

Baumrind, D. (1977). Some thoughts about childrearing. In S. Cohen & T. J. Comiskey (Eds.), *Child Development: Contemporary Perspectives.* Itasca, IL: F. E. Peacock.

Coletta, A. J. (1977). *Working together: A guide to parent involvement.* Atlanta: Humanics.

Coopersmith, S. (1967). *The antecedents of self-esteem.* Princeton, NJ: Princeton University Press.

Gazda, G. M. (1977). *Human relations development: A manual for educators* (2nd ed.). Boston: Allyn & Bacon.

Hoffman, M. L. (1963). Parent discipline and the child's consideration of others. *Child Development 34,* 573-595.

Katz, L. G. (1977). What is basic for young children? *Childhood Education 54*(1), 16-19.

Kostelnik, M. J. (1978). *Evaluation of a communication and group management skills training program for child development personnel.* Unpublished doctoral dissertation, The Pennsylvania State University.

Kostelnik, M. J. (1987). *Development practices in early childhood programs.* Keynote Address, National Home Start Day, New Orleans, LA.

Kostelnik, M. J., Stein, L. C., Whiren, A. P., & Soderman, A. K. (1988). *Guiding children's social development.* Cincinnati, OH: Southwestern.

Maccoby, E. E. (1980). *Social development—Psychological growth and the parent-child relationship.* New York: Harcourt Brace Jovanovich.

Openshaw, D. K. (1978). *The development of self-esteem in the child: Model interaction.* Unpublished doctoral dissertation, Brigham Young University, Provo, UT.

Rogers, C. R. (1961). *On becoming a person.* Boston: Houghton Mifflin.

Swayze, M. C. (1980). Self-concept development in young children. In T. D. Yawkey (Ed.), *The self-concept of the young child.* Provo, UT: Brigham Young University Press.

Avoiding "Me Against You" Discipline

? **I see why they are termed the terrible 2s. I have constant discipline problems with most of the children in my group. There are several children who give me trouble one incident on top of another. Last year I had 4-year-olds. They were not so bad, but what do you do when children *are* bad? Some of my co-workers do not seem to believe in discipline.**

Some adults see each individual child as being at this moment "good" and at that moment "bad." It all adds up to a view of a child as, overall, either a "good child" or a "bad child": She's a good girl; he's a hateful child, a really naughty boy.

Other adults, and certainly those of us well educated in child development, think differently about children. We consider all infants, toddlers, and young children *potentially* good people, naive little people with a very small amount of experience on Earth, who have much to learn, and *a great deal of motivation to please, to be accepted, to be approved, to be loved, to be cared for*. We see young children as generally recep-

tive to guidance and usually eager to "do it right." (There are exceptional instances, and they sure keep us from falling asleep on the job!)

It's hard to imagine a sensible adult who does not "believe in discipline." You don't find mainstream adults trained in child development, child psychology, early childhood education, or parenting who don't believe in discipline. How would a young child learn self-control, daily self-help and family/school life, procedures how to get along with other children, values, parents' and teachers' standards, and "right from wrong" without explanations and expectations (discipline)? How would a child develop "good character"? *Our profession believes in discipline, but rather than thinking of good versus bad children thinks of good versus bad approaches to discipline.*

● *Bad approaches to discipline* diminish a child's self-esteem, make her feel worthless, make her feel victimized, make it impossible for her to begin to feel in control of—and to take responsibility for—some aspects of her own "destiny," make her blame "them,"

make her apathetic and disengaged, make her leave it all up to "fate," and make her not even try to "be good."

● *Good approaches to discipline* increase a child's self-esteem, allow her to feel valued, encourage her to feel cooperative, enable her to learn gradually the many skills involved in taking responsibility for some aspects of what happens to her, motivate her to change her strategy rather than to blame others, help her take initiative, help her relate successfully, and help her problem solve.

Getting into a pattern of "me against you" confrontations with a crawler, toddler, or young child of any age can only lead to failure for the adult and bad news for the child's healthy emotional development.

If the adult is doling out harsh orders, humiliating insults, or sharp smacks intended to make the child *stop* doing something (touch it, climb up it), she may superficially succeed: The giant adult is three or four times as big and strong as a young child, and the adult can terrorize the vulnerable little child,

From *Young Children*, Vol. 44, No. 1 (November 1988), pp. 24-29. Copyright © 1988 by the National Association for the Education of Young Children, 1834 Connecticut Avenue, N.W., Washington, DC. Used by permission.

through the child's fear of loss of love and care, into compliance. But the adult will have *only* superficial success because each such incident in which the child's shaky, emerging sense of individuality and independence is crushed leaves him angry (he will get revenge) and leaves him with lowered self-confidence.

If the adult is attempting to make the child *start* doing something (eat, sleep, be friendly, learn), she will undoubtedly fail and feel frustrated. (You can lead a horse to water but....)

So one reason not to sink to the level of fighting with a 2-year-old is that it is not likely to work even in the short term. A second reason not to resort to frequent "no-no's," arguments, put-downs, and punishments when relating to young children is that a pattern of this treatment is permanently damaging to the child's long-term self-esteem.

Methods of discipline must seldom interfere with the lifelong need for self-esteem

The search for a sense of personal worth steers much of what well-adjusted adults do (adults who have made an *unfortunate* adjustment may have *given up* the search and settled for *low* self-esteem). The search for a sense of personal worth is of pivotal importance to teenagers in their tumultuous identity struggles and is critical in the lives of small children.

Beyond providing physical care, perhaps the main child caring job of parents and other primary caregivers is providing a feeling of self-esteem to children, from earliest infancy onward. Not only adults and adolescents, but in young children and even infants, the search for a sense of personal worth motivates much of each individual's ceaseless striving to develop and maintain meaningful attachments and meaningful work. The beginnings of a sense of being a valued individual come from loving interactions between mother and infant, and from loving interactions with other primary caregivers; *and* from encouragement of initiative and independence: Mother wants me to become myself, to make choices, to do it my way, to learn to do it acceptably without having my spirit broken. Nothing is more consistently and intimately linked to a wide variety of emotional and behavioral disturbances than is a low

opinion of oneself. Low self-esteem is always found in children/teens/adults who regularly do poorly in family life, friendships, school, jobs, and their lives in general.

Positive or negative self-image starts in infancy

Very early in an infant/toddler's development, before he or she has effective language, an embryonic ability to self-evaluate has begun to evolve. This is the capacity (to some people the curse) to assess the aggregate of one's feelings, behaviors, competencies, and relationships—to judge oneself. Even toddlers, in an intuitional way if not in a way they could explain, pervasively feel they are perceived as precious, a pest, clever, stupid, wonderful, naughty, capable, helpless, or whatever. Astonishingly early, babies develop a *sense* of self as good or as unable and unworthy. We know people who seem to have a weak sense of self; they seem not to know who they are, where they're going, what they want, or even what they have already accomplished. They do not appear to understand the coherence of their core *self*. Worse yet, we know people who have a strong sense of *negative* self: They feel that at the center of themselves they are less than equal to others, a loser, deficient, dumb, unkind, unconscientious, incapable of successes—the ultimate success being that of feeling like a lovable person.

One's self-image, at all ages, but all the more so in infancy and early childhood, is dependent upon and interconnected with the judgments of higher authorities.

Adults, in many cases, will work hard without promotions or salary increases if they get encouragement, a degree of praise, and recognition from their supervisors.

Adolescents, confused as to whether they are going to be popular and make it in life, if fortunate enough to have loving and effective parents, get a significant amount of calming, stabilizing, and focus from parental conviction that *of course* they are going to find friends and mates, *of course* they are going to make it in life. In short, teenagers' positive self-image is reinforced by their parents' positive image of them.

Children will work hard in school for their teacher's approval; under normal, nonremedial circumstances, grades and stickers are not required. At the same time that parents and teachers strive to help each child develop independence, autonomy, individuality, and satisfaction in a job well done (intrinsic reward), we know that our opinion of the child, and how we convey it to her, is a critical variable in her feeling of self-worth.

The human self is not solitary, self-contained, and completely autonomous. Human beings are social animals. We live in groups, we need each other to survive, and so we care what people think of us. Largely based on what the most significant people in our early lives think of us, we develop high, adequate, or low self-esteem.

Helping infants and toddlers develop self-esteem *and* self-discipline

We can structure our spaces at home and in the center, the schedule, diet, outings, frequency of visitors, and so on, to bring out the best in easily overwrought, easily exhausted babies and young children whose emotional and social systems quickly "short circuit" under stress. We can also structure our *own* lives to provide enough sleep, healthy food, time off, rewarding projects beyond the child, and other friends so that we can act with maxi-

Nothing is more consistently and intimately linked to a wide variety of emotional and behavioral disturbances than is a low opinion of oneself.

mum maturity—can muster maximum patience and understanding. (Because they are egocentric, young children experience grown-ups' grumpiness as disapproval of *them;* feeling constantly disapproved of leads to low self-esteem.) All this is *preventive discipline.* Nonetheless, situations calling for limits to be set, standards to be established, and desired behaviors to be encouraged will arise with mobile infants, into-everything toddlers, and increasingly independent preschoolers. Therefore, we are continuously faced with the questions: Am I disciplining in a way that hurts or helps this child's self-esteem? Am I disciplining in a way that attempts to control (to disempower) the child or in a way that attempts to develop *self*-control in the child (personal empowerment)?

Methods of discipline that promote self-worth

1. Show that you recognize and accept the reason the child is doing what, in your judgment, is the wrong thing:

"You want to play with the truck but ..."

"You like to climb but ..."

"You want me to stay with you but ..."

This validates the legitimacy of the child's desires and illustrates to the child that you are an understanding person. It also is honest from the outset: The adult is wiser, in charge, and not afraid to be the leader, and occasionally has priorities other than the child's wishes.

2. State the "but"

"You want to play with the truck

Creating a Positive Climate Promotes Self-Discipline

The stronger a child's motivation "to be good," the more effort he will exert in this direction. Therefore, there will be fewer "me against you" situations. If the child believes *you* believe he *is* good and is *capable* of learning new aspects of being good, and if he feels that you like him, he will be easier to live with.

Creating a positive climate for the very young includes
- spending lots of leisurely time with an infant or young child;
- sharing important activities and meaningful play;
- listening and answering as an equal (not as an instructor; for example, using labeling words when a toddler points inquiringly toward something, or discussing whatever topic the 2-year-old is trying to tell you about);
- complimenting the child's efforts: "William is feeding himself!" "Juana is putting on her shoe!" (even if what you are seeing is only clumsy stabs in the right direction); and
- smiling, touching, caressing, kissing, cuddling, holding, rocking, hugging.

The young child should not have to "be good" to "earn" these indicators of caregivers' enjoyment. Children should freely be given affection and approval solely because they *exist.*

Even to babies and toddlers, it's important that we say every day

"Good morning!"

"Hi" (from time to time)

"Will you play with me?" or "Let's play _____ together."

"Come with me. We will ..."

"I love you," or "You're my friend."

"Let's (sit, ride, rest, etc.) together."

"I'm glad you're in *my* (class, group, family)."

"I like to hug you."

Harmful, Negative Disciplinary Methods

1. Frequently saying, "Stop that!" "Don't do it *that* way!" "That's not so bad considering that *you* did it." "If it weren't for you, ..."
2. Criticizing
3. Discouraging
4. Creating constant obstacles and barriers
5. Blaming, shaming
6. Saying "You always ...," "You never ..."
7. Using sarcastic, caustic, and cruel "humor"
8. Physical punishment
9. Using removal from the group or isolation (the time-out chair, the corner, the child's room)

Any adult might *occasionally* do any of these things. Doing any or all of them more than once in a while means that a bad approach to discipline has become a habit and urgently needs to be addressed, analyzed, and altered before the child experiences low self-esteem as a permanent part of her personality.

but Jerisa is using it right now."
"You like to climb *but this will fall and hurt you; it's my job to keep you safe."*

"You want me to stay with you *but now I need to (go out, help Jill, serve lunch, etc.)."*
This lets the child know that others

have needs too. It teaches "perspective taking" and will lead later to the child's ability to put himself in other people's shoes. It will also gain you the child's respect; you are fair. And it will make the child feel safe; you are able to keep *him* safe.

3. Offer a solution:

"Soon you can play with the truck." One-year-olds can begin to understand "just a minute" and will wait patiently if we always follow through 60 seconds later. Two- and 3-year-olds can learn to understand "I'll tell you when it's your turn" if we always follow through within two or three minutes.

This assists children in learning how to delay gratification but is not thwarting in view of their short-term understanding of time, and teaches them to trust because you are fair.

4. Often, it's helpful to say something indicating your confidence in the child's ability and willingness to learn.

"When you get older I know you will (whatever it is you expect)."

"Next time you can (restate what is expected in a positive manner)."

This affirms your faith in the child, lets her know that you assume she has the capacity to grow and mature, transmits your belief in her good intentions, and establishes your expectation that "next time" she will do better.

5. In some situations, after firmly stating what is not to be done, you can demonstrate "how we do it," or "a better way":

"We don't hit. *Pat* my face *gently*" (gently stroke).

"Puzzle pieces are not for throwing. Let's put them in their places together" (offer help).

This sets firm limits yet helps the child feel that you two are a team, not enemies.

6. Toddlers are not easy to distract, but frequently they can be redirected to something similar but OK. Carry or lead the child by the hand, saying,

"That's the gerbil's paper. Here's Lindsay's paper."

"We don't jump in the scrub bucket. Lindsay can jump on the rug."

"Peter needs that toy. Here's a toy for Lindsay."

This endorses the child's right to choose what she will do, yet begins to teach that other people have rights too.

7. Avoid accusing. Even with babies, communicate in respectful tones and words.

This prevents lowering the child's self-image and promotes his tendency to cooperate.

8. For every "no," offer two *acceptable* choices:

"No! Rosie cannot bite Esther. Rosie can bite the rubber duck or the cracker."

"No, Jackie. That book is for teachers. Jackie can have *this* book or *this* book."

This encourages the child's independence and emerging decision-making skills, but sets boundaries. Children should *never* be allowed to hurt each other. It's bad for the hurter's self-image as well as for the self-esteem of the hurt.

9. If children have enough language, assist them in expressing their feelings, including anger, and their wishes. Assist them in thinking about alternatives and in thinking of a solution to the problem. Adults should never fear children's anger.

"You hate me because you're so very tired. It's hard to feel loving when you need to sleep. When you wake up, I think you'll feel more friendly."

"You feel terribly angry because I won't let you have candy. I *will* let you choose a banana or an an apple. Which do you want?"

This encourages characteristics we want to see emerge in children, such as awareness of feelings and reasonable assertiveness, and gives children tools for solving problems without unpleasant scenes. It shows them that we are strong, so they are safe: We will not fall apart or cave in or harm them even if their rage scares *them*.

10. Until a child is a year and a half or almost 2 years old, adults are completely responsible for his safety and comfort, and for creating the conditions that encourage "good behavior." After this age, while we are still responsible for his safety, adults increasingly, though extremely gradually, begin to transfer responsibility for behaving acceptably to the child. Adults establish firm limits and standards as needed. They start expecting the child

to become aware of other people's feelings. They begin to expect the child to think simple cause/effect (consequences) thoughts, if guided quietly through the thinking process. This is teaching the rudiments of "self-discipline."

11. When talking to children 1 year old and older, give clear, simple directions in a firm, friendly voice.

This avoids confusion, miscommunication, overwhelming a person new to the art of comprehension with a blizzard of words, and resulting refusal to comply.

12. Be aware that the job of a toddler, and to an extent the job of *all* young children, is to taste, touch, smell, squeeze, tote, poke, pour, sort, explore, and *test*. At times, toddlers are greedy, at times grandiose. They do not share well; they need time to experience ownership before they are expected to share. They need to assert themselves ("No," "I can't," "I won't," and "Do it myself"). They need to separate to a degree from their parents (individuate). One way to do this is to say *no* and not to do what is asked, or to *do* what is not wanted.

If adults understand children in this age range, they will create circumstances and develop attitudes that permit and promote development. *Development includes learning self-discipline.* It's better learned through guidance than through punishment. It's better learned through a "We are a team, I am the leader, it's my job to help you grow up" approach than it is through a "me against you," self-esteem reducing, hostility-generating approach.

* * * * *

None of us control our own destiny. Our moment in history and our geographic place, the socioeconomic circumstances of the family we happen to be born into, disabilities or extra blessings we may find ours, our genetic inheritance and birth order, whether we have dreadful, sensational, or adequate parents, educational and other opportunities available or unavailable to us, and much, much more are matters, from an individual's point of view, of good or bad luck. But the goal of a good approach to discipline is to give each child ever-increasing control of his life.

UNDERSTANDING AND ALTERING AGGRESSION

Janis Bullock

Janis Bullock is Instructor of Early Childhood Education at Montana State University in Bozeman.

One of the most difficult challenges teachers must face is successfully managing the aggressive behavior of young children. A teacher may have to deal with strong emotional feelings of one or more children while trying to come up with appropriate responses and courses of action. Trying to assist a child in finding alternative ways of interacting or attending to a hurt child can be a challenge to many teachers. Consequently, handling aggressive children can be an emotionally draining and perplexing problem.

In fact, a major problem in dealing with aggressive children is the strong feeling of anger or resentment experienced by the teacher. Learning to deal with aggression can be a manageable process for both teachers and children. Teachers who understand childhood aggression can in turn help children understand their own aggressive feelings. This understanding will provide a basis for guiding and directing children to more productive courses of action.

Different Types of Aggression

Aggression is defined generally as those behaviors that result in injury or anxiety to another person such as hitting, kicking, yelling, or verbal attacks; causing damage to property; and resisting requests (Caldwell, 1977). More specifically, aggression is defined in terms of accidental and intentional aggression (Marion, 1981). Understanding the distinctions between these types can aid in dealing with aggressive encounters among children.

ACCIDENTAL AGGRESSION.

Several children interacting in close proximity are bound to encounter accidental aggression which is incidental to the interactions. A child may knock over another child's block structure while attempting to build his own or a child's foot may be stepped on while playing ball outside. Because young children have difficulty distinguishing between accidental and intentional acts, they may react with aggression. Therefore, it is important for teachers to help children understand these differences and prevent them when possible. A teacher may say, "Brian didn't mean to knock your blocks down. He was trying to help you build and the blocks fell down," or "Lori didn't mean to step on your foot. You two were running toward the ball at the same time and it was an accident." Other types of accidental encounters might be prevented by stating clear rules to children such as, "We need to walk inside," or "Only four people are allowed in one area at a time so there is enough room to build."

INTENTIONAL AGGRESSION.

A second type of aggression is intentional aggression. Intentional aggression includes two types of aggression, instrumental and hostile in which the resulting injury is a major part of the behavior. Instrumental aggression is associated with a particular goal of the child (Marion, 1981). A child who pushes another child off of a bicycle because she wants to ride it has a clear goal in mind. In this situation, a teacher may ask herself, "What

can I teach these children so that they can better deal with the dilemma?" There are several appropriate courses of action such as, encouraging turn taking ("In 10 minutes you can give Kathy a turn"), teaching coping ("Susan really wants to ride the bike. Let's find something else for you to do until she is finished"), or modeling verbal skills for a child to use ("You've been riding the bike a long time and I would like a turn").

Hostile aggression occurs when a child injures someone because of feelings of anger. Hostile aggression may occur immediately when a child hits or shoves another child suspected of taking a toy away or may be deferred until a later time (Marion, 1981). A child who shoves and pushes another child on the playground several hours later after a morning squabble is showing deferred hostile aggression. Again, it is the teacher's responsibility to assist these children in working out their differences. This might be accomplished by encouraging the children to use assertive phrases such as "Please don't hit me," or "You can play with this toy when I'm finished."

Why Children Might Behave Aggressively

Aggression is considered one outcome of frustration. Frustration often occurs when (1) children are stopped from participating in an activity, (2) a child fails to achieve a desired goal, (3) activities are too difficult, (4) children are made to wait unnecessarily, (5) there are insufficient toys and crowded play spaces, and (6) there are unexpected changes in routines or transitions (Hildebrand, 1980).

Children respond to frustration in a

From *Day Care and Early Education*, Spring 1988, pp. 24-27. Published by Human Sciences Press. Reprinted by permission.

variety of ways. Some children may withdraw while others might cry, hit, scream, or throw temper tantrums. Encountering frustrating experiences seems to be inevitable part of growing up, therefore it is important for young children to learn to deal with their feelings in a constructive manner. Finding alternative ways of dealing with frustration may be particularly difficult for some children because of their tendency to center on one aspect of thought. Once a child decides on a course of action, it may be quite difficult to consider other options. It is important for caregivers to be sensitive to this so that they can help children understand that alternatives do exist.

Accepting and Supporting Children's Feelings

Regardless of the type of aggression a child may express, it is important to work toward an attitude of acceptance of the child. This can be a real challenge because aggression is often equated with being "bad," therefore children who are aggressive may be perceived as being "bad." Instead, it is important to recognize that aggression is often accompanied by strong feelings of frustration and anger with which children need to learn to cope.

Our intent, therefore, should not involve making children feel guilty about their feelings. Rather, it is important to concentrate on accepting children's feelings and helping them find alternate ways of expressing themselves. Feelings should never be denied, rather they must be recognized, acknowledged and treated with respect. However, this does not mean that children's aggressive acts toward another be accepted. Rather children may need assistance in finding more appropriate ways of interacting.

Because young children are egocentric and often lack basic social skills, telling children what we find unacceptable about their actions may be insufficient. Rather, children need to be taught those behaviors or actions that are more appropriate and acceptable. A teacher might first solicit more acceptable responses from the children by asking, "I see you two have a problem here. How else might you handle it instead of hitting?" Sometimes it is necessary to be more direct by stating, "I can't let you hit Dennis when you are mad, and I won't allow

anyone to hit you if they are mad," or, "When this happened to Steve and Josh this is what they did and it worked for them."

In order to respond in the most appropriate manner to young children, it helps to have an understanding of some of the reasons associated with aggression. Although several correlates have been discussed in the past such as the effects of role modeling, television, and punishment, the following discussion will focus on those aspects most important in early childhood settings.

Some Classroom Antecedents of Aggression

DAY CARE AND AGGRESSION.

Does day care precipitate aggression in young children? Some studies (Finkelstein, 1982; Haskins, 1985) are beginning to suggest that children who have been in day care centers since infancy may be more aggressive with their peers than home-reared children. Some children may not be learning the basic rules for interacting from their caregivers. These studies suggest that when children behaved aggressively, caregivers did not intervene or found it difficult to intervene. When the caregivers did intervene, however, these children were found to be no different in aggression from a control group. It may not be that children are being taught to be aggressive, but in schools with low teacher-child ratios the social needs of children are not adequately met. Children in schools need to be in groups with an adequate amount of caregivers. This means that for infants a 1:4 ratio is recommended; for toddlers it is a 1:6 ratio, and young children a 1:7 ratio (Farran, 1982). Although an appropriate child-adult ratio is essential, it is not the only factor of importance. Children need adults who are sensitive to their needs and actively guide behavior.

THE TEACHER'S STYLE AND AGGRESSION.

A teacher may unknowingly respond to a child or situation in a way which might actually facilitate or encourage aggressive behavior. In an attempt to maintain order in a classroom some teachers are overly controlling. These

authoritarian teachers are likely to have many classroom rules; value obedience, respect for authority, and order; discourage verbal exchanges; and use harsh disciplinary measures as a means of controlling aggression (Hendrick, 1984). Sometimes authoritarian teachers feel these measures are necessary to control large groups of children or to meet parental expectations.

Children's responses to the authoritarian teacher will vary. Some children, in an attempt to please the teacher, will withdraw out of fear of doing something wrong, while others may work hard at conforming in order to receive favorable feedback. Other children will attempt to challenge the teacher by engaging in inappropriate behavior such as pocketing a small toy, ruining a child's blockbuilding, or disobeying a classroom rule as a way of asserting oneself.

At the other end of the continuum are teachers who are overly permissive. These teachers are likely to be accepting of children's impulses and actions even when they may be inappropriate; use little discipline; allow children to regulate their own activities and interactions; and avoid control and order (Hendrick, 1984). Classrooms of this type are boisterous, loud, and lacking in teacher guidance.

In this situation, children are often confused about rules and limitations and may "push" a teacher until she responds in some manner. Other children soon learn that aggression pays off for them because there is no intervention to stop the act. In turn, these aggressive children may be acting as role models for less aggressive children. Permissive teachers increase the likelihood that aggression will occur by either directly or indirectly rewarding such behavior.

Still other teachers may reward or encourage aggression by behaving or acting in inconsistent ways (Hendrick, 1984). Interacting inconsistently with children actually increases aggression. A child will quickly learn that rules that are erratically enforced can be challenged. For example, a child who screams at a peer and is reminded one time to use a lower voice and ignored other times will most likely continue to use a loud voice. This intermittent reinforcement schedule used by the teacher, therefore, is likely to cause the child's behavior to persist, especially when the "payoff" is desirable.

Being consistent in the classroom involves being certain about desirable ways of guiding children's behavior and carrying through with classroom rules and requests. This will undoubtedly involve an understanding of the importance of being consistent on a child's behavior as well as a great deal of energy and patience. Therefore, when a certain rule has been established, it is important to make sure that it is clear to the children and that it is followed through.

Helping Children Deal With Aggressive Feelings

Because children learn to be aggressive, they can also learn to be cooperative. A goal of teachers should include an emphasis on interactions and expression of feelings which take into account the rights of others. Staff, teachers, and parents can work together to prevent or modify a child's aggressive tendencies in a number of ways.

Create an Environment Incompatible with Aggression

Because teachers have control over the school environment, they need to be aware of how this aspect contributes to children's behavior. Programs need appropriate resources and planning in order to prevent aggressive encounters among children. Teachers therefore need to critically evaluate the environment to determine how children are responding. Children respond more favorably to environments which offer a variety of play opportunities and choices, sufficient time to become involved in play, lots of materials, plenty of indoor and outdoor space, nutritious snacks, and appropriate climate control.

Furthermore, aggressive models can be discouraged in planning activities for young children. Toys, activities, games, and books can be chosen which emphasize cooperation. Language experiences, puppets, and dramatic play can be utilized to help children understand alternative points of view.

Provide Cooperative Role Modeling

Because children learn through modeling, it is important to provide many cooperative experiences for them. Provide children with opportunities to observe cooperative interactions and encourage their involvement. Statements such as: "I like the way you two are building together," or "When we all help with cleaning up it makes the job a lot easier," show the value of cooperation.

Help Children Understand Their Feelings

Young children are beginning to learn about feelings and how to label and express them. Consequently, angry feelings are often expressed by aggressive actions. Teachers can help children understand angry feelings as well as learn to deal with these feelings more constructively. Angry feelings are inevitable and should not be denied. Aggressive actions however should not be permitted because they are ineffective and lead to more aggression. What seems to be effective is acknowledging the angry behavior while helping children find more constructive ways of dealing with aggressive behaviors. Say: "I can see that you are really mad at Susan right now because she won't share the ball with you, but you may not pinch her. Tell her you really want a turn when she is finished."

Do Not Ignore Aggressive Acts

Occasionally an aggressive act may occur which does not result in a confrontation. For example, Chuck may push Wes because he is in his way and Wes moves quickly out of the way with no further response. This situation may be easy to ignore because neither child complained about the situation. However, ignoring aggressive encounters conveys a message to children that aggression will be tolerated and thus the act becomes reinforcing.

A teacher should intervene in this situation to make it clear that the aggressive act is unacceptable. One way to do this is to attend to the victim and help him assert himself against the attacker. "Tell Chuck how you feel about being pushed," or more directly, "Tell Chuck not to push you," lets Chuck know that his behavior is inappropriate. At the same time, the teacher is acting as an important and concerned role-model for other children who may have witnessed the encounter.

Teach Children the Value of Verbal Skills

One effective way to control aggression is to teach children to use verbal skills. Verbalizing gives children the opportunity to express themselves which often reduces aggressive acting out. Many children are unskilled in expressing themselves and benefit from coaching. We can assist children by saying, for example, "Tell Jason not to hit you because it hurts," or "Jason, use your words to tell Nick what you would like." Such statements provide children with alternate ways of coping.

Use Reasoning as a Guidance Technique

An important goal of teachers should include teaching children internalized self-control. Children who have learned inner control are more likely to control their impulses and less likely to act out. We can help children learn self-control by reasoning with them about their actions and behavior.

Instead of scolding a child at the snack table who grabs most of the fruit before other children have had their share, the child may be reminded, "When you take most of the fruit other children do not get their share and are hungry." Reasoning with the child rather than punishing helps the child understand and accept responsibility for the inappropriate behavior. The child then is able to change the behavior without fear of punishment.

Use Time-Out Procedures Sparingly

One way of dealing with children who are acting in inappropriate ways is to "time them out" by having them sit in a chair for two to three minutes or separating them from the scene and allowing them to come back "when they are ready to play again." Although these techniques often appear to work, they do little in the way of teaching self-control or social skills. These procedures are often used in place of teaching children alternate ways of dealing with aggression.

Maintain Contact With Parents

There are often many factors that contribute to aggression in children. Although there is much that teachers can do to alleviate aggression in the classroom, they alone should not be responsible. The family, peers, media, and community all contribute to children's aggressiveness or lack of it. By maintaining contact with parents teachers are showing them that they are concerned about their child and value their input. Teachers can communicate and share their concerns in a number of ways.

When a particular child is behaving aggressively over a period of time, it helps to document the behavior, the particular strategies used and the outcomes. Teachers can then share this information with parents as well as elicit some of their suggestions, such as "I am interested in how you might handle this situation." This provides insights to how the parent might deal with the situation and allows us to suggest additional strategies if necessary.

Most parents are genuinely interested in learning about more effective ways of interacting with their children. Teachers can assist parents by planning a meeting and inviting a child development specialist or psychologist to speak and address particular concerns. Parents can be urged to discuss ideas that work for them. Providing parents with resources such as bibliographies, a lending library, examples of toys which promote cooperation, short articles on how children learn aggression, or the effects of television and aggression are greatly appreciated.

Make Referrals When Necessary

Although these are several strategies useful for teachers, occasionally a situation may arise where a child does not respond to guidance techniques and little change is apparent over time. The concerned parent may be pushing the teacher to work harder with the child or asking for additional suggestions on how to handle the child at home. Teachers may feel uncomfortable coming up with readymade advice. In fact, teachers should not be acting as a therapist or parent educator, if this is not their training.

In this case, teachers should acknowledge their concern to parents and suggest additional resources. A professional teacher should take the time to compile a list of resources from the community which can be shared with parents. This information should include a variety of carefully screened services such as mental health clinics; child, family, and marriage counselors; psychologists; and developmental screening clinics.

Summary

Aggression in children is precipitated by a variety of events. Because of this, it is difficult to develop a neat, orderly plan to prevent and control aggression. Rather, the preceding strategies have been suggested because they are generally effective in altering behavior in the classroom. Teachers who use these suggestions will help children develop more appropriate ways of interacting and will feel more competent in their role.

REFERENCES

Caldwell, B. M. (1977). Aggression and hostility in young children. *Young Children, 32,* 4-13.

Farran, D. (1982). Now for the bad news. *Parents,* 80-82, 145.

Finkelstein, N. W. (1982). Aggression: Is it stimulated by day care? *Young Children, 37,* 3-9.

Haskins, R. (1985). Public school aggression among children with varying day care experiences. *Child Development, 56,* 689-703.

Hendrick, J. (1984). *The whole child.* St. Louis: Time Mirror/Mosby.

Hildebrand, V. (1980). *Guiding young children* (2nd Ed.). New York: Collier MacMillian Publishers.

Marion, M. (1981). *Guidance of young children.* St. Louis: the C. V. Mosby Company.

Curricular Applications

- **Creating and Inventing (Articles 27-29)**
- **Emergent Literacy (Articles 30-31)**
- **Motor Development (Articles 32-33)**
- **Content and Process (Articles 34-36)**

Unlike the job of a secondary teacher who concentrates on one academic area, the job of an early childhood teacher is to meet the needs of a young child in many different areas. Hendrick (1990) looks at the child as five different selves that combine to form the whole child. It is the job of the teacher of young children to plan developmentally appropriate activities to meet the physical, emotional, social, creative, and cognitive selves of the young child. Only then can the curriculum truly be centered on the children and appropriate for their growth and development.

Contrary to popular opinion, greater professional expertise and effort are required to plan, monitor, and evaluate a play-based cooperative learning program for young children (which provides activities that encourage healthy development of the five selves of the child) than a program that is teacher-directed and contains many sit-and-listen activities. There are many commercial kits and packaged curriculum guides that can be purchased that suggest everything from activities for group time on a particular day to dittoed sheets for the children to color for "creative art." The problem with these teaching aids is they are generic and do not meet the developmental needs of children of varying levels or in one specific program, but are intended for all children in general. The teacher's job is to read the lesson from the printed sheet provided for each day. Many commercial curricula use the popular theme "Winter" and plan activities centered around snow and wintertime activities. Teachers in Maine as well as Alabama may use the same plan on any given day. It is difficult for a child in Alabama, sitting in shorts and a short-sleeved shirt, to be excited about gluing torn tissue pieces which are to resemble snow onto a dittoed picture of a snowman.

Teachers who plan localized curricula and have an understanding of the life-styles of the children in their class are better able to develop a true working relationship with the young children in their care and their families. Teachers sensitive to the different ways families spend money, occupy themselves during leisure time, or relate to school personnel are able to affect the relationship between home and school.

Teachers often devote a great deal of thought and time to planning activities and selecting materials in which the children can participate during free choice or discovery time. A teacher may run all around town getting colored cotton balls, donated banana split and float dishes, and pom-pom balls from the fabric store to use in an ice cream parlor, or stack boards, tires, and hoops in a pile for the children to arrange while creating an obstacle course but never give a thought as to how to help children and parents separate at the beginning of the day, or how to dismiss children from group time. Routine day-to-day activities such as arriving, snack, toileting, and nap, as well as transition times, may encompass over 75 percent of the time a child is in a program, but these are often not recognized as being an important part of the child's day. Teachers spend time planning for the 60 to 90 minutes of free choice or discovery time in the morning, which is a very small percentage of time a child is at a full-day center. The rest of the day deserves the same comprehensive and child centered planning.

Time children spend in appropriate large muscle development is time well spent when one reads the numerous research studies detailing the inferior physical condition of children in America today. As noted above, teachers often are so focused on planning for the brief choice time each morning, which often centers on creative and cognitive activities, that gross motor development is left to the 30 minutes of free time spent running around on a poorly equipped and unsafe playground. The National Survey of Playground Equipment in Preschools concludes that preschool playgrounds are dangerous and require much-needed attention to improve the quality of experiences children gain while outside.

Playing with materials and language is the way the young child conquers the world of objects and symbols and constructs knowledge about their properties. Part of the teacher's role is to provide information to parents on the benefits of play in the young child's development. Thus, developing a philosophy for and implementing an early childhood program that focuses on the developmental needs of young children requires, in addition to time and money, a thorough knowledge of how to select play materials and media for children of differing ages, abilities, and backgrounds. It also means teachers are responsible for sharing with parents the ways in which their children spend their day and the activities in which they participate. If the only concrete evidence parents receive of their child's day are pictures done at the easel or collages made from stickers, chalk, and feathers, they will continue to see art as the only creative endeavor in which their child can participate and not see the value in blocks, puppets, movement, or music. Teachers must show they appreciate and value creative endeavors made with non-expendable as well as expendable materials.

When children begin to communicate through print, they are embarking upon one of the most challenging yet rewarding skills one can develop. The young child who writes; "One sapona time petr pan savd wende from the pirets," should be encouraged to continue to put words on paper, not discouraged from creative writing by being told to only use words he knows how to spell correctly. Teachers who are aware of steps children take in emergent literacy recognize the unique skills children bring to the reading process and capitalize upon their eagerness for learning and their insatiable appetite for encouragement while they are learning.

The reader will note there are two articles on play and two on kindergarten curriculum in this unit. "Learning to Play: Playing to Learn" and "Conceptualizing Today's Kindergarten Curriculum" are included for the student who has had some prior experience with young children and reading literature. "Creative Play" and "How Good Is Your Kindergarten Curriculum?" have broader appeal to a wide variety of readers.

Looking Ahead: Challenge Questions

What do young children actually learn by playing? How can play materials be evaluated for their contribution to children's development?

What are some ways teachers can plan effectively for times during the day when children are engaged in daily routines such as arrival, toileting, and mealtime?

How can teachers demonstrate to parents and children that all types of creative endeavors are valued?

What are the benefits of invented or temporary spelling in assisting the child to become literate?

What are fundamental movement skills, and how can they be enhanced in the early childhood setting?

What are the components of a quality kindergarten curriculum? How can they best be implemented?

How can local issues affect the curriculum offered in a kindergarten?

What needs to be done to make many of the play-gounds in America today safe for all children to use?

Learning to Play: Playing to Learn

Pauline Davey Zeece and Susan K. Graul

Have you ever heard comments such as "In this program we focus on learning — *not* playing" or "Is this a day care program where children learn or play?" At a time when the importance of early life experiences has gained public attention, there is the temptation to overlook or at least misunderstand the value and importance of play.

Pauline Davey Zeece and Susan Graul are at the Department of Human Development and the Family, University of Nebraska - Lincoln, Lincoln, NE.

For many decades, play has been considered an integral part of childhood (Rubin, Fein, & Vanderberg, 1983; Smilansky, 1968). As such, it serves vital functions by integrating and balancing all aspects of human functioning (Rogers & Sawyer, 1988). Through play, young children gain mastery over their bodies, discover the world and themselves, acquire new skills, and cope with complex and conflicting emotions (Bruner, 1972; Papalia & Olds, 1986; Rubin et al., 1983; Vygotsky, 1976). This makes play an important part of early childhood programming. Play is one of the most effective ways children learn about their ever-changing world.

In a historical overview, Christie (1985) concluded that caregivers' and teachers' attitudes toward their role in children's play have changed since the 1960s. Before 1960, adults assumed not only that play was trivial, but that interference in children's play was not beneficial (Sutton-Smith, 1986). However, Smilansky's 1968 study provided evidence that play training impacted on the quality of children's play and enhanced various areas of their cognitive development. It was gradually accepted that intervening in children's play could be beneficial to children in many ways.

Importance of Play

Defining Play

Exact definition of *what* constitutes children's play appears to be more difficult to determine than recognition of *when* children are actually playing. Although a universal agreement on the definition of play has not yet been established, Rubin and colleagues (1983) identified six criteria from the research literature that characterize children's play behavior:

1. *Play is intrinsically motivat-motivated.* Children play because they want to and not because they are required by adults to act in certain ways. Thus, the motivation for engaging in play behavior comes from the child, rather than the adult (Gottfried, 1985; Rogers & Sawyer, 1988).

2. *Play involves attention to the means rather than the end.* Because behavior during play is most often spontaneous, children's play may begin as a make-believe trip to the moon, change to racing cars, and end in making spaghetti. The focus of play is on the activity rather than the end product.

3. *Play is dominated by the child.* Children gain a sense of mastery and self-worth in play because they are in control. When playing, children can become a mommy or a monster, a dancer or a doctor, or even a child care teacher! In addition, objects may perform magic (e.g., "This is my shield, no one can get me now" or "My doll can fly").

4. *Play is related to instrumental behavior.* Children may appear to "shoot" a gun when they pick up a block and yell "bang." Actually, they are only pretending to shoot. The key to this characteristic of play is pretense. Pretense helps to widen chil-

From *Day Care and Early Education*, Fall 1990, pp. 11-15. Published by Human Sciences Press, 72 Fifth Avenue, New York, NY 10011. Reprinted by permission.

dren's perspectives and lessen their egocentrism (Grusec & Lytton, 1988).

5. *Play is not bound by formal rules.* Unlike games, the flexibility of real play allows young children to change rules as they interact. A stool may be a table one minute and a bed the next. In the first instance, the "rule" of play would dictate children to eat from the stool; in the second instance, they would sleep on it.

6. *Play requires active participation.* Unlike daydreaming, play requires children to move and create. Thus, behaviors are considered play only when children engage in them actively.

In addition to these six criteria of play, there are several developmental characteristics of young children's play which impact on their overall growth.

Understanding Developmental Characteristics of Play

Play stimulates children's thinking. The value of play can be conceptualized in cognitive terms (Butler, Gotts, & Quisenberry, 1978). To study the relationship between thinking and play, Smilansky (1968) developed one of the most widely used descriptions of children's cognitive levels of play. Accordingly, it was proposed that children's activities are directly related to the way they think as they play. Thus, activities may be categorized by cognitive levels which include functional, constructive, and dramatic play, as well as games with rules.

In *functional* play, children use their bodies to practice and test their physical limits and to explore the immediate environment. Children try a wide variety of new actions through the use of imitation. Even very young infants engage in functional play as they first entertain themselves with things as simple as watching their own hands move. Later, children engage objects as they use their bodies in this kind of play. Functional play consistently occurs in solitary and parallel social play situations and declines as children get older (Hetherington, Cox, & Cox, 1979; Rubin, Maroni, & Hor-

nung, 1976: Rubin, Watson, & Jambor, 1978).

Constructive play is the most common form of cognitive play activity used by preschool children (Rubin et al., 1983). Children manipulate objects to construct or create. From manipulating materials, children learn various uses for them. By learning to use materials effectively, young children see themselves as the creators of events. This gives them a sense of confidence in themselves and a feeling of power in an otherwise adult-controlled environment.

Dramatic play begins around the age of two. It includes role playing and/or make-believe activities (Rubin et al., 1983). For example, a child may pretend to be a firefighter, a chef, or a cat. When such activities are supported, dramatic play develops social tendencies in children and allows them to act simultaneously as actors, observers, and participators in a common endeavor (Smilansky, 1968).

The most sophisticated form of dramatic play is sociodramatic play, which emerges around three years of age. This play depends on the child's ability to talk and provides for the recreation of real-life happenings. Children assume roles they have learned from experiences with adults and other children. Many experts believe that participation in sociodramatic play is critical to cognitive, as well as social, development (Golomb & Cornelius, 1977; Rubin et al., 1983; Smilansky, 1968).

The fourth kind of cognitive play is *games with rules.* This play typically does not begin until children are school-aged and continues through adulthood. Children must be able to control their behavior, actions, and reactions to play games with rules effectively (Piaget, 1962; Rubin et al., 1983). This may explain why preschoolers so often cry, pout, or even cheat when they try to participate in formal games with stringent rules.

Play enhances language development. The effects of play on verbal cognition and language development are found throughout the research lit-

erature (Levy, 1984; Rubin et al., 1983). For example, Bruner (1983) found that children use some of the most complicated grammatical forms of speech while playing. Play also provides a safe way to try out new words and phrases and to experiment with their meanings and usage.

Play promotes the acquisition of verbal forms of interpersonal contacts which precede thought and writing (Garvey & Hogan, 1973). Children learn not only the words but the nuance of language that is so important in human communication. They enjoy playing with the sounds and rhythms of language and connecting these to the words and reactions of others.

Play provides an arena for social learning. In play, the way children group themselves among their peers is referred to as the *social level of play.* As children become older and more mature, their play becomes increasingly more complex, and the social level of their play changes (Johnson, Christie, & Yawkey, 1987; Parten, 1932; Rogers & Sawyer, 1988; Smilansky, 1968). In social play, activities may be ordered from those which require the least amount of involvement to those which require the most. There is an increase in interactive play as children become older.

Infants' first social play usually involves interacting with an adult. In this play, each participant is intently involved with the other. The adult and infant exchange sounds and smiles in a turn-taking system which is sometimes called the beginning of social conversation (Rogers & Sawyer, 1988). As infants become older (i.e., between 6 and 18 months), they spend less time with adults and more time with objects (Rogers & Sawyer, 1988). Around the age of two and through the preschool years, children become increasingly involved in social play with peers. Through social play, preschool children are eventually able to repeat their own behavior, understand and imitate their peers' behavior, get the attention of others, and engage in social interaction (Rogers & Sawyer, 1988; Smith & Vollstedt, 1985).

More than a half century ago, Parten (1932) developed one of the most elaborate categorizations of children's social play. Based on observations of children in free play in a nursery school setting, Parten arrived at six play categories: solitary, parallel, associative, cooperative, unoccupied, and onlooking.

In *solitary* play, children play alone and independent of those around them. They play with materials that are different from those used by other children in the immediate playing area. The key to this play rests in the notion that children center their interest on their own play when they play alone (Parten, 1932).

Closely related to this type of play is *parallel* play. In parallel play, children play independently with similar objects and side by side with other children. They do not attempt to play with other children or to control those who came into or leave the play area. However, the activities that children choose in parallel play naturally bring them closer to other playing children (Parten, 1932).

Children interact with one another in *associative* play. They engage in similar, if not identical, activities, but there is no clear division of labor or organization. Children do not impose their individual ideas on the group, and each child plays as he or she wishes. Yet there is overt recognition by the playing children of common interests and relationships (Parten, 1932).

In *cooperative* play, one or two children assume the role of leader. This encourages a marked sense of belonging or not belonging to the group. Leaders control the play by directing and assigning roles and telling other children what needs to happen in the play (e.g., "I'll be the dad and you be the baby" or "That can't be the car; the car only runs here"). Play leaders change frequently, just as play itself changes. Thus, children may take on a variety of responsibilities or roles as they engage in cooperative play (Parten, 1932).

Finally, young children may not always be directly involved in play. Instead, they may stand back and watch other children play or may simply watch anything that happens to be of interest to them at a certain time (Rogers & Sawyer, 1988). This kind of play is referred to an *unoccupied* or *onlooking* play behavior. The onlooking child spends time watching others play; the unoccupied child participates in a variety of nonplay behaviors (Parten, 1932).

Play allows for testing of feelings and emotions. As young children learn to play, they learn social rules and test the limits of permissible behavior without getting into trouble (Grusec & Lytton, 1988). They are able to make "mistakes" without punishment and to interpret the reactions of others in safe ways.

In play, children also learn to deal with emotionally overwhelming experiences by re-creating them in their minds and play (Erikson, 1963). For example, children may play monster when they are afraid of the dark, tiny baby when they are anxious about the arrival of a new sibling, or child care provider when they are unsure of a change in child care arrangements. Additionally, play affords young children a safe way to say such things as "I hate you" or "Go away!"

Play also allows an avenue for the expression of positive feelings and emotions. Children may re-create happy times and special events; they may become their own heroes or heroines. In such sociodramatic play, children explore new roles and are helped to see things from others' point of view. They begin to understand the needs and feelings of others by acting these out in their play.

Optimizing Children's Play: The Adult Role

Although children may play without adult intervention, the quality of their play may be enhanced by adults. This occurs best when adults understand that play is learning for children, advocate for play in early childhood education programming, model play for children, and create an environment that optimizes play experiences.

Understanding That Play Is Learning for Children. One of the most effective ways to enhance children's play is to understand the critical role it assumes in all areas of development. As they play, children use their minds and their senses to explore and learn. They make meaningful and exciting discoveries: banging pan lids together creates sounds or echoes; being the "boss" is difficult at times; building high structures with small blocks is tricky; finishing the last piece of a difficult puzzle is wonderful. Children learn when they play — and they learn in ways that will ideally sustain them throughout their entire life. Understanding all of this creates an attitude of support for play in young children's lives. Play is learning for children.

Advocating the Importance of Play to Others. Advocacy for play begins with accurate information about its effect on children. If parents, providers, and policymakers are not well informed, young children may be pushed to excel in "academics" (i.e., flashcards and worksheets) at the expense of developmentally appropriate learning (Bredekamp, 1986; Elkind, 1986). But with accurate information about the role of play in development, programs and curricula may be developed and implemented in ways which foster optimal growth. Children need adults to advocate for the importance of play.

Modeling Play for Children. The need to play continues throughout the life span. Although the props and language of play may change as children age, the goal of play is similar for all living beings. Play functions as a release of feelings and an avenue for learning. It acts as a mechanism by which affective and cognitive energies may be renewed. When adults engage in the play of children, they commit to a mutual and unique sharing with the children entrusted to their care.

Thus, modeling play becomes an important job for adults. Children may need adults to help them initiate play or to enter a play group. They may require encouragement to negotiate the language or rules of play. Others may need to play with adults. However, it is important that adults not interfere with or dominate spontaneous play behaviors. Thus, modeling entails an understanding of developmental and individual differences in children, as well as insight into the situations which surround their play.

Creating an Environment Conducive to Play. Greenman (1988) suggests that an environment is an ever-changing system. More than the physical space, it includes the way time is structured and the roles people are expected to play. It conditions how children and adults feel, think, and behave; it dramatically affects the quality of living. A well-conceptualized environment is critical to children's play. Therefore, it ideally provides children with opportunities for decision making, motor, social, and cognitive skill development (Weinstein & David, 1987).

There are many ways adults can contribute to the development of an effective play environment for young children. Some of these include:

1. *Using a variety of play materials.* The environment should include a variety of materials (e.g., puzzles, blocks, play dough, and books), with the quantity of materials great enough so children need not wait to begin playing. Children in transitional and nonplay behavior often become bored or restless. Age-appropriate variety and quantity of materials reduce the opportunities for off-task behavior.

2. *Ensuring accessibility of toys.* Toys located on low, open shelves create an atmosphere where children are free to move about the room without total dependence on adults. If children feel in control of their playing environment, they begin to become independent in their actions and to develop an internal ability to act autonomously.

3. *Promoting diversity in play.* Children enjoy engaging in a variety of activities with each one, ideally leading to developmental gain. To foster a variety of interests and play behaviors, children need access to art

materials, dramatic play props, blocks, and manipulative toys.

Art materials (e.g., scissors, markers, crayons, scraps of paper and materials, collage materials, glue, and tape) should be out and accessible to children at all times. Providing this opportunity encourages children to be creative on their own timetable. It supports the notion that art is creation and not craft.

Dramatic play props should be changed frequently and related to children's real-life experiences. It may be useful to store dramatic play materials in easily movable prop boxes whose contents can be continually added to over time. These different props allow children to role play a variety of life experiences and to determine how these experiences affect them.

The block area is one of the spaces in which dramatic play is most likely to occur. Ideally, it should be filled with interesting props to complement block play. Children enjoy being challenged with many blocks. Thus, it is better to rotate a large set of blocks and props between two groups or programs than to divide the blocks into smaller sets.

Providing children with three-dimensional objects to manipulate enhances their interest in and curiosity about the world. Children seek more information about objects they are allowed to touch, compared to those they are not allowed to touch. Thus, question asking among young children can be maximized by the thoughtful placement of manipulatable objects in children's environment. The use of such material does not need to be limited to a table or counter. Many children enjoy playing on the seat of a chair, an overturned box, or even the floor. The trick is to conceptualize all areas in an environment as potential, usable space.

4. *Structuring traffic patterns.* Environments need to provide not only a variety of play materials, but also a variety of play spaces organized to define play areas. An environment should have open spaces for such things as block building and other

construction; small and cozy places for reading books, talking to a friend, or being alone; and clearly defined areas for manipulative, art, and dramatic play. Traffic patterns should allow children to have a sense that what they are doing will not be interrupted or destroyed by passing children and adults.

5. *Allocating time effectively.* Transition times should be minimal between play activities. Planning for children should be built around their need to play, rather than using play to "fill in" gaps in planning. Young children require long periods of time to play because it often takes them awhile to organize and begin their play activities. Without considerable blocks of time to play, children may not be able to follow through to the end of their play activity.

6. *Facilitating a positive atmosphere.* The environment includes not only physical and temporal components, but also interpersonal ones. When adults demonstrate mutual regard for one another and communication is positive, the feeling within the environment will be one of support and encouragement for everyone. When relationships between adults break down, children may sense tension or stress. This may make it difficult for children to communicate, create, and play constructively.

Conclusion

Quality play is not a luxury but a necessity in the lives of young children. With adult support, children's play becomes a catalyst for optimal growth and development. Play contributes to learning and cognitive maturity as children consolidate what they know with what they are learning as they play. Indeed, children play to learn as they learn to play!

References

Bredekamp, S. (Ed.). (1986). *Developmentally appropriate practice.* Washington, DC: National Association for the Education of Young Children.
Bruner, J. (1972). The nature and uses of immaturity. *American Psychologist, 27,* 687-708.

Bruner, J. (1983). Play, thought, and language. *Peabody Journal of Education, 60*, 6-69.

Butler, A., Gotts, E., & Quisenberry, N. (1978). *Play as development.* Columbus, OH: Charles E. Merrill.

Christie, J. F. (1985). Training of symbolic play. *Early Child Development and Care, 19*, 43-52.

Elkind, D. (1986). Formal education and early childhood education: An essential difference. *Phi Delta Kappan,* pp. 631-636.

Erikson, E. (1963). *Childhood and society.* New York: Norton.

Garvey, C., & Hogan, R. (1973). Social speech and social interaction: Egocentrism revisited. *Child Development, 44*, 565-568.

Golomb, C., & Cornelius, C. (1977). Symbolic play and its cognitive significance. *Developmental Psychology, 13*, 246-247.

Gottfried, A. (1985). Intrinsic motivation for play. In C. C. Brown & A. W. Gottfried (Eds.), *Play interactions: The role of toys and parental involvement in children's development* (pp. 45-52). Skillman, NJ: Johnson & Johnson.

Greenman, J. (1988). *Caring spaces, learning places.* Redmond, WA: Exchange Press.

Grusec, J., & Lytton, H. (1988). *Social development: History, theory, and research.* New York: Springer-Verlag.

Hetherington, E. M., Cox, M., & Cox, R. (1979). Play and social interaction in children following divorce. *Journal of Social Issues, 35*, 26-49.

Johnson, J. E., Christie, J. F., & Yawkey, T. D. (1987). *Play and early childhood development.* Glenview, IL: Scott Foresman.

Levy, A. (1984). The language of play: The role of play in language development. *Early Child Development and Care, 17*, 49-62.

Papalia, D., & Olds, S. (1986). *Human development* (3rd ed.). New York: McGraw-Hill.

Parten, M. B. (1932). Social participation among pre-school children. *Journal of Abnormal and Social Psychology, 24*, 243-269.

Piaget, J. (1962). *Play, dreams, and imitation in childhood.* New York: Norton.

Rogers, C., & Sawyer, J. (1988). *Play in the lives of children.* Washington, DC: National Association for the Education of Young Children.

Rubin, K. H., Fein, G. G., & Vanderberg, B. (1983). Play. In E. M. Hetherington (Ed.), *Handbook of child psychology* (pp. 693-774). New York: Wiley.

Rubin, K. H., Maroni, T. L., & Hornung, M. (1976). Free play behaviors in middle- and lower-class preschoolers: Parten and Piaget Revisited. *Child Development, 47*, 414-419.

Rubin, K. H., Watson, K., & Jambor, T. (1978). Free play behaviors in preschool and kindergarten children. *Child Development, 49*, 534-536.

Smilansky, S. (1968). *The effects of sociodramatic play on disadvantaged preschool children.* New York: Wiley.

Smith, P., & Vollstedt, R. (1985). On defining play: An empirical study of the relationship between play and various criteria. *Child Development, 56*, 1042-1050.

Sutton-Smith, B. (1986). The spirit of play. In G. Fein & H. Rivkin (Eds.), *Reviews of research: The young child at play* (Vol. 4). Washington, DC: National Association for the Education of Young Children.

Vygotsky, L. S. (1976). Play and its role in the mental development of the child. In J. Bruner, A. Jolly, & K. Sylva (Eds.), *Play — Its role in development and evolution* (pp. 537-554). New York: Basic Books.

Weinstein, C., & David, T. (1987). *Spaces for children: The built environment and child development.* New York: Plenum Press.

CREATIVE PLAY

—

CHILDREN

LEARN...

ADULTS DO,

TOO!

—

SANDRA WAITE-STUPIANSKY

Sandra Waite-Stupiansky is an assistant professor at the Center for Teacher Education at the State University of New York at Plattsburgh.

Laura and David, building next to one another, decide to join their structures to make one big building. Branching out, they reach Larissa's "territory," and after an involved discussion, succeed in getting her to join their play. At the same time, Peter and Nicky hurry out of the dramatic-play area to make a sign for their new clothing store, letting everyone know the shop is ready for business. Miguel stands immersed in his art at the easel, while Katya announces that she has successfully balanced not one, but two objects on the raft that she's making at the water table.

The room is alive with creative play! Children are inventing, pretending, negotiating, and involved. What fosters this creative energy? Opportunities—for children to originate their own themes, generate their own solutions, and come up with unique uses for materials. Creative play happens when children engage in activities because they have chosen to do so—when the *process* of playing is regarded by adults as more important than any product or end result—during free-play time.

WHAT DO CHILDREN LEARN FROM PLAY?

Through play, children develop emotionally, socially, cognitively, physically, and of course, creatively. Because their play is alive with social interaction, young children learn about the power of words, practice cooperation and negotiation skills, and realize that the perspectives of others are different from their own. Free play gives children time and opportunities to explore creatively, using their imaginations to experiment with reality, and to learn about themselves and their worlds. Whether children are involved in creating a painting, examining an anthill, or acting out the drama of going to the dentist, during free play they make choices, solve problems, plan what they are going to do, and feel a sense of control.

RECORDING YOUR OBSERVATIONS

Observational records of children's creative play can be a wonderful source of information to share with parents, as well as other adults who are working with children now and who will in the future. Here are a few guidelines to help you master techniques so that you can record play observations easily.

● **Start by observing a small group of children.** Rather than trying to record something about every child every day, select one or two children to focus on closely each day. For instance, if two adults are responsible for a group of twelve children, divide the group in half. Each adult can be the primary recorder for six children. (Try to record at least one observation a week for each of your six.)

● **Watch for episodes that indicate growth or skills in each of the developmental levels — social, emotional, cognitive, creative, and physical.** Then over the course of a year, you will have a rich source of information as each child changes and develops.

● **Keep a pencil and paper handy.** Tuck a small pad of paper and a pencil in a roomy pocket or handy place. You never know when a bit of dialogue or a fascinating comment will come from a child. You may be walking to the duck pond or sitting at the lunch table when a child says something or makes an observation that gives you insight into his or her development or presents an example of growth.

● **Keep observations objective and nonjudgmental.** Record exactly what happened as if you were a video camera. Avoid using any words that express an opinion. Rather than write, "His painting was beautiful," or "She was being lazy," use objective, descriptive language such as, "He selected a variety of colors for his painting — blue for the hair, red for the eyes, and green for the mouth." or "She sat in the corner of the block area for approximately 15 minutes watching the other children." When possible, include actual examples of art work and dialogue.

● **Keep observational records organized and in a common place.** You may want to use a notebook or file box for your records, adding new entries as soon as possible. Naptime and after children leave are good times to routinely add your latest observations. Because observations are recorded without opinions they can be easily shared with staff members and parents.

● **To make sure your observations are well-rounded, take time to read over previous ones.** Because you want to develop a profile of the whole child, check to see whether your observations tend to focus on a particular time of the day or tap only one or two specific areas of development. If so, consciously look for episodes that focus on areas of development you've missed, making observations in a number of settings, such as small and large group and individual play, and at structured and unstructured times. As the year progresses, patterns of behavior may become apparent such as the times of day when a child is particularly lethargic or unusually energetic.

● **Include relevant information.** All records need to have the date of the observation, the name of the person making the observation, location, other children involved, and if possible, verbatim conversations. (Also note whether any information should remain confidential such as the name of the victim in a biting incident.)

● **Know what to look for.** Finally, it is important to know what you are looking for in children's play and interactions. Signs of cognitive reasoning, social competence, and creative thinking abound. You can be a connoisseur of play by recognizing the subtle and natural clues children share about themselves as they play with one another.

During free play children make decisions — where to play, what and with whom to play, and where the play will lead. Social, emotional, cognitive, and physical growth take place before your eyes as children learn to negotiate, cooperate, compromise, and accept limits. Close observation can provide rich insights into individual children's development. Here are suggestions of what to look for and why.

Social Development - Observations of children's play can provide invaluable tools in identifying a child who is having difficulties with social development. When children have recurring difficulties interacting, plan to help by fostering healthy conflict resolution skills.

Emotional development - It is within the context of play that self-concepts can be recognized and nurtured. If you sense and observe that certain children are feeling rejected or less capable, observations can help you find special qualities and accomplishments to warmly acknowledge. Remember, children who are consistently successful also need your recognition. Because you are observing behaviors, you can praise their efforts, too.

Language Development - Language is involved in most play, as children learn to manipulate words to achieve their goals and to express their desires. Because young children tend to see the world in egocentric terms, disagreements are often a part of their play. By observing, you can learn how individual children use language to resolve conflicts, negotiate objects and territories, and make their points of view known to others. Observations can help you identify which children may still need help using words to express their thoughts and feelings.

Cognitive development - Whether playing in a group or by themselves, children display their abilities to order their physical and social worlds, try out new ideas, speculate on outcomes, alter plans, etc. Consider the cognitive thinking that goes into block construction. You may see a child experiment with one-to-one correspondence as she builds identical walls; explore spatial relationships as she builds a bridge; estimate which of the long blocks will span the gap by trying this one or that. Observations such as these provide clues as to how you can help to expand her growing repertoire of concepts and abilities.

Physical development - Fine-motor and gross-motor skills develop as children play. Assess the pace of physical development as they ride tricycles, climb on jungle gyms, fingerpaint, etc. Frustration with motor skills often surfaces as children go about their play. Set up their environments so children experience physical challenges one step at a time.

Diana Scarselletta-Straut received her master's degree from the State University of New York at Plattsburgh. Her master's thesis was on observing children's social play. She collaborated with Sandra Waite-Stupiansky on this portion of the article.

SETTING THE STAGE FOR CREATIVE PLAY

Some play areas just call out: Come be creative here! What is it about these spaces children find so inspiring and alluring? First of all, they are child-friendly. A safe and secure atmosphere enables children to take risks and pursue their ideas. As you share in their joy of discovery, children feel supported and accepted, comfortable and able to express themselves. Though atmosphere is important, there are additional ways you can help to create a play-conducive environment. The space, time, and materials you provide help to determine how creative children will be.

Caution: Imaginations on the Loose! - The space you provide for play needs to be roomy enough for children to feel comfortable. Boundaries between play areas are clearly marked but not impenetrable. If the firefighters in the block area need a bucket from the housekeeping area, it isn't difficult for them to retrieve one. When several children decide to make the book corner a library, it's easy for them to create signs with materials from the art shelf. Children can easily reach items to use and to put back because materials are accessible and organized. This encourages children to impose their own order and make many of their own choices. Your role is to monitor decisions, making sure children are safe and stimulated—being careful that your need for order doesn't stifle their creative expression.

To make sure your environment fosters and enhances children's creative play, look around your setting. Do the materials in each area (blocks, manipulatives, art, etc.) offer children open-ended experiences? Opportunities to make their own choices and decisions? Generate their own themes? Is your setting arranged so children can safely reach and put back the items they want to use in their play? Does the room arrangement allow children to move about freely from one area to another? Bring materials they need from one place to another?

The opportunities you open up, along with your personal enthusiasm and interest, set the stage for creative growth and development.

Just Five More Minutes - Time is another component that influences children's involvement and creativity. Children need at least 30-45 minutes to get immersed in their play, as well as opportunities to build on their themes and explore ideas over days. During your next several free-play times, notice how much time children have to explore and create. Observe individual children, paying close attention to the amount of time each seems to need to go from one activity to another or to get really involved in one particular thing. Do children seem to feel rushed? Do they have enough time to get involved? Is there enough notice when the time will end so they can draw their play to closure with feelings of satisfaction and completion? Are there opportunities, for those who want to, to carry on their theme and/or their creating over the next few days?

Remember, children don't necessarily need a product such as a painting or a block building to show for time they've spent. It's not important whether or not a specific block structure looks like a castle to adults; if Caroline and Nikko have determined that it works for them, it does. Left up, it may remain a castle tomorrow or perhaps become a hospital. What is important is their involvement in the process. If after playing at the art table for a lengthy time, Hillary has only a satisfied look, that is enough, too. In both cases, the children have had enough time to explore in their own unique ways—creatively.

So Many Possibilities - The materials you offer need to invite multiple uses and a variety of interpretations. For example, of course an indoor climber has to be fairly small and safe, but that's where its definition stops. Children may choose to define it as a rocketship one day, a house, igloo, or cave another, depending on what they might need for their play. This means that materials are *process-,* rather than *product-,* oriented.

Again, look around at the various areas in your room: Does the block area contain a variety of shapes and sizes? Is there a shelf with easy-to-reach small props, such as non-stereotyped people, vehicles, and animals, that children can bring to their play throughout the room? Does the house-keeping area offer props that inspire children to art out the dramas of their lives? Do these props represent children's various backgrounds and home lives, as well as places they may have been to or heard about such as the library, a restaurant, the doctor's office, etc.? Do props change as children express their interests and share their experiences? At the manipulative table, are there materials children can choose to use for building, making designs, and sorting? Does the sand table offer tactile stimulation as well as props for pretend play? Is the act corner filled with interesting, creative materials that inspire children to make creations all their own? Is there a writing shelf with pads, paper, fat pencils, and markers so children can create their own signs, lists, letters, etc.? Is your room filled with materials children can use to create imaginative, participatory experiences?

YOUR ROLE IN ENHANCING CREATIVE PLAY

Knowing how to involve yourself in children's play — when to enter and when to withdraw—will help you enhance, rather than interfere with, creativity. These important skills are based on listening from afar; timing your involvement so that it doesn't interrupt important and natural creative flows; being sensitive to each child's right to create worlds that don't necessarily parallel adults'; and, of course, respecting children's creative expression.

These examples highlight such situations:

"Hide Me! Hide Me!" - At the sand table, four-year-olds Jacob and Maria giggle and hoot with surprise as they pour sand from various vessels onto one another's hands. Then quickly, they pull their hands out of hiding. Judith, their teacher, stands nearby carefully watching to see whether too much sand is flying about. After keeping a close eye on their play, she determines that directly intervening may deflate their joy so she quietly positions herself at an empty space at the table. Slowly, she begins to bury a few plastic props, afterwards searching for them by burrowing her hands into the sand mounds she's created. Jacob and Maria turn to watch her, and also begin burying and searching, squealing with delight at each discovery. Sand is no longer flying and their game of burying and retrieving continues. Judith leaves

quietly. Without discouraging their involvement or delight, she successfully directed their play to a safer process.

"How Far Does This One Go?" - Three-year-old Audri rolls a toy truck back and forth on the floor in the block area. Clifford, a teacher's aide, watches for several minutes as she listlessly pushes and pulls. Deciding a few props could help extend her play, he sets up a makeshift ramp and selects a vehicle similar to her's to roll down the plank. Sharing his reasoning out loud he says, "I wonder how far this car will roll. I wonder if it will go farther if I put it up higher. Look how much faster the car goes when I tip the ramp up!" After watching a bit, Audri and several other children begin to roll their vehicles down the ramp. Using some of Clifford's words as well as language of their own, they discuss which goes the fastest and farthest as they experiment with changing the tilt. Soon they try an array of vehicles, even a few blocks of different shapes and sizes, discovering that some roll and some don't. As the children become involved and interact with one another, Clifford quietly moves away. Through his involvement, he was able to pick up on Audri's interest, expand on it, and, at the same time, help her interact with other children.

"I'll Huff, and I'll Puff, and . . ." - At the outdoor climber several five-year-olds act out their own version of "The Three Pigs." Max, playing the wolf, pretends to "huff and puff and blow the house (climber) down." The other three children squirm and squeal in delighted fear. They agree that the house is made of bricks so the wolf can't blow it down. But Max insists that the house must be made of straw. A shouting match begins: "Bricks!" "Straw!" "Bricks!" "Straw!" Clarisse, their family day-care provider, hears the commotion and moves a bit closer so she can see and hear better. Deciding that their happy play may be disintegrating, she crouches by the edge of the climber and listens as Max unsuccessfully tries to convince the others to follow the traditional storyline. At this point, she gently asks the children, "What could the wolf do if your house is made of bricks?" One of the children calls out, "He could climb down the chimney!" Immediately, Max climbs to the top of the climber and pretends to lower himself down the chimney. The play resumes. The pigs run out from the climber with the wolf close on their tails! Clarisse watches as she walks to the other side of the playground. Her subtle intervention extended and facilitated their play.

LEARNING FROM CHILD'S PLAY

Just as children learn from their play, so can adults. By watching children as they play, you can gain insight into emotional, social, cognitive, and physical development. In the three scenarios described earlier, each adult observed before he or she stepped in. Each enhanced the play and stepped away, allowing the play and the children's skills to develop further. What the adult learned relates directly to what the children were learning.

In "Hide Me! Hide Me!" Jacob and Maria's play at the sand table offered several indicators of their social, cognitive, and physical development. Socially, they were able to coordinate their actions with one another, taking turns burying hands and fingers. Of equal importance, their

FOSTERING CREATIVE PLAY

To encourage creative play:

● **Wait to enter. Then be careful that you maintain and/or extend children's general theme and direction.** Make sure you understand the play before you help build on it. For example, if children are involved with a block structure, wait to see what they have defined it to be — a rocketship, fort, cave, or whatever. Be careful that your intervention doesn't identify it for them.

● **Enter by making statements that reflect what the child or children are doing.** For example, if a child is lining up a number of small animals, you might comment, "Look at all the animals you've used." Observational statements communicate approval without judgement. They let children know you recognize that what they are doing is important.

● **Next, ask open-ended questions.** These kinds of questions require no specific or correct response but inspire a variety of answers. For example, if a child is in the midst of painting you might say, "You've used so many colors. How do they make you feel?"

● **Step away so children can resume their play, or when they gain control over the play themselves.** As your conversation continues, be careful that it enhances children's play rather than monopolizes it.

these skills — social, cognitive, and physical — are important to later academic success.

With an adult's help, three-year-old Audri's play in "How Far Does This One Go?" was extended to resemble the process a scientist might go through. Cognitively, she became involved in the process of discovering the laws of the natural world. She experimented, observed, modified, and continued to investigate. The block corner became her laboratory. Socially, an observer would see her as able to take turns with the other children who joined her play, and cooperate in experimenting with a variety of objects. A watchful adult might also note her physical dexterity, as she manipulated small vehicles and the large plank. Also apparent would be her language and thinking skills as she formulated predictions and conclusions.

The five-year-olds in "I'll Huff, and I'll Puff, and . . ." demonstrated memory and sequencing skills. Cognitively, they remembered the storyline well enough to follow it in their play. Max, in particular, knew that a straw house preceded the brick one. Observation shows that the children used language effectively to communicate their ideas to one another. Socially, the play demonstrated their ability to cooperate with one another and to coordinate their play— important milestones in development.

Obviously, all three of these play episodes provide insights into children's development. By keeping records of observations, you can track developmental progress and plan further learning experiences based upon the children's interests. For example, Jacob and Maria might be encouraged to extend their sand play into an exploration or a dig in the sand box or outside. Audri might like to do further experiments using velocity and gravity with other types of materials, possibly charting the results. The children in "The Three Pigs" might be encouraged to dictate and illustrate their own version of the story. Perhaps Max would want to tell the story from the wolf's point of view.

Observations not only help us understand the many different parts of the whole child, but aid us in tuning in to children as individuals, gaining clues to their unique interests in order to open up other truly exciting, developmentally appropriate opportunities that they have initiated. Remember, we are taking their cues and building on them.

laughter indicated the joy each experienced from the company of the other.

Cognitively, the game was a sophisticated version of hide-and-seek. The children were able to sequence their actions to follow a predictable format: hide, search, and discover. They were also able to apply the same rules to a different set of objects when they varied their game from hiding hands to hiding props. Physically, their fine- and gross-motor skills allowed them to fill various containers and burrow through the sand to find the objects. All of

There is no magic formula to fostering and learning from children's creative play. With the support of an inviting environment and understanding adults, children usually know just what to do. Like an assistant director of an impromptu theater production, set the stage, provide the necessary props, and do what you can to subtly keep creative action and energy flowing. Then sit back and watch! Creative play will provide invaluable learning experiences, not just for your children but also for you.

"Put Your Name on Your Painting, But... the Blocks Go Back on the Shelves"

David Kuschner

David Kuschner, Ed.D., is Associate Professor of Early Childhood Education at the University of Cincinnati. He has done research and writing in the area of children's play and material use.

My daughter's schoolwork has covered our refrigerator door for the past six years. During these six years, there has been a change in what she brings home from school as evidence of the day's activities. For the two years she was at the child care center, all that we saw were various forms of artwork: scribbles and beginning scenes done with tempera paints, broad washes of color applied with little fingers, and tissue, yarn, and glitter stuck together with gobs of glue. Then, starting in kindergarten, a shift occurred: Worksheets began to be mixed in with the artwork. Instead of pieces of paper with her own inventions expressed on them, we saw pieces of paper with somebody else's inventions, but with our daughter's connecting lines, colored in shapes, and traced letters. In first grade, the ratio of worksheets to artwork began to change in favor of worksheets, and now in third grade, when she pulls her "work" out of her backpack to show us, the pile of papers is mostly worksheets of one kind or another.

When I think about those art projects and worksheets, I do so both as a parent *and* as an early childhood educator. As a parent, I have been familiar with all of my daughter's teachers and classrooms: The teachers have been good and the environments rich and stimulating. Children in those classrooms were doing much more than just art projects and worksheets. As a teacher educator, I spend time in early childhood programs from preschool through third grade and I see children playing with blocks and puzzles, creating elaborate make-believe scenes, reading and listening to stories, engaging in language play, testing themselves on the playground, and negotiating relationships with their peers. While I am sure that the same activity has been occurring in my daughter's classrooms, the only "evidence" I have had about what my daughter does during her day has been the art projects and the worksheets, the portable products of some of the day's activities.

I also know that an emphasis on the importance of play for children's development is a part of our profession's long history and tradition. Our textbooks suggest how best to foster all types of children's play and our profession's major position statement, *Developmentally Appropriate Practice in Early Childhood Programs Serving Children From Birth Through Age 8* (Bredekamp, 1987) reinforces and supports these suggestions. The important voices of our history, from Froebel and Montessori

Expendable materials such as paper and clay easily become permanent objects that children own and parents too are proud of. Nonexpendable materials such as blocks and dramatic play props are used with creativity but impermanence. A child does not "own" the blocks in the way she "owns" a painting.

through James Hymes and David Elkind, have continually emphasized the need to provide opportunities for children to play. We also need to show children we value their play, in all its forms. Why, then, do we have worksheets dominating so many of our first grade classrooms and now creeping down into many of our kindergarten programs? Why, as a parent, have I had only art projects and worksheets as tangible evidence of my daughter's school life?

Teacher's differential responses to children's forms of play

Consider the following two observations of children at play in a typical preschool or kindergarten. We'll begin with *Ralph, the artist.*

During free time, Ralph chooses to paint at one of the easels. He is very definite about whether his paper should be placed horizontally or vertically on the easel and about the colors he wants to use. As he paints you can observe how he uses empty space in his painting and how he knows that shades of color can be created by blending paints together.

When Ralph is finished, he brings a teacher over to see what he has done. After a minute or so of admiring nods and interested questions, the teacher asks Ralph if he wants to put his name on the painting and then hang it on the line so that it will dry and he will be able to take it home. Ralph agrees, signs his name, finds a spot on the drying line, and runs off to find something else to do in the room.

Now consider the activity of *Jamie, the block player.*

As soon as activity time begins, Jamie makes her way over to the block area. After a few minutes, her block structure begins to take some shape: She is building a zoo. Soon Ryan comes over and joins in the construction. He adds to the structure by erecting more enclosures for the plastic animals Jamie has gathered from the toy shelf. Once they place their animals in the zoo, they become animal trainers and zoo keepers, giving orders to and caring for their beasts.

About 40 minutes after Jamie had first started to build, a teacher walks over and watches for a few minutes. She asks the two zoo keepers a few questions, expresses her admiration for how well they built their zoo, and then tells them that it is time to clean up because snack time is approaching. Together they quickly put the blocks back on the shelves and the animals back into their boxes. Jamie and Ryan then join their classmates on the carpet for a story.

In each of these play episodes, children were involved in meaningful activity. Both types of play are vitally important for children's development. There are, however, important differences between the ways in which the teachers responded to the ending of each play episode.

Expendable and nonexpendable materials

In order to understand the differences between the teacher behaviors with the artist and the block players it is first necessary to think about the materials the children were using. I previously described a framework for thinking about children's material use (Kuschner & Clark, 1976, 1977) that in part consists of analyzing the *nature* of the materials in question. Blocks, for example, are rigid, three-dimensional, often natural in color, and are usually symmetrically balanced. Paints, on the other hand, are colored, fluid, essentially two-dimensional, and applied with some sort of applicator (e.g., brush, finger) to some sort of surface (e.g., paper, table). This type of analysis highlights a very important difference between blocks and paints: Blocks are *nonexpendable* materials, paints are *expendable* materials.

Expendable materials—crayons, paints, paper, glue, tape, and glitter—will be used up by the chil-

dren. These materials are bought, used, and replaced. Materials that are expected to have a relatively long, functional life—blocks, puzzles, books, manipulative toys, and role-playing props—fall into the nonexpendable category. When a hundred dollars or so is spent on a set of blocks, the assumption is that the blocks will get years of use. Toys do break and puzzle pieces do get lost, but for the most part the expectation is that nonexpendable materials will have a long "shelf life."

Understanding this distinction helps make us aware of the socially determined constraints placed upon the use of various materials. The child who is encouraged to cut colored paper into the shapes he wants, glue the shapes onto construction paper in any design he wants, and then use markers he chooses to color the design is definitely not encouraged to make the same choices with units from the block set. Even though he may need a block of a particular shape for the farm he is building, he is not encouraged to take a block piece to the woodworking bench and cut it into that shape, nor is he encouraged to take a piece to the art area to paint it the color he needs.

A sense of ownership and permanency. This distinction not only suggests constraints on what children can do with materials but also suggests ways in which the behavior of *teachers* is influenced by the type of material children are using. Think again about the observations of Ralph and Jamie and how the teachers related to the endings of the play episodes. In the case of Ralph, the teacher helped him attach a sense of ownership (writing his name on the painting) and permanency to the activity (taking the painting home). In the case of Jamie, as interested in the block play as the teacher might have been, she did not encourage Jamie to sign her work (as a sculptor might), nor did she suggest that the zoo structure could have any permanent existence (certainly not to be taken home). What the teacher did do was to remind Jamie that her creation had to be dismantled and that the blocks needed to be put back on the shelves to be used another day by other children.

We all have some typical responses to the endings of children's play, and these responses differ *depending* upon the type of play it is and the type of material involved. If the child is playing with expendable materials—materials that result in a product the child can possess—we tend to focus on whether or not she has completed what she was doing. If the child is playing with nonexpendable materials—materials that belong to the classroom and need to be used again by other children—we tend to focus on the return of these materials to their storage places.

Understanding the messages we send. Our typical differential reponses to children's play may be sending some unintended messages to both children and parents about the relative value of different types of play. Since all parents don't necessarily believe that play is important (Almy, Monighan, Scales, & Van Hoorn, 1984; Rothlein & Brett, 1984; Ramsey & Reid, 1988), we need to be aware of how our responses to children's play do and do not reinforce its value. As Rivkin (1986) writes, "In considering their interactions with children during play, teachers have to be simultaneously aware not only of developmental stages, but also of their own attitudes and values" (p. 214).

Consider the very language we use to talk about different types of children's play. What Timmy is doing at that table is *playing* with puzzles, while Juan and Alicia dressed up as firefighters are engaged in make-believe, role, and sociodramatic *play*. But Jerome over at the easel is doing his art*work*, and Nicole sitting at the table drawing lines between objects printed on a piece of paper is doing a *work*sheet. When Jerome and Nicole are fin-

ished, they will put their *work* in their cubbies to be taken home at the end of the day. When Alicia and Juan are finished the teacher may ask them if they had a good time *playing* firefighter and will remind them to put the props away. Jerome and Nicole's *work* may be displayed for parents' night and put in folders to be shared at parent-teacher conference time. Our language and actions regarding children's activity can socialize children into adult conceptions of the differences between work and play, thus suggesting which type of activity is more important (Suransky, 1982; Klein, Kantor, & Fernie, 1988). Spodek (1986) suggests that children's interests and what *they* believe is important may be influenced by the value messages sent by adults: "Children's interests, however, do not grow naturally from the child but rather are influenced by the social context in which the child functions... needs do not arise naturally but are related to elements that adults value" (p. 33).

The importance of ownership and permanency. We shouldn't underestimate the power of having names attached to activities. When a name is connected to something a child has done, a sense of pride may be fostered and a valuing of the activity engendered. Beardsley and Zeman-Marecek (1987) capture this power as they answer their question, "What's in a name?"

As children progress through preschool experiences that allow them to explore the power of language in a social context, no symbol, no word emerges more powerfully than the child's own name. A 3- or 4-year-old who is encountering his first school experience finds that in this

world of many peers, his name—that ordered progression of letters that means him—takes on heightened significance. At home, he may be the only small person; what is his is obvious by its size and child-appeal. In the classroom, there are many small people; teachers can help the young child realize that what he *has* and what he *does* become uniquely recognizable by using the powerful label of his name. (p. 162)

The sense of permanency is also important because it can set the stage for children's reflection about their activity. When the product of a child's activity lasts past the immediate time of the activity, the child can literally and figuratively sit back and consider what he has done. He can reflect on the reasons for why he did it in the way he did and consider how he might change it or do it differently next time. When there is tangible evidence of the activity to reflect upon, there is the opportunity for revision and the evolution of activity that revision embodies.

Children are assisted in the reflection and revision process by teachers, peers, and parents who ask questions or make statements about what they have done. Asking children about their intentions, the materials they used, and the difficulty they might have had carrying out their intentions can help children focus on their activity. Asking children about how they plan on changing, modifying, or revising their activity can help them understand the relationship between what they have done now and what they might do in the future. High/Scope has incorporated such reflection under its "Plan-Do-Review" curriculum organization (Hohmann, Banet, & Weikart, 1979), and Was-

---

The policy of cleaning up all materials should sometimes be set aside to honor children's creations. An intricate Lego™ truck or block zoo is worth looking at and talking about for a day or so.

---

serman (1988) has proposed a "Play-Debrief-Replay" instructional model for elementary science curriculum. Wasserman suggests that the debriefing process is important because it helps children "extract meanings from their experiences" (p. 233).

How to attach ownership and permanency to all types of play

There are a number of ways in which teachers can help children attach a sense of ownership and permanency to all forms of their play.

Use photography to capture interesting activity. Photography is a wonderful way to capture the excitement of children's activity. I walked into a kindergarten once to find the teacher taking a picture of a large group of children standing behind this massive block structure sprawling across the carpet. All of the children had contributed to the

building and every face was beaming.

Display photographs on walls, send them home to parents, or organize them into albums. I worked with one program that compiled albums depicting a year's worth of play and activity. The parents loved to look through these albums and often would order reprints of particular pictures. You can use photographs as story starters to encourage children to describe, both orally and in writing, what they had been doing.

Show slides, films, and videos at parent nights as a way of explaining what the goals and curriculum of the program are and as a terrific way of valuing all forms of children's play. Parents enjoy watching their children, as do the children themselves. Film and video, although more costly, offer the advantage over prints and slides of including sound and the dynamic aspect of children's activity.

Send notes home to parents. Teachers should find efficient and effective ways of sending home written notes about children's play. Keep pads of paper close by so that you can make quick notes when you witness something interesting. (It is important to remember that this "something interesting" doesn't have to involve concrete activity. It may have been some language play or the resolution of social conflict.) I have known teachers who wore aprons with pockets to hold a pad and pencil just to make the note-taking process easier. Other teachers have created and duplicated notepaper with such starter sentences as, "You should have seen what _____ did today!" (Of course, such notepaper should only be used to communicate positive happenings!) Write the note when you see the interesting episode and leave it in the child's cubby or mailbox for him to take home or for his parent to find at arrival or departure time—a time during which a great deal of parent-school communication often occurs (Herwig, 1982). Share the note with the child to let him know that you noticed and valued what he had been doing. He will then have the pleasure of anticipating his parent finding the note.

Attach signs to the products of children's activity. I have seen teachers very effectively attach a sense of ownership and permanency to children's activity by helping the children make a sign to identify the product as theirs. When Jamie and Ryan spent 40 minutes constructing their zoo, instead of taking it down, the teacher could have helped them print a sign saying, "Jamie and Ryan carefully built this zoo together. Please do not disturb." Such a message serves a number of functions. A sense of ownership is attached to the activity. A sense of valuing is communicated because the teacher took the time to help the children make the sign. By placing the sign in front of the structure, some permanency is established—the sign

Marietta Lynch

Some children can guess-spell their own signs, labels, or captions. Others can copy them. Any child can dictate. Good preschool, kindergarten, and primary grade teachers have been integrating play, print, self-esteem building, and documenting children's school successes since our profession took shape 100 years ago.

serves as a bit of protection for the zoo itself. And, of course, the children are exposed to the functional power of the printed word in a very meaningful context, an experience important for the development of literacy (Schickedanz, 1986).

Create a "favorite toy" display. If some tabletop, cabinet top, or bookshelf space is available, it can be reserved for children to have their favorite *school* toy displayed with their name in front of it, much as artwork is often displayed. Displaying these toys or materials shows the child herself, other children, and parents that the activity represented by the toy is valued and that even though the toy or material cannot go home and doesn't *belong* to the child, the type of play supported by the toy is just as important as play that does result in products that can be sent home. As Levin and Klein (1988) suggest, the school environment can be used to foster communication between parents and children.

Have the children write about what they do. Encourage children, when developmentally appropriate, to write or dictate stories and descriptions about what they have been doing. This not only attaches ownership and permanency to the activity but again supports the development of reading and writing. These stories can be displayed on walls, made into books, or sent home. The stories and the process of creating them can also be part of the "plan-do-review" format as described in the High/Scope curriculum (Hohmann, Banet, & Weikart, 1979).

Rethink attitudes about cleanup. There is one last—and very important—suggestion as to how we can help children understand the importance of all of their play activity: Rethink our sometimes compulsive approach to cleanup time. It is true that some early childhood programs suffer from

constraints on the use of physical space—somebody else is going to use the space after the children leave and therefore all materials need to be put away. In addition, sometimes space is limited and parts of the classroom must serve multiple functions. Even with these constraints, we need to reflect upon the rules we create to manage the transitions from activity to activity. We tend to get caught up in what comes next as opposed to focusing on what the children are doing at the moment. There are probably more opportunities than we realize to let the products of children's activity remain visible for awhile. It may take some coordination with other teachers or custodians. By suggesting to the children that their efforts can have some permanence beyond the moment, we let them know that we found what they were doing then at least as interesting as what everyone is supposed to be doing next. As Ramsey and Reid (1988) write, "teachers can plan flexibly so that rigid schedules and routines do not disrupt the flow of play" (p. 233).

Valuing all of children's play

The six suggestions just described do not comprise an exhaustive list. Undoubtedly, teachers have already found many more ways to attach a sense of ownership and permanency to the wonderful variety of children's play activity. We need to continue to find ways of doing so if we want to make sure that the message we send to children, parents, and other professionals is the one we intend: Play, in *all* of its forms, is what children do and is the way children grow, learn, and develop.

References

Almy, M., Monighan, P., Scales, B., & Van Hoorn, J. (1984). Recent research on play:

The teacher's perspective. In L. Katz (Eds.), *Current topics in early childhood education* (Vol. 5, pp. 1–25). Norwood, NJ: Ablex.

Beardsley, L. V., & Zeman-Marecek, M. (1987, February). Making connections: Facilitating literacy in young children. *Childhood Education, 63*, 159–166.

Bredekamp, S. (Ed.). (1987). *Developmentally appropriate practice in early childhood programs serving children from birth through age 8* (exp. ed.). Washington, DC: NAEYC.

Herwig, J. E. (1982). Parental involvement: Changing assumptions about the educator's role. In *How to involve parents in early childhood education* (pp. 6–30). Provo, UT: Brigham Young University Press.

Hohmann, M., Banet, B., & Weikart, D. (1979). *Young children in action: A manual for preschool educators.* Ypsilanti, MI: High/Scope.

Klein, E. L., Kantor, R., & Fernie, D. E. (1988). What do young children know about school? *Young Children, 43*(5), 32–39.

Kuschner, D., & Clark, P. (1976, November). *A framework for analyzing children's interactions with materials.* Paper presented at the annual conference of the National Association for the Education of Young Children, Anaheim, CA.

Kuschner, D., & Clark, P. (1977). Children, materials, and adults in early learning settings. In L. Golubchick & B. Persky (Eds.), *Early childhood education* (pp. 122–127). Wayne, NJ: Avery Publishing.

Levin, D.E., & Klein, A. (1988). What did you do in school today? Using the school environment to foster communication between children and parents. *Day Care and Early Education, 15*, 6–10.

Ramsey, P., & Reid, R. (1988). Designing play environments for preschool and kindergarten children. In D. Bergen (Ed.), *Play as a medium for learning and development* (pp. 213–239). Portsmouth, NH: Heinemann.

Rivkin, M. S. (1986). The educator's place in children's play. In G. Fein & M. Rivkin (Eds.), *The young child at play: Reviews of research, Volume 4* (pp. 213–217). Washington, DC: NAEYC.

Rothlein, L., & Brett, A. (1984). *Children's, teachers', and parents' perceptions of play.* Coral Gables, FL: University of Miami. (ERIC Document Reproduction Service No. ED 273 395)

Schickedanz, J. A. (1986). *More than the ABCs: The early stages of reading and writing.* Washington, DC: NAEYC.

Spodek, B. (1986). Development, values, and knowledge in the kindergarten curriculum. In B. Spodek (Ed.), *Today's kindergarten: Exploring the knowledge base, expanding the curriculum* (pp. 32–47). New York: Teachers College Press, Columbia University.

Suransky. V. (1982). *The erosion of childhood.* Chicago: University of Chicago Press.

Wasserman, S. (1988). Play-Debrief-Replay: An instructional model for science. *Childhood Education, 64*, 232–234.

Thinking, Playing and Language Learning: An All-in-Fun Approach with Young Children

Judy Spitler McKee

Judy Spitler McKee is the editor of several volumes on Early Childhood Education (1976-1987) and Professor of Early Childhood Education and Educational Psychology at Eastern Michigan University. She teaches specialized courses devoted to play and Piaget.

There is no better play material in the world than words. They surround us, go with us through our work-a-day tasks, their sound is always in our ears, their rhythms on our tongue. . . . But when we turn . . . to hearing and seeing children, to whom all the world is as play material, who think and feel through play, can we not then drop our adult utilitarian speech and listen and watch for the patterns of words and ideas? Can we not care for the *way* we say things to them and not merely *what* we say? Can we not speak in rhythm, in pleasing sounds, even in song for the mere sensuous delight it gives us and them, even though it adds nothing to the content of our remark? If we can, I feel sure children will not lose their native use of words: more, I think those of six and seven and eight who have lost it in part . . . will win back their spontaneous joy in the play of words.

Lucy Sprague Mitchell

All around the cobbler's bench,
The monkey chased the weasel.
The monkey thought 'twas all in fun.
Pop goes the weasel!

Bruner, a cognitive psychologist, summarizing two decades of research on children's language in the U.S. and Great Britain, has stated that while language is innate to human beings, language must be nurtured through try-out and experience to be mastered. Moreover, a child's "mother tongue is most rapidly mastered when situated in playful activities" rather than the duress of striving for goals (1983, p. 65). Knowledgeable adults have noted that healthy children talk spontaneously and fluently when they are secure, absorbed in an activity, and when the adults significant to them "come alive." When there is mutual adult-child engrossment in a chosen activity, reciprocal conversation flows. The best and preferred medium for "alive" or vivid interpersonal exchanges is play. Clearly, thinking, play and language are a dynamic, interrelated trio, and they appear together in "all-in-fun" situations.

Garvey (1977) has shown the multiple ways in which communication is central to play, how language and play interact to produce widening levels of competence. Researchers have shown how the most complicated grammatical and pragmatic (conversational) forms of language are initiated in play (Pellegrini, 1983; Pellegrini and Galda, 1984; Bruner, 1983). And Piaget, the Swiss scholar of cognitive research (1969; 1977), has explicated the intimate linkage between language and play, both representational forms of intelligence difficult to define or study in isolation or in the laboratory. Chukovsky (1963) collected samples of Russian children's play with language itself, which validated how they joyfully explored and manipulated sounds, words and phrases as if they were play materials with innumerable possibilities for forming and reforming, combining and re-combing, ordering and reordering, adding and deleting parts from wholes.

CHARACTERISTICS AND CIRCUMSTANCES OF PLAY

Play, manifold in form and variety, has been studied by researchers for decades; some of the circumstances under which it occurs and some of its elusive characteristics have been identified. For our purposes, those circumstances and characteristics related to children's thinking, play and language include: Attitude, Control, Relaxation, Absorption and Vivification.

When children and adults have an ATTITUDE of playfulness, failure or fear of consequences is suspended; the players are free to feel, think, do or say whatever they want in the play arena. Play is cherished by the world's children because it is voluntary, SELF-CONTROLLED. They choose

Reprinted from *Play: Working Partners of Growth*, 1986, pp. 15-28. Reprinted by permission of Judy Spitler McKee and the Association for Childhood Education International, 11141 Georgia Avenue, Suite 200, Wheaton, MD. Copyright © 1986 by the Association.

whether to play or not, with whom, with what, where, how and how long. As Sutton-Smith (1979) has pointed out, this is a reversal of most of life when we are controlled by others, or when we engage in activities of necessity rather than desire or choice.

RELAXATION of mood is necessary since the player must feel some inner security and competence in the situation. This explains why children new to a program often do not play with the materials, or why distressed or abused children cannot play. But when play occurs, whether it is individual or social, construction or social-dramatic in form, an ABSORPTION occurs; the player is not easily distracted from the engrossing play.

While researchers in many countries have quibbled about what *is* and what *is not* play, playing children, *oblivious* to any of the aforementioned circumscribing aspects of characteristics, tell us simply and profoundly why they play and what immediate benefits they derive: Play is Fun. As several hundred surveyed children ages 4 to 10 years indicated to adults: "Play is funner. Play is funner than anything." Sutton-Smith argues that the vividness and excitement of play, the FUN part, is the VIVIFICATION effect. The thrill, the fun, the natural "high" that can be psychomotor, affective, cognitive and/or aesthetic may be short-lived—as when a child spends an hour raking leaves in order to jump joyously into them for ten seconds. Children around the world play for the vividness, the fun-ness, the thrilling-ness of play—and so do many early childhood educators who say they teach because they "simply love" their work with children.

PLAY AND LEARNING

How play correlates to learning is a question that has been asked by philosophers, historians, researchers, educators and parents; their respective answers vary with the perspective on play with which they originated their investigations. Theorists and researchers in the areas of child development, cognition, and social and behavioral learning have shown us that human learning occurs most readily through active, investigative, experiential and cooperative interactions with the world (Piaget, 1977; Bruner, 1962; Erikson, 1963). Play permits all of these and, without the child's intent or knowledge, produces a FUNdamental understanding about the inner self ("in here") and the outer world ("out there"). Moreover, because play is pleasurable and failure-free, the child is able to move from the personal nucleus of the self that regulates all experiences to non-self (others). The child's expressive interpretations—movement, play, laughter, music and art—are interdependent with conceptual and language abilities. Thus, one area such as play stimulates and elaborates the other such as language (Piaget, 1969; 1977).

In summary, thinking, play and language—along with movement, laughter, music and art—are primary ways the young child symbolizes the outer world; tests and modifies its form, functions and meanings, and grows in curiosity and competence. Adults and children who take delight in each other's play and language will "come alive" for each other. Let us recall Mitchell's observation that "There is no better play material in the world than words," as Chukovsky's vignettes reveal. How can playful adults, able to surrender some control to children and experience vivification in return, become "partners in play" (Singer and Singer, 1977) with chil-

dren from 2 through 10 years—enabling them to delight in sounds, words, phrases and meanings so they will benefit from using language as free-play materials to be endlessly explored? Let us be mindful that an "all-in-fun" approach, like the monkey in the song, releases and develops children's thinking, play and language.

THE TODDLER STAGE: 1½ TO 3 YEARS

Play Patterns

Healthy toddlers are busy, energetic people, who have a passion to explore their physical and social surroundings in their attempts to order them. Ironically, their ceaseless attempts at ordering their world on their terms look like disorder to adults; for instance, when they rearrange and cart away food left out for eating. They delight in "fill-and-dump" play, tirelessly carting materials from one place to another, filling up containers and then dumping them out. Their play is solitary and, gradually, parallel or side by side with other children who may share the same space and materials such as blocks or sand, but without sharing of ideas. Sensory-motor play enjoyed during babyhood continues. Around 18 to 24 months, healthy children achieve a cognitive milestone in beginning to use the symbolic function (Piaget, 1969; 1977), which is manifested in language, symbolic play, deferred (remembered) imitation and art. Now the toddler is able to store direct, vivid, immediate experiences of daily living in cognitive schema—similar to a mental filing system—and later translate them into another highly personal form wherein something (e.g., a blanket, pan, doll, scribble or a few words) is used to stand for something else (e.g., an image, memory, animal, person or story fragment).

Their gradually emerging attempts to order and control their world are reflected most clearly in their *locomotor* and *language skills*, areas where action and thinking are linked and where playful adults can assist this stage child. Toddlers who are mastering locomotor skills play with *space*: they tirelessly scoot, tumble, climb up, slide down, crawl around, run, swing, roll, jump, leap or rock. They fall into laundry baskets, boxes and wastebaskets. Language is facilitated as adults talk with them and they joyously play with *sounds* and *words*, giving them much-desired *control* over their environment. They delight in *repeating names* (K-Mart), *animal noises, silly sounds*, especially those associated with toilet-training (poo poo, pee pee, kaka); *chants* (Row, row; Ashes, all fall down; chinney, chin chin; Fuzzy Wuzzy was a bear); and *jingles* (Plop, plop, fizz, fizz). Adults can assist toddlers as they engage in these exploratory and play activities by bathing them in a pleasant stream of language as they care for and play with them. Three types of conversation useful for building language performance are:

1. *Descriptions*: "What big shoes you are wearing!" "My, what a large purse you are carrying!" Many songs and stories popular with this age use this format, such as "Mary wore her red dress . . . " or *The Three Little Pigs*.

2. *Simple questions* involving where or who: "Where is your dolly today?" "Whose shoes are these under the bed? Are these Care Bear's shoes?" Questions involving motivation and purpose, the *why* type, are generally too cognitively complex for toddlers.

3. *Expansion* (to adult grammatical form) and *extension* (to add new information): Model the correct grammatical

forms to children's language, but do *not* correct their grammar at this stage since this stops the flow. For instance, when a toddler states, "Fro truk," you can respond in a natural voice and expand the form: "Yes, you did throw the truck, a long way." You can provide extension by offering more information for the child to assimilate: "Let's pick up the truck now from the driveway. Elizabeth will be coming home soon, and she might hit your truck with her bicycle."

Let Fluency Precede Accuracy

At all levels of expression in the symbolic function—language, symbolic play, deferred imitation and art—children's fluency (flow) of production precedes their accuracy of execution. By nature, children are both young and inexperienced. Adults who demand precision in any of the symbolic forms greatly inhibit the child's spontaneous and playful productions. Preoccupation with accuracy—to "say it right" or "draw it right," or to play the story in a certain way—moves the adult from mediating at children's level of proficiency to trying to instruct them in becoming an adult. When the situation becomes work-like and controlled by the adult, the child may feel tense or insecure, and play exits the situation. If we corrected a child's early eating habits or early attempts at drawing or singing (as some adults correct children's speech and language productions), most children would not eat or draw or sing in our presence—and many do not. Instead, we should offer supportive, encouraging feedback in a playful mood rather than only corrective, accuracy-laden feedback.

Movement Activities

Toddlers enjoy simple movement chants. Three of their favorites are "Ring A-round a Rosey," "Pop Goes the Weasel" and "Motor Boat," which have the reverse actions of falling down and popping up, moving slowly and moving fast. Examine the words and you will see that the actions are the same that toddlers are engaged in as they explore and try to understand the complex concepts of *space* and *cause and effect*:

1. Ring a-round a rosey. Pocket full of posies. Ashes, ashes. We all fall down!

2. All around the cobbler's bench. The monkey chased the weasel. The monkey thought 'twas all in fun. Pop goes the weasel!

3. Motor boat, motor boat. Goes so fast. Motor boat, motor boat. Step on the gas!

Of course, the parts that cause the greatest anticipation, laughing, and cognitive and affective thrill (vivification) are the ending lines: "We all fall down," "Pop goes the weasel" and "Step on the gas." Adults who make playful fun of these simple movement chants are assisting the twin symbolic functions of symbolic play and language to burst forth in individual ways. Favorite play materials of toddlers are the push-and-pull variety that are accompanied by clacking and sounds, such as popcorn poppers, lawn mowers, push-downs, pop-up figures, and animals on moveable legs (dogs, penguins).

Musical Activities

Adults working with toddlers note their favorite songs are often rhymes with an action component. For example, "Clap, clap. Clap your hands. Clap your hands together." This can be varied to "Stamp your feet," Shake your head," "Tap your knees" or "Roll your arms" (Oppenheim, 1984, p. 50). These are the forerunner of a beloved early childhood song requested even by 8-year-olds: "If you're happy and you know it, clap your hands." Other musical favorites include "Row, Row Your Boat" (which older children can sing as a round), "Jingle Bells," "Are You Sleeping?," "I'm a Little Teapot," and "Where Is Thumbkin?" (Bayless and Ramsey, 1982).

Depending on the maturity of the children, the adults will do most of the singing and movements, but this is critically important for modeling effects. After all, no human baby plays "Peek-a-Boo," "Hear-a-Boo," "Hide and Find Me," "This Little Piggy" or "Pat-a-Cake" unless a playful, responsive and often clown-ful adult initiates these bodily and social games with them. Issues associated with autonomy and control by others make "Five Little Monkeys" and "Taking a Bath" especially rewarding for toddlers, who must feel controlled by everyone around them:

1. Five little monkeys, jumping on a bed. One fell off and bumped his head. Mama called the doctor. The doctor said, "No more monkeys jumping on the bed!"

2. Every night I take a bath. I scrub and rub and rub. Every night I take a bath. I splash around the tub. Every night I take a bath. Face, nose, and ears. Arms and hands and legs and feet. Enough to last for years. (Bayless and Ramsey, 1982, p. 45)

Another favorite of toddlers is:

> Two Little Blackbirds. Sitting on a hill. One named Jack, and one named Jill. Fly away, Jack. Fly away, Jill. Come back, Jack. Come back, Jill.

Books

Books popular with toddlers include *The Three Bears*, *Three Little Pigs* and *Three Little Kittens* (with varying voices), *The ABC Bunny* (Gag), *Goodnight Moon* (Brown), and Dr. Seuss's *Hop on Pop* and *One Fish Two Fish Red Fish Blue Fish*. Other books replete with language play are *Hand, Hand, Fingers, Thumb* (Perkins), *The Berenstains' B Book* (Berenstains) and *Fox in Socks* (Seuss). Speech pathologists report that "wonderful noises" children like to repeat are found in *Gobble, Growl, Grunt* (Spier) and *Mr. Brown Can Moo! Can You?* (Seuss).

Healthy toddlers exhibit great energy, curiosity and exploratory drives, and they laugh a lot. Accordingly, the adults who work with them need to possess adult levels of energy, curiosity and exploratory drives, and be able to laugh a lot so they can enjoy the children's playful pursuits and assist them for the purposes of growth.

THE PLAY STAGE: 3-7 YEARS

Play Patterns

Erik Erikson (1963) calls the period from 3 to 7 years the Play Stage where there is intimate linkage of thinking, play and language, and where pretending and "as-if" play are more readily observed. Play is now more clearly "creating model situations . . . to master reality by experiment and planning" (Erikson, 1963, p. 222). There is greater variety in children's use of materials and media, as well as a movement from purely random to more systematic approaches. Play can still be solitary but parallel, associative and cooperative forms (with shared rules and roles) can appear, indicating the exceptional importance of adapting to the many rule systems set by adults. Hence, inventing your own rules in play and getting others to follow them become a developmental milestone (Sutton-Smith, 1981).

The types of play that predominate at this stage are sensory-motor, continuing since babyhood, and symbolic play, continuing since toddlerhood. Richer, more elaborated content appears in play vignettes and is associated with home, school or medical themes; and there is more detail and discussion over constructive projects with blocks or home settings. More children can sing and dance to music or carry on telephone conversations with unseen listeners.

Astute child care workers and kindergarten teachers have long noted that the children who possess the best oral language skills and social play skills generally seem the most "ready" for the next educational experience. Children of this stage who have poor expressive language and cannot play for any sustained amount of time often lack other readiness skills. Again, the linkage among thinking, language and play is apparent.

Movement Activities

Favorite finger plays and movement exercises enjoyed at earlier ages can still be used; children do not become bored with "There Was a Little Turtle" or "Where Is Thumbkin" at 4 just because they knew them at 3 years. Now, clapping hand rhythms can be added for older children, first by saying, then singing, then hand-clapping them. Two favorites are:

1. Mary Mack, mack, mack. All dressed in black, black, black. With silver buttons, buttons, buttons. All down her back, back, back.

2. Say, say my playmate. I cannot play with you. My dolly has the flu. Boo, hoo, boo, hoo, hoo, hoo.

Many simple chants and rhymes can be made more complicated in rhythm patterns, which again builds awareness of language qualities and possibilities. For example, "Hickory, Dickory Dock" is a favorite of this stage, but older children can be divided so that one group recites the rhyme while the other group recites "Tick Tock" in rhythm.

Musical Activities

Songs with clear beats, rhyme, movement and repetition continue to be popular: "Row, Row Your Boat"; "Are You Sleeping?"; "Mary Had a Little Lamb"; "Twinkle, Twinkle Little Star"; "If You're Happy"; "Wheels on the Bus"; "Puff, the Magic Dragon"; "This Old Man" ("Knick, knack, paddy whack" is pure word play). "Frosty, the Snowman," "Jingle Bells," "Rudolph, the Red-Nosed Reindeer" and "Happy Birthday" (written by Mildred and Patty Hill) are requested regardless of the weather or status of birthdays. More language-mature children may add playful phrases such as "Tingo, Lingo, Mingo" to "Bingo," or "He Had a Care Bear" to "Old MacDonald." This then requires the talents of the adult to continue the "all-in-fun" singing and exploring activity and to add similar variations. Children can now be exposed to ascending and descending scale songs such as "Five Little Monkeys," earlier enjoyed as a movement and finger play. Some will want to substitute other animals such as donkeys or puppies, thus learning the enormous variability of language as well as demonstrating knowledge of syntax and semantics (word order and meaning).

Directions during transition times can be happily sung to the children: "Time to put your toys away. Safe to play another time. Clean-up time." "Good-bye, boys and girls. We had a playful day. I'll see you tomorrow." Children can be taught simple dances such as the Cha-Cha, with a rhythm of 1-2, 1-2-3, 1-2 or car-rots, broc-co-li, cabb-age. The Bunny Hop can be hilariously modified to The Froggy Jump or Doggy Scratch. In the Hokey Pokey, children become literally and figuratively absorbed in putting their "whole" selves "in" the doing, which is what we want them to do with thinking, play and language. Songs with dramatization possibilities and musical changes in loudness, softness and voice intonations—such as "The Old Gray Cat" is (creep-ing, sleep-ing)—are favorites with kindergartners.

Books

Dr. Seuss stories and other stories with repetitive phrases, silly-sounding words and voice changes enable children to anticipate, repeat and memorize the story elements, building the foundations for later re-enactments in social-dramatic play and reading (Pellegrini, 1983). A surprising number of adults have reported that the first book they think they were able to "read" was either *Hop on Pop* or *One Fish Two Fish Red Fish Blue Fish*, both by Seuss. If reading is, among other things, bringing enjoyment, engagement and expansive meaning to printed words of others, then those adults had playful adults, either at home or in early childhood programs, who encouraged them to enjoy the selections many, many times. At the end of *Hop on Pop* are the "beau-tee-ful" sounding *Timbuktu* and *Constantinople*, enjoyed by word lovers of all ages. *Green Eggs and Ham* (Seuss), *The Three Bears* and *Three Little Kittens* are favorites, as are the language pictures found in *The Three Billy Goats Gruff*, *The Pokey Little Puppy* (Lowrey) and *The Nonsense Alphabet* (Lear). Children delight in the repetitive line from Gag's *Millions of Cats*: "Cats here, cats there. Cats and kittens everywhere. Hundreds of cats, thousands of cats. Millions and billions and trillions of cats."

Children can re-enact nonverbally and verbally their favorite stories in small groups, if provided with the encouragement, modeling and appropriate props such as head coverings or colored clothing, masks and simple block enclosures to simulate a setting. These can be re-enacted many times or re-told with the aid of flannel board figures, which builds both self-confidence and language competence. To maintain an *attitude* of play, a *relaxation* of mood and the child's internal *control*, plus *fun*, children should not be required to practice the stories under adult direction for productions for other children or adults. The play spirit vanishes under such duress. Many children delight in Silverstein's poem, "Boa Constrictor." This can be followed up with books such as *Crictor* (Ungerer). Coody reports that kindergarten children used the following adjectives to describe Crictor: "curvey, wiggly, slitherly, long, coiled, colorful, beautiful, and graceful" (1983, p. 73).

Play Props

The provision of judiciously selected play props can spark interest, engagement and elaborations of play and language. For instance, a nursery school teacher compiled a "Three Bears Play Kit" for a child with low language skills. She included several storybooks on bears, homemade and purchased bear puppets, a tape recording of *The Three Bears*, small bowls and furniture, a "bear costume" made from a brown terry towel, two different flannel boards, and felt and laminated figures as well as art materials to draw, cut, paste and color. After several playful explorations with the Three Bears Play Kit, the child's self-esteem noticeably improved, his language was more fluent, and he asked to keep the kit so he could "read" to his family.

A gifted kindergarten teacher very successfully adapted for language production the "tent" or "blanket" type of play that children have engaged in for generations. She created a four-side red felt covering for a card table that included a door flap, a window and several velcro strips on each side for adding felt props. She added felt and realistic props for: (a) a post office with envelopes and postal box signs; (b) a gas station with plastic hoses and gas signs and prices; (c) a fire station with hats and hoses; (d) a McDonald's restaurant with yellow sponge fries, hats and paper food containers. She tested the materials over a period of weeks in several kindergartens where children had scored low on earlier language testing. Without exception, all the children talked when they used the highly stimulating materials. Many talked fluently for lengthy periods of time. During play with the fire station props, some kindergarteners created their own "burn center" play episodes.

Topsy-Turvey Talking

As Chukovsky has shown in his research (1963), children love topsy-turveys, indicating they comprehend the "sense" of the situation and its embedded meaning or they could not invert it or transform it into "nonsense." The poem "Elete-phony" (Richards) is enjoyed because of its mixed-up words. Mention to children that you would like to sing "Rudolf, the green-eared reindeer," or that "purple means stop and brown means go"; note who corrects you when you comment on the "humongous old shoes you have on today." During transition times, notice the responses to: "Let's put on your mittens for outside. Give me your toes, now." Or, "Lunchtime, everyone wash their paws!" Two gifted speech pathologists reported they used this topsy-turvey approach to help language-delayed children feel in control of the situation, laughing at the adult's errors and speaking naturally in the process.

Research on Early Childhood Activities and Language Usage

The views of Symbolic Interaction writers such as Dewey (1933) and Mead (1934), that humans grow and develop their abilities through widening social interaction experiences, have been shown to be valid by contemporary researchers (Geneshi and DePaola, 1982; Ross, 1983; Almy, 1984). Observers of early childhood programs and classrooms often report that the two most popular play areas generate both the greatest social interaction (social-dramatic) play and accompanying social usage of language (person-to-person communication). These are the home and family centers and the constructional materials centers (blocks).

In both the home and family and the constructional materials centers, children are required by the dictates of time, space, materials and the presence of peers to become engaged, cooperate, compete, squabble and negotiate very complex social-cognitive rules, roles and plots. Recall the characteristics and circumstances of play. Immersed in the situations of home and family or constructional materials, the children can control the variable uses of the materials, decide on playmates and the use of space. Much time is spent in those areas talking about play (meta play) and social relationships. For example, "I'm mother, you're the baby! No *coffee* for you!" The astute adult hears much bantering and negotiating for identity and power, or what researchers call "social cognition." The implications are clear: thinking, play and language grow with expanding social-dramatic engagements and with partner play (Singer and Singer, 1977). Thus, home and family centers and constructional materials centers are absolutely indispensable for dramatic (solitary) and social-dramatic play interactions that allow higher levels of thinking, play and language to blossom. Unfortunately, as programs for the Play Stage child become more highly structured, formal and adult-controlled, children are provided less time, space and materials for enjoyable engagements that build the templates for developmental readiness. Or, as one 2nd-grader angrily told a kindergarten neighbor: "Stay in kindergarten! Don't go to 1st grade. First and 2nd grade is awful. All we do is work, work, work. We never get outta our seats. It's awful!"

THE WORK STAGE: 7-10 YEARS

Play and Game Patterns

Children 7 to 10 years (and to 11) are identified by Erikson (1951) as being in the Work Stage, when work habits, school accomplishments and the learning of cultural literacy become central to a child's psychosocial well-being.[1] The play of children 7 to 10 years changes from "pure" play to more time spent on *interplay* since children are increasingly more social; and games with rules set by other persons become an important yardstick for measuring one's competency and popularity. Board games, card games, games of skill (tag, ball games, jump rope) and games of strategy (checkers, Tic Tac Toe, team sports) become favorite pastimes. Solitary play takes the forms of reading for pleasure, collections, and arts and crafts, each of which requires persistence, concentration and self-discipline, which are necessary for schoolwork and the learning of work and study skills. Friends and after-school gatherings assume a key role as social-dramatic play centers on family, school, power and morality themes. As children arduously master—and many do not—new social roles and expectations, they often tattle on those who do not. Teachers who provided a picture or three-dimensional model of a robot named "Beepo," for 1st- and 2nd-graders "to tattle to," reported many children talked fluently to Beepo and then were able to return to their "seatwork" without disturbing others or wasting work time.

The Work Stage child has much more skill: psychomotor, social, cognitive and academic. The child is generally more reasonable (able to reason out things) and is able to be instructed in school information. Very often, however, while this Work Stage child is more mature in thinking, play and language, elementary classrooms are basically teacher-controlled, teacher-talk dominated, highly structured and *quiet*—with time blocks for required school work but not for play. Many observers report that 1st-, 2nd- and 3rd-grade children can no longer talk or play with other children or exercise thinking skills other than memorization. An intelligent prescription for elementary school classrooms—based on research on growth, development and learning—would be to *continue* providing the enjoyable, engaging, expanding and skill-building activities and materials of play and games. Such play and games approaches are an investment in the child's present and future growth.

Musical Activities

Children's most requested songs can be continued with zest, such as "Bingo" and "Old MacDonald." Useful additions

[1]Erikson (1951, 1963) refers to the period from 7-11 years as the Industry (accomplishment) vs. Inferiority stage. For our purposes, the period from 7-10 will be used since this is the upper end of the Early Childhood Era.

with language play include: "I Know an Old Lady Who Swallowed a Fly," "I've Been Working on the Railroad," "Erie Canal," "I Love the Mountains," "The Mocking Bird" and "The Fox Went Out on a Starlit Night."

The Cruciality of Double Meanings

The learning of double meanings is a vital social and cognitive learning for this stage child (Sutton-Smith, 1981). Children need to be assisted by playful adult partners to create their own (a) riddles that deal with word meanings and (b) secret languages that deal with letter meanings.

Dinosaur tales and riddles are much loved, partially due to the beauty and power of the names: Brontosaurus, Tyrannosaurus Rex. So, change children's names—and yours, also—to a dinosaur name, or to the name of another current play material. For instance, Christopherosaurus, Aliciaosaurus, Care Bear Jose, Care Bear Tomika. Recall that an earlier generation of children delighted in learning to say, sing and spell Supercalifragalisticexpialidocious.

Word play and word games are a natural adventure and occur in the "riddles, jokes, puns, double meanings, multiple meanings, rhymes, sound fun, and word games" children of this stage use in conversing with each other (Tomkins and Tway, 1985, p. 361). Favorite children's literature that is built on word and concept play includes: *Amelia Bedelia* (Parish), *A Chocolate Moose for Dinner* (Gwynne) and *The King Who Rained* (Gwynne), *Morris and Boris* (Wiseman), *Otter Nonsense* (Juster) and *Daffy Dictionary* (Rosenbloom).

Home and Family and Constructional Materials Centers

Since professionals have observed that the greatest quantitative and qualitative language fluency occurs in the home and family centers and the constructional materials (blocks) centers, which invite social interactive play and language, these two centers are irreplaceable in value for school-age children. The centers may have to be modified in form depending upon the constraints of the 1st, 2nd and 3rd grades. A group of adventuresome teachers in the elementary grades, who had been taught how to make systematic observations of their students at play and how to select and evaluate play materials, carefully added either a home and family center or a constructional materials center to their individual classrooms. Each reported greater student persistence to academic tasks and fewer behavioral and social problems. Teachers of compensatory eduation and learning disabled students who experimented by adding these centers to their programs reported similar findings, as well as improved study skills. The teachers found that play themes occurring in the home and family centers indicated a consolidation of acquired language and academic learnings as children explored confusing changes in their home and school relationships (such as divorce, separation and school failure). Some children preferred to continue "working" on a block construction over several days as it changed form and function. Again, the linkage of thinking, play and language is observable to adults when a complicated space center, airport or metropolitan park system is built and modified within the classroom setting.

Language Centers

Jokes and riddles about pickles, monsters, elephants, gorillas, salamanders, mice and moose abound in healthy children's language exchanges. Knowledgeable teachers can capitalize upon these to promote language curiosity and competence. A creative 2nd-grade teacher had her students create their own booklets based on the theme of double meanings, using the format of Gwynne's *The King Who Rained* and *A Chocolate Moose for Dinner*. The project lasted all year, and students' language understanding and achievement test scores grew. Another playful 2nd-grade teacher overheard her students telling moose jokes. She included a joke-telling time each day, and they quickly began to create their own responses. For example, "What does a moose have for breakfast?": Moose juice, moose eggs, moose toast, moose flakes, moose oatmeal. During successive weeks, mice and gorilla jokes were used. In each of these instances, the children were playing with the enormous (enormoose) flexibility and variability of thinking and language, something that takes a lifetime to master.

Poetry, a daily *must* for this stage child, can be selected from potent sources. Leland B. Jacobs, Langston Hughes, Louise Binder Scott, Shel Silverstein and Ogden Nash are beloved mesmerizers of children.

An area of the classroom can be designated a "Joke Center," "Linger, Laugh and Learn Location," "Rib-Tickler Spot" or "Collections of Funny Stuff."

Books

Books with cartoon characters will promote enjoyment as well as language expansion and concept attainment; moreover, they can inspire reluctant children to read and more able children to create other language, jokes, stories and poetry. Books based on family fun and animal happenings include: *Peanuts, Snoopy, Garfield, Marmaduke, Heathcliff* and *The Family Circus*. Favorite books can be read aloud and used for journal artwork and compositional writing include the *Ramona* series (Cleary), *Charlotte's Web* (White) and *The Jungle Book* (Kipling). The possibilities are limited only by the playful vision of the teachers.

SUMMARY

Adults who are playful and love language and its beauty, power, elegance and flexibility have innumerable opportunities to help young children grow in language fluency, enjoyment and competence by linking people, play and the production of sounds, words and concepts. Whether you are working with children in the Toddler Stage (1½ to 3 years), the Play Stage (3-7 years) or the Work Stage (7-10 years), remember:

- Bathe children in a pleasant, rhymical stream of language while engaged in everyday tasks, routines and transitions: Scrub and Rub time in the Tub!
- Model playful attitudes and actions for growing children. Surrender some control and gain enjoyment and vivification.
- Provide less corrective criticism, which blocks free expression, and more supportive feedback.
- Help young children fall in love with sounds and words and phrases: "Fuzzy Wuzzy was a bear."
- Link the self-expressive arts of movement, play, language, music and art. Do the Cha-Cha with language. Put your "whole self" in.
- Use playful interchanges: "Five Little Monkeys," topsy-turvey talk.
- Use playful songs children ask to sing over and over: "If You're Happy," "Old MacDonald."

- Select children's literature that has beautiful, repetitive, silly or elegant language: Dr. Seuss, Leland B. Jacobs or Shel Silverstein.
- Arrange play centers or language arts centers that spark higher levels of thinking, play and language: home centers, construction materials centers, joke and riddle areas.
- Include rhymes, chants, riddles and jokes that are lovely to the ear, delicious to the palate, tickling to the torso and generative to the emerging mind.

Researchers studying language for two decades in varying countries and settings have shown that it is critical that young children have accepting, responsive, playful adults who help them try out language, who model correct forms and who expand and extend their language, provide play activities and materials, and enjoy language possibilities with them. In serving as playful models, appreciative listeners, play partners and extenders, we encourage children's thinking, play and language in their manifold forms and limitless variations.[2]

[2]Why did Judy the Moose dislike typing? She made so many moose-takes.

REFERENCES

Almy, A. "A Child's Right to Play." *Childhood Education* 60 (1984): 350.

Bayless, K.M., and Ramsey, M.W. *Music: A Way of Life for the Young Child.* St. Louis, MO: Mosby, 1982.

Bruner, J.S. *The Process of Education.* Cambridge, MA: Harvard University Press, 1962.

_____. "Play, Thought, and Language." *Peabody Journal of Education* 60 (1983): 60-69.

Coody, B. *Using Literature with Young Children* (3rd ed.). Dubuque, IA: Brown, 1983.

Chukovsky, K. *From Two to Five.* Berkeley, CA: University of California Press, 1963.

Dewey, J. *How We Think.* Boston: D.C. Heath, 1933.

Erikson, E.H. "A Healthy Personality for Every Child." Mid-Century White House Conference on Children and Youth, 1951.

_____. *Childhood and Society.* New York: Norton, 1963.

Garvey, C. *Play.* Cambridge, MA: Harvard University Press, 1977.

Genishi, C., and DiPaola, M. "Learning Through Argument in a Preschool." In L.C. Wilkinson, ed., *Communicating in the Classroom.* New York: Academic Press, 1982.

Gruber, H.E., and Vonèche, J.J. *The Essential Piaget.* New York: Basic, 1977.

Hutt, C. "Exploration and Play." In B. Sutton-Smith, ed., *Play and Learning.* New York: Gardner, 1979.

Mead, G.H. *Mind, Self and Society.* Chicago: University of Chicago Press, 1934.

Mitchell, L.S. *The Here and Now Story Book.* New York: Dutton, 1948.

Oppenheim, J.F. *Kids and Play.* New York: Ballantine, 1984.

Piaget, J., and Inhelder, B. *The Psychology of the Child.* New York: Basic, 1969.

Pellegrini, A.D., DeStefano, J.S., and Thompson, D.L. "Saying What You Mean: Using Play To Teach 'Literate Language.' " *Language Arts* 60 (1983): 380-84.

Ross, D.D. "Competence, Relational Status and Identity Work: A Study of the Social Interactions of Young Children." Paper presented at Annual Conference of National Association for the Education of Young Children, Washington, D.C., 1983.

Singer, D.G., and Singer, J.L. *Partners in Play.* New York: Harper and Row, 1977.

Sutton-Smith, B., ed. *Play and Learning.* New York: Gardner, 1979.

_____. "Play Isn't Just Kid's Stuff." Reprinted in J.S. McKee, ed., *Early Childhood Education 80/81.* Guilford, CT: Dushkin, 1981.

Tompkins, G.E., and Tway, E. "Adventuring with Words: Keeping Language Curiosity Alive in Elementary School Children." *Childhood Education* 61 (1985): 361-65.

Emergent Literacy:

How Young Children Learn to Read and Write

New insights into how children learn to read and write are changing—dramatically—the teaching of literacy.

Dorothy S. Strickland

Dorothy S. Strickland is State of New Jersey Professor of Reading, Rutgers University, Graduate School of Education, 10 Seminary Place, New Brunswick, NJ 08903.

Judy, aged 4, and Mikey, aged 5, are huddled close together looking at a picture storybook. Mikey begins to "read" to Judy. He is self-assured as he turns each page, his face displaying the knowledge of someone very familiar with the text. Although the words he utters are not always exactly those appearing in the written text, his rendering is an extraordinarily close approximation. Moreover, the meanings conveyed by Mikey are consistently appropriate, as are his intonation and style of storybook reading.

Judy notices that Mikey's attention seems rooted to the pictures and asks, "Mikey, what are all those black marks at the bottom of the page for?"

With unwavering confidence, Mikey answers, "Oh, those are for people who can't read the story from the pictures."

Anecdotes such as this one have been told many times, most often as cute vignettes describing a child's view of the world. However, recent research on young children's literacy development has shed new meaning on these stories. Researchers investigating children's explorations into reading and writing now regard stories like this one of reading "imitation" as highly significant demonstrations of literacy learning. Although early childhood educators have always been aware that young children enter school with a remarkable knowledge of oral language, it is only recently that awareness of their written language has received serious attention.

Current investigations build on the work of John and Evelyn Dewey (1915/1962), who contrasted the functional, meaning-driven learning that children engage in before they enter school with "the practices of the schools where it is largely an adornment, a superfluity and even an unwelcome imposition" (p.2). More recently, the work of Marie Clay (1982) has provided the foundation for new ways of studying and thinking about early literacy. Teale and Sulzby (1989) outlined the distinctive dimensions of the new research. Among its chief characteristics, they found:

- The age range studied has been extended to include children 14 months and younger;
- Literacy is no longer regarded as simply a cognitive skill but as a complex activity with social, linguistic, and psychological aspects;
- Literacy learning is perceived as multidimensional and tied to the child's natural surroundings, so it is studied in both home and school environments.

Literacy is no longer regarded as simply a cognitive skill but as a complex activity with social, linguistic, and psychological aspects.

New Perspectives

The study of literacy learning from the child's point of view has given us new insights into how young children learn to read and write.

Learning to read and write begins early in life and is ongoing. When two-year-old Josh rushed to his Mom with the newspaper in his hands and shouted, "Peanut, peanut," she was puzzled at first. After noticing the advertisement for his favorite brand of peanut butter, she was both surprised and pleased at the connections he was making. Young children who live in a "print-rich" environment are constantly observing and learning about written language. Most of their learning occurs as a natural part of their daily lives, not as something rare or mysterious.

Learning to read and write are interrelated processes that develop in concert with oral language. The old

Dorothy S. Strickland, "Emergent Literacy: How Young Children Learn to Read and Write," *Educational Leadership*, Vol. 47, No. 6, March 1990, pp. 18-23. Reprinted with permission of the Association for Supervision and Curriculum Development.

belief that children must be orally fluent before being introduced to reading and writing has been replaced with the view that the language processes—listening, speaking, reading, and writing—develop in an interdependent manner. Each informs and supports the other. Recognizing the value of informal activities with books and other print materials, one teacher in an urban program for four-year-olds sets aside a short period of time each day especially for "book browsing." Children are encouraged to find a book they like and a comfortable place to read. They may read alone or with a friend. Book browsing usually follows a read-aloud session. The teacher uses this time to observe children as they recreate renderings of stories read to them. Children discuss and argue about their favorite pictures and characters. The teacher is amazed at how these children, most of whom have rarely been read to at home, have become so absorbed with literature. They constantly make connections between the content in books and related discoveries inside and outside the classroom. And, not surprisingly, the books that have been read to them are also their favorites for independent browsing.

Young children who live in a "print-rich" environment are constantly observing and learning about written language.

Learning to read and write requires active participation in activities that have meaning in the child's daily life. Participating in listing all of the items needed to prepare a particular recipe, for example, can be an important literacy event for a young child. Helping to check off each item as it is purchased and then used in the recipe makes oral and written language come together through an activity that has current meaning for the child. This immediacy makes the activity much more meaningful than one that serves

merely as preparation for something to be learned in the future.

Learning to read and write involves interaction with responsive others. As parents, caregivers, and teachers become increasingly aware of the importance of young children's attempts to write, they take time to listen to the stories and messages evoked by scribbling, which may be intelligible only to the writer. One kindergarten teacher shared her amusement as she recalled how an eager writer confidently began to share a story elicited from an entire page of scribbling. After a few minutes of reading, the youngster stopped abruptly and in an apologetic tone exclaimed, "Oops, I wrote that twice!"

Learning to read and write is particularly enhanced by shared book experiences. Family storybook reading plays a special role in young children's literacy development, and researchers have learned much through observations of this familiar ritual. Sharing books with young children has long been recognized as a crucial aid to their language and literacy development and as a socializing process within families. Teachers and caregivers can further support this process when they use "big books" to encourage children to participate in reading. These allow children to see the print as the story is being read to them at school in much the same way they do when being read to at home. The highly predictable language and storylines of these picture storybooks permit groups of youngsters to "read along." Saying aloud the repeated refrains and rhymes with the reader helps give them a sense of what it means to be a reader.

Traditional Perspectives

Traditionally held views about reading and writing differ fundamentally from the concept of emergent literacy. Although learning to speak is accepted as a natural part of the maturation process that doesn't require formal instruction, the mastery of reading and writing has been considered an arduous learning task, requiring a period of intense readiness. Only after children were thoroughly primed with the necessary prereading skills was "real" reading instruction begun. "Getting them ready" consisted largely of direct instruction in learning letter names, letter-sound relationships, and a vari-

Content of interest and importance to children is the basis for learning language, learning through language, and learning about language.

ety of visual-perceptual tasks. The task of learning to write waited until reading was well underway. Children were considered literate only after their reading and writing began to approximate adult models.

In contrast, an emergent literacy curriculum emphasizes the ongoing development of skill in reading and writing and stresses participation in literacy activities that are meaningful and functional from the child's point of view. In operation, here is how the two viewpoints might look in a kindergarten classroom.

Old Ways Versus New

Teacher A has spent considerable time planning a program that will ensure her students are ready for the 1st grade curriculum. Preparing them for the reading program is of particular interest to her, since that is a high priority of the parents and of the 1st grade teachers. The entire year has been blocked out so that each letter of the alphabet is given equal time for in-depth study.

Using a workbook as her guide, she teaches the children the names of the letters of the alphabet, their corresponding sounds, and how to trace them in upper and lower case. The children play numerous games and engage in a variety of activities based on each letter. *All* of the children go through *all* of the activities in the order prescribed by the workbook, regardless of their previous knowledge. Reading instruction takes place during a specified time each day, and except for occasionally reading a story aloud, the teacher does very little to make literacy connections beyond that time.

Since kindergarten children are

thought to be incapable of and uninterested in writing, the teacher makes no provision for it in the curriculum. She gives workbook unit tests periodically. These closely resemble the nationally normed readiness test that will be given at the end of the year. The tests help Teacher A to identify those children who may be falling behind. Although she tries to give these children extra help, the very nature of the program allows little differentiation of instruction.

Thus, children who fail to catch on early keep falling farther and farther behind. By the end of the year, they either repeat kindergarten or are assigned to transition classes. Even those children who do well on the standardized test must often repeat the phonics program in 1st grade—this is a consequence that has baffled both Teacher A and the 1st grade teachers.

Teacher B relies heavily on the classroom environment to prompt student involvement with literacy. There is an inviting reading center filled with books within reach of the children. Most of the titles are familiar, since the books have already been read aloud. A writing center is also available with plenty of writing tools, paper, magnetic letters, and an alphabet chart at the eye level of the children. Children are encouraged to use these centers daily. Printed materials are everywhere. There is a message board where they record important news and reminders each day, and personal mailboxes made of milk cartons encourage note writing. Teacher B values scribbles, pictures, and beginning attempts at spelling as engagement in the writing process.

Adorning the walls are numerous charts depicting graphs, poems, lists, and other important information related to the theme currently under study. Read-aloud time occurs at least twice each day. Stories, poems, and informational books are shared. Books with highly predictable language and storylines are stressed, since they encourage group participation and independent rereading in the reading center.

Although Teacher B has definite goals regarding the concepts and skills she wishes to foster, she sees no need to organize them hierarchically or to introduce them in isolation. Rather, the print environment and related activities are carefully orchestrated to

allow children to build on what they already know about literacy, refine it, and use it for further learning. Although a unit of study about bugs might lead to a poem about a busy buzzy bumblebee and an opportunity to discuss the letter *b*, the emphasis is not placed on merely matching letter to sound but on helping children gain an understanding of a pattern in their language—that certain letters and sounds are often related.

Teacher B looks for evidence of these understandings and assesses learning through observation and analysis of children's independent reading and writing and through their participation during storytime. She is distressed when what she has documented about a child's knowledge is not always revealed on a standardized test.

In this classroom, literacy learning is not relegated to a specific time of day. Rather, it is integrated into everything that occurs throughout the day. Most important, content of interest and importance to children is the basis for learning language, learning through language, and learning about language.

It is important to recognize that both Teacher A and Teacher B are caring, concerned professionals. Each is a fine example of the theoretical framework from which she operates. Teacher A operates from a traditional readiness framework, in which the teacher is both keeper and dispenser of knowledge. Her lesson plans are segmented and preorganized into what are thought to be manageable bits and pieces, dispensed in small increments over a specified time. All children receive the same instruction, and little use is made of the knowledge about language that children bring with them to school.

Teacher B sees her role as that of facilitator of children's learning. The classroom environment is structured so that certain events are very likely to occur. Learning stems as much from these incidental literary events that occur by virtue of living within a print-rich environment as from the numerous daily activities planned to involve children in oral and written language. Teacher B expects differences in the way children respond to the activities she plans. She carefully monitors their responses and plans accordingly. She emphasizes helping children build on

Child, teacher, and parent should celebrate each new learning by focusing on what is known rather than what is lacking.

what they already know in order to make connections to new learning.

Issues for Instruction
The move toward full-day kindergartens and programs for four-year-olds has prompted increased concern for developmentally appropriate instruction. Many schools are addressing this concern by implementing programs reflecting an emergent literacy perspective.

Not surprisingly, interest in emergent literacy has brought with it a host of issues. The issues reflect the problems schools face as they attempt to serve a younger population and, at the same time, change perspective on a host of long-held beliefs. Issues that predominate are those related to the place of writing and invented spelling, the development of skills, assessment, and continuity.

Writing and invented spelling. Because the importance of paying attention to young children's writing is a relatively recent concern, teachers and parents often feel uneasy about how they should respond to children's scribbles, strings of letters, and one-letter words. Traditional writing lessons have been associated with neatness, correct spelling, and proper letter formation. Teachers need to learn as much as they can about the early spellings that children produce independently. Encouraging children to scribble and invent their own spellings does not lead them to think that phonetic spelling is systematically being taught; they are aware that their inventions may not conform to adult norms. The children know that, as with other areas of their development, they are simply functioning as young learners moving gradually toward adult standards. Child, teacher, and

Learning to read and write requires that children participate in activities that have meaning in their daily life. Learning must be interesting and important to the child. (United Nations photo by John Isaac)

parent should celebrate each new learning by focusing on what is known rather than what is lacking. Providing daily opportunities for varied experiences with literacy is the best assurance that children will begin to demonstrate what they know about writing and spelling as they compose stories and messages. Spelling errors should never be allowed to interfere with the composing process.

The development of skills. As educators, we must be careful not to give parents the impression that we are anti-skills; we are not. Rather, we need to help them see the differing ways that skills are developed through an emergent literacy perspective: not as an accumulation of information about a task but embedded within the child's growing ability to actually do the task. For example, children learn letter names and the sounds they represent as a part of the purposeful reading and

writing they do, not as a set of meaningless fragments of information. Stress is placed on helping children think with text and helping them to become independent learners. Unfortunately, poor and minority children—who would benefit most from holistic approaches that require them to think with text and encourage them to become independent learners—are often the least likely to get this type of instruction.

Appropriate assessment. Although standardized tests have undergone severe criticism as screening devices and evaluative measures of young children's literacy, they unfortunately continue to be highly regarded by some policy makers as definitive evidence of young children's learning (Chittendon 1989). Challenges regarding the assumptions underlying such tests, particularly the narrowness with which literacy is defined, raise serious ques-

tions about their use (Valencia & Pearson 1987). Children's initial explorations with literacy involve a variety of experiences with books and print, which may be used for assessment. Among these are their knowledge of print conventions, their understandings about the relationships between letters and sounds (invented spellings), and their growing interest in listening to and making sense of stories. Standardized tests tap but a few of these. Yet, even as early as kindergarten, standardized test results are used to make important decisions about placement, retention, and promotion.

The integration of assessment and instruction is fundamental to an emergent literacy perspective. Increased reliance on systematic observation, record keeping, and analysis of children's classroom participation and work products and less reliance on standardized tests are the hallmarks of student evaluation and teacher planning.

The need for continuity. Continuity in the early grades is critical. Children who are supported by an emergent literacy curriculum in the prekindergarten and kindergarten years, only to be faced with a subskills approach in 1st grade, will not only be confused, they will be unable to demonstrate what they do know about literacy. Collaborative curriculum decision making with teachers and administrators within a particular school and with those in the early childhood centers that feed into them is essential. In addition to supporting articulation between schools and grades within a school, educators must help parents understand new approaches to literacy that may be outside their experience. Children benefit from consistency in their lives. They function best when the adults they care about most reflect a comfortable harmony in their expectations and beliefs.

References

Chittendon, E. (1989). "Assessment of Young Children's Reading: Documentation as an Alternative to Testing." In D. S. Strickland & L. M. Morrow (Eds.) *Emerging Literacy: Young Children Learn to Read and Write*. Newark, Del.: International Reading Association.

Clay, M. (1982). *Observing Young Readers*. London: Heinemann.

Dewey, J. and Dewey, E. (1915/1962). *Schools of Tomorrow*. New York: Dutton.

Teale, W. and Sulzby, E. (1989). "Emergent Literacy: New Perspectives." In D. S. Strickland and L. M. Morrow (Eds.). *Emerging Literacy: Young Children Learn to Read and Write*, pp. 1-15. Newark, Del.: International Reading Association.

Valencia, S. and Pearson, P. D. (1987). "Reading Assessment: Time For a Change." *The Reading Teacher*, 40, 726–733.

Resources on Emergent Literacy

Bissex, G. (1980). *GNYS AT WRK: A Child Learns to Write and Read*. Cambridge, Mass.: Harvard University Press.

Clay, M. (1975). *What Did I Write?* Portsmouth, N.H.: Heinemann.

Ferreiro, E. & Teberosky. (1982). *Literacy Before Schooling*. Portsmouth, N.H.: Heinemann.

Genishi, C. & Dyson, A.H. (1984). *Language Assessment in the Early Years*. Norwood, N.J.: Ablex.

Hall, N. (1987). *The Emergence of Literacy*. Portsmouth, N.H.: Heinemann.

Harste, J., Woodward, V. & Burke, C. (1984). *Language Stories and Literacy Lessons*. Portsmouth, N.H.: Heinemann.

Holdaway, D. (1979). *The Foundations of Literacy*. New York: Ashton Scholastic.

Schickedanz, J. A. (1986). *More Than the ABC's: The Early Stages of Reading and Writing*. Washington, D.C: NAEYC.

Strickland, D. S. & Morrow, L. M. (Eds.) (1989). *Emerging Literacy: Young Children Learn to Read and Write*. Newark, Del.: International Reading Association.

Taylor, D. & Strickland, D. (1986). *Family Storybook Reading*. Portsmouth, N.H.: Heinemann.

Teale, W. & Sulzby, E. (Eds.). (1986). *Emergent Literacy: Writing and Reading*. Norwood, N.J.: Ablex.

Temple, C. A., Nathan, R. G., Burris, N.A. & Temple, F. (1988). *The Beginnings of Writing*. Boston, Mass.: Allyn and Bacon.

—Dorothy S. Strickland

EARLY CHILDHOOD PHYSICAL EDUCATION

The Essential Elements

CARL GABBARD

Carl Gabbard is a professor and director of the Child Movement Lab, Department of Health and Physical Education, Texas A&M University, College Station, TX 77843.

During the last 10 years a considerable amount of attention has been focused on physical activity programs for children three to five years of age (traditionally designated as preschoolers). Much of the support for this interest is a result of several factors, including research findings that suggest early intervention with health-related fitness and motor development programs as an appropriate means of enhancing children's academic development and physical wellness. Several educators and researchers contend that intervention during this phase of child development is crucial in developing a foundation that may be a significant influence on the quality of life and intellectual productivity in a child's later years. Another significant factor in the popularity of early childhood programs is the concern for improving the quality of day-care.

Unfortunately, several of the suggestions for early childhood physical education content have been scaled-down versions of curricula designed for older children. Some recommendations have been based on the more traditional activities approach, which focuses primarily on the selection of simple games and dances as the core of the curriculum. An alternative to this general curricular model is a format based more upon our understanding of motor development/human movement and the developmental needs of children (Gabbard et al., 1987; Gallahue, 1982). A common characteristic among models of this type is the use of teaching themes that have been identified as essential elements related to the child's fundamental movement characteristics and physiological needs.

Closely associated with this human movement theoretical model is the identification of phases of motor development that characterize the developmental motor skill capabilities and performance of individuals. Gabbard, LeBlanc, and Lowy (1987) identify the early childhood state (approximately 2-7 years of age) with the fundamental movement phase of motor development (Table 1). Gallahue (1982) also describes this association in a similar theoretical model. The characteristic psychomotor behaviors that originate from this phase are categorized as locomotor skills, nonlocomotor (stability) skills, manipulative skills, and movement awarenesses.

Theoretically, these movement components may be referred to as the foundation or essential elements of motor skill performance. Figure 1 represents an illustrative example of the foundation from which more complex motor tasks can be performed. Acceptance of this developmental concept would also lend support to the critical importance of specifically designed physical activity programs during the early childhood years. As the illustration in figure one depicts, the first level of efficient movement prerequisites is the movement awareness category. Along with emphasis on developing basic fundamental skills, this category should be the primary focus of the early childhood motor skill curriculum and may be viewed as one distinction from the basic elementary physical education program.

The following discussion briefly describes the essential elements of the movement foundation and health-related physical fitness. Table 2 provides a sample of the fundamental movement skills, movement awareness, and physical wellness components that are suggested as essential elements for the early childhood curriculum.

Movement awareness

This category refers to specific elements of the perceptual-motor system that are basic and essential to movement efficiency and motor skill performance. The execution of all motor tasks requires the use of sensory information and perceptual mechanisms. The components of movement awareness are, in essence, the substructure of the movement foundation. Basic com-

This article is reprinted with permission from the *Journal of Physical Education, Recreation & Dance*, September 1988, pp. 65-69. JOPERD is a publication of the American Alliance for Health, Physical Education, Recreation and Dance, 1900 Association Drive, Reston, VA 22091.

TABLE 1. Phases of Motor Behavior

Developmental Stage (Approximate Age Range)	Phase	Characteristic Psychomotor Behaviors
Prenatal-Infancy (−5 mo. to 1 year)	Reflexive	Initial flexion & extension, postural adjustments
Infancy (birth to 2 years)	Rudimentary	Rolling, sitting, crawling, creeping, standing, walking, grasping
Early Childhood (2 to 7 years)	Fundamental Movement (and perceptual efficiency)	Locomotor skills, nonlocomotor skills, manipulative skills, movement awarenesses
Middle-late Childhood (8 to 12 years)	Specific	Refinement of fundamental skills and movement awarenesses; use of foundation in specific dance, game (sport), gymnastics, and aquatic activities
Adolescence Adulthood (12 to adult years)	Specialized	Recreational or competitive level activities

ponents such as eye-hand and eye-foot coordination, for example, may be viewed as the foundation for proficiency with fundamental manipulative skills (e.g., throwing, catching, kicking, trapping). Activities within an eye-hand and eye-foot category would be much more diverse and generalized than fundamental throwing or catching themes, therefore merit separate and specific emphasis. An eye-foot theme for example, may include kicking and trapping activities as well as jumping, leaping, hopping, and walking with eye focus on lines or between ladder rungs. Eye-hand activities would also be quite generalized and include several gross motor skill activities (e.g., rolling, bouncing, throwing, catching, striking) and fine-motor tasks. Vestibular awareness (stability) is another example of a basic component that influences the execution of virtually all fundamental skills.

In reference to the human movement model, body, spatial, directional, and temporal awarenesses are generally associated with kinesthetic perception, that is, information derived from within the body, as opposed to stimuli received from the environment (i.e., visual, auditory, and tactile information). A feature that makes this information uniquely appropriate for this period of child development is that several of the concepts associated with movement awareness are also the concepts basic to an early childhood education. The introduction of these concepts (e.g., directions, size, shapes, body parts) through the use of movement activities is a well-accepted teaching strategy that not only brings fun to the learning process, but may also enhance learning retention.

Body awareness. Also referred to as *body concept* or *body knowledge,* this component is associated with the internal awareness of the location of one's body parts and their relationship to each other. An understanding of one's capabilities and movement pattern execution is also involved.

Spatial awareness. An extension of body awareness, this component refers to the child's perception of spatial relationships, based upon internal information and frequently, visual input. Descriptors include the ability to locate objects in space in relation to oneself, and locating the position of two or more objects in relation to each other. With this awareness (of space and the position of one's body), the child has additional information upon which to project the body.

Directional awareness. This component refers to the internal awareness of the two sides of the body (laterality) and the ability to identify dimensions of external space (directionality). It is through these elements that the child is able to understand the dimensions of space (e.g., left/right, up/down, in/out, front/back/sideways) and move the body through self-effort and guidance.

Vestibular awareness. The vestibular apparatus (located in the inner ear) provides information about the body's relationship to gravity. Thus, it serves as the basis for the body's sense of body position as it relates to stability (balance).

Temporal awareness. This component involves the awareness and timing mechanism required for coordinated, rhythmical movements. Since all movements are based upon an understanding and coordination of spatial-temporal characteristics, a well-developed time structure is another essential ingredient in the movement foun-

TABLE 2. The Essential Elements

Movement Awarenesses	Fundamental Locomotor Skills	Fundamental Nonlocomotor Skills	Fundamental Manipulative Skills	Health-Related Fitness
Body	Walking	Dodging	*Propulsive*	Aerobic
Spatial	Running	Stretching/	Ball Rolling	Endurance
Directional	Leaping	Bending	Throwing	Flexibility
Temporal	Jumping/	Turning/	Bouncing	Muscular
Rhythm	Landing	Twisting	Striking	Strength/
Eye-hand	Hopping	Pushing/	Kicking	Endurance
Eye-foot	Galloping	Pulling		
Vestibular	Sliding	Swinging/	*Receptive*	
Visual	Skipping	Swaying	Catching	
Auditory	Body Rolling		Trapping	
Tactile	Climbing			

dation. From this general structure, three teaching themes are suggested: eye-hand coordination, eye-foot coordination, and rhythmic awareness.

Visual awareness. Approximately 75 percent of the information derived from the environment is in the form of visual stimuli. Fundamental to the performance of virtually all motor tasks is the child's ability to judge depth, distance, and distinguish an object from its surrounding background (figure-ground discrimination).

Auditory awareness. The ability to discriminate, associate, and interpret auditory stimuli is prerequisite to all learning situations. The physical education setting is an excellent medium for introducing the basic characteristics of auditory discrimination, sound localization, and auditory figure-ground perception.

Tactile awareness. The ability to interpret sensations from the surfaces (skin) of the body is described as a sense of touch. Children increase their knowledge base and tactile awareness through touch and the manipulation of objects. From

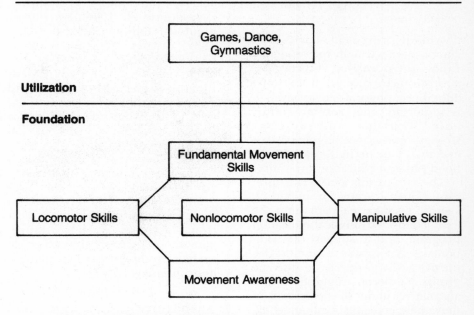

Figure 1. Foundation of Movement Skills Leading to More Complex Tasks

(e.g., run, jump, skip); (2) nonlocomotor skills—movements are executed with minimal or no movement of one's base of support,

fine-motor and gross-motor tasks, children learn and are guided by their sense of feel.

Fundamental movement skills

Along with a diverse and efficient movement awareness base, the acquisition of fundamental skills form the movement foundation upon which more complex game, dance, and gymnastic activities can be performed. The three categories of fundamental movement are (1) locomotor skills—movements that propel the individual through space

sometimes described as skills of stability (e.g., twist/turn, swing/sway); and (3) manipulative skills—movements that focus upon the control of objects primarily with use of the hands and feet. Two classifications of manipulative behavior are used: propulsive (e.g., throw, kick, strike) and receptive (catch, trap).

Health-related physical fitness

Including health-related fitness components in the early childhood curriculum has gained enormous support in recent years.

Two national fitness programs (AAHPERD, 1988; Fitnessgram, 1988) provide fitness standards and instructional suggestions for children five years of age and older. A preponderance of evidence suggests that early intervention with strategies for developing positive attitudes toward healthful physical activity may be a significant factor in enhancing one's physical and mental wellness in ensuing years.

AAHPERD (1988) and the American Academy of Pediatrics (1987) describe these essential elements related to health-related physical fitness:

- *Aerobic (cardiorespiratory) endurance* is the ability of the heart, lungs, and vascular systems to function efficiently at moderate to high intensity over extended periods of time.

- *Flexibility* is the ability to move muscles and joints through their full range of motion.

- *Muscular strength/endurance* is the ability of muscles to produce force at maximum effort (strength) and to sustain work at low to moderate intensities over extended intervals of time (endurance).

- *Body composition* is defined as the

> ## Early intervention with motor development programs may be a significant influence on the child's quality of life and intellectual productivity in later years.

relative percentages of fat to lean body mass.

While improvement of one's body composition is usually the result of a fitness program that incorporates several factors (e.g., nutritional adherence, physical activity level), it is important that aerobic endurance, flexibility, and muscular strength/endurance be regarded as essential elements in the early childhood physical education program.

The aim of this article is to present a justification for including specific essential elements into the early childhood physical education program, and to suggest the components that appear to be most distinctive and appropriate for this age group. Numerous suggestions and alternatives under the descriptors of movement concepts (Graham et al., 1987), movement framework (Logsdon et al., 1984), and movement variability (Gabbard et al., 1987) discuss the framework or method by which the essential elements may be presented. Use of these strategies adds strength and diversity to the movement foundation and provides the child with a movement vocabulary which is vital to understanding how the body moves. While the activities approach was not recommended as the curricular content by which the program should be held accountable, the use of carefully selected educational activities such as dance, games, and gymnastics as a vehicle to develop the essential elements is appropriate.

References

AAHPERD. (1988). *Physical best*. Reston, VA: American Alliance for Health, Physical Education, Recreation and Dance.

American Academy of Pediatrics. (1987). Physical fitness and schools. *Pediatrics, 80*(3), 449-450.

Fitnessgram. (1988). Dallas, TX: Institute for Aerobics Research in cooperation with Campbell Soup Company.

Gabbard, C., LeBlanc, B., & Lowy, S. (1987). *Physical education for children: Building the foundation*. Englewood Cliffs, NJ: Prentice-Hall.

Gallahue, D. (1982). *Understanding motor development in children*. New York: John Wiley & Sons.

Graham, G., Holt/Hale, S., & Parker, M. (1987). *Children moving* (2nd ed.). Palo Alto, CA: Mayfield.

Logsdon, B, Barrett, K., Broer, M., McKee, R., & Ammons, M. (1984). *Physical education for children: A focus on the teaching process* (2nd ed.). Philadelphia, PA: Lea & Febiger.

The State of American Preschool Playgrounds

JOE L. FROST
LOUIS E. BOWERS
SUE C. WORTHAM

Joe L. Frost is the Parker Centennial Professor at the University of Texas at Austin, Austin, TX 78712. Louis E. Bowers is a professor of physical education in the Department of Physical Education at the University of South Florida, Tampa, FL 33620. Sue C. Wortham is an associate professor in the Division of Education at the University of Texas at San Antonio, San Antonio, TX 78285.

How safe are our nation's playgrounds? Playgrounds for children are the subject of growing interest throughout the industrialized world, particularly in the United States. Two major reasons exist for this: (1) Evidence that play contributes to child development—social, cognitive, affective, motor—is accumulating at an accelerating rate, and (2) a growing awareness of preventable hazards on playgrounds. In the United States, these hazards, frequently resulting in child injuries or fatalities, are increasingly the basis for legal litigation.

Although some members of the general public believe that play is frivolous, wastes children's time, and detracts from academic success, little controversy exists among play scholars as to its overall value for child development.

Similarly, the issues of whether playgrounds are hazardous, and to what extent hazards exist, are being resolved. Data collected from hospital emergency rooms show that the number of playground injuries grew from about 118,000 in 1974 to more than 200,000 in 1988. "About 60% of all playground equipment-related injuries (for both public and home equipment) are a result of falls to the surface below the equipment... nine out of ten of the serious injuries" resulted from falls to the surface (U.S. Consumer Product Safety Commission, 1990, p. 1). Since most of these injuries were to young children (ages three to six) it is particularly important to examine the safety of preschool playgrounds.

> **The worst of the lot are accidents waiting to happen, sterile in play value, and essentially unfit for children's play.**

Recently published, the results of the first national surveys of American public elementary school playgrounds (Bruya & Langendorfer, 1988) and American public parks playgrounds (Thompson & Bowers, 1989) revealed an overall pattern of antiquated design, hazardous conditions, and poor or absent maintenance.

In the National Survey of Playground Equipment in Preschool Centers (Wortham & Frost, 1990) 349 centers located in 31 states were examined. Centers were randomly selected from lists of all state licensed centers within the area. Surveys were conducted by 62 trained early childhood and physical education professionals.

Survey Results: Equipment and Provisions' Play Value.

In evaluating results of the survey, two major factors were considered; play value and safety. The preschool outdoor environment that is rich in play value takes into account the developmental needs of the age groups involved. Three through five-year-old children engage in several types of play: exercise, dramatic (make-believe), constructive, and organized games. In addition, their play is affected by complexity, novelty, creative and problem-solving potential, and aesthetic qualities of equipment and materials.

The preschool survey revealed that a broad array of equipment, portable materials, and other provisions were available to young children. The permanent, fixed, equipment on a typical playground included one or more swings, slides, balance beams, overhead ladders, rocking apparatus, and climbers. Fewer than 20 percent of the playgrounds included see-saws and merry-go-rounds.

Among the portable materials, tricycles were most often available, with an average of about three per playground. Loose tires, sand, wagons, barrels and loose boards (building material, stacking blocks) were available, in descending order, ranging from about two tires per playground to about one barrel or board to every three playgrounds. Building materials and tools were absent on most playgrounds or from adjacent storage facilities.

Most playgrounds included grassy areas for organized games, accessible water, sand play areas, hard

This article is reprinted with permission from the *Journal of Physical Education, Recreation & Dance*, October 1990, pp. 18-23. JOPERD is a publication of the American Alliance for Health, Physical Education, Recreation and Dance, 1900 Association Drive, Reston, VA 22091.

surfaces for games and man-made shade structures. Storage, adjacent to or on the playground, was absent at over half of the sites. This is a critical omission, since convenient storage is essential to the provision of play materials for children's dramatic and constructive play and for organized games.

Cars and boats for dramatic play, water and earth (digging) play areas, and natural areas (plants, gardens) were found on fewer than one-third of the playgrounds. Toilet facilities, provisions for animals, and amphitheaters were found at only a few centers.

Playground Equipment: Safety.

Swings. There were 554 swing structures and 1,455 swing seats on the 349 playgrounds surveyed. About one-third (191) of the swing structures were designed for younger children (infants and toddlers) and 13 percent (194) had swivel suspensions to support tire swings. Hazardous elements were common, including 73 metal or wood seats, which constituted five percent of total swing seats. The United States Consumer Product Safety Commission (1981, p.8) guidelines recommend that seats be "constructed of light-weight material such as plastic, canvas, or rubber." Support structures were not firmly anchored on 45 swings; 21 percent of the structures had sharp corners, edges and projections; moving parts were in poor repair on 24 percent of the structures. Only 11 percent had barriers (e.g., low fences) to keep children from running into the path of swings.

The survey identified 531 slides or about 1.5 per playground. One hundred ten (110) of these were wide slides (over 3' wide). Six percent (34) of the slides had broken or missing parts; 18 percent (94) had sharp corners, edges, or projections; 16 percent (85) were not firmly anchored; 50 percent (264) had no deceleration chute at the slide exit.

Climbers. Combining all climbing equipment, the survey found that 16 percent were not firmly anchored; nine percent had unsecured or loose parts; ten percent had open holes at the end of pipes; 15 percent had sharp edges or protrusions; 39 percent lacked a guard rail around the highest platform; 44 percent contained openings between 4 1/2" and 9" that could entrap children's heads or necks. In addition, over 13 percent of the climbers were over eight feet in height and 24 percent were over seven feet high.

Merry-go-rounds. Among the 72 merry-go-rounds identified in the survey, 35 percent were not securely anchored; 60 percent had parts that were not securely fastened; 14 percent contained sharp edges and protrusions. Very hazardous conditions included open areas in the base around rotation post (16%); shearing actions in mechanism under the

Play's Contributions to Child Development

The evidence that play contributes to child development is impressive. Sources reveal that play *promotes cognitive development* (Sutton-Smith, 1967, 1977; Piaget, 1962; Saltz & Brodie, 1982; Fein, 1979; Saltz, 1980; Bruner, 1972; Bruner, Jolly & Sylva, 1976). Play *promotes social development* (Shure, 1981; Ladd & Mize, 1983; Eisenberg & Harris, 1984) and *leads to discovery, verbal judgment and reasoning.* It is also important in *developing manipulative skills, imaginative art, discovery, reasoning and thought* (Isaacs, 1933; Pepler & Ross, 1981). Play with objects *results in divergent production or expands uses for objects* (Sutton-Smith, 1968; Goodnow, 1969; Dansky, 1980b) and *improves problem-solving* (Sylva, 1977; Smith & Dutton, 1979; Dansky & Silverman, 1973; Eisenberg & Harris, 1984). Play *enhances language* (McCune-Nicolich, 1981; Schirmer, 1989).

Culture arises in the form of play (Huizinga, 1950). From a therapeutic perspective, play is *a means for overcoming fears* (Klein, 1932; Isaacs, 1933; Axline, 1947; Erikson, 1950). *Motor abilities are formed through play* (Bennett, 1980; Seefeldt, 1984; Staniford, 1979) and *playgrounds enhance motor development* (Gabbard, 1979; Myers, 1985).

Play training for children enhances imaginative play (Smilansky, 1968; Feitelson & Ross, 1973; Smith & Sydall, 1978), *enhances creativity* (Feitelson & Ross, 1973; Dansky, 1980a), *enhances language development* (Vygotsky, 1967; Lovinger, 1974; Saltz, Dixon & Johnson, 1977), and *enhances group cooperation* (Rosen, 1974; Smith & Sydall, 1978). Finally, *play training for teachers improves their interaction with children during play* (Busse, Ree & Gutride, 1970; Wade, 1985).

base (seat) of the device (9%); gear boxes that could crush fingers (4%).

Rocking equipment. The 175 pieces of rocking equipment (primarily spring-mounted animal seats) included the following hazards: 67 percent were not firmly anchored; 17 percent had missing parts; pinching was possible in 47 percent of the devices.

See-saws. The 76 see-saws identified in the survey included: 56 percent that were not firmly anchored; 40 percent with internal moving parts accessible to fingers; 28 percent with loose joints or fasteners; 26 percent with sharp corners or projections. Only 19 percent included cushioned impact devices between the end of see-saws and the ground.

Surfacing. A wide range of surfacing material was found under and around playground equipment, including loose materials (sand, pea gravel, mulch), commercial surfacing and hard surfaces (packed earth, asphalt, concrete), and grass. Only the loose materials and commercial playground surfacing meet CPSC guidelines for safety. Less than half (48%) of the material under swings (sand, pea gravel, commercial matting) met this requirement; 53 percent of the material under slides and 63 percent under climbers met the requirement. The survey did not ascertain whether the acceptable materials were in a properly maintained condition (8" to 12" deep under and around equipment). Two of the authors participated in the surveys in about a dozen states. None of the playgrounds they surveyed met common guidelines for depth and maintenance of surfacing material.

Implications: Play Value

Overall, most of the preschool playgrounds surveyed were developmentally sterile and lacking in play value. The major emphasis, judging from equipment and materials available, was on exercise or motor activity. The equipment for such activity was essentially the same as that provided

Tricycles were the most frequently available portable materials available on playgrounds.

for older children at public schools and public parks. Since play is the primary vehicle for learning and development (intellectual, social, physical) in the early years, it is essential that all preschool playgrounds include a broad, rich selection of age/size-scaled equipment for motor development and portable materials (with storage) and other provisions for dramatic play, constructive play (with proper supervision), and organized games. In addition, the well-designed environment will feature nature areas, amphitheaters, toilet and drinking facilities, and places for gardening and animal care.

The availability of infant-toddler play areas and appropriate equipment designed especially for infants and toddlers was difficult to determine from the survey. Infants were served at many of the centers surveyed, but data on numbers of infants and toddlers served compared to older preschool children were not available. Smaller equipment for younger children was found on almost half of the playgrounds, and only 36 percent of the playgrounds had large and small equipment separated.

There were other indications that provisions for infant and toddler play were included on the preschool playgrounds. Tricycles, push and pull toys, small vehicles, balls, and materials for sand and water play were available at many of the sites surveyed.

Survey results indicate that some provisions are being made for the youngest children on preschool playgrounds. However, it appears

that designers of these playscapes do not understand the developmental differences between infants and toddlers and older children. Many of the playgrounds surveyed included opportunities for play experiences for younger children, but few of the play environments that served infants and toddlers provided for their unique play needs. The inclusion of smaller equipment and a sprinkling of toys seemed to be the norm, rather than providing environments designed specifically to enhance emerging physical, social, language, and cognitive skills in children between the ages of birth and three years.

Safety

The overall results show that preschool playground equipment is smaller in size and better maintained than public school equipment (Bruya & Langendorfer, 1988) or public park equipment (Thompson & Bowers, 1989) and the array of equipment and materials is more varied. However, this finding only intensifies the concern for safety at school and park playgrounds: overall, the safety of preschool play equipment is unconscionably bad. All three locations feature playgrounds that are remarkably consistent with the antiquated 1928 guidelines of the National Recreation Association (1928). The worst of the lot are accidents waiting to happen, sterile in play value, and essentially unfit for children's play.

Four fundamental factors contribute to the hazardous state of playgrounds: (1) design of equipment, (2) zoning (arrangement) and installation of equipment, (3) maintenance, and (4) play leadership or supervision.

Given the current state of preschool playgrounds, school administrators should conduct careful evaluations of existing playgrounds, using professional expertise, followed by the development of a master plan replacing or rebuilding their playgrounds. Selection of equipment and related activities are guided by the master plan.

Much of the playground equipment now available from manufacturers and distributors violates CPSC safety guidelines. An analysis of equipment in the 1989 catalogs of 24 national companies showed that only three companies had "no violations." Nine additional companies had "limited violations" or "some violations." Twelve companies, or half of those surveyed, advertised play equipment with "extensive violations" or "extreme violations" (Frost, 1990). This analysis used catalog photographs, equipment specifications, and firsthand inspection of equipment. The original analysis by the author was verified in blind analyses by two additional playground specialists. The violations found in playground equipment catalogs included head entrapment areas, open base merry-go-rounds, excessive heights (up to 16'), heavy, rigid swing seats, and pinching/crushing mechanisms. Consequently, consumers should seek expert help and/or secure copies of CPSC guidelines and related professional literature to guide equipment selection. (See references for relevant literature.) A growing number of play equipment manufacturers/distributors are studying play and play environment research and are making dramatic improvements in their equipment. Such companies are valuable sources of playground assistance.

Once equipment has been selected, it must be properly installed. Some manufacturers provide directions for installation of their equipment. It is wise to secure experienced installers and require that they sign written confirmation that the equipment is installed according to manufacturer and CPSC guidelines. For additional security, the manufacturer's representative should inspect the installation and certify proper installation.

It is the rare preschool that provides regular, comprehensive maintenance for the playground, or that

provides staff training for playground supervision. The maintenance program should include the selection or development of a safety checklist (see Thompson, Bruya & Crawford, 1990), regular inspection of equipment and grounds, and prompt, thorough repairs. Teachers, administrators and custodians should receive annual training about playground safety and supervi-

Almost half of the climbing equipment had openings that could entrap a child's head.

sion. They, in turn, should conduct safety sessions with children, including playground walk-throughs, discussions, and examples of safe and unsafe play practices. Staff training can begin with workshops staffed by play specialists, literature reviews, and visits to model playground programs.

Playgrounds are an essential component in the educative process for preschools. They contribute to child development and to academic goals such as language and reading. The play value of playgrounds is complemented by playground safety. The National Survey of Playground Equipment in Preschools concluded that preschool playgrounds are in a state of general disrepair and, overall, they are hazardous. Those concerned with preschool playgrounds should reevaluate their playgrounds, taking into account equipment design, safety, installation, maintenance, and supervision. The safety issue is of sufficient concern to involve school administrators, regulatory agencies, and legislators. Such groups, working with professionals in play, child development, physical education, and design, can collectively rebuild American playgrounds

and ensure that they meet the developmental needs and safety requirements of young children.

References

Axline, V. (1947). *Play therapy.* Boston: Houghton Mifflin.

Bennett, C. (1980). Planning for activity during the important preschool years. *Journal of Physical Education, Recreation & Dance, 15*(7), 30-34.

Bruner, J. S. (1972). The nature and uses of immaturity. *American Psychologist, 27,* 687-708.

Bruner, J. S., Jolly, A., & Sylva, K. (Eds.) (1976). *Play: Its role in development and evolution.* New York: Penguin.

Bruya, L.D., & Langendorfer, S.J. (Eds.). (1988). *Where our children play: Elementary school playground equipment.* Reston, VA: American Alliance for Health, Physical Education, Recreation and Dance.

Busse, T., Ree, M., & Gutride, M. (1970). Environmentally enriched classrooms and the play behavior of Negro preschool children. *Urban Education, 5,* 128-140.

Dansky, J.L., & Silverman, I.W. (1973). Effects of play on associative fluency in preschool-aged children. *Developmental Psychology, 9,* 38-43.

Dansky, J. L. (1980a). Cognitive consequences of sociodramatic play and exploratory training for economically disadvantaged preschoolers. *Journal of Child Psychology and Psychiatry, 20,* 47-58.

Dansky, J.L. (1980b). Make believe: A mediator of the relationship between free play and associative fluency. *Child Development, 51,* 576-579.

Eisenberg, N., & Harris, J.D. (1984). Social competence: A developmental perspective. *School Psychology Review, 13,* 267-277.

Erikson, E.H. (1950). *Childhood and society.* New York: Norton.

Fein, G. (1979). Play in the acquisition of symbols. In L. Katz (Ed.), *Current topics in early childhood education.* Norwood, NJ: Ablex.

Feitelson, W., & Ross, G.S. (1973). The neglected factor—play. *Human Development, 16,* 202-223.

Frost, J. L. (Summer, 1990). Playground equipment catalogs: Most can't be trusted for safety. *Texas Child Care Quarterly.* Austin, TX: Corporate Child Development Fund of Texas and Texas Department of Human Services.

Gabbard, C. (1979). *Playground apparatus experience and muscular endurance among children 4-6.* (ERIC Document Reproduction Service, SP 022 020; ED 228190).

Goodnow, J. J. (1969). Effects of handling, illustrated by use of objects. *Child Development, 40,* 201-212.

Huizinga, J. (1950). *Homo Judens: A study of the play element in culture.* London: Routledge & Kegan Paul.

Isaacs, S. (1933). *Social development in young children: A study of beginnings.* London: Routledge & Kegan Paul.

Klein, M. (1932). *The psychoanalysis of children.* London: Hogarth.

Ladd, G., & Mize, J. (1983). A cognitive-learning model of social-skill training. *Psychological Review, 90,* 127-157.

Lovinger, S.L. (1974). Sociodramatic play and language development in preschool disadvantaged children. *Psychology in the Schools, 11,* 313-320.

McCune-Nicolich, L. (1981). Toward symbolic functioning: Structure of early pretend games and potential parallels with language. *Child Development, 52,* 785-797.

Myers, G.D. (1985). Motor behavior of kindergartners during physical education and free play. In J.L. Frost & S. Sunderlin (Eds.), *When children play.* Wheaton, MD: Association for Childhood Education International.

National Recreation Association (1928). *Report of committee on standards in playground apparatus.* New York: National Recreation Association.

Pepler, D.J. & Ross, H.S. (1981). The effects of play on convergent and divergent problem solving. *Child Development, 52,* 1202-1210.

Piaget, J. (1962). *Play, dreams and imitation in childhood.* New York: W.W. Norton.

Rosen, C.E. (1974). The effect of sociodramatic play on problem solving among culturally disadvantaged children. *Child Development, 45,* 920-927.

Saltz, E. (1980).*Pretend play: A complex of variables influencing development.* Paper presented at the Annual Meeting of the American Psychological Association.

Saltz, E., & Brodie, J. (1982). Pretend-play training in childhood: A review and critique. In D.J. Pepler & K.H. Rubin (Eds.), *The play of children: Current theory and practice.* New York: S. Karger.

Saltz, E., Dixon, D., & Johnson, J. (1977). Training disadvantaged preschoolers on various fantasy activities: Effects on cognitive functioning and impulse control. *Child Development, 48,* 367-368.

Schirmer, B.R. (1989). Relationship between imaginative play and language development in hearing-impaired children. *American Annals of the Deaf, 134,* 219-222.

Seefeldt, V. (1984). Physical fitness in preschool and elementary school-aged children. *Journal of Physical Education, Recreation & Dance, 55* (9), 33-40.

Shure, M.B. (1981). Social competence as problem solving skill. In J.D. Wine and M.D. Smye (Eds.), *Social Competence* (pp. 158-185). New York: Guilford Press.

Smilanski, S. (1968). *The effects of sociodramatic play on disadvantaged preschool children.* New York: John Wiley.

Smith, P.K. & Dutton, S. (1979). Play and training in direct and innovative problem solving. *Child Development, 50,* 830-836.

Smith, P.K., & Syddall, S. (1978). Play and non-play tutoring in preschool children: Is it play or tutoring which matters? *British Journal of Education Psychology, 48,* 315-325.

Staniford, D.J. (1979). Natural movement for children. *Journal of Physical Education and Recreation, 50*(8), 14-17.

Sutton-Smith B. (1967). The role of play in child development. *Young Children, 22,* 361-370.

Sutton-Smith B. (1968). Novel responses to toys. *Merrill-Palmer Quarterly, 14,* 151-158.

Sutton-Smith, B. (1977). Play as adaptive potentiation. In P. Stevens (Ed.), *Studies in the anthropology of play.* Cornwall, NY: Leisure Press.

Sylva, K. (1977). Play and learning. In B. Tizard & D. Harvey (Eds.), *Biology of play.* London: Heineman.

Thompson, D., & Bowers, L. (Eds.). (1989). *Where our children play: Community park playground equipment.* Reston, VA: American Alliance for Health, Physical Education, Recreation and Dance.

Thompson, D., Bruya, L.D., & Crawford, M.E. (1990). In S.C. Wortham and J.L. Frost (Eds.), Maintaining play environments: training, checklists, and documentation. *Playgrounds for Young Children: American survey and perspectives.* Reston, VA: American Alliance for Health, Physical Education, Recreation and Dance.

U.S. Consumer Product Safety Commission (February 26, 1990). *Focus projects on playground surfaces—transmittal of hazard analysis.* United States Government memorandum. Washington, DC: U.S. Consumer Product Safety Commission.

Vygotsky, L.S. (1967). Play and its role in the mental development of the child. *Soviet Psychology, 12,* 62-76.

Wade, C. (1985). Effects of teacher training on teachers and children in playground settings. In J. Frost (Ed.), *When children play.* Washington, DC: Association for Childhood Education International.

Wortham, S.C., & Frost, J.L. (Eds.). (1990). *Playgrounds for young children: American survey and perspectives.* Reston, VA: American Alliance for Health, Physical Education, Recreation and Dance.

Transition Time:
Make It A Time of Learning for Children

Young children spend much of their day in transition, passing from one place or activity to another. Caregivers can use this time for planned activities which reinforce learning.

Betty Ruth Baker

Betty Ruth Baker is Assistant Professor of Curriculum and Instruction and Director of Early Childhood Education at Baylor University in Waco, Texas.

The first major transition occurs when children come from home to the preschool or child care center. There are periods when children move from place to place in the classroom as well as throughout the building. There are times when children complete activities before others and there are times when the group must prepare for a new activity. Too often during these times young children are told to "Sit down, be quiet, and wait," rather than shown how to use the time effectively.

Transition activities are teaching techniques and are used to prepare children to relax, to listen, to sit down, to move from place to place and activity to activity with ease while providing an opportunity to think and reason, to apply and reinforce concepts, and to learn. Transition activities differ from regular activities in purpose, length, and frequency, but they require the same consideration and planning. If planning is adequate children will move with ease through the routine (Hildebrand, 1981).

The best transition activities may come from ideas generated from a lesson or other activities (Ramsey & Bayless, 1980). These activities usually require simple or easily available materials or no materials at all. They may be active or quiet and teacher directed or independent. Transition activities should be selected according to the developmental characteristics, needs, and interests of the children to provide optimum learning.

Questions to Consider When Planning Transition Times

The following questions may prove helpful in planning for transition times:

• What is the purpose of the activity?

• What kind of activity preceded transition time and what kind of activity will follow?

• What kind of instructional materials will be needed for the activity?

• What is the space or physical setting needed for the activity?

• Will the activity be teacher directed or independent?

• Will the activity be for large group, small group, or individuals as needed?

• What directions will be needed for the activity?

• What are the learning opportunities involved in this activity?

• What are the developmental characteristics and needs of the children participating in the activity?

• How much time should be spent in transition?

Caregivers and teachers find that activities go along smoothly until it is time to clean up, until children begin to complete activities or need to move to another place. Children need positive direction during these times and teacher attitude is important. The teacher/caregiver's sense of calm and order will help children overcome problems (Spodek, 1985).

Ideas for planning transition activities may be derived from a variety of sources. Resource and activity books, records, stories, games, poetry, songs, and finger games provide ideas to be adopted into transition activities.

The following transition activities should offer ideas for planning.

From *Day Care and Early Education*, Summer 1986, pp. 36-38. Published by Human Sciences Press, 72 Fifth Avenue, New York, NY 10011. Reprinted by permission.

Arrival at the Center or Preschool

• Greet the children with a smile or welcome and show them what activity to do.

• Greet the children and provide choices for them for the first activity of the day.

• Make name cards for each child. On arrival give the child the name card to place in a box or basket decorated for the season. Count and see how many names are in the box or basket and who is present. Note: The name card can be used for other activities during the day.

• Construct an attendance chart and on arrival have each child place a star, seal, or mark by his or her name.

• Construct a choice board to identify learning centers in the room. Allow each child to select a learning center to work in independently.

Cleaning Up or Putting Away Materials

• Listen to music while putting away materials. Tell the children something to listen for in the music.

• Group the children in teams to be responsible for different centers in the room.

• Construct a "Helpers' Chart" listing the clean-up responsibilities.

• Sing while putting away materials or cleaning up.

• Write words to familiar tunes. Example (to Mary Had a Little Lamb):

It is time to clean up
To clean up, to clean up.
It is time to clean up
Put your work away.

This transition time period requires children to use memory and recall to know where to put materials. It also encourages pride in the environment and develops skills in accepting responsibility.

Preparing for Another Activity

• Use puppets to give directions.

• Make a cover for a picture or chart about the activity or topic of discussion by folding a piece of butcher paper the size of the picture or chart and cutting three-sided openings in the paper. Number the openings. Place over the picture. Open the numbers and have children guess the activity or topic of discussion.

• Repeat finger games or poems about the activity.

• Walk in imaginary shapes. Example: circle, square, rectangle.

• Walk in the shape of numerals and letters.

• Tell the children a riddle.

• Construct a "feel" box or bag. Place an item in the box or bag that suggests the next activity. Let each child feel the item to determine the next activity or topic.

• Construct a "look" box or bag. Place objects in the bag or box that identify the next activity. Let each child look at the item to determine the next activity.

Ideas for Relaxing

• Have children pretend they are a bowl of jello and shake all over.

• Have children pretend they are blowing up a big balloon, to blow harder and harder until the balloon bursts. Then have them sit and relax.

• Clap hands in a rhythm pattern.

• Use rhythm instruments to form rhythm patterns.

• Use exercise records to provide an opportunity to release extra energy.

• Play games. Examples: "Simon Says," "I Spy," and "Moving Water — Still Water."

• Sing familiar action songs. Examples: "Did You Ever See a Lassie" and "The Farmer in the Dell."

• Tell children to wiggle body parts and conclude with wiggling whole self; then sit with hands in lap.

Rest Time

• Tell children to imagine they are tired puppies — yawn, stretch, and roll on the floor. Then have them be very still.

• Listen to music. Identify various instruments. Then have children listen for various instruments.

• Repeat rhymes. Example:

I know it's best to take a rest.

I have a little key.
I lock my lips
Pull down my shades (close eyes)
I can not talk or see.

• Show a filmstrip on the ceiling with or without narration.

• Select a book and read only part of the story each day.

Preparing for Listening

• Lock lips and put the "key" on your shoulder.

• Put on elephant ears, rabbit ears, or cat ears.

• Have children pretend to be a snowflake, raindrop, leaf, or feather. Quietly whirl around and sit quietly.

• Clap hands beginning loud and fast. Then get softer and slower until hands are in lap and all is quiet. You can also substitute a poem or rhyme for hand clapping.

Moving from Place to Place in the Building

• Direct children to walk like animals — bears, elephants, etc.

• Have children pretend to wear invisible shoes or moccasins and to walk as quietly as possible.

• Tell children to pretend to be birds or butterflies.

• Have children form a line with each child a passenger in an airplane. The leader is the pilot.

• Have children form a line with you as the engine. Assign the last child to be the caboose to turn the light off in the room and close the door as you leave.

• Walk down the hall or to the playground looking for color, shapes, letters, numbers, or other designated items.

• Turn a jump rope into a worm or caterpillar by attaching a head to one end and a tail to the other. Children form the body and legs by holding on to the rope with one hand.

• Holidays can provide ideas for transition. Have children move like ghosts, bats, witches, turkeys, reindeer, Santa's elves, snowflakes, leprechauns, and bunnies.

Grouping Children, Changing Centers, or Completing Activities

• Use signals to indicate time to change centers, complete activities, or clean up. Flash lights, ring a bell, play a musical instrument, or set a timer or alarm clock.

• Have a get-ready signal such as a flashing light or a ringing bell for the children to know they have five more minutes to complete a task and clean up for the next activity.

• Group children by shirt/dress color or article of clothing; by home address; by a common number, shape, letter, or picture which they hold.

• With masking tape place a line on the floor by the various centers or work areas. As children finish a task at one center they go to the line and with the next signal move on to the next place.

• Children make a "train" by forming a line and walking around the room, stopping at each center. You are the conductor and tell who will stop and work in the center.

• Play a record or a piano and stop the music. When the music stops call names of children and where they will work.

• Hold up a card with each child's name written on it to identify time to move.

• Write the child's name on the chalkboard to indicate time to move.

Waiting for Others to Complete Activities

• Cut out pictures of available classroom materials from teacher supply catalogues. Mount on cards. Place cards in a file box. On completion of activity the child may select a card and go to work with the pictured material.

• Make an apron with different color pockets. In each pocket place activity cards. On completion of an activity each child selects a color and takes a card or is assigned a color and activity.

• In folders, large envelopes, or boxes provide activities for children to use when they have completed an assigned task. Plan a special table, space in the room, or area rug for this activity.

• Prepare a listening station with a tape player, record player, and headsets. Select stories, music, and poetry for independent listening.

• Construct a planning board to identify learning centers in the room. Allow each child to select a center for independent activity after completing assigned tasks.

Conclusion

Transition should be a learning time for young children. Activities must be appropriately selected and well planned, and should meet the developmental needs of the young child. Planned and implemented in a comfortable setting, transitional activities provide opportunity for imaginative and creative thinking, develop appropriate social behaviors, and motivate, relax, reinforce, and prepare children for the continuing learning experience.

References

Hildebrand, Verna. *Introduction to Early Childhood Education.* New York: Macmillan, 1981.

Ramsey, Marjorie E., and Bayless, Kathleen M. *Kindergarten Programs and Practices.* St. Louis: The C. V. Mosby Co., 1980.

Spodek, Bernard. *Teaching in the Early Years.* Englewood Cliffs, NJ: Prentice-Hall, 1985.

Conceptualizing Today's Kindergarten Curriculum

Bernard Spodek

University of Illinois

Abstract

As kindergartens have become an almost universal experience for American children, there is a need to rethink the concepts underlying kindergarten education. Child development research and theory can help educators understand what young children can know. What children need to know is determined by what society thinks is important. Kindergartens have taught children various things at different times. Kindergarten programs that have developed from diverse traditions also teach young children different things. Educators today need to make explicit what they believe children should learn in kindergarten. Kindergarten programs can be responsive to children's developmental levels while emphasizing cultural knowledge and the foundations of academic scholarship. Such programs should be evaluated both in terms of their developmental appropriateness and in relation to their educational worth to the children taught and the communities served.

As kindergarten attendance has become nearly universal, and more than half of all children now enter kindergarten with prior early childhood education experience, disagreements have arisen about what kindergarten education should include. Some educators see kindergarten as primarily a socializing experience, allowing children to adjust to life in the elementary school. Others believe that kindergartens should focus more on teaching academic skills.

These competing conceptions of kindergarten education, sometimes characterized as academic versus developmental kindergartens, or child-centered versus content-centered kindergartens, reflect different ideologies. One ideology conceives of early childhood education as supporting children's personal development, with educa-

tion following development. The other ideology views early childhood education as supporting children's learning and is concerned with teaching content.

The purpose of this article is to make the possible purposes of kindergarten education explicit in order to promote better conceptualization and research. A historical review of the field indicates that the definition of appropriate kindergarten experiences has changed over time. Different educational traditions also lead to different conceptions of what constitutes appropriate kindergarten experiences for young children.

Historical Purposes and the Kindergarten Curriculum

The kindergarten was originally created in Germany over 150 years ago. It has been reconstructed many times since to serve different purposes. The original Froebelian kindergarten was designed to teach children philosophical idealism. They learned about the unity of Man, God, and Nature through activities and materials that symbolized aspects of that unity. The Froebelian Gifts, Occupations, and Mother Songs and Games were used in prescribed ways. The ideas symbolized by the materials were more important than the attributes of those materials and what could be discovered by exploring these attributes. This characterizes the original ideal of the kindergarten, which was brought to America in 1856.

With the development of scientific progressive education in the first quarter of the twentieth century, kindergarten theory and practice changed. Influenced by developmental theorists like G. Stanley Hall and learning theorists like Edward L. Thorndike, kindergartens were redesigned to teach children proper habits that would be the basis for adult behavior. Later, as psychoanalytic theory rose to popularity, kindergartens were redesigned to provide emotional prophylaxis. Children would use kindergarten play activities to rid themselves of childhood conflicts that could lead to neurotic complexes in adulthood.

Large numbers of immigrants needed to be assimilated into American society during the latter third of the nineteenth century and the first third of the twentieth century. To meet this need, the kindergarten was used to socialize and Americanize young immigrant children and their parents.

During this same period, kindergartens began to be incorporated into the elementary school, serving as a transition between children's homes and the elementary school. Kindergartens allowed children to be socialized into the role of student, making a gradual adjustment to the rigors of the primary grades while academic demands were increased. More recently, kindergartens have been viewed as just another primary grade, offering the content of elementary subjects now taught to children 1 year younger. Reading instruction, for example, may be considered appropriate for 5-year-olds and is incorporated into some kindergartens (Spodek, 1973a).

Kindergartens stood apart from the other grades when they were first introduced into the public schools. These early kindergartens were different from the rest of the elementary school in their philosophy, goals, and methods. Kindergarten education was seen as resulting from children's play and manipulative activities rather than from lessons and recitations. Music, art, and nature study were legitimate kindergarten subjects of study for young children, while teaching the three R's was postponed.

It can be seen that the issue of whether kindergartens should be academic or developmental is a fairly recent one. Although, as noted earlier, few practitioners view development as a focus of kindergarten education, many scholars, researchers, and teacher educators in early childhood education reflect this view in their exhortations to practitioners. Indeed, the controversy of the 1960s over the potential of early childhood education, reflected in Jensen's (1969) article and the many responses to it, centered around the issue of whether, or how much, early experiences can influence development.

Child Development and the Early Childhood Curriculum

Teachers in the early Froebelian kindergartens had few concerns about child development. The original approach to kindergarten education was based on philosophical speculation about the nature of childhood rather than on scientific studies of childhood and the effects of particular experiences on children's growth and development. Indeed, the field of child development did not originate until well after Froebel created the kindergarten.

It was with the development of the child study movement and the work of G. Stanley Hall, starting in the 1890s, that the close association of early childhood education and child development began. The establishment of the field of child development as a scientific discipline and of the progressive education movement helped to fuse the two fields (Weber, 1984). The relation between child development and early childhood education during this period also reflected the progressive reconstruction of kindergarten education that took place during the first quarter of the twentieth century. Since that time, early childhood educational theories have been bonded to related theories of child development.

Kohlberg and Mayer (1972) discuss the three ideologies that characterized Western education and that also characterize developmental theories. The *romantic* ideology reflects the work of Rousseau, Froebel, Gesell, Freud, and others who viewed development as maturation and education as the unfolding of inner virtues and abilities. The *cultural transmission* ideology conceives of education as passing knowledge, skills, values, and social and moral rules from one generation to the next. Behaviorism provides the psychological principles for a technology of education within this ideological stream. The *progressive* ideology views education as helping the child achieve higher levels of development as a result of structured, though natural interactions with the physical and social environment. The idea of education as the attainment of higher levels of development reflects this relation between human development and education that has resulted in a conception of the teacher as a child development specialist. This ideology is consistent with a constructivist conception of development based upon Piaget's work.

Using Developmental Knowledge to Match Children to Programs

There are two uses that can be made of developmental theory in designing early childhood programs within these ideologies. One is to match program elements to children's level of development; the other is to use developmental theory as a basis for early childhood education programs.

The first use of child development theory is reflected in the guidelines, *Developmentally Appropriate Practices* (Bredekamp, 1986), issued by the National Association for the Education of Young Children (NAEYC). In proposing guidelines that address only developmental appropriateness, NAEYC rejected the need to use additional criteria to judge early childhood educational programs. No guidelines were proposed to allow a judgement to be made about whether a program is educationally worthwhile, or whether children are being adequately socialized, either for life in school or in the community—both legitimate early childhood educational goals.

The judgment, based on developmental appropriateness alone, obscures the quest for the answer to the question: What does the early childhood teacher teach and how well is it taught? A judgment about what one teaches young children seems irrelevant in determining the quality of a program, except to the extent that it nurtures the general development of the child. An early childhood education program is not evaluated in relation to children's achievement of that program's outcomes or in relation to the worth of program outcomes.

It is questionable whether early childhood programs, including kindergarten programs, should be judged as worthy based on developmental appropriateness alone. Enhancing children's knowledge may be equally as important as enhancing their development, and possibly a better goal for early childhood education.

Basing Programs on Developmental Theories

The second use of developmental theory is found in the view that early childhood education is the practical application of the principles of child development (Caldwell, 1984). This suggests that early childhood education programs reflect only child development research and theory. One indicator of such a belief is that Head Start programs are viewed as comprehensive child development programs and are located in *child development centers* rather than in schools or even preschools. Another indicator is the use of different developmental theories as the basis for the various early childhood curriculum models developed in the 1960s (Evans, 1975).

This view is closely related to the traditional goals of early childhood education programs. For decades, early childhood teachers were taught that the purpose of their programs was to foster the social, emotional, physical, and intellectual development of children. Although these programs have focussed more on cognitive development and less on socioemotional and physical development since the mid-sixties, early childhood education programs are still evaluated in terms of their effects on development. The programs that were developed for children of low-income families in the 1960s, for example, were evaluated in terms of their effects on IQ scores, an index of cognitive development. Long-term effects were sought related to the continuing intellectual development of children who had been in these programs.

It is difficult to find empirical evidence, however, to support the claim that early childhood programs significantly affect children's cognitive development. The evidence of long-term effects of these programs leaves open the question of the effects of these programs on developmental processes while supporting the value of these programs for improving academic achievement and school success. In the studies of long-term effects of early childhood education, IQ gains—indices of intellectual development—fade by about third grade, while the effect of early education on later school achievement continues through the high school (Consortium for Longitudinal Studies, 1978). Today's response to Jensen's (1969) earlier query: "How much can we boost IQ and scholastic achievement?" might be that we can be more confident about boosting scholastic achievement than about boosting IQ.

The confounding of early childhood education with child development may result from a confusion of developmental theory with educational theory. There is a significant difference between development and education and between developmental theory and educational theory. Fein and Schwartz (1982) have clarified the difference, suggesting that theories of development are universalistic and minimalist. They describe what is considered a normal course of growth and change within an environment with a minimal core of features. In contrast, educational theories are particularistic and maximalist, dealing with practice related to particular individuals in specific settings aimed at maximizing the benefits of deliberate interventions. In addition, developmental theory views change in the individual as a result of multiple influences, while educational theory looks essentially on the influence of practice on individuals. Although one type of theory can inform the other, one cannot be derived from the other.

Although developmental theory can be viewed as a resource to the early childhood curriculum, it is inappropriate to conceive of it as its source (Spodek, 1973b). Biber (1984) suggests that the starting place for an educational program "should be a value statement of what children ought to be and become" (p. 303).

The Content of Early Childhood Programs

In viewing early childhood education, we need to analyze its content, *what is taught*, separately from its process, *how it is taught*. The process of educating young children is closely related to their level of development. Knowledge of child development can help educators understand what young children are capable of knowing, how children come to know what they know at a particular stage in their development, as well as how they come to know that what they know is true (how they validate their knowledge). What young children need to know is not solely determined by what certain children are capable of knowing. It also is determined by what society thinks is important for children to know. These goals of early childhood education need to be made explicit.

The need to articulate the content of kindergarten education reflects a need to articulate the content of education at all levels. The National Endowment for the Humanities has recently issued a report criticizing elementary and secondary schools for being too involved with "process" and not involved enough with helping children and youth become deeply knowledgeable of the roots of our culture (Cheney, 1987).

This criticism might also be applied to early childhood education programs. Most individuals will agree that some things are more worthy of learning or knowing than others. Educators need to define the content of early child education as something more that a set of skills that will enable children to function adequately and meet the demands of the primary-grade curriculum. Specifying the various domains of development as the goals of early childhood education without a concern for what is being learned is also inadequate.

Making explicit the content of early childhood education to be learned by children does not require that all children learn the same thing or that there be a single standard early childhood curriculum. Indeed, there are many ways that kindergarten content can be defined and many possible kindergarten programs that can be justified.

It is helpful to look at early childhood education programs that result from traditions different from our own to see other possibilities. These alternative programs need not serve as models of ideal education. Rather, they can help us reflect on kindergarten education from a different vantage point. China has a very different kindergarten program than our own; analyzing a study of Jewish kindergartens in America provides a second alternative.

Kindergartens in China

Education in the People's Republic of China was significantly influenced by Soviet educational practice at every level in the 1950s. This influence continues, though relations with the Soviet Union have not been close for some time. As a result of this influence, kindergarten programs found in China before Liberation in 1949, which were based on the American progressive education model, were replaced by a model based on the Soviet kindergarten.

The Chinese kindergarten curriculum emphasizes academics. The formal program contains six areas of learning: music, language, mathematics, physical education, art, and general knowledge (a combination of science and social studies). In addition to the formal curriculum, opportunities for play are provided (Lu, 1987). Since Chinese kindergartens also function as child-care centers, meals, snacks, health inspections, naps, and informal activities are included in the daily program.

The six areas of the curriculum are taught through formal *lessons*. Three- to 4-year-olds have one or two lessons a day of about 15 minutes duration, 4–5-year-olds have two 20–25-minute lessons, and 5–6-year-olds have two to three 25–30-minute lessons each day. (Kindergartens, like all schools and businesses in China, operate 6 days a week.) The lessons are taught through direct instruction, with teachers lecturing to children, often using teacher-made teaching aids to illustrate the concepts presented and to maintain the children's interest. The children remain attentive and well behaved during these lessons, sitting around tables, often with their hands behind their backs. After the teachers' presentations, time is provided for the children to participate in related activities (Spodek, in press).

The Chinese kindergarten educators' concern that their programs be developmentally appropriate is expressed by not placing undue stress on the children. Their program, however, is based on the subjects that are taught rather than on developmental theory. The source of the kindergarten curriculum is the same as that of later school curricula. Kindergarten lessons, while simpler and designed to be more interesting to young children, are no different in kind from those offered to older children and youth.

Although the lessons taught in Chinese kindergartens are academic, they also represent a form of socialization. Children are socialized into the life of the school. The academic work of the kindergarten provides children with a basis of common knowledge that represents the foundation for later studies. In addition, the kindergarten teaches children to function properly as students in a school. The socialization experience is equally important as the lessons learned.

American Jewish Early Childhood Programs

A very different approach to determining early childhood curriculum is suggested by Feinberg (1988), who studied the curriculum choices of Jewish nursery schools and kindergartens. Rather than identify the goals of these programs as the enhancement of social, emotional, intellectual, and physical development—goal statements associated with many early childhood programs—she looked at what Jewish early childhood educators want children to know, searching within traditional Jewish knowledge for the source of an early childhood Jewish curriculum. The areas she identified included Bible Study, the Jewish Way of Life, the Hebrew Language, Israel, Jewish Peoplehood, Faith in God, and Jewish Values and Attitudes.

The American Jewish early childhood schools with which Feinberg was concerned serve a particular subpopulation in our nation, with traditions, values, and other cultural elements different from those of the majority culture. Since these programs value different learnings from those valued in non-Jewish early childhood programs, the content of these programs is also different. Of course, there is also much content in common with other American early childhood schools since there is much that both groups commonly value.

The Jewish early childhood programs Feinberg studied are very much concerned with socializing children into a culture—in this case, a minority American culture. The curriculum that young Jewish children should learn in these schools is necessarily made explicit, since it is doubtful that this knowledge could be transmitted through the many informal interactions the children have in their lives or through their contacts with the mass media or with other community agencies. Although this curriculum emphasizes socialization, it is also rich in content. There is much that children are expected to learn—the roots of Jewish culture—and the programs that are developed are designed to transmit that culture in a way that is developmentally appropriate, that is, in a way that enables the children to derive meanings from what is taught, not just learn it by rote.

American Kindergarten Programs

It is obvious that the curriculum constructs of Chinese kindergartens are different from those of American kindergartens. Each program is based on a distinct theoretical orientation with unique standards for what constitutes appropriate kindergarten activities. But what about the differences between the American Jewish early childhood programs and secular American kindergarten programs? The teachers and program developers in these Jewish early childhood schools hold the same theoretical orientation as do those in non-Jewish American schools. The preparation of teachers in American Jewish early childhood programs is similar to that of other American early childhood teachers, as are their views of development, education, and learning. Because sectarian Jewish early childhood programs serve different cultural needs than do secular American kindergartens and are based in a culture that is not reflected in everyday American life, the content of these programs must be made explicit.

In reality, one can find a parallel content to Feinberg's categories of knowledge in traditional American early childhood programs. However, the knowledge transmitted in most American programs is implicit; it is often not discussed or studied. Standard American early childhood programs teach about the American way of life, about the English language, about America, about American peoplehood, and about American values and attitudes, parallel topics to those identified for Jewish programs.

The day-to-day curriculum experiences offered in early childhood programs relate to the American way of life. The knowledge our society wants young children to acquire is embedded in the books read to them, the stories told, the songs sung, the experiences offered, and the relations nurtured among children and between children and adults.

One of the most important elements of all early childhood programs is language. Literacy education for young children is being viewed as increasingly significant. However, literacy skills are only part of the language learnings provided to young children. Schools teach about American language to both bilingual and monolingual children. They also share rich oral and written traditions of children's literature and poetry, folk stories, and fairy tales. Many of the holidays celebrated with children in school—from Columbus Day, to Thanksgiving Day, to President's Day, to Martin Luther King Day, and so on—relate to American history and American traditions. These are celebrated in school to instill a sense of

American peoplehood. These celebrations and the learnings related to them help all children, whatever their cultural background and cultural heritage, develop a sense of belonging to the American culture, while not necessarily denying their own. It is as if each child's own forebears had celebrated that first New England Thanksgiving, no matter when they or their ancestors actually arrived on our shore (Spodek, 1982). These elements are not absent from kindergarten programs. They are an implicit part of them. However, because they are unarticulated, they remain unstudied by early childhood educators.

Explicating the Early Childhood Curriculum

Making the content of early childhood education programs more explicit does not make it less developmentally appropriate. These two characteristics of programs are not mutually exclusive. Judging programs on the basis of developmental appropriateness alone, however, is not enough. In addition to developmental appropriateness, the values of our culture and the nature of the knowledge children need to gain should determine the content of kindergarten programs (Spodek, 1986).

Some early childhood educators are attempting to make program content more explicit. Elkind (1988), for example, has recently addressed the issue of what to teach in early childhood education. He suggests that early childhood teachers should begin to teach young children the content, the concepts, and classification of the different disciplines such as science, social studies, and history. Young children should also be taught different colors, shapes, and sizes, learning to match, categorize, discriminate, and order things according to the similarities and differences of their attributes.

Elkind also addresses the issue of how to teach, suggesting that the most appropriate way of doing this for young children is through projects. Elkind's suggestion of an appropriate teaching method in kindergarten is similar to that of the progressive kindergartens of the first quarter of the twentieth century (Weber, 1984). As progressive education influenced early childhood education programs then, kindergartens changed. Froebel's games and materials were modified, and new activities to help children better understand their physical and social environment were introduced. Children explored the world immediately accessible to them, the "here and now," representing that world in their play, in their construction, in their art products, and in the stories and discussions they shared. Because the world that children experienced was an organic one—not organized by subjects or categories—units or projects, which integrate subject knowledge around themes or experiences, became the vehicle for educating young children.

Elkind's suggestion needs more elaboration before being implemented. Although it requires rethinking the assumptions underlying current early childhood educational curricula and changing how early childhood educators design programs for young children, his suggestion has its basis in the traditions of the field.

Programs that develop from such suggestions will be consistent with those suggested by Robison and Spodek in their book, *New Directions in the Kindergarten* (1965). This book, written more than 2 decades ago, proposed that kindergarten curricula be based on key ideas or concepts from various fields of knowledge. These key ideas could be used to test the intellectual worth of kindergarten content. Activities that would be integrated into units or projects would be designed to be developmentally appropriate.

Kindergarten educators do not have to make a choice between providing content-rich programs, as suggested here, and socializing children into the school and into the culture while providing a preparation for later schooling. Nor is there a conflict between programs that are responsive to children's developing understandings and abilities and programs that emphasize cultural knowledge and academic scholarship.

Conclusions

In designing kindergarten programs for children in contemporary American society, early childhood educators need to reconsider the assumptions upon which their teaching is based. The knowledge base of early childhood programs also needs to be made more explicit. In doing this, these programs would become appropriate for today's children.

Parents and teachers should not be misled by the false dichotomy between socializing kindergartens and academic kindergartens. Socialization is a continuous process, within the society at large and within each social institution or social group. Kindergarten children need socialization experiences just as all students do. However, the socialization of kindergartners includes learning the student role, learning the importance of academic learning, and learning basic literacy and mathematical skills. Being socialized does not mean learning to follow teachers' directions, to be quiet and compliant. It should mean becoming an independent seeker of knowledge and a creative thinker.

If kindergartens are to improve, educators must make explicit what is being taught and why. Educators can design programs that help socialize children, prepare them for later school learning, and that teach significant content. Kindergarten programs need to be evaluated, not only in terms of their developmental appropriateness, but also in relation to their educational worth, to the children taught and the communities served. Only when that content becomes public can it be evaluated as to its effectiveness, its worth, and its practicality.

References

Biber, B. (1984). *Early education and psychological development*. New Haven, CT: Yale University Press.

Bredekamp, S. (1986). *Developmentally appropriate practices*. Washington, DC: National Association for the Education of Young Children.

Caldwell, B. (1984). From the president. *Young Children*, **39**(6), 53–56.

Cheney, L. V. (1987). *American memory: A report on the humanities in the nation's public schools*. Washington, DC: National Endowment for the Humanities.

Consortium for Longitudinal Studies. (1978). *Lasting effects of preschool education*. Washington, DC: Government Printing Office.

Elkind, D. (1988). Early childhood education on its own terms. In S. L. Kagan & E. Zigler (Eds.), *Early schooling: The national debate* (pp. 98–115). New Haven, CT: Yale University Press.

Evans, E. D. (1975). *Contemporary influences in early childhood education*. New York: Holt, Rinehart & Winston.

Fein, G., & Schwartz, P. M. (1982). Developmental theories in early education. In B. Spodek (Ed.), *Handbook of research in early childhood education* (pp. 82–104). New York: Free Press.

Feinberg, M. P. (1988). *Placement of sectarian content for Jewish nursery schools and kindergartens in the United States.* Unpublished doctoral dissertation, University of Maryland, College Park.

Jensen, A. R. (1969). How much can we boost IQ and scholastic achievement? *Harvard Educational Review, 39,* 1–123.

Kohlberg, L., & Mayer, R. (1972). Development as the aim of education. *Harvard Educational Review, 42,* 449–496.

Lu, L. (1987). *Kindergartens in China.* Paper presented at the University of Illinois, Urbana-Champaign.

Robison, H. F., & Spodek, B. (1965). *New directions in the kindergarten.* New York: Teachers College Press.

Spodek, B. (1973a). Needed: A new view of kindergarten education. *Childhood Education, 49,* 191–195.

Spodek, B. (1973b). What are the sources of early childhood curriculum? In B. Spodek (Ed.), *Early childhood education* (pp. 81–91). Englewood Cliffs, NJ: Prentice-Hall.

Spodek, B. (1982). Early childhood education: A synoptic view. In N. Nir-Janiv, B. Spodek, & D. Steg (Eds.), *Early childhood education: An international perspective* (pp. 1–13). New York: Plenum.

Spodek, B. (1986). Development, values and knowledge in the kindergarten curriculum. In B. Spodek (Ed.), *Today's kindergarten: Exploring its knowledge base, extending its curriculum* (pp. 32–47). New York: Teachers College Press.

Spodek, B. (in press). Chinese kindergarten education and its reform. *Early Childhood Research Quarterly.*

Weber, E. (1984). *Ideas influencing early childhood education.* New York: Teachers College Press.

HOW GOOD IS YOUR KINDERGARTEN CURRICULUM?

Carol Seefeldt

Carol Seefeldt is a professor and director of the Institute for Child Study at the University of Maryland in College Park.

If you can answer these ten questions correctly, you've got a model kindergarten.

Here is a little test that should help principals evaluate the kindergarten curriculum in their schools. Circle the answers that best fit.

1. How many kindergarten teachers hold specialized degrees in early childhood education?
    100%   50%   under 25%

2. How many centers of interest are in any one kindergarten classroom? (A center of interest might be a place to build with blocks, easels and paints, a library corner, or a game center.)
    none   5 or 6   over 10

3. Is there a dramatic play area in which children can dress up and "make believe"?
    yes   no

4. Is the kindergarten nice and quiet? For example, are children taught to raise their hands before speaking?
    yes   no

5. What is the average age of kindergarten children at midyear?
    6½   6   5½

6. How often do kindergarten children take walking field trips in the school building or neighborhood?
    once a week   once a month
            once or twice year

7. Are children taught to recognize all 26 letters of the alphabet, both lower and upper case, and to make letter-sound correspondence?
    yes   no

8. How many children fail kindergarten and are placed in some other program before attending first grade?
    none   less than 20%
            more than 20%

9. How many poems, songs, or finger plays should a kindergarten child know by the end of the year?
    less than a dozen   a couple
            more than a dozen

10. Before children are permitted to attend kindergarten, must they pass a test or some type of developmental screening to guarantee that they can do the work successfully?
    yes   no

How did you do? Let's find out.
1. *How many kindergarten teachers hold specialized degrees in early childhood education?*

Give your kindergarten 10 points if all teachers have had training in early childhood education; 5 if about 50 percent of them have; and 0 if fewer than 25 percent.

You really need teachers with early childhood background for a successful kindergarten progrm. A successful kindergarten curriculum is not found in a commercial kit, prescribed lesson or unit plans, predetermined competencies, or programmed materials. It is found in teachers who have knowledge in three critical areas:

Knowledge of Children

The world has changed but children's growth and development have not. Five-year-olds are still about 36 inches tall, weigh about 40 pounds, and are active and energetic. Their thinking is grounded in the concrete, and although they are beginning to use symbols, they cannot think abstractly. They confuse reality and fantasy, believe inanimate objects have thoughts and motives, and do not understand that properties remain the same even if the shape or spatial arrangement has been changed.

Teachers should systematically observe children, talk with them, and try to uncover each child's thinking processes. In this way teachers can adapt

From *Principal*, Vol. 68, No. 5, May 1989, pp. 11-15. Copyright © 1989, National Association of Elementary School Principals. All rights reserved.

each curriculum experience to meet an individual child's needs for challenge and successful achievement.

Knowledge of Content

If anything is characteristic of five-year-olds, it is their desire to learn. Curious, enthusiastic kindergarten children want to know all about "ants, worms, cars, boats, water, air, space, foreign countries, letters, machines, trees, colors, families, seeds, rocks. And their deepest concerns are the timeless ones—love, hate, birth, death, friendship, war, peace, cosmic forces, good and evil" (Martin 1985).

Because of children's broad interests, teachers must have in-depth knowledge accessible to young children. Bruner (1966) advocated the idea that each content area has its own structure. Teachers who are knowledgeable of the structure of each content area are better able to determine the scope and sequence of learning experiences, and to make each one more meaningful for children.

Knowledge of Process

When teachers are familiar with both child and content, they are able to capitalize on every opportunity for teaching and learning. The learning potential in the simplest of activities, such as blowing bubbles, are seized. For some children, the goal of that activity might be to develop physical control. Others may be challenged to blow the largest, smallest, or most bubbles, or to measure how long a bubble lasts. Back in the classroom, children can describe their bubble experience in original stories and poems.

Teachers should share control of activities with the children. A good kindergarten curriculum is like a ballet between a sensitive adult and enthusiastic children. Both are in control, both initiate, both respond, and both take cues from one another.

Teachers should not be permissive. Froebel (1912) reminded kindergarten teachers that although they had to follow the natural laws of child growth and development, as gardeners they were also responsible for removing obstacles to growth. Teachers have the re-

sponsibility not only to tend, fertilize, and increase productivity of children but also, with sympathetic understanding, to redirect, guide, and prune undesirable growth.

Through systematic observing and recording of children's behavior, or structured interviews or tasks, teachers must evaluate children's progress continually. The object, however, should not be to grade children or determine whether they have passed or failed a set of predetermined competencies, but to better plan, monitor, and foster each child's growth and achievement.

2. *How many centers of interest are in any one kindergarten classroom?*

Your program gets 10 points for 10 or more centers of interest; 5 points for 5 or 6; and 0 points if there are none.

Because children, as all humans, learn through experiences, they must be able to touch, handle, move, taste, pound, see, hear, and do something in order to have an experience.

Centers of interest, arranged throughout the room, are one way teachers provide children with first-hand experiences. There should be spaces for block-building, art activities, music, reading, board games, puzzles, sociodramatic play, writing, science, and math. Children must be given time and freedom to explore, experiment, and engage in hands-on activity, alone or with others.

Raw materials—sand, wood, water, boxes, paints, paper—should be featured. These foster thinking because children have to figure out what to do with these raw materials and how to do it.

Children should choose the centers in which they work and make choices within those centers. For example, a child may choose the writing center and then make a choice of assembling a word with plastic alphabet blocks, printing it with letter stamps, typing it on a computer, or writing it on paper. In control, and making their own choices, children do not fail.

3. *Is there a dramatic play area in which children can dress up and "make believe"?*

You get 20 bonus points if you have a sociodramatic play area; 0 if you do not have one.

You get extra points because it takes real courage in today's pressured climate to recognize the value of sociodramatic play for children's intellectual growth and development and to provide an area for it in the classroom.

4. *Is the kindergarten nice and quiet? For example, are children taught to raise their hands before speaking?*

Take away 10 points if the kindergarten room is quiet. Give yourself 10 points if there is a hum of activity present and children are talking and arguing with one another.

Children must be encouraged to converse freely with one another, for it is through their informal conversations and interactions that "intellectual development in general, and literacy growth in particular" (Dyson 1987) take place. Children should be encouraged to talk about what they are doing as they work together on a puzzle, rotate the eggs in an incubator, or build with blocks.

More formal conversations should take place during group times when teachers encourage children to tell how they completed a project, found their way to the nurse's office, or why they think the fish died. As children talk, listen, and discuss shared experiences, they gain insights into one another's perceptions and views.

5. *What is the average age of kindergarten children at midyear?*

Take away 10 points if children are over six at midyear; take away 5 if they are about six; and give your program 10 points if the average age is between five and five and a half.

Kindergarten is for children between the ages of five and six. If children are over six at midyear you have a clear sign that the kindergarten curriculum is simply "too soon, for too many young children" (Uphoff and Gilmore 1988).

Years ago, the kindergarten program and curriculum were adjusted to the nature of five-year-olds. Today, however, pressures for academic excellence and accountability have resulted in greater demands being placed on kindergarten children. An increasingly academic and accelerated curriculum of worksheets, drill and practice, and rote recitation have replaced the once cognitively rich kindergarten curriculum. The five-year-olds are being pressured to master knowledge of letter names, corresponding sounds, and math facts once only required for first- and second-grade children.

To protect children from this accelerated curriculum, many parents hold their five-year-olds out of kindergarten until they are six and have a better chance of succeeding. Some school systems, responding similarly to the unrealistic demands of the accelerated kindergarten curriculum, have raised the entrance age for enrollment.

6. *How often do kindergarten children take walking field trips in the school building or neighborhood?*

You get 10 points for weekly walking field trips; 5 for monthly trips; and 0 for once or twice a year.

A sound kindergarten curriculum expands children's experiences by taking frequent walking field trips through the school building and into the community. On these walking trips, children observe and participate in the social life of others. The relationships of occupations and social systems are observed and experienced. Representatives from the community should also be invited to visit the kindergarten and demonstrate skills, occupations, or hobbies.

When walking trips are used, continuity can be planned. For example, a trip through the building to identify all of the signs with words leads to a trip into the neighborhood to find other signs. Once back in the classroom, children can then create their own signs.

Walking field trips also give children a base for their own social activity and sociodramatic play. A behind-the-counter trip to a fast food restaurant may result in children playing restaurant and taking on the roles of cooks, servers, and customers.

One group of children walked to a nearby police station and, after returning, began building a police car in the room with large blocks. The teacher added a steering wheel, a piece that looked like an instrument panel, and some boards. The block structure was expanded and became a more identifiable "car" with seats, dashboard, horn, and shift. Picture books were consulted as children tried to make the car ever more realistic.

Throughout, children were the chief learners and teachers. They used their past experience of visiting the police station to initiate a cooperative effort in which they made plans, evaluated their progress, checked one another, offered criticism and information, and exchanged ideas. The result was a real and invaluable experience in intellectual growth and academic achievement.

7. *Are children taught to recognize all 26 letters of the alphabet, both lower and upper case, and to make letter-sound correspondence?*

You get 10 points if children do NOT have to master knowledge of the ABCs. If mastery of ABCs IS the curriculum, take away 10 points.

It's not that children will not learn to recognize and even write some of the letters. In a quality program, however, knowledge of letters and how to write them is secondary to children's real learning.

When the curriculum is based on children's activity and experiences, the need for reading and writing is soon demonstrated. Experiences demand expression. As children think about their experiences, they develop images, feelings, and ideas about them. Expression can take a number of forms. Children may draw or paint a picture about their experience, dance or tell about it—or they may dictate or write about their ideas.

Little by little, children take responsibility for their own writing. They begin by copying letters, words, and sentences, or by actually writing—figuring out and inventing their own spelling as they go. Volunteers, perhaps upper-grade students or members of the National Retired Teachers Association, can help in this process either by taking dictation or showing children how to form a letter or write a word.

When read aloud several times a day, books help to extend and expand first-hand experiences so that children have a richer mental model of their world and the vocabulary to describe it (Snow 1983). The entire range of literature, from poetry and folk tales to encyclopedia entries, serve to help children sum up and clarify ideas.

Kindergarten children DO achieve academic skills in a good program. But the knowledge of letter names and their sounds, numerals, and number facts all have more meaning when they become tools for the broader goal of teaching children to think.

8. *How many children fail kindergarten and are placed in some other program before attending first grade?*

Give your program 10 points if no children are placed in a transitional class; take away 5 points if less than 20 percent must attend a second year of kindergarten; and take away 10 points if more than 20 percent fail.

If too many children must attend a second year of kindergarten, then it is apparent that the program's curriculum is not appropriate. Unrealistic academic demands are being made and too many five-year-olds simply cannot master an accelerated academic curriculum. Transitional or second-year kindergartens have been established to handle large numbers of children who are unable to succeed. The problem is that children placed in transitional groups know they have failed (Shepard and Smith 1988). Repeating kindergarten seems to carry a negative stigma and harms self-esteem. Further, the extra year does not seem to boost achievement.

Kindergarten children should not be expected to have the abilities and capabilities of six- or seven-year-olds. When the curriculum is designed for five-year-olds and individualized with experiences selected to match each child's developmental abilities, capabilities, and interests, children do not fail.

9. *How many poems, songs, or finger plays should a kindergarten child know by the end of the year?*

Give yourself 10 points if children know more than a dozen songs, poems, or chants by the end of kindergarten; 5 if they know less than a dozen; and 0 if they only know a couple.

Children memorize things that have appeal. Every single day in a good kindergarten, poems are read, songs sung, chants, rhymes, and finger plays repeated over and over. Although not required to memorize them, children will learn many by heart if they are integral parts of the curriculum.

Auditory memory develops as children listen to poems and sing songs and chants. By listening and repeating, children are building the base for the phonics and word attack skills they will need when they are in the second or third grade.

Poetry, chants, and songs are essential for another reason. It is through the oral tradition of reading aloud to children that the cultural heritage is transmitted. The nursery rhymes, folk tales, silly finger plays, and songs carry with them significant messages about who we are, and our cultural traditions.

10. *Before children are permitted to attend kindergarten, must they pass a test or some type of developmental screening to guarantee that they can do the work successfully?*

If your system uses any type of screening to keep children OUT of kindergarten, then you have to take away 20 points. You get 10 points if you do not use any type of screening procedures to keep unready children out of kindergarten.

No public school program should deny access to children of legal entry age on the basis of lack of maturational readiness (NAEYC 1986). Children should enter school on the basis of their chronological age and legal right to enter, not on the basis of what they already know.

We know that all children are ready and eager to learn many things. To deny them access to learning is to say that "the choice has been made to serve the needs of the system rather than those of an individual child" (Shepard and Smith 1988).

Screening, raising the entrance age, or adding a second year of kindergarten may do more harm than good, and none address the real problem: an accelerated, academic, and inappropriate kindergarten curriculum.

Add up your score. Congratulations if you scored 100 on your kindergarten report card. If you scored the maximum 110 you have an outstanding kindergarten program.

If your program rated over 80, you have a pretty good kindergarten. Which questions did you fail? Can you make changes in the program to get the extra points that would make the kindergarten outstanding?

If you rated your program between 70 and 80, then certainly your program isn't a failure. But this score raises the fear that too many children may fail.

A score of under 70 is a sign that things need to be changed. There are plenty of resources available (*box*) to help in moving toward an appropriate and successful curriculum for all young children. Contact some of these associations, read some of the listed books, and start improving your kindergarten curriculum. □

REFERENCES

Bredekamp, S. *Developmentally Appropriate Practice in Early Childhood Programs Serving Children from Birth Through Age 8: Expanded edition.* Washington, D.C.: National Association for the Education of Young Children, 1987.
Bruner, J. *Toward a Theory of Instruction.* Cambridge, Mass.: Belknap Press (Harvard University Press), 1966.
Dewey, J. *Democracy and Education.* New York: The Macmillan Company, 1944.
Dyson, A. H. "The Value of 'Time Off Tasks': Young Children's Spontaneous Talk and Delib-

FOR FURTHER INFORMATION

These books are valuable resources for information on kindergarten curriculums:

Association for Childhood Education International. *The Child Centered Kindergarten.* Wheaton, Md.: The association, 1987.
Bredekamp, S. *Developmentally Appropriate Practice in Early Childhood Programs Serving Children from Birth Through Age 8.* Washington, D.C.: National Association for the Education of Young Children, 1987.
Early Childhood Literacy Development Committee of the International Reading Association. *Literacy Development and Pre-First Grade: A Joint Statement of Concerns about Present Practices in Pre-First Grade Reading Instruction and Recommendations for Improvement.* Newark, Del.: The association, 1985.
National Association of State Boards of Education. *Right From the Start: The Report of the NASBE Task Force on Early Childhood Education.* Washington, D.C.: The association, 1988.
Peck, J. T.; McCaig, G.; and Sapp, E. *Kindergarten Policies: What Is Best for Children?* Washington, D.C.: National Association for the Education of Young Children, 1988.
Seefeldt, C., and Barbour, N. *Early Childhood Education: An Introduction.* Columbus, Ohio: Charles E. Merrill, 1987.
Texas Association for the Education of Young Children. *Developmentally Appropriate Kindergarten Reading Programs.* Denton, Tex.: The association, 1986.
Warger, C. *A Resource Guide to Public School Early Childhood Programs.* Alexandria, Va.: Association for Supervision and Curriculum Development, 1988.

Contact these associations for additional information:

Association for Childhood Education International
11141 Georgia Avenue
Wheaton, Maryland 20902

Association for Supervision and Curriculum Development
125 North West Street
Alexandria, Virginia 22314-2798

Black Child Development Institute
1463 Rhode Island Avenue, N.W.
Washington, D.C. 20005

ERIC Clearinghouse on Elementary and Early Childhood Education
University of Illinois
805 W. Pennsylvania Avenue
Urbana, Illinois 61801

International Reading Association
P.O. Box 8139
800 Barksdale Road
Newark, Delaware 19714

National Association for the Education of Young Children
1834 Connecticut Avenue, N.W.
Washington, D.C. 20009

National Association of Elementary School Principals
1615 Duke Street
Alexandria, Virginia 22314-3483

erate Text." *Harvard Educational Review* 57, No. 4, 1987.

Elkind, D. "The Resistance to Developmentally Appropriate Educational Practice with Young Children: The Real Issue." In C. Warger, ed. *A Resource Guide to Public School Early Childhood Programs.* Alexandria, Va.: Association for Supervision and Curriculum Development, 1988.

Eisner, E. "The Primacy of Experience and the Politics of Method." *Educational Researcher* 17, No. 5, 1988.

Froebel, F. *The Education of Man.* Translated by D. Hailman. New York: Appleton & Co., 1912.

Gesell, A.; Ilg, F. L.; and Ames, L. B. *Infant and Child in the Culture of Today.* New York: Harper & Row, 1974.

Hatch, J. A., and Freeman, E. B. "Kindergarten Philosophies and Practice: Perspectives of Teachers, Principals, and Supervisors." *Early Childhood Research Quarterly* 3, No. 2, 1988.

Hiebert, E. F. "The Role of Literacy Experiences in Programs for Four- and Five-year-olds." *Elementary School Journal,* September 1988.

Hill, P. S. "Kindergarten." In *The American Educator Encyclopedia.* Chicago: The United Educators Group, 1942.

Hunt, J. McV. *Intelligence and Experience.* New York: The Ronald Press, 1961.

Langer, S. *Philosophy in a New Key.* Cambridge, Mass.: Harvard University Press, 1942.

Louglin, C., and Sunian, J. *The Learning Environment: An Instructional Strategy.* New York: Teachers College Press, 1982.

Martin, A. "About Teaching and Teachers." *Harvard Educational Review* 55, No. 3, 1985.

National Association for the Education of Young Children. "NAEYC Position Statement on Developmentally Appropriate Practice in Early Childhood Programs Serving Children from Birth Through Age Eight." *Young Children* 41, 1986.

Piaget, J. *The Psychology of the Child.* New York: Basic Books, 1969.

Shepard, L. A., and Smith, M. L. "Escalating Academic Demand in Kindergarten: Counterproductive Policies." *Elementary School Journal,* September 1988.

Snow, C. E. "Literacy and Language: Relationships during Preschool Years." *Harvard Educational Review* 53, No. 3, 1983.

Uphoff, J. K., and Gilmore, J. E. "Pupil Age at School Entrance—How Many Are Ready for Success" *Young Children* 41, No. 2, 1986.

Weikart, D. P. "Quality in Early Childhood Education." In C. Warger, ed. *A Resource Guide to Public School Early Childhood Programs.* Alexandria, Va.: Association for Supervision and Curriculum Development, 1988.

Vygotsky, L. *Thought and Language.* Cambridge, Mass.: Harvard University Press, 1986.

Teaching

- **Education and Support (Articles 37-38)**
- **International Perspectives (Articles 39-41)**

We are ushering in a decade that has begin with nations turning toward democracy at the same time that superpowers turn toward armaments. No more walls between the two Germanys and their swift unification could signal the redesign of a wholly new European community, one committed to cooperation across national lines. Countries of Asia, China in particular, still seek their own new identity—a painful, sometimes violent process.

International prospects during the 1990s prove again how tenuous human relationships can be across borders. A year or two ago, the world thought the end of the cold war would begin lasting peace. While the world's economies are intricately bound together, peace is becoming more remote.

It is these controversial and paradoxical worldwide situations we must understand in order to live through the 1990s. Turbulent and serious changes in other lands always gain our attention. This is true of religions, cultures, and education. The international perspectives section of this unit is new, an acknowledgement that the status of early childhood education elsewhere affects the United States as well. It is particularly valuable to see how the world teaches new generations going into the twenty-first century.

In a quieter place in the world, New Zealand continues to lead in its literacy rate. It has clung to its consistent, highly valued philosophy of teaching reading through a whole language approach. The contrast of New Zealand's singular approach with the diverse approaches used in the United States is stark. While the two nations are certainly not comparable in size or ethnic and cultural composition, what the smaller nation has done to advocate one type of instructional approach has resulted in the highest literacy rate in the world, while the larger nation languishes with a much lower rate, due largely to diffuse, conflicting approaches.

Italy is in the middle of shifts in the European community. As a heritage from the economic outcome of World War II, its towns and municipalities benefit from subsidized child support and other social services. For one northern Italy town, the result is public preschools of high quality for all three- to six-year-old children. The distinctive feature of Reggio Emilia's centers is how they use space for children's work, a unique twist on what Americans typically think of as Eurodesign. And beyond simply using creative arts as design, teachers emphasize valuing the projects of the children.

A country previously closed to our eyes is China. Because of historic links with that Asian nation, many early childhood educators have been anxious for borders to open and have taken advantage of recent freedom to travel within in its provinces. Surprising stories are brought back, stories of cheerful learners in pleasant, though highly regulated, settings. Attention to detailed tasks of forming letters, creating fluid movements, and giving serious respect to elders occupies young children. The contrast is clear: originality and independence are preeminent goals of American teachers while the Chinese value approved form and group procedures. What can be learned from these children and their teachers may help American educators keep the balance of process and product.

Back home in the United States, outcomes of a national child care staffing study are bleak but not surprising. Child care teachers are undertrained, underpaid and undervalued. The results are a predictably high turnover rate, which leaves young children insecure and the workplace unstable, and a low morale among adults who need a large measure of satisfaction to function effectively with children. The net effect is less quality in programming and a weaker education overall for the children.

The need for expansion of child care continues as adults with small children feel the economic pressure for employment. An increase in demand for child care is not being met with a supply of trained teachers, however. Enter a program offering hope for people entering the early childhood teaching profession—the Child Development Associate. Economically and politically, the newly revised CDA training program holds much promise for the remainder of the 1990s.

Early childhood education continues to undergo change. All over the world, as nations regroup, the care and education of the youngest are affected. In the United States, we are attracted to prosperity, but are actually deeper in debt. This too affects the youngest.

We need to learn from each other to teach new generations going into the twenty-first century.

Looking Ahead: Challenge Questions

What aspects of the adult work environment in early childhood education make it high quality? Which make it low quality?

What are average salaries in your region for full-time child care teachers? Assistant teachers? Part-time aides? What benefits accompany these salaries?

In your state, what training is required for child care staff? What training is required for entry staff positions in particular?

What basic training should child care entry staff complete?

How are children in America taught to read? What are some of the instructional methods of kindergarten and the primary grades?

Can you estimate the current literacy rate in America?

What are fundamental techniques used in the whole language approach for teaching reading?

In your community, what percentage of young children attend preschool? What percent kindergarten?

In what ways can teachers validate children's work and projects in the classroom?

Which do you consider more important, the process or product of teaching/learning? Is this true in all situations?

When would direct instruction be a useful teaching method to use with young children?

Child Care Teachers and the Quality of Care in America

Marcy Whitebook, Carollee Howes, Deborah Phillips, and Caro Pemberton

Marcy Whitebook, M.A., is Project Director and Principal Investigator for the National Child Care Staffing Study. She is the Executive Director of the Child Care Employee Project, Oakland, California.

Carollee Howes, Ph.D., is Principal Investigator for the National Child Care Staffing Study. She is an Associate Professor of Education at the University of California at Los Angeles.

Deborah Phillips, Ph.D., is Principal Investigator for the National Child Care Staffing Study. She is an Assistant Professor of Psychology at the University of Virginia.

Caro Pemberton is the Associate Director of the Child Care Employee Project in Oakland, California.

As a nation we have been reluctant to acknowledge child care settings as a work environment for adults or to commit the necessary resources to improving salaries and working conditions for teaching staff. This inattention has had its costs: Child care centers throughout the country report difficulty in recruiting and retaining adequately trained staff. Nearly half of all child care teachers leave their jobs each year, many to seek better paying jobs. By failing to meet the needs of the adults who work in child care, we are threatening not only their well-being but that of the children in their care. As the nation deliberates on what is best for its children, the question of who will care for them grows increasingly critical.

Who Cares? Child Care Teachers and the Quality of Care in America is the report of the National Child Care Staffing Study, which the Child Care Employee Project coordinated. The Study was the most comprehensive examination of center-based care in the United States undertaken in over a decade. Below is a synopsis of this report. For a full description of the Study and discussion of the findings, obtain both the Executive Summary and the Final Report from the Child Care Employee Project (6536 Telegraph Ave., A201, Oakland, CA 94609).

From *Young Children*, Vol. 45, No. 1, November 1989, pp. 41-45. Copyright © 1989 by the authors. Reprinted by permission.

The National Child Care Staffing Study explored how teachers and their working conditions affect the caliber of center-based child care available in the United States today. To begin our investigation, we identified the aspects of child care represented in Figure 1. Our purpose was to describe each of the areas and examine the relations among them. Our experiences in child care and previous research suggested the pathways between these components of center-based care.

This investigation targeted three major goals

Goal #1: To examine relations among child care staff characteristics, adult work environments, and the

quality of child care provided for children and families in center-based care.

Goal #2: To examine differences in child care quality, child care staff, and adult work environments in centers that varied with respect to standards, accreditation status, auspice, and the families served.

Goal #3: To compare center-based child care services in 1988 with those provided in 1977. In order to identify trends in center-based care over the last decade, we compared our findings to those of the National Day Care Supply Study conducted by Abt Associates in 1977 (Coelen, Glantz, & Calore, 1978).

The National Child Care Staffing Study examined the quality of care in 227 child care centers in five metropolitan areas in the United States—Atlanta, Boston,

Figure 1. **Guide to the National Child Care Staffing Study**

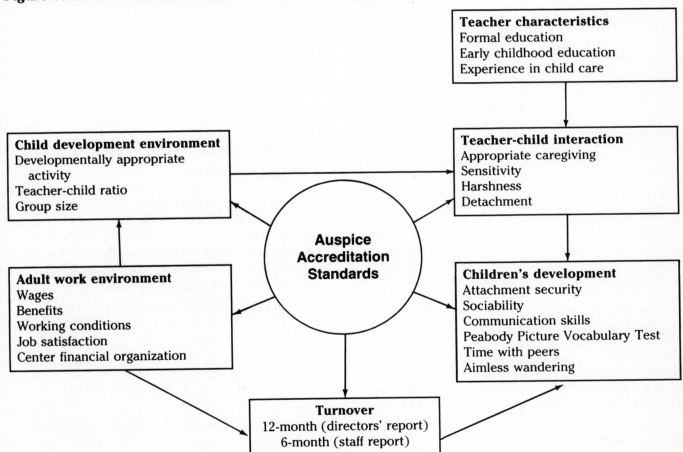

Key: ——→ = **Predicts**

Note: The following analysis plan was used to test the model. Within each area (e.g., Teacher characteristics, Turnover), we used multivariate analyses of variance to compare centers with difference auspices, coincidence with Federal Interagency Day Care Requirements provisions, accreditation, and family income. We used multiple regression techniques to test relations indicated by arrows on the diagram and to test the relative contributions of auspice, correspondence with regulation, accreditation, and percentage of government funding to explain variance within each domain. All findings reported in the text are statistically significant.

Detroit, Phoenix, and Seattle—which represent the diversity of center-based care throughout the country. We began collecting data in February 1988 and finished in August 1988. Classroom observations and interviews with center directors and staff provided data on center characteristics, program quality, and staff qualifications, commitment, and compensation. In addition, in Atlanta, child assessments were conducted to examine the effects of varying program and staff attributes on children.

The sample

We used a stratified random sampling strategy to generate a sample of child care centers that matched the proportion of licensed centers serving low-, middle-, and high-income families in urban and suburban neighborhoods in each study site (see Table 1). Of the final 227 participating centers, 107 were for-profit and 120 were nonprofit.

Table 1.
Final Sample of Participating Centers

	Low-income census tract	Middle-income census tract	High-income census tract
Urban	35	64	10
Suburban	4	96	18

In each center, three classrooms were randomly selected for observation, one each from among all infant, toddler, and preschool classrooms. We randomly chose an average of two staff members from each participating classroom to interview and observe. Sixty-six percent (865) of the final sample of 1,309 teaching staff were teachers (805 teachers and 60 teacher/directors) and 34% (444) were assistant teachers (286 assistant teachers and 158 aides).

Two children, a girl and a boy, were randomly selected for assessment from each target classroom in Atlanta. Two hundred and sixty children constituted the child sample: 53 infants, 97 toddlers, and 110 preschoolers.

The measures

The complexity of the investigation required a varied approach to collecting data. On average, the research team in each site, consisting of trained observers and interviewers, spent three days in each center.

Quality observations

The research team measured quality by observing overall quality, classroom structure, and interactions between the teaching staff and children.

Overall quality was assessed with the Early Childhood Environment Rating Scale (Harms & Clifford, 1980) for each observed preschool classroom and the Infant-Toddler Environment Rating Scale (Harms, Cryer, & Clifford, 1986) for each of the observed infant and toddler classrooms. From a factor analysis of the scale items, we derived two subscales: (1) *developmentally appropriate activity* (e.g., materials, schedule, and activities), and (2) *appropriate caregiving* (e.g., supervision, adult-child interactions, and discipline).

Investigators recorded ratios and group size at regular intervals during a two-hour observational period per classroom. Hour-by-hour staffing patterns were obtained through interviews with directors.

We observed staff-child interaction in each classroom using a scale of staff sensitivity (Arnett, in press) to derive scores for *sensitivity* (e.g., warm, attentive, engaged), *harshness* (e.g., critical, threatens children, punitive), and *detachment* (e.g., low levels of interaction, interest, and supervision). Scores range from routine caregiving (e.g., touching without any verbal interaction) to intense caregiving (e.g., engaging the child in conversation, playing with an infant while changing diapers).

Director and staff interviews

In interviews about structural aspects of the program, including limited budget information and staff characteristics, each director provided information about the teaching staff's demographic and educational backgrounds, compensation, working conditions, and turnover. Directors also provided their estimates of the socioeconomic status (low-, middle-, and high-income) of all children enrolled in the center.

The six staff members from each of the observed classrooms participated in an individual interview consisting of seven sections: personal background, child care experience, wages and benefits, other jobs, educational background, professional satisfaction, and recommendations for improving the child care profession. Six months after the initial staff interview (August 1988 – February 1989), we reached 71% of the staff by phone to obtain data on actual turnover rates.

We assessed children's development in several ways. The child's security of attachment to adult caregivers and sociability with adults and peers were measured using the Waters and Deane Attachment Q-Set (Waters & Deane, 1985) and the Howes Peer Play Scale (Howes & Stewart, 1987). Teachers rated communication skills using the Feagans & Farran Adaptive Language Inventory (Feagans & Farran, 1979). To assess preschool children's language development, we administered the Peabody Picture Vocabulary Test (Dunn, 1984) to them.

Highlights of major findings

The education of child care teaching staff and the arrangement of their work environment are essential determinants of the quality of services children receive.

- Staff provided more sensitive and appropriate caregiving if they completed more years of formal education, received early childhood training at the college level, earned higher wages and better benefits, and worked in centers devoting a higher percentage of the operating budget to the teaching personnel. Too few teaching staff held competency-based credentials, such as CDA, for these to be evaluated in the study.

The most important predictor of the quality of care children receive, among the adult work environment variables, is staff wages.

- The quality of services provided by most centers was rated as barely adequate. Better quality centers had:
  - higher wages
  - better adult work environments
  - lower teaching staff turnover

- better educated and trained staff
- more staff caring for fewer children
- Better quality centers were more likely:
  - to be operated on a nonprofit basis
  - to be accredited by the National Association for the Education of Young Children's National Academy of Early Childhood Programs
  - to be located in states with higher quality standards
  - to meet adult-child ratios, group size, and staff training provisions contained in the 1980 Federal Interagency Day Care Requirements

Despite having higher levels of formal education than the average American worker, child care teaching staff earn abysmally low wages (see Tables 2 and 3).

Teaching staff turnover has nearly tripled in the last decade from 15% in 1977 to 41% in 1988.

- The most important determinant of staff turnover, among the adult work environment variables, was staff wages (see Table 4).
- Teaching staff earning the lowest wages are twice as likely to leave their jobs as those earning the highest wages.
- Teaching staff belonging to either a professional organization or a union had more specialized training and experience, earned $1.50 more per hour, and were less likely to leave their jobs.

Table 2. Wages of Child Care Teaching Staff Versus Civilian Labor Force*

| | Teaching staff, 1988 | Civilian labor force, 1987** | |
		Women	Men
High school diploma or less	$ 8,033	$15,806	$24,097
Some college	$ 9,275	$19,369	$29,251
B.A./B.S. or more	$11,568	$26,066	$42,422

*Full-time annual earnings based on 35 hours per week/50 weeks per year.
**1988 data not available.
Source: *Money Income of Households, Families, and Persons in the United States: 1987*, Current Population Reports, Series P-6, No. 162, Table 36.

Table 4. Turnover Rates for Teaching Staff With Differing Wages

Hourly wage	Percentage earning wage	Six-month turnover
$4 and under	28%	54%
Between $4 and $5	29%	36%
Between $5 and $6	16%	33%
Over $6	27%	27%

Table 3. Educational Level of Child Care Teaching Staff and of the Female Civilian Labor Force, Ages 25–64

	Assistant teachers	Teachers	Female civilian labor force*
Less than high school	10.8%	4.7%	12.4%
High school diploma	33.3%	21.1%	43.3%
Some college	37.4%	43.5%	21.2%
B.A./B.S. degree or more	18.5%	30.7%	23.1%

*U.S. Department of Labor, Bureau of Labor Statistics, unpublished tables from March 1988 *Current Population Survey*.

- The average hourly wage is $5.35 for this predominantly female work force.

- Most child care teaching staff, even full-time staff, received minimal employment benefits. Out of the entire sample, two out of five received health coverage and one out of five had a retirement plan. Other than sick leave and paid holidays, the only benefit offered to a majority of the staff was reduced fees for child care. Those earning the lowest wages received the fewest benefits.

- In the last decade, child care staff wages, when adjusted for inflation, have decreased more than 20%.

- Child care teaching staff earn less than half as much as comparably educated women and less than one-third as much as comparably educated men in the civilian labor force.

Children attending lower quality centers and centers with more staff turnover were less competent in language and social development.

- Children in centers with higher turnover rates spent less time engaged in social activities with peers and more time in aimless wandering. They also had lower *Peabody Picture Vocabulary Test* scores compared to children in centers with more stable teaching staff.

- Low- and high-income children were more likely than middle-income children to attend centers providing higher quality care.

Compared to a decade ago, child care centers in the United States receive fewer governmental funds, are more likely to be operated on a for-profit basis, and care for a larger number of infants.

Recommendations

Improving the quality of center-based child care and addressing the staffing crisis demand the commitment of more public and private resources. The National Child Care Staffing Study findings suggest the following recommendations.

1. Raise child care teacher salaries as a means of recruiting and retaining a qualified child care work force.

2. Promote formal education and training opportunities for child care teachers to improve their ability to interact effectively with children and to create developmentally appropriate environments.

3. Adopt state and federal standards for adult-child ratios and staff education, training, and compensation in order to raise the floor of quality in America's child care centers.

4. Develop industry standards for the adult work environment to minimize the disparities in quality between types of child care programs.

5. Promote public education about the importance of adequately trained and compensated teachers in child care programs in order to secure support for the full cost of care.

Conclusion

Amidst the child care debate facing our nation, a consensus is emerging that high-quality early childhood services are essential to the developmental and economic well-being of our children and families. The National Child Care Staffing Study raises serious concerns about the quality of services many American children receive. But our findings also clearly indicate how services can be improved if, as a society, we will devote the necessary resources to accomplish this. America depends on child care teachers. Our future depends on valuing them.

References

Arnett, J. (in press). Caregivers in day care centers: Does training matter? *Journal of Applied Developmental Psychology.*

Coelen, C., Glantz, R., & Calore, D. (1978). *Day care centers in the U.S.: A national profile, 1976–1977.* Cambridge, MA: Abt Associates.

Dunn, L.M. (1984). *Peabody Picture Vocabulary Test* (revised). Circle Pines, MN: American Guidance Service.

Feagans, L., & Farran, D. (1979). *Adaptive Language Inventory.* Unpublished, University of North Carolina at Chapel Hill.

Harms, T., & Clifford, R. (1980). *Early Childhood Environment Rating Scale.* New York: Teachers College Press, Columbia University.

Harms, T., Cryer, D., & Clifford, R. (1986). *Infant-Toddler Environment Rating Scale.* New York: Teachers College Press, Columbia University.

Howes, C., & Stewart, P. (1987). Child's play with adults, toys, and peers: An examination of family and child care influences. *Developmental Psychology, 23,* 423–430.

Waters, E., & Deane, K.E. (1985). Defining and assessing individual differences in attachment relationships: Q-methodology and the organization of behavior in infancy and early childhood. In I. Bretherton & E. Waters (Eds.), Growing points of attachment theory and research (pp. 41–65). *Monographs of the Society for Research in Child Development, 50*(1–2, Serial No. 209).

The Child Development Associate Program:

Entering a New Era

Carol Brunson Phillips

*An early childhood educator, **Carol Brunson Phillips** has for 20 years been involved in writing, research, and teacher education, specializing in cultural influences on development. Currently she is Executive Director of the Council for Early Childhood Professional Recognition in Washington, D.C.*

". . . The challenge of CDA is not complete; rather it is . . . constantly changing to keep pace with its own accomplishments."

Thus wrote Edward Zigler and Sharon L. Kagan in a 1981 article describing the Child Development Associate (CDA) program as a "challenge for the 1980s" (Zigler & Kagan, 1981, p. 10). True to form, as the program enters the '90s, it brings with it both the challenge of its initial vision and the changes wrought by the '80s. NAEYC has been central to the CDA effort since its conception, and as the new era unfolds, the Association will continue to have a special place in CDA's future.

Background

In January 1971, 30 leaders in the field of early childhood education/child development met to discuss the establishment of a new professional credential, the Child Development Associate. The need for such a credential was felt in the growing national concern for increasing the abilities as well as the numbers of child care personnel, thus increasing the quality of care provided to children. Subsequently, NAEYC convened a task force to outline a set of CDA Competencies and refine them into six broad areas.

By 1972, a planning group of representatives from the American Association of Elementary/Kindergarten/Nursery Educators, the Association for Childhood Education International, and NAEYC established a consortium of organizations concerned with the welfare of children, the major task of which was to develop the assessment and credentialing system. This CDA Consortium reviewed and formally adopted the six broad competency areas that guide the program today.

In 1973, the design and implementation of CDA competency-based training began with 13 pilot training projects. These projects developed innovative approaches to training based on the CDA Training Guidelines and the CDA Competencies. During 1974, the CDA Consortium established the definition of a Child Development Associate and further delineated the six Competencies into 13 Functional Areas. As defined, a Child Development Associate is an early childhood professional who

assumes primary responsibility for meeting the specific needs of a group of children in a child development setting by nurturing the child's physical, social, emotional, and intellectual needs; sets up and maintains the child care environment; and establishes a liaison relationship between parents and the child development center. (*CDA Pilot Projects,* 1978, p. 1)

These are the guiding principles and philosophical base of the Child Development Associate program. Working since that time to make this new category of early childhood professional a reality, the national CDA effort focuses on improving the quality of care for children by increasing the competency of the staff.

Since the award of the first credential in 1975, more than 30,000 individuals have received the CDA credential, and 42 states and the District of Columbia recognize CDAs as qualified staff in their child care licensing regulations. A consistent pattern emerges in profiling a CDA. According to data from two national surveys conducted by the CDA National Credentialing Program in 1983 and 1988, CDAs have, on the average, more than 10 years experience working with young children. Approximately 60% have at least some college (30% have two-year degrees or better). CDAs are overwhelmingly female (98%), averaging age 38 at the time of the credential award. Eighty percent are employed by Head Start programs. In addition, CDAs come from every state, plus the U.S. territories of Guam, Puerto Rico, and the Virgin Islands.

In 1985, the year of the 10th anniversary of the first credential award, the program's administration was transferred to a permanent national body newly created by NAEYC, the Council for Early Childhood Professional Recognition. The Council now administers the CDA National Credentialing Program.

From 1985 to 1988, through a cooperative agreement between the federal government, represented by the Administration for Children, Youth and Families (ACYF), and the early childhood profession, represented by NAEYC, the Council engaged in the following projects:

• reviewing all aspects of the CDA program to identify strategies for implementing new practices;

• establishing standards for CDA training programs;

• developing an approval process for CDA training programs to provide competency-based training that meets national standards; and

• improving the efficiency, credibility, affordability, and quality of assessments.

The CDA Council Model

During the three years of collaborative work, the Council designed a model that linked training and assessment as a way to strengthen the program's ability to meet this country's child care personnel needs for the 1990s and beyond. The goal of restructuring was for the program to become an even stronger participant in meeting the growing demand for trained personnel and to have a long-term commitment to increased professional status for early childhood education professionals. By 1989, with the new plans approved by ACYF, the Council was able to sever its formal ties with NAEYC and become the independent entity necessary to launch a new era for the CDA program.

The new Council Model has two parts. One involves a training program leading to the CDA credential; the other involves revised procedures for direct assessment.

The Professional Preparation Program

The training program, which will begin in the fall of this year, is called the CDA Professional Preparation Program. Its aim is to develop, nationally, a strong core of child care workers who are uniquely qualified in the early childhood profession.

This one-year training program is for individuals 18 or older with a high school diploma or GED. Previous early childhood experience is not a requirement. Enrollment consists of submitting an application and fee ($1,500) to the Council.

The Council has designed a model curriculum for early childhood training built around the six Competency Goals and the 13 Functional Areas. The teaching-learning strategies embody developmentally appropriate child care practices that address the needs of infants, toddlers, preschoolers, and their

families. The Competency Goals are:

1. To establish and maintain a safe, healthy learning environment.

2. To advance physical and intellectual competence.

3. To support social and emotional development and provide guidance.

4. To establish positive and productive relationships with families.

5. To ensure a well-run, purposeful program responsive to participant needs.

6. To maintain a commitment to professionalism.

The program's three phases are outlined below.

PHASE I: *Fieldwork.* During fieldwork, students will participate in child care programs on a daily basis. They will follow written materials prepared by the Council. These materials will consist of a series of readings and exercises to help the candidate build the skills needed to work with young children. The fieldwork will be guided by an advisor, an early childhood professional who will mentor the candidate through hands-on experience with young children. Advisors will also use Council-designed manuals in their work with CDA candidates.

PHASE II: *Instructional course work.* The candidate will attend a series of group seminars provided by a local college, university, or other postsecondary educational institution. Designed by the Council, the instructional curriculum content will cover the knowledge base in early childhood education. The institutions may supplement this curriculum content from their own resources. The Council will work directly with the postsecondary institutions to monitor them and provide resources and technical assistance. In addition, students will frequently refer to the practical experiences they have had during their fieldwork.

PHASE III: *Integration and evaluation.* Toward the end of the year of study, the candidates will integrate their fieldwork with their instructional course work and participate in a final evaluation. The student will return to hands-on work in a child care setting and at the same time complete a series of exercises and a performance-based assessment, guided by Council-written material. A Council Representative will conduct a series of interviews and review written documents submitted by the candidate. All materials and the Council Representative's assessment will be submitted to the Council for review. Successful candidates will receive their CDA credential, which will be valid for life.

Direct assessment

In addition to the Professional Preparation Program, the Council will continue to offer the direct assessment route to candidates who have received their CDA training elsewhere. The procedures will remain a competency-based evaluation of a candidate's performance, but will also include a written assessment of the candidate's knowl-edge of good early childhood practice. Documents citing the candidate's competence will be submitted to the national office for review, and the credential will be awarded for life.

CDA of the future

The 1990s promise to be an era of increased public support for high-quality care for young children. With this support, early childhood professionals can expect to be in greater demand and must be ready to take a position of higher status in the work place. The preparation and continuing education of the work force thus becomes the real challenge to the profession—to early childhood membership associations such as NAEYC, as well as to other agencies that deliver child care programs and to institutions of higher education.

A clear picture of the standards for professionalism is emerging from NAEYC's work on the new *Model for Professional Development.* This is a proposed revision of the NAEYC Position Statement on Nomenclature, Salaries, Benefits, and the Status of the Early Childhood Profession that will set up a concrete framework for creating (and recreating) staff qualifications, career ladders, training, and staff development. As the CDA credential becomes more associated with higher education and recognized as the entry-level qualification for the profession, the status of CDAs will be enhanced. As the credential becomes uniformly acessible across the country, more trained personnel will be available to replace the child care workers who have no training at all.

With these accomplishments, the CDA effort can contribute to achieving the profession's goals for increased status and recognition for early childhood professionals in the '90s and beyond. And with the continued collaboration and leadership of NAEYC in establishing and monitoring standards for professional practice, new levels of collaboration, organization, and advocacy will become possible.

References

CDA pilot projects: Innovations. (1978). Washington, DC: University Research Corporation.

Zigler, E., & Kagan, S.L. (1981). Viewpoint. The Child Development Associate: A challenge for the 1980s. *Young Children, 36*(5), 10–15.

Learning to Read in New Zealand

*A brief look at beginning reading instruction
in the world's most literate nation*

BRIAN CUTTING
AND JERRY L. MILLIGAN

Brian Cutting is Education Director for Wendy Pye Ltd.
Auckland, New Zealand. Jerry Milligan is Professor of Education, Washington State University, Pullman, WA.

There is at the present time an increasing concern in the United States about the rate of reading failure and the general level of literacy as compared to other industrialized nations. In light of this concern, it occurred to us that it might be useful to identify a country where reading is taught more effectively, go there and observe firsthand how it's done.

New Zealand was chosen for an obvious reason: It is considered to be the most literate country in the world. The United States, according to a recent study, ranks 49th in literacy among the 159 countries of the world.

It should be noted that comparing the ways beginning reading is taught in the two countries is complicated by the fact that beginning reading is taught in diverse ways in the United States. For example, we found many classrooms in the United States where the approach was closer to the approach used in New Zealand than to the one used in most American classrooms.

In contrast, New Zealand has a single national school authority whose policies on reading instruction apply throughout the country. Thus, the small variations found in New Zealand classrooms must be attributed to differences in teachers, not policies.

With that in mind, let's take a look at some of the most significant differences.

Age of beginning readers. In the United States, formal reading instruction usually begins early in the first grade. Since most states require a child to be five or older before entering kindergarten, most first graders are at least six by the time they receive formal reading instruction.

New Zealand children, however, are permitted to enter school on their fifth birthday. And, as we will discuss later, they receive reading instruction on their first day of school. The only children beginning school on the first day of the school year are those who had summer birthdays.

We found that New Zealand educators value the system of having the school year begin with a small group of five-year-olds which gradually increases in size until the group is somewhat over 30. They believe that this arrangement allows them to provide for more individualized instruction. Indeed, it forces individualized instruction.

Reading readiness. Most children in the United States receive prereading instruction prior to formal reading instruction. This instruction normally takes place during kindergarten and the beginning of first grade, and usually focuses on what American educators refer to as reading readiness—for example, developing such skills as visual discrimination, auditory discrimination and letter recognition.

In New Zealand, there simply isn't time for reading readiness. Reading instruction begins the very first day that children enter school. An effort is made to have the children impress their families by taking home a book they can read very soon after they enter school. The book is likely to be a short one that they have heard read aloud regularly

Reprinted with permission of the publisher, Early Years, Inc., Norwalk, Connecticut 06854. From the August/September 1990 issue of *Teaching/K-8*, pp. 62-65.

and have read in unison with a fluent reader until they nearly know it by heart.

Beginning reading. The prevailing approach to beginning reading in the United States is the word-centered skills approach. The focus here is on enabling young readers to recognize an increasing number of words and on providing children with the skills they need to unlock words they do not recognize by sight so they can derive meaning from print.

Reading instruction in New Zealand is predicated on a holistic theory of language teaching methods. What is known as the whole language approach is the policy throughout New Zealand. Any deviation from this approach is regarded as being counter to policy.

In practice, the word-centered skills approach used in the United States involves breaking language into small units such as words and parts of words, and then teaching these units in a planned sequence of skills developed. In contrast, reading instruction in New Zealand is based on the assumptions that children can best learn to read by reading, and that reading improvement comes mainly as a result of reading.

Balanced reading. New Zealanders refer to their beginning reading program as a balanced reading program. This program is comprised of five approaches (see accompanying diagram) which are part of the teaching routine nearly every day. Each of these approaches serves a specific purpose:

Reading to Children is used, in both New Zealand and the United States, to demonstrate to children that reading can be a source of delight and to familiarize them with book language and story structure.

Shared Reading, with its goal of having children read aloud without the support of either teacher or classmates, is clearly aimed at building the young reader's enthusiasm and self-confidence.

The *Language Experience Approach* introduces five-year-olds to writing and crystallizes their concepts of words, sentences, letters and other conventions of language.

Guided Reading leads children to know reading as a process of actively reconstructing meaning by predicting one's way through print, not as a process of recognizing words.

Independent Reading is, of course, an end in itself. One feature of this approach is that reading is made as pleasant as possible. In a

THE UNITED STATES	NEW ZEALAND
Reading usually regarded as a subject like math or science.	Reading regarded as a skill that everyone masters.
Basal reading series used for beginning reading instruction. The series is augmented by trade books and other reading materials.	All children begin reading via a group of small paperbacks, published by the government. Each book contains only a single story. Other books, mainly paperbacks, containing poems and short stories are also used.
Basal books feature scope and sequence of reading skills, as well as vocabulary control.	Beginning books do not include scope and sequence of reading skills or vocabulary control. Nor are materials designed to be read in any particular order.
Workbooks and work sheets often used to teach beginning reading. Work sheets frequently designed to teach a specific skill.	Workbooks and work sheets not used to teach beginning reading. Teaching a specific skill inconsistent with the stated policy of the national school authority.
Homogeneous grouping of children to practice reading fairly common. Such groups frequently labeled "low" "medium" or "high".	Reading groups more likely to be ephemeral, own-choice groups or children working in pairs. Groups rarely labeled.
Widespread use of criterion-referenced tests designed to periodically assess reading progress.	No elaborate system for measuring student reading progress.
Teachers assess reading development by observing student's progress as part of daily teaching routine.	Teachers refer to the monitoring of student reading progress as "keeping a running record." Learning to keep a running record is quite formal and part of the teacher training program.
Extensive use of remedial reading programs to treat reading difficulties. These services usually provided from the primary grades through secondary school.	Extensive remedial reading services provided for only a very small percentage of children beyond second grade.

New Zealand classroom, one will see stuffed chairs and sofas, carpeted areas and many large pillows. Also, children are free to seek assistance from either the teacher or a classmate when they need help in making sense out of what they're reading.

Reading Materials. Big books are an integral part of beginning reading instruction—particularly the shared reading approach—throughout New Zealand. Upon entering school, a child becomes part of a small group of pupils gathered together by the teacher. The teacher reads aloud from a big book and while reading, points to the print and pictures.

We observed both teacher-made as well as commercially-prepared big books being used. The print in these books is large enough to be seen easily by a fairly large group of children. The pictures, particularly in the commercially-prepared big books, are colorful, while the language is predictable and often humorous and rhythmical.

Most of the commercially-prepared big books are also available in regular size paperback texts, which the children can take home to impress friends and family with their reading.

In addition to the big books, teachers in New Zealand use a variety of regular size books containing a single story, multiple copies of books containing poems or chants, and books (mainly paperbacks) containing poems and short stories. The journals written by the children as part of the Language Experience Approach are also a source of reading material.

Reading recovery. Although the term *remedial reading* is not a term New Zealand educators would likely use, they do have a program for six-year-olds that one might consider remedial. They refer to this early intervention program as *reading recovery*.

The reading recovery program is based on the assumption that it's better to prevent reading difficulties than treat them. As many

SHARED READING
The teacher rereads a story from a big book until the children are able to read aloud as the teacher points to the print. Eventually, each child reads without support from the group.

READING TO CHILDREN
The teacher reads stories aloud to children. If listening centers are available, the children can later listen to the stories while they follow the print in small books.

LANGUAGE EXPERIENCE APPROACH
The child dictates a story to the teacher. Together, child and teacher polish a draft of the story. Within a few months, children are writing independently, using invented spellings.

BALANCED READING PROGRAM

INDEPENDENT READING
Children read independently in a variety of comfortable places. After they have read a story, the teacher discusses favorite or puzzling parts with them and whether they enjoyed the book.

GUIDED READING
The teacher begins by reading part of a story and asking children to predict what happens next. After the children have read a part silently, they are led to react and retell the part in their own words.

as 30 to 50 percent of the children in some schools receive, as they reach their sixth birthday, what is known as the *six-year-check*, a formal observation of children's orientation to print. As a result of the six-year-check, about 15 percent of the children, depending upon the school, may receive help from special teachers outside the classroom for part of their second year in school.

It should be kept in mind that this special help is provided during the children's seventh year of life. In the United States, it is not until the children's seventh year of life that formal reading instruction is begun.

Final thoughts. From studying the development of reading instruction in the two countries, it is apparent that the differences have become institutionalized. Administrators and teachers in New Zealand grew up in a school environment dominated by the whole language philosophy. Since they learned what they needed to know about reading *from* reading, they do not see the need for systematic skills instruction.

While basal readers and other controlled vocabulary have been an integral part of reading instruction in the United States since early in this century, they have not been in New Zealand. Nor have the workbooks and work sheets which accompany basal series. The teachers fail to see the merits of basals and workbooks because this is not the way they learned.

At the present time, American educators are divided in their views regarding beginning reading instruction. While they debate such issues as phonics instruction and the best way to introduce decoding skills, New Zealand educators do not seem to be divided. They all seem to agree that beginning reading instruction should be a balance of the five approaches described earlier.

Finally, teachers colleges in New Zealand appear to be much more involved with schools than in the United States, and they all seem to be advocating the same type of beginning reading instruction. This makes the preparation of teachers easier and tends to produce teachers who have similar views about the way reading should be taught.

Excellent Early Education:

A City In Italy Has It

Rebecca New

Rebecca New, Ed.D., is an Assistant Professor of Early Childhood Education at the University of New Hampshire. She has lived and worked in Italy, and has visited preschool and infant/toddler classrooms in Reggio Emilia on numerous occasions.

Who knows what's best for children—their parents or their teachers? Can children's creative and intellectual potentials be maximized without sacrificing their need for play and exploration? How can we use available space to support our curriculum goals? For the past three decades, these questions have been part of discussions among parents, educators, and community members in Reggio Emilia, Italy—site of one of the most renowned examples of community-supported child care systems in Western Europe. This municipal preschool and infant/toddler day care program challenges notions of adverse effects of out-of-home care for young children and illuminates the potential of early childhood programs that are truly responsive to young children's interests and capabilities. To understand this unique and exciting program and its implications for early childhood education here in the United States, a brief description of the cultural setting is necessary.

The town of Reggio Emilia is in a wealthy region of northern Italy well known for its agricultural and industrial productivity as well as for its art and architecture. Child welfare is a major priority of Reggio Emilia's well-subsidized social services (Rankin, 1985), as evidenced by the community's response to child care needs of dual-earner families since the end of World War II. Well in advance of the 1968 national law that established funding of public preschools for *all* three- to six-year-old Italian children, the town council of Reggio Emilia established the first public preschools. Today, Reggio Emilia has 22 community preschools and 13 infant/

Ongoing exchanges with Reggio Emilia personnel—including director Sergio Spaggiari, former director Loris Malaguzzi, and curriculum coordinators Tiziana Filippini and Carla Rinaldi—and with American early childhood educators Lella Gandini, Carolyn Pope Edwards, George Forman, and Baji Rankin—also serve as a basis for this discussion.

toddler centers serving, respectively, 49% of all three- to six-year-old children and 37% of those under the age of three. (Virtually all preschool-aged children in Reggio Emilia attend *some* form of preschool; church-affiliated programs serve 33% of the population, private and state-run preschools the remaining 18%. Of the 42% of infants and toddlers in day care, 88% are in the municipal centers [Department of Education, 1989].)

This municipal early childhood program incorporates high-quality day care beginning in infancy with a preschool program built around a philosophy of education that has evolved over 25 years of intense collaboration, discussion, and work with young children. Classrooms are organized to support a problem-solving approach to learning, with extensive reliance on the arts as a natural form of expression and exploration; parents and teachers are mutually involved in observing and evaluating children's growth and development. Since 1979, the Reggio Emilia program has attracted thousands of visitors worldwide from countries as diverse as Sweden, West Germany, Argentina, Japan, and the United States. Two traveling exhibitions sponsored by the City Administration of the Municipality of Reggio Emilia—one for European, the other for English-speaking countries—were created to convey central themes and characteristics of the program. **The English version of *The Hundred Languages of Children* exhibit, on an extended tour of the United States, is scheduled for October 1 through December 1, 1990 at the Capital Children's Museum, Washington, D.C.**

Numerous aspects of the Reggio project are intriguing to American educators, including the level of community support for quality programs for children. (Twelve percent of the annual Town Council budget is allocated to the preschool and infant/toddler program. Program fees are assigned on a sliding scale, with a maximum fee for full-time infant care less than $150 per month U.S. equivalent.) While we continue to ponder the ways and means of reaching such a level of consensus *and* support in our own communities, other features may prove more immediately useful in our own efforts to provide high-quality early childhood

From *Young Children*, Vol. 45, No. 6, September 1990, pp. 4-10. Copyright © 1990 by Rebecca New. Reprinted by permission.

Virtually every three- to five-year-old attends some form of preschool. Outstanding programs in which parents are deeply involved make the "home is best" argument much less meaningful than in the United States.

programs. Three aspects are particularly relevant: the community of families and schools; the curriculum, based on projects and the arts; and the use of space to support curriculum goals.

School is a community of exchange

The Reggio Emilia program reflects a long-standing commitment to cooperative and supportive home/school relationships, advocating a partnership among parents, teachers, and community members. A blending of beliefs about what is best for young children and their families facilitates this partnership in a number of ways. Contrary to prevalent perceptions in the United States, citizens of Reggio Emilia don't see day care as an issue of maternal substitution, even though a majority of children in the program are from dual-earner households with 75% of the mothers of the preschool children and 88% of the mothers of children in infant/toddler day care employed (Department of Education, 1988). From the outset, teachers acknowledge the critical role of both parents, emphasizing that the child is also capable, at a very young age, of developing other quality relationships. Because teachers and parents consider isolation from one another a hindrance to professional and child development, they have designed formal and informal strategies to establish a rich community of exchange.

Groups are long-lasting, like families

Schools begin the process of collaboration by keeping the same group of children and teachers together for a three-year period, so that children who begin as infants remain together at the *asilo nido* ("nest" or day care) until the third birthday, at which time they move into preschool classrooms where they remain with a new preschool teacher for another three years. Each classroom of children, varying in number from 12 infants to 25 preschoolers, has two teachers, with occasional assistance from the school art teacher, the cook, and auxiliary staff. Besides creating a stable and secure environment for children, the three-year grouping provides a degree of continuity and familiarity that enables more effective relationships among parents and teachers, and results in a large community of adults around a group of children.

Parents actively collaborate

Parents are initiated into the program as soon as a

child is enrolled. Teachers solicit information about each child's daily routines and sleeping and eating preferences, and urge parents to stay in the classroom for the first few weeks of school if their work schedules allow, until the child is comfortable without a family member. Albums are created for each child upon entry to a class, for family members and school personnel to fill with observations, photographs, and anecdotal records; by the time the child leaves for elementary school, there may be as many as three or four volumes. As one teacher notes, the notebooks (1) serve as a method of communication between parents and teachers, (2) document the child's progress relative to other children, and (3) provide evidence to the child of the importance attributed to this period of her life (Carlina Rinaldi, personal communication, June 13, 1989). Regular meetings with the cook to share favorite family and school recipes also foster a sense of shared responsibility.

These long-term home/school relationships have the flavor of the traditionally typical Italian extended family (New, 1988). Another advantage for parents is the opportunity to develop among themselves a stable network of families of young children. The strength of this

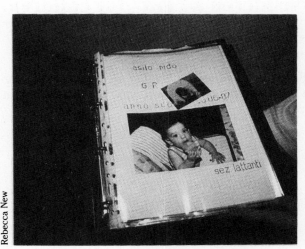

Rebecca New

Notebook

network is apparent in the subsequent level of parent cooperation and participation in school projects. Field trips, for example, become major social events for the adults as well as the children. One preschool class of 25 children that was studying outer space took a field trip with 50 parents, two classroom teachers, an art teacher, the school custodian, and the cook to dinner at a local pizzeria followed by a late-night visit to the small observatory several miles outside town.

Parental involvement extends beyond individual classrooms to include decision making at the school and community levels. Each school has a Parent-Teacher Board made up of elected representatives of staff, parents, and citizens; parents consider this board important enough that 85% of eligible families participated in recent elections. To accommodate working parents, meetings are held in the evening, often beginning at 9:00 P.M. and running past midnight. The Board deals with problems specific to the school. It also elects one person for membership to *La Consulta,* a committee that includes representatives from the directorial staff, the town council, and the local Department of Education and asserts significant influence over local government policy.

This community of adults shares the understanding that no one has a monopoly on deciding what is best for the children. Reggio Emilia citizens acknowledge the difficulties of such a cooperative relationship; the process of maintaining a dialogue between parents and teachers has been described as one "which is and *should be* complicated" (Department of Education, 1989, p. 11).

Perhaps no topic has provoked more thought and discussion among these adults than what pedagogical approach to take in the Reggio Emilia classrooms. The resulting curriculum is a testimony to the virtues of ongoing staff development, parent involvement, and respect for children's interests and capabilities.

Even a rain puddle is considered a "gift" for children.

Problems, projects, and the symbolic languages: A natural combination

Reggio Emilia teachers believe that children's learning is facilitated by actively exploring problems that

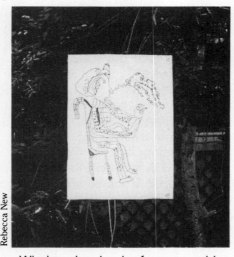

Window drawing by four-year-old

children *and* teachers help determine. They also believe that art is inseparable from the rest of the curriculum, and in fact is central to the educational process as a form of both exploration and expression (Gandini & Edwards, 1988). Reflecting this centrality, children's efforts with various media are referred to as "symbolic representations" rather than "art."

Each school has an art teacher who is available to work with the children and their teachers throughout the day, and children are given many opportunities to discover the properties of artistic materials, in the belief that exploration is essential for emerging aesthetic awareness. More importantly, teachers believe in the need to nurture children's natural tendency to use the symbolic languages—including drawing, painting, constructing, and creative dramatics—as a way to make sense of their world.

Art

Project-based teaching

One strategy that provides numerous reasons for symbolic representation and maximizes opportunities for shared problem solving is the use of short- and long-term projects. The "art" work that results from such projects astounds and delights most viewers, and conveys a broad interpretation of the typical preschool thematic approach, not to mention children's creative, communicative, and intellectual potentials.

Though some projects last only several days, others may continue for months, reflecting a belief in the need for long periods of time for both children and teachers to stay with an idea, to "enter inside a situation, to enjoy . . ., to discover . . ., and finally—to find one's own way out" (Filippini, 1989). Projects, which may involve the entire class or only a small group of children, are of three broadly defined types: those resulting from a child's natural encounter with the environment, those reflecting mutual interests on the part of the teacher and children, and those based on teacher concerns regarding specific cognitive and/or social concepts (Gandini & Edwards, 1988; Edwards, Forman, & Gandini, in preparation).

For example, a child's spontaneous play on a sunny day can turn into an extensive exploration of the properties and magic of *l'ombra,* or shadow. Observing such play, the teacher "captures" the event through a photograph, which leads to more elaborate attempts at variations in the forms shadows might take. As other children join in, they are encouraged to explain (by drawing) their understanding of shadows. Thus they must not only come to terms with their own beliefs about the event, but they must find a way to communicate those perceptions to others. Children and teachers then spend many more days, outside as well as inside the classroom, creating and observing shadows. As children begin to develop theories about the properties of light and the magical shadow, the teachers follow their lead by providing props and questions for additional experimentation. This sequence of events—playing, documenting, exploring, hypothesis building, and testing—characterizes most classroom projects.

Another type of project that involves more advance planning is based on the teachers' understanding of the keen interest young children display in themselves—their bodies, their feelings, their sense of being alive. Such a project also corresponds to a curriculum goal of helping children learn to appreciate themselves as unique individuals who are also contributing members of the class group. Children have repeated opportunities to contemplate the image they present to others, in mirrors and other reflective surfaces as well as in frequent photographs taken by the teacher. Children are encouraged to create images of themselves (through drawing, clay, wire sculptures). These activities and ensuing discussions are repeated throughout the time that children are in a particular class, providing multiple opportunities to increase observational and representational skills. Discussions of children's images often lead to other related problems, such as discovering how we communicate through body language, how our voices convey emotion, and exploring the variations in the human form associated with movement.

The third type of project is one that is initiated by the teacher(s) in response to an observed need on the part of some or all of the children. For example, teachers and parents were concerned about the major role that war toys, especially action figures based on popular television cartoons, were assuming in children's dramatic play. Rather than insisting that the action figures be left at home, parents and teachers decided to redirect the interest in war play, suggesting that the children create the space scene in which the typical battles took place. Children constructed several space vehicles out of cardboard boxes and recycled material, and previously uninvolved children were invited to assist in the creation of an "outer-space" atmosphere. Within a short time the action figures were put aside as new challenges and problems associated with the space project (including how to communicate with an alien being) took their place. Such an approach not only gave

The curriculum is played out in projects that emerge from children's expressed interests, teachers' knowledge of what interests children, and teachers' observations of children's needs. Parents' concerns are also sources of curriculum.

teachers the opportunity to gain a better understanding of children's fascination with war toys and war play in general, but also provided them with a more direct way to encourage prosocial values and foster critical thinking about such issues as conflict and negotiation (Edwards, 1986; Carlsson-Paige & Levin, 1990).

In these and other Reggio Emilia projects, children are given problems to solve, opportunities to explore and interact with each other, and materials and objects related to the quest. They are encouraged to reflect and reconsider their perceptions and understandings, and to share their ideas and experiences with parents and other children through one or more means of symbolic

Rebecca New

Outer space

representation. Throughout, teachers serve as the "memory" of the group, making photographs and tape recordings of children's activities and discussions. Other roles of the teacher include provoking theory building and engaging children in conversation of the sort that encourages "reflection, exchange and coordination of points of view" (Lay-Dopyera & Dopyera, 1989). Typically, such projects involve the use of "little money and a lot of fantasy."

Children represent their understanding and learning in a great variety of ways—pictures, sculptures, constructions, collections, and creations fill the school.

The use of space supports the curriculum

Visitors to Reggio Emilia are often astonished by the visual appeal of the preschool and infant/toddler classrooms. One Reggio Emilia parent, reflecting on her first impressions, remembers an ambience that was . . . *"molto luminoso, sereno e stimolante nello stresso tempo"* (luminous, serene, and stimulating at the same time) (Department of Education, 1986). While the furnishings are of good quality, what is compelling about the appearance of the schools and classrooms is the result *not* of a higher-than-average budget but of a creative, meticulous consideration of the potentials of the environment to meet program and curriculum goals.

The environment informs and stimulates

What one sees upon entering any one of the community preschools includes the work of children (drawings, paintings, sculptures) and their teachers (photographs and displays of projects in process), often with the dramatic use of graphics. Such displays convey ongoing curriculum and research projects in a manner that keeps families informed about and interested in children's school activ-

ities and captures the interest of other children in the projects.

There is more to see, however, than evidence of children's thinking. Everywhere you turn, there is something else to ponder. Art supplies, including paints and clay as well as recycled or naturally found materials (leaves, bottle caps, fabric scraps) are pleasingly arranged, often by color, on shelves within children's reach. Groupings of found objects, including flower petals and plastic bags filled with "memories" from field trips, are carefully displayed so as to acknowledge the importance children attribute to the objects as well as the aesthetic qualities (shape, texture, color) of the objects themselves (Gandini, 1984). This attention to visual stimuli extends beyond the classroom walls. Doors, windows, and other translucent surfaces highlight children's image making. Lunchrooms are inviting and personal, and the daily menu is a vivid display of close-up color photos of the foods to be served that day, enticing children to comment on the shape of the pasta or the color of a vegetable.

Rebecca New

Lunchroom

The environment fosters sustained working and a sense of community

When discussing the issue of space, teachers make reference to more than the physical plant, alluding to the social environment as well. Each classroom includes a large central area where all children and teachers can meet, in addition to smaller work spaces, and a *"mini atelier"* (small art room) where children can

The environment and curriculum are inseparable. Rooms connect in ways that promote community, yet allow space for children's works-in-progress that require weeks of effort. Multiple mirrors and reflective surfaces constantly invite children to interact with themselves.

work on long-term projects. Schedules and supplies are flexibly arranged so that children hard at work on a project may continue in their efforts throughout the school day without the need to return things to their places before completing the activity. Each school also has a large central *atelier* (workroom) where the art teacher works with children as well as teachers.

Classrooms typically open to a large area that connects each individual classroom to the entire school. Kitchens, centrally located when possible, are often surrounded by glass windows so that the activities are always observable. Children are frequently invited to participate in the cooking process. Bathrooms, important centers of social exchange, are decorated with mobiles, paintings, and colorful arrangements of towels and toothbrushes. Mirrored-tile arrangements in the bathrooms and hallways encourage children to perform antics to the amusement of their peers, puzzle over the cognitive task presented by a missing piece, or simply contemplate their growing bodies. Gardens and courtyards also extend the classroom, and each school has rooms in which parents can meet and families can gather.

Such features are characteristic of renovated as well as modern facilities, each planned to support program goals, including facilitating social exchanges among and between adults and children and nurturing children's interests in problem solving and symbolic representation. This use of school space draws attention to unique aspects of the environment while making the everyday atmosphere more appealing.

What are the implications of this Italian program for early childhood education in the United States?

While some features described certainly reflect Italian cultural values, and, as such, might not be applicable to American programs, there are many lessons to be learned from the teachers and children of Reggio Emilia. For example, given the strong Italian view that mothers should be the major influence with young children, perhaps the tight home-school relationship is natural. Yet even without this cultural view, there are ample theoretical grounds to support the development of cooperative home-school relations (Powell, 1989), particularly in the early years (Honig, 1979), despite the difficulties inherent in establishing such relations (Kontos & Wells, 1986). Teachers in Reggio Emilia emphasize the *value* of multiple points of view and reciprocal participation, as they purposely seek out diversity of opinion.

The significance of the environment as a source of opportunities for social exchanges among adults as well as children reflects a cultural appreciation of group *discussione* (Corsaro, 1988). Yet attention to a classroom's social climate is equally important in the United States if schools are to be places where children and adults can truly learn from and with each other (Bruner, 1985; Slavin, 1987).

Bathroom

Dramatic play space

The emphases on the arts and aesthetic sensibilities reflect an appreciation of detail and sensitivity to design consistent with the Italian cultural tradition of creative endeavors. Though Americans purportedly also value creativity and individual expression, we historically neglect the expressive arts in favor of competing demands within the curriculum. Yet the contribution of the arts, within a personally meaningful and intellectually stimulating environment, to developmentally appropriate early childhood curriculum is well acknowledged by American educators (Bredekamp, 1987; Hoffman & Lamme, 1989).

Katz and Chard (1989) have recently reminded us of the importance of providing for and enabling children's engagement in meaningful work. Extensions of children's experiences not only validate their interest in the world around them but afford children multiple opportunities to reflect on their understanding of the world—as we saw in their studies of shadows, self, conflict, and outer space. Yet American teachers too seldom provide children with the luxury of time to explore their ideas; our insistence on "clean-up time" even as a block structure begins to take shape routinely inhibits opportunities for growth within our classrooms.

Our unrealized potential

Perhaps the greatest contribution the preschools of Reggio Emilia might make to American education is to reveal the potential for enhancing children's creative and intellectual development. The works produced by three-, four-, and five-year-old children in Reggio Emilia are the results of prolonged efforts on the part of children, fostered by a set of parent and teacher expectations about what children can do, which clearly exceeds the expectations of the average American parent and teacher. Such beliefs are based not only on cultural "folk wisdom" but also actual experiences with children (Edwards & Gandini, 1989). We have much to gain by providing ourselves and our children such opportunities for learning.

References

Bredekamp, S. (Ed.). (1987). *Developmentally appropriate practice in early childhood programs serving children from birth through age 8.* Washington, DC: NAEYC.

Bruner, J. (1985). Vygotsky: A historical and conceptual perspective. In J. V. Wertsch (Ed.)., *Culture, communications, and cognition: Vygotskian perspectives,* (pp. 21-34). New York: Cambridge University Press.

Carlsson-Paige, N., & Levin, D. (1990). *Who's calling the shots? How to respond effectively to children's fascination with war play and war toys.* Santa Cruz, CA: New Society.

Corsaro, W. (1988). Routines in the peer culture of American and Italian nursery school children. *Sociology of Education, 61,* 1–14.

Department of Education. (1989). *A historical outline, data and information.* Reggio Emilia, Italy: Center for Educational Research.

Department of Education. (1988). *Scuole dell'infanzia e asili nido: Ieri e oggi.* Reggio Emilia, Italy: Center for Educational Research.

Department of Education. (1987). *I cento linguaggi dei bambini/The hundred languages of children.* Reggio Emilia, Italy: Center for Educational Research.

Department of Education. (1986). *Dieci anni di nido.* Reggio Emilia, Italy: Center for Educational Research.

Edwards, C. (1986). *Promoting social and moral development in young children: Creative approaches for the classroom.* New York: Teachers College Press, Columbia University.

Edwards, C., Forman, G., & Gandini, L. (Eds.). (in preparation). *Education for all the children: The multi-symbolic approach to early education in Reggio Emilia, Italy.*

Edwards, C. P., & Gandini, L. (1989). Teachers' expectations about the timing of developmental skills: A cross-cultural study. *Young Children, 44*(4), 15–19.

Filippini, Tiziana. (1989, June 12). Presentation to Syracuse University students, Reggio Emilia, Italy.

Gandini, L. (1984 Summer). Not just anywhere: Making child care centers into "particular" places. *Beginnings: The magazine for teachers of young children,* p. 17–20.

Gandini, L., & Edwards, C. P. (1988). Early childhood integration of the visual arts. *Gifted International, 5*(2), 14–18.

Hoffman, S., & Lamme, L. L. (1989). *Learning from the inside out: The expressive arts.* Wheaton, MD: Association for Childhood Education International.

Honig, A. (1979). *Parent involvement in early childhood education* (rev. ed.). Washington, DC: NAEYC.

Katz, L., & Chard, S. (1989). *Engaging children's minds: The project approach.* Norwood, NJ: Ablex.

Kontos, S., & Wells, W. (1986). Attitudes of caregivers and the day care experiences of families. *Early Childhood Research Quarterly, 1,* 46–67.

Lay-Dopyera, M., & Dopyera, J. (1989). The child-centered curriculum. In C. Seefeldt (Ed.), *Continuing issues in early childhood education* (pp. 207–222). Columbus, OH: Merrill.

New, R. (1988). Parental goals and Italian infant care. In R. A. LeVine, P. Miller, & M. West (eds.), Parental behavior in diverse societies (pp. 51–63). *New Directions for Child Development,* no. 40, San Francisco, CA: Jossey-Bass.

Powell, D. R. (1989). *Families and early childhood programs.* Washington, DC: NAEYC.

Rankin, M. (1985). *An analysis of some aspects of schools and services for 0–6-year-olds in Italy with particular attention to Lombardy and Emilia-Romagna.* Unpublished master's thesis, Wheelock College, Boston.

Slavin, R. (1987). Developmental and motivational perspectives on cooperative learning. *Child Development, 58,* 1161–1167.

LEARNING,
CHINESE—STYLE

Is it better to let kids learn a task by experimenting— or to teach them exactly how to do it? The answer depends on whether your values are American or Chinese, says a leading educational psychologist.

Howard Gardner

Howard Gardner, author of Frames of Mind (1983) *and* Mind's New Science (1985), *is professor of education at Harvard University, and holds research appointments at the Boston Veterans Administration Medical Center and the Boston University School of Medicine.*

For a month in the spring of 1987, my wife Ellen and I lived in the bustling eastern Chinese city of Nanjing with our 1½-year-old son Benjamin while studying arts education in Chinese kindergartens and elementary schools. But one of the most telling lessons Ellen and I got in the difference between Chinese and American ideas of education came not in the classroom but in the lobby of the Jinling Hotel where we stayed in Nanjing.

The key to our room was attached to a large plastic block with the room number embossed on it. When leaving the hotel, a guest was encouraged to turn in the key, either by handing it to an attendant or by dropping it through a slot into a receptacle. Because the key slot was narrow and rectangular, the key had to be aligned carefully to fit snugly into the slot.

Benjamin loved to carry the key around, shaking it vigorously. He also liked to try to place it into the slot. Because of his tender age, lack of manual dexterity and incomplete understanding of the need to orient the key just so, he would usually fail. Benjamin was not bothered in the least. He probably got as much pleasure out of the sounds the key made as he did those few times when the key actually found its way into the slot.

Now both Ellen and I were perfectly happy to allow Benjamin to bang the key near the key slot. His exploratory behavior seemed harmless enough. But I soon observed an intriguing phenomenon. Any Chinese attendant nearby would come over to watch Benjamin and, noting his lack of initial success, attempt to intervene. He or she would hold onto Benjamin's hand and, gently but firmly, guide it directly toward the slot, reorient it as necessary, and help him to insert it. The "teacher" would then smile somewhat expectantly at Ellen or me, as if awaiting a thank you—and on occasion would frown slightly, as if to admonish the negligent parent.

I soon realized that this incident was directly relevant to our assigned tasks in China: to investigate the ways of early childhood education (especially in the arts), and to illuminate Chinese attitudes toward creativity. And so before long I began to incorporate this key-slot anecdote into my talks to Chinese educators.

Two Different Ways to Learn

With a few exceptions my Chinese colleagues displayed the same attitude as the attendants at the Jinling Hotel. Since adults know how to place the key in the key slot, which is the ultimate purpose of approaching the slot, and since the toddler is neither old enough nor clever enough to realize the desired action on his own, what possible gain is achieved by having the child flail about? He may well get frustrated and angry—certainly not a desirable outcome. Why not show him what to do? He will be happy, he will learn how to accomplish the task sooner, and then he can proceed to more complex activities, like opening the door or asking for the key—both of which accomplishments can (and should) in due course be modeled for him as well.

We listened to such explanations sympathetically and explained that, first of all, we did not much care whether Benjamin succeeded in inserting the key into the slot. He was having a good time and was exploring, two activities that *did* matter to us. But the critical point was that, in the process, we were trying to teach Benjamin that one can solve a problem effectively by oneself. Such self-reliance is a principal value of child rearing in middle-class America. So long as the child is shown exactly how to

The learning style in China is based on teaching children exactly how to do a certain task, and not have them experiment and solve the problem themselves. These kindergarten children are following their teacher closely so that they can learn to dance. (United Nations photo by A. Holcombe)

do something—whether it be placing a key in a key slot, drawing a rooster or making amends for a misdeed—he is less likely to figure out himself how to accomplish such a task. And, more generally, he is less likely to view life—as Americans do—as a series of situations in which one has to learn to think for oneself, to solve problems on one's own and even to discover new problems for which creative solutions are wanted.

Teaching By Holding His Hand

In retrospect, it became clear to me that this incident was indeed key—and key in more than one sense. It pointed to important differences in the educational and artistic practices in our two countries.

When our well-intentioned Chinese observers came to Benjamin's rescue, they did not simply push his hand down clumsily, hesitantly or abruptly, as I might have done. Instead, they guided him with extreme facility and gentleness in precisely the desired direction. I came to realize that these Chinese were not just molding and shaping Benjamin's performance in any old manner: In the best Chinese tradition, they were *ba zhe shou jiao*—"teaching by holding his hand"—so much so that he would happily come back for more.

The idea that learning should take place by continual careful shaping and molding applies equally to the arts. Watching children at work in a classroom setting, we were stunned at their facility. Children as young as 5 or 6 were painting flowers, fish and animals with the dexterity and panache of an adult; calligraphers 9 and 10 years old were producing works that could have been displayed in a museum. In a visit to the homes of two of the young artists, we

learned from their parents that they worked on perfecting their craft for several hours a day.

Interested as I was in the facility of the young artists, I wondered whether they could draw any object or only something they had been taught to portray. After all, in the practice of calligraphy, the ordinary method involves painstaking tracing of the same characters over and over. Suddenly I had a minor inspiration. I decided to ask three 10-year-olds to draw my face. The assignment at first nonplussed my three guinea pigs, but soon they undertook it with gusto, and each produced a credible job. To be sure, one picture had me looking like one of the Beatles, the second like a Chinese schoolboy, the third as Charlie's aunt is usually portrayed, but each of them bore at least a family resemblance to its subject. I had found out what I wanted: Chinese children are not simply tied to schemata; they can depart to some extent from a formula when so requested.

Creativity: Evolutionary or Revolutionary?

If I had to indicate the typical Chinese view of creativity, it would run as follows: In every realm, there are accepted means for achieving competence — prescribed and approved performances. There is really no good reason for attempting to bypass a long-established route, although a modest degree of latitude can be tolerated as the traditional form is acquired. Though the point of acquisition may never be totally reached (Zen Buddhist masters ask their charges to create the same sound or form or movement thousands of times), competent performers are sanctioned to introduce increasing departures from the approved forms. By this distinctly evolutionary path, the products of the master eventually come to be reasonably deviant from the canon. This is "approved creativity." Even so, the relationship to the canon continues to be evident, and critical discussion of an adult master may center on fruitful as opposed to idiosyncratic deviations.

While these views of the creative realm are not the modern Western ones, they seem entirely viable to me. We might contrast the Western, more "revolutionary" view, with a more "evolutionary" view espoused by the Chinese. There is a virtual reversal of priorities: the young Westerner making her boldest departures first and then gradually reintegrating herself into the tradition; and the young Chinese being almost inseparable from the tradition, but, over time, possibly evolving to a point as deviant as the one initially staked out by the innovative Westerner.

One way of summarizing the American position is to state that we value originality and independence more than the Chinese do. The contrast between our two cultures can also be conceptualized in terms of the fears we both harbor. Chinese teachers are fearful that if skills are not acquired early, they may never be acquired; there is, on the other hand, no comparable hurry to inculcate creativity. American educators fear that unless creativity has been acquired early, it may never emerge; on the other hand, skills can be picked up later.

However, I do not want to overstate my case. There is certainly creativity in China:

creativity by groups, by selected individuals in the past and by numerous Chinese living in diverse societies around the world today. Indeed, as a society, China compares favorably with nearly every other in terms of the scientific, technological and aesthetic innovations that have emerged over the centuries.

There is also the risk of overdramatizing creative breakthroughs in the West. When any innovation is examined closely, its reliance on previous achievements is all too apparent (the "standing on the shoulder of giants" phenomenon). Perhaps as Claude Levi-Strauss has argued, it is misleading to speak of creativity as though it ever occurs from scratch; every symbolic breakthrough simply represents a certain combination of choices from within a particular symbolic code.

But assuming that the antithesis I have developed is valid, and that the fostering of skills and creativity are both worthwhile goals, the important question becomes this: Can we glean, from the Chinese and American extremes, a superior way to approach education, perhaps striking an optimal balance between the poles of creativity and basic skills?

Reflections

- The Present (Articles 42-43)
- The Future (Article 44)

The purpose of the three articles in this unit is to challenge us all to become very familiar with the state of childhood in America today, and then to become advocates and act to change the conditions and outlook for these young people.

Articles for the *Annual Editions: Early Childhood Education 91/92* come from many sources, and the editors are often surprised to pick up a business journal and read an article focusing on young children. The lead article in this unit comes from a source new to *Annual Editions: Early Childhood Education*, but it demonstrates the scope of the problem facing children today. Sharing page space with advertisements for retirement homes in Florida and an application for membership in the American Association for Retired Persons is a look at the state of childhood today written for individuals who do not have daily contact with young children facing the perils of life in the '90s. Early childhood educators and parents of young children are familiar with children's issues but have a responsibility to assist others in becoming aware of the lack of quality child care or the effects of teenage pregnancy. Marion Wright Edelman, Director of the Children's Defense Fund, is quoted in the article as saying, "Children don't vote, they don't lobby. Children are powerless: Adults have to be a power and a voice for them if we're to protect our great nation."

The authors of the second article address issues that have received a great deal of attention lately. What are the effects of long-term child care on young children? Will relationships be difficult to maintain for children who spend 7 A.M. to 6 P.M. days during their preschool years in child care? There are no simple answers to these questions.

We have chosen to end this edition with "The Costs of *Not* Providing Quality Early Childhood Programs," written by Ellen Galinsky, the immediate past president of the

National Association for the Education of Young Children. Many times people feel there is not much they can do as one person to initiate change, but Galinsky suggests we challenge this attitude. We can educate parents on what to look for when choosing child care, and discuss the importance of consistent and knowledgeable caregivers. During these hard economic times, some states are considering budget-cutting that would eliminate the Division of Child Day Care Licensing or drastically reduce grants to local centers. With changes such as these pending, we have the responsibility to write legislators and detail the benefits of quality early childhood programs and the devastating effects if quality child care is not available for all families seeking it.

It takes passion about an issue for people to become involved. Think of the children, families, and educators you know who would benefit from your involvement in issues and then act on their behalf.

Looking Ahead: Challenge Questions

What effects has the breakdown of the American family had on children? What can be done to assist families who are at risk?

In "A Promise at Risk" what similarities are drawn between children of poverty during the Depression and children being raised in poverty today? What can be done to break that cycle of poverty?

What can be learned from research on the effects of infant care, given the contradictory findings? What questions should parents ask of infant caregivers?

What are some of the benefits of increasing the salaries of child care workers? How can this best be accomplished?

How does the quality of the child care program affect the parents of children in that program? What role do relationships play in the child care experience?

A PROMISE AT RISK

Can America rouse itself to conquer the perils facing its children?

Susan Champlin Taylor

In his three years of life, Bobby* has seen an undue share of suffering. Born in Southern California to a drug-addicted mother, Bobby went through withdrawal at the age of two weeks. He has lived in two foster homes, barely survived a life-threatening case of spinal meningitis, and is now back with his natural mother despite allegations by her relatives that she has abused Bobby and his three siblings.

Tim is a New Jersey teenager. He started drinking at age 11, had a poor relationship with his mother, and constantly acted up in class. After getting into some serious trouble he was referred to the state's School Based Youth Services program, through which he stopped drinking, got counseling, and improved his school performance. Tim is the lucky one.

* The names of all the children in this story have been changed.

Mary grew up in Memphis, Tennessee, in a home headed by her single mother, an alcoholic. By age 12 Mary had been moved into foster care. At 15, she was pregnant with her first child. She and the baby were then put into separate foster homes. At 16, Mary was pregnant again.

These are children at risk. The dangers to them are formidable and tragic enough: threats of lifelong ill health—most likely *not* covered by any kind of health insurance; of dropping out of school; of going on the welfare roles and never getting off.

Multiply these children by several million living under equally daunting circumstances. Then broaden the picture to include these children's children, who may be destined to repeat their parents' grim lives, and one sees a national catastrophe in the making.

Looking at children as America's prospective workers, parents, voters

and taxpayers, it becomes a frightening prospect to realize that one in five of them—13 million children in all—live in poverty; that 12 million have no health insurance coverage and often go without medical care; that one-fourth of all teenagers drop out of high school; that countless thousands more will graduate with reading, writing and reasoning skills inadequate for the job market; and that nearly half a million teenage girls will become mothers this year, virtually guaranteeing a continuation in the cycle of poverty.

There is hope—in the form of hundreds of thousands of dedicated individuals working to better the lives of children. And there is hope for the future—if the country acts now to forestall the looming crisis. Says Philip Porter, M.D., founder of Boston's Healthy Children program, "Early intervention is better than late intervention, but prevention is best of all."

Part of the solution

Programs that work

Many government programs for children have outstanding track records; the Children's Defense Fund, the Committee for Economic Development, and *American Agenda* recommend they be expanded. Figures are based on the 1985 report of the House Select Committee on Children, Youth and Families:

• A Special Supplemental Food Program for Women, Infants and Children has reduced rates of infant mortality and low-birthweight babies among participants; $1 invested in the prenatal component of WIC saves up to $3 in short-term hospital costs.

• Prenatal coverage by Medicaid has led to a decrease in neonatal and infant mortality; $1 spent on comprehensive prenatal care saves $3.38 in future medical costs.

• The success of the Childhood Immunization program has meant dramatic decreases in mumps, rubella, measles, polio and other diseases; $1 spent saves $10 in later medical costs.

• Head Start, a preschool program for disadvantaged three- and four-year-olds, has had great results in preparing youngsters for school; $1 invested in quality preschool saves $4.75 in costs of special education, public assistance and crime.

• Extra educational help provided by Chapter 1 Compensatory Education to disadvantaged students, has been linked to achievement gains in reading and mathematics; an investment of $500 per child for one year can save $3,000 for repeating a grade.

• Job Corps and the Youth Employment Training Program resulted in gains in employability, wages and success while in school and afterwards; $1 invested in Job Corps yields $1.45 to American society. . . .

One route to prevention is public awareness. "We've got to make a critical mass of Americans understand that the breakdown of the American family is a great threat," says Marian Wright Edelman, president of the Children's Defense Fund. "It's greater than the Soviet threat, greater than the Libyan threat, greater than the savings-and-loan crisis."

Children are the concern of every citizen, whether because of simple humanity or just because our own self-interests are at stake when children's futures are at risk. It is self-interest that's motivating the business community to get involved: Corporations worry about the potential dearth of trained, educated employees if today's children aren't given the right building blocks to become productive workers. Older people are realizing that their own Social Security is threatened if children don't enter the workforce.

"If we're to support the quality of life we value, we must have a highly trained and highly competent workforce," says Representative Nancy Johnson (R-Connecticut), a four-year member of the House Select Committee on Children, Youth and Families. "The economic consequences of failing to act are great, but the human consequences are even greater."

The Reverend Jesse Jackson also stressed the moral imperative of looking out for our children in a speech to the Children's Defense Fund's annual conference last March: "The critical issue is not left-wing or right-wing, it's the moral center," Jackson said, adding, "How we treat children in the dawn of life, and how we treat old people in the sunset of life, are measures of our character."

The problems are many and complex, but all of them boil down to the increasingly familiar three-word phrase, "children at risk." While the words are generally applied to poor and disadvantaged children, middle-class families face risks of their own. Says Representative Patricia Schroeder (D-Colorado), "They're having to work twice as hard to stay even. Like the hamster in the wheel, they run and run and run but they're still at the bottom. Health-care insurance, homes, automobiles—those are the basic American dream items, and they're being priced out of the range of a lot of people we define as middle-class. If you can't attain those things, you feel you're losing your status."

Sometimes it doesn't take much to push people over the line into poverty. Says Edelman, "In the last few years we've seen a growth in poverty and a loss in health insurance. This is happening to people who thought it couldn't happen to them: the white, the middle-class."

Sandra Kessler Hamburg, deputy director of information for the Committee for Economic Development, edited CED's 1987 report, *Children in Need: Investment Strategies for the Educationally Disadvantaged.* Hamburg says, "All children are at risk to the extent that we have a very changing society where the rules and structures most of us remember fondly no longer exist. It is atypical for a child today to grow up in a two-parent

Everyone's children deserve the concern of all citizens

household. Estimates are that 60 percent of children will live in a single-parent household at some point in their lives. Families structured in the 1950s model, with two parents and the mother staying home full-time, make up only 18 percent of all families."

The problems, of course, are most grave for children growing up in poverty, and families headed by single women have the highest poverty rates. Many of these single mothers are teenagers unlikely to ever finish high school or make it off the welfare roles. Their children in turn are most likely to become poor adults.

In a bitter irony, while the nation as a whole has gotten wealthier, children as a group have gotten poorer. In 1969, one in seven children in America were poor. Today, though the country is better off, that number has increased to one in five. By the year 2000, if present trends continue, it will be one in four. Children now make up the largest segment of America's poor population. Though black children have the greatest likelihood of being poor (because a disproportionate number of them are poor compared to their population), most children in poverty today are white.

"There's this notion of the 'unworthy poor,'" says Edelman, "and that most people on welfare are black and brown. The truth is that most poor people are white and working." In fact, according to *American Agenda*, a 1988 report in which former Presidents Gerald Ford and Jimmy Carter collaborated on recommendations to the new President, "About 15 percent of poor households are headed by someone who works full-time all year at the minimum wage, earning roughly $7,000. The poverty line for a family of four is $11,203 [as of 1986]."

But regardless of who the poor are,

what color poor children's skin may be, they need help—and America needs its children to be given that help. "Our economic competitiveness depends on what we do with the poorest and blackest child," Edelman says.

The risks to poor children start even before they are born: The lack of health insurance means poor mothers are more likely to go without prenatal care, resulting in higher rates of infant mortality and low-birthweight babies. Says R. Scott Fosler, vice president and director of government studies for the Committee for Economic Development, "If a mother gives birth to a low-birthweight child, the consequences are astronomical right off the bat." Poor children may not get necessary immunizations, even though it has been shown that $1 spent on the Childhood Immunization program averages a $10 saving in later medical costs. These children are at far greater risk of suffering ill health throughout their lives.

worried about having a roof over their heads and food in their child's stomach, this does not take precedence."

Drugs pose another active threat to children's health, education, and well-being. Unfortunately, for many children in poor neighborhoods, drugs are seen as the only ticket out of poverty. As CED's Hamburg says, "In the inner city there's this pernicious underground economy fueled by the drug trade. That is the only source of wealth people in those communities see that is tangible—the drug dealers who flaunt their wealth conspicuously. If a 13-year-old can make money running crack for a drug lord and buy his mother a new coat with the money he makes, what do you think he's going to do?"

Babies of drug-addicted mothers are also at risk before birth. Many are themselves born addicted, and may have physical or mental problems lasting long past childhood. They may be put into foster care, or end up living with aging grandparents because their mothers (when the fathers have long since disappeared) cannot care for them. Says Representative Nancy Johnson, "Drug-addicted parents have lost the basic instincts of food-gathering and nurturing. Welfare checks are being spent on drugs; that means the children go without food."

Education is one key to ending the cycle of poverty

A five-year-old in Pasadena, California, went for a state-funded physical and was discovered to have a draining ear. When questioned, her mother admitted that the child had had the condition since she was a baby. "We of course refer them to medical care," says Louise Singleton, who runs the local school district's Child Health, Disability and Prevention Program funded by the state of California. "But if the parents don't have the means to pay, and they're

Adolescent girls are faced with an equally life-altering threat: teenage pregnancy. CED notes that one out of six babies born in the United States today is the child of a teenage mother, and 96 percent of these girls keep their babies. There is often a sad connection between family poverty and teenage pregnancy: Having grown up in poor homes, perhaps themselves the children of teenage mothers, these girls tend to feel hopeless; they feel they have no control over the course of their own lives. Getting pregnant, then, is less an active choice than a virtual inevitability.

In the April 1989 issue of *Harpers*, writer Elizabeth Marek tells of visiting a group of teenage mothers in the Bronx, New York. "In all their stories, I hear again and again how little volition these girls feel they have, how little control over the events of their lives," Marek writes. "[Group director] Sophie-Louise told me once that these girls exert no more control over their lives than a 'leaf falling from a tree.'"

Says Sandra Hamburg, "The biggest deterrent to breaking the cycle of poverty is this mentality of no hope. These girls have babies because they want someone to love them back, no questions asked. It's very difficult to convince somebody who has no hope that it's important to prepare for the future, forgo childbearing, go into the work world and do something with their lives before they have families."

These women-children may then raise their babies in similar environments of hopelessness, perpetuating another generation of children in poverty. Adds CED's Scott Fosler, "The really grave problem is the substantial proportion of kids who are not even developing the personal wherewithal to take advantage of the opportunities that are there. They just don't have the drive or the role models or the motivation."

it," says Fosler. "They looked at the children of today and wondered why they couldn't overcome their obstacles. What they came to understand is that the key is not just whether a family is poor, it's whether the kids are getting the kind of parenting that can provide them with the support and the nurturing and the motivation to overcome those obstacles. Today so many kids who are poor are not getting that kind of parenting. In many cases there's only one parent, usually a mother with limited education, often a teenager herself, struggling to make ends meet. It's very difficult for kids in that situation to break out."

In an effort to help the mothers—and in turn their children—"break out," more and more cities now have school programs allowing pregnant teenagers or teenage mothers to stay in school; the mother can leave her child in on-site day care while she attends classes. At Bethany Home for unwed mothers in Memphis, Tennessee, residents are strongly urged to attend the nearby high school for pregnant girls, or take vocational classes if they've already graduated. "We stress education and job skills," says assistant executive director Elizabeth Anne Carver. "We feel that is the key to breaking this cycle and ending welfare dependency."

But national statistics still say that fewer than half of teenage mothers finish high school. In fact, the overall

poverty or overly stressful family circumstances often suffer from a wide variety of physical and emotional problems that can delay normal social and intellectual development or impair their ability to function effectively in the typical public school setting. . . . most educators believe that potential dropouts can be clearly identified by third grade."

For children who start out disadvantaged, schooling can become a long downward spiral. Thus, as the CED report states, "Teenagers rarely make a sudden, conscious decision to leave school at the age of 15 or 16; the act of dropping out is the culmination of years of frustration and failure."

CED puts the cost to society in forgone earnings and taxes at more than $240 billion for each year's dropouts, and the figures climb higher if one considers the costs of incarceration, welfare and other public-assistance costs often associated with dropouts. Even among those who do complete school there are alarming rates of functional or actual illiteracy and inadequate job skills. Carnegie Foundation for the Advancement of Teaching president Ernest L. Boyer and former Secretary of Education Terrel H. Bell write in *American Agenda*, "Of those who do graduate, too many lack the skills and technological literacy that will be necessary for the workforce of the 1990s and beyond."

An additional consideration is the changing make-up of the workforce: By the year 2000 only 15 percent of new workers will be U.S.-born white males. The majority will be women; one-third will be minorities and the poor—the ones currently receiving the least education and training.

All of this has serious implications for America as a competitive and economically strong nation. Says Marian Wright Edelman, "One of our real challenges is to have the discipline to invest in our children now to yield a 21st century workforce capable of competing in the global arena. We have to decide whether we're willing to sacrifice consumption or short-term pleasure now, because if we're not ready to make those choices, we'll sell

'Children are powerless: Adults must be a voice for them'

Fosler uses the idea of parents as motivators to make a comparison between today's children growing up in poverty and those who grew up during the Depression. Many of those who worked on the CED *Children in Need* report are now successful businessmen who themselves grew up during the 1930s. "Their families were very poor but they worked hard and made

number of high school dropouts is staggering—in some inner city neighborhoods as high as 80 percent. *American Agenda* cites a 26.7 percent overall dropout rate. And the rates are even higher for black and Hispanic students.

Seeds for dropping out of school are sown early. As the 1987 CED report notes, "Children who are born into the country to foreign competitors."

But it is not just as future workers that today's children are unprepared. Their lack of education, of general preparation for life, make them ill-equipped to handle the responsibilities they face as citizens, as voters, as parents. Says Scott Fosler, "Unless we turn today's kids into good citizens who will vote wisely, take part in their communities, and become good par-

older children (dropping out of school, adolescent pregnancy) have their roots develop in early childhood—or even prenatally. Haveman, Wolfe, Finnie and Wolff write in The Vulnerable (Urban Institute Press, 1988): "Children's well-being has important life-cycle consequences. The productivity and attainments of adults rest on their well-being as children and on the investments their parents—and soci-

The problem is that insufficient funding means these programs usually serve only a fraction of the eligible children—or the eligibility requirements preclude many who need the services. The Head Start program currently serves only 18 percent of eligible three- and four-year-olds. In 1987, less than half of America's poor pregnant women and children were covered by Medicaid. Thus the Children's Defense Fund, CED and *American Agenda* call for increased federal funding for and expansion of these programs. The CED and CDF proposals ask for new funding ranging from $11.5 billion to $22 billion over the next four to five years.

Children who grow up without hope can't break out of poverty

ents to *their* children, we will develop a permanent underclass."

Though the connection may not be immediately apparent, today's older population is and will continue to be affected by many of the desperate circumstances facing children. Representative Pat Schroeder notes that we don't even need to wait until the next century to feel the effects of children's deprivation: "Every major city in America is having tremendous problems with drugs, violence, gangs, teenage pregnancy. Older people are often the victims of the decline in quality of life—they're the easiest victims."

On an economic level, as mentioned earlier, future Social Security recipients will feel the pinch if today's children do not become productive workers contributing to the Social Security fund. Notes Edelman, "Those who are 50 now will be 62 when today's first-graders graduate from high school. If they're dropping out and not becoming productive, your tax dollars will be paying to support them instead of having those workers helping to support your Social Security." Adds Fosler, "We may find ourselves in the next century with a workforce unable to provide basic services to the elderly."

It's important to realize that the many risks and problems affecting children are intertwined, and that many of the symptoms that appear in

ety generally—have made in them during their formative years."

This idea of investment in children is the key to proposals made by the Children's Defense Fund, CED and *American Agenda*. Says Marian Wright Edelman, "We need a comprehensive approach, we need prevention so we don't have to deal with problems after they've become intractable, and we need to sustain that investment into adulthood."

Says Sandra Hamburg, "CED recommends early and sustained intervention from prenatal care through adolescence, with cost-effective, specific programs focused on infants and preschool education for three- and four-year-olds. But you can't just do any of those things in isolation. You have to sustain the intervention and simultaneously change their environment and the education in inner city schools, which is typically the worst education in any city."

Adds *American Agenda*, "Spending public funds for these young Americans is not wasteful; it is wasteful *not* to invest in the medical attention, the education and the job training that will provide poor children with their share in the American opportunity."

All three organizations point to the success of established programs that have proved cost-effective (see "Part of the Solution").

Admits Sandra Hamburg, "It's a matter of convincing the powers that be to make these programs more widely available so that down the road we will have saved seven times what it cost initially. But in an era of tighter budgets and escalating budget deficits, it's hard to make that case."

Edelman disagrees: "We're asking for a *quarter* of what the country was able to find to bail out the savings-and-loan industry. Our children didn't create this deficit. If we deny the money for prevention we'll spend far, far more later on. It's not a money issue. The country can always find the money when it wants to."

Naturally, though, there is resistance in some areas to increased federal spending—or an increased federal role, generally—in these issues. Sandra Hamburg explains why the government typically avoids up-front spending that would save money down the road: "We work on a crisis mentality: We don't prevent problems before they happen, we try to solve them when they occur. That's been the problem with pregnancy-prevention programs. It's hard to quantify how many pregnancies you prevented, because you can't count a pregnancy that didn't happen. It's easier to take a girl who's already pregnant and target programs to help her."

There also are some who feel that families should make it on their own, without government help. Sheila B. Kamerman and Alfred J. Kahn write in *The Vulnerable*, " . . . this country has chosen individualism as a central value. It has sustained its complex multi-cultural and multi-religious diversity, and avoided value confrontations by . . . keeping national government out of the family, unless it can define a particular family as dangerous or endangered."

Says Edelman, "There's a privatistic view of families, a sense that they should be self-sufficient and independent. There's a fear of government involvement. The truth is we all benefit from the government's help in one way or another."

Then there is the pragmatic truth that in Washington it all comes down to power, and who's got it. Children don't. As Senator Christopher Dodd (D-Connecticut), co-sponsor of the Act for Better Child Care, has said, "Never before has there been a constituency so popular but with so little political clout." Representative Pat Schroeder puts it more bluntly, "The tragedy is that the power base in Washington is not built around children's issues. You don't gain power talking about children, you gain power talking about tanks and missiles and all that crap."

Further, adds Edelman, "Children don't vote, they don't lobby. Children are powerless: Adults have to be a power and a voice for them if we're to protect our great nation."

It is this call to arms that groups like CDF, *American Agenda* and CED are issuing in the form of sobering reports on the economic status of children and recommendations to the federal government. CED's *Children in Need* report also calls upon the members of the business community to raise their powerful voices in support of children's issues—if for no other reason than pure self-interest.

Dee Topol, vice president of the American Express Foundation, speaks of the challenges facing American Express in the future; similar problems face businesses throughout the country: "Our biggest challenge will be in the workforce: how to attract, motivate and retain talented people as the workforce declines and there are fewer trained people."

Ultimately, however, the real voice must come from the electorate, and Marian Wright Edelman is confident that it will. "I have enough faith in our country's basic decency to believe that when we get the message through that

this is our nation's crisis, they will do the right thing with proper leadership. We're not suicidal as a people. We have to create a climate where it's unthinkable not to take care of our kids, where it's un-American for children to live in poverty. Out of this is hope, if we're to remain who we are."

Edelman and others call on the country's older population to lend their voices and support to children's causes. She says, "You're a powerful voice, and a compassionate voice, potentially. We should be natural allies. The elderly are strong because they vote. Children are weak. Use your strength to lift the weak."

And, adds Fosler, "There needs to be a powerful coalition built that says we've got to make the investment in our children early, and the older population has got to be a part of that coalition if it is to have any effect."

Whether through advocacy efforts, political support or direct action through intergenerational programs, older people can make a vast difference in the lives of America's children. When that happens, everyone benefits: you, your children and grandchildren, and all future generations of Americans.

The Day Care Generation

PAT WINGERT
AND BARBARA KANTROWITZ

Meryl Frank is an expert on child care. For five years she ran a Yale University program that studied parental leave. But after she became a new mother two years ago, Frank discovered that even though she knew about such esoteric topics as staff-child ratios and turnover rates, she was a novice when it came to finding someone to watch her own child. Frank went back to work part time when her son, Isaac, was 5 months old, and in the two years since then she has changed child-care arrangements *nine* times.

Her travails began with a well-regarded day-care center near her suburban New Jersey home. On the surface, it was great. One staff member for every three babies, a sensitive administrator, clean facilities. "But when I went in," Frank recalls, "I saw this line of cribs and all these babies with their arms out crying, wanting to be picked up. I felt like crying myself." She walked out without signing Isaac up and went through a succession of other unsatisfactory situations—a babysitter who couldn't speak English, a woman who cared for 10 children in her home at once—before settling on a neighborhood woman who took Isaac into her home. "She was fabulous," Frank recalls wistfully. Three weeks after that babysitter started, she got sick and had to quit. Frank advertised for help in the newspaper and got 30 inquiries but no qualified babysitter. (When Frank asked one prospective nanny about her philosophy of discipline, the woman replied: "If he touched the stove, I'd punch him.") A few weeks later she finally hired her 10th babysitter. "She's a very nice young woman," Frank says. "Unfortunately, she has to leave in

May. And I just found out I'm pregnant again and due in June."

That's what happens when a *pro* tries to get help. For other parents, the situation can be even worse. Child-care tales of woe are a common bond for the current generation of parents. Given the haphazard state of day care in this country, finding the right situation is often just a matter of luck. There's no guarantee that a good thing will last. And always, there's the disturbing question that lurks in the back of every working parent's mind: *what is this doing to my kids?*

The simple and unsettling answer is, nobody really knows for sure. Experts say they're just beginning to understand the ramifications of raising a generation of youngsters outside the home while their parents work. Mothers in this country have always had jobs, but it is only in the past few years that a majority have gone back to the office while their children are still in diapers. In the past, most mothers worked out of necessity. That's still true for the majority today, but they have also been joined by mothers of all economic classes. Some researchers think we won't know all the answers until the 21st century, when the children of today's working mothers are parents themselves. In the meantime, results gathered so far are troubling.

Some of the first studies of day care in the 1970s indicated that there were no ill effects from high-quality child care. There was even evidence that children who were out of the home at an early age were more independent and made friends more easily. Those results received wide attention and reassured many parents. Unfortunately, they don't tell the whole story. "The problem is that much of the day care available

Child care has immediate problems. But what about the long-term effect it will have on kids?

in this country is not high quality," says Deborah Lowe Vandell, professor of educational psychology at the University of Wisconsin. The first research was often done in university-sponsored centers where the child-care workers were frequently students preparing for careers as teachers. Most children in day care don't get such dedicated attention.

Since the days of these early studies, child care has burgeoned into a $15 billion-a-year industry in this country. Day-care centers get most of the attention because they are the fastest-growing segment, but they account for only a small percentage of child-care arrangements. According to 1986 Census Bureau figures, more than half of the kids under 5 with working mothers were cared for by nonrelatives: 14.7 percent in day-care centers and 23.8 percent in family day care, usually a neighborhood home where one caretaker watches several youngsters. Most of the rest were in nursery school or preschool.

Despite years of lobbying by children's advocates, there are still no federal regulations covering the care of young children. The government offers consumers more guidance choosing breakfast cereal than child care. Each state makes its own rules, and they vary from virtually no governmental supervision to strict enforcement of complicated licensing procedures for day-care centers. Many child-development experts recommend that each caregiver be responsible for no more than three infants under the age of 1. Yet only three states—Kansas, Maryland and Massachusetts—require that ratio. Other states are far more lax. Idaho, for example, allows one caregiver to look after as many as 12 children of any age (including babies). And in 14 states there are absolutely no training requirements before starting a job as a child-care worker.

Day-care centers are the easiest to supervise and inspect because they usually operate openly. Family day care, on the other hand, poses big problems for regulatory agencies. Many times, these are informal arrangements that are hard to track down. Some child-care providers even say that regulation would make matters worse by imposing confusing rules that would keep some potential caregivers out of business and intensify the shortage of good day care.

No wonder working parents sometimes feel like pioneers wandering in the wilderness. The signposts point every which way. One set of researchers argues that babies who spend more than 20 hours a week in child care may grow up maladjusted. Other experts say the high turnover rate among poorly paid and undertrained child-care workers has created an unstable environment for youngsters who need dependability and consistency. And still others are worried about health issues—the wisdom of putting a lot of small children with limited immunities in such close quarters. Here's a synopsis of the current debate in three major areas of concern.

There's no question that the care of the very youngest children is by far the most controversial area of research. The topic so divides the child-development community that a scholarly journal, Early Childhood Research Quarterly, recently devoted two entire issues to the subject. Nobody is saying that mothers ought to stay home until their kids are ready for college. Besides that, it would be economically impossible; two thirds of all working women are the sole support of their families or are married to men who earn less than $15,000 a year. But as the demographics have changed, psychologists are taking a second look at what happens to babies. In 1987, 52 percent of mothers of children under the age of 1 were working, compared with 32 percent 10 years earlier. Many experts believe that day-care arrangements that might be fine for 3- and 4-year-olds may be damaging to infants.

Much of the dispute centers on the work of Pennsylvania State University psychologist Jay Belsky. He says mounting research indicates that babies less than 1 year old who receive nonmaternal care for more than 20 hours a week are at a greater risk of developing insecure relationships with their mothers; they're also at increased risk of emotional and behavioral problems in later childhood. Youngsters who have weak emotional ties to their mothers are more likely to be aggressive and disobedient as they grow older, Belsky says. Of course, kids whose mothers are home all day can have these problems, too. But Belsky says that mothers who aren't with their kids all day long don't get to know their babies as well as mothers who work part time or not at all. Therefore, working mothers may not be as sensitive to a baby's first attempts at communication. In general, he says, mothers are more attentive to these crucial signals than babysitters. Placing a baby in outside care increases the chance that an infant's needs won't be met, Belsky says. He also argues that working parents have so much stress in their lives that they have little energy left over for their children. It's hard to find the strength for "quality time" with the kids after a 10- or 12-hour day at the office. (It is interesting to note that not many people are promoting the concept of quality time these days.)

Work by other researchers has added weight to Belsky's theories. Wisconsin's Vandell studied the day-care histories of 236 Texas third graders and found that youngsters who had more than 30 hours a week of child care during infancy had poorer peer relationships, were harder to discipline and had poorer work habits than children who had been in part-time child care or exclusive maternal care. The children most at risk were from the lowest and highest socioeconomic classes, Vandell says, probably because poor youngsters usually get the worst child care and rich parents tend to have high-stress jobs that require long hours away from home. Vandell emphasizes that her results in the Texas study may be more negative than those for the country as a whole because Texas has minimal child-care regulation. Nonetheless, she thinks there's a "serious problem" in infant care.

Other experts say there isn't enough information yet to form any definitive conclusions about the long-term effects of infant

Who's Minding the Children?

Even with the sharp rise in working mothers, most children are still cared for at home—their own or someone else's.

Percent of Mothers Working

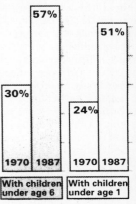

SOURCE: CHILD CARE INC.

Day Care

WHO LOOKS AFTER CHILDREN UNDER AGE 5 WHILE THEIR MOTHERS WORK

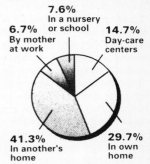

7.6% In a nursery or school

6.7% By mother at work

14.7% Day-care centers

41.3% In another's home

29.7% In own home

SOURCE: U.S. CENSUS BUREAU

Day care that might be fine for 3- or 4-year-olds may be damaging to infants

care. "There is no clear evidence that day care places infants at risk," says Alison Clarke-Stewart, a professor of social ecology at the University of California, Irvine. Clarke-Stewart says that the difference between the emotional attachments of children of working and of nonworking mothers is not as large as Belsky's research indicates. She says parents should be concerned but shouldn't overreact. Instead of pulling kids out of any form of day care, parents might consider choosing part-time work when their children are very young, she says.

For all the controversy over infant care, there's little dispute over the damaging effects of the high turnover rate among caregivers. In all forms of child care, consistency is essential to a child's healthy development. But only the lucky few get it. "Turnover among child-care workers is second only to parking-lot and gas-station attendants," says Marcy Whitebook, director of the National Child Care Staffing Study. "To give you an idea of how bad it is, during our study, we had tiny children coming up to our researchers and asking them, 'Are you my teacher?' "

The just-released study, funded by a consortium of not-for-profit groups, included classroom observations, child assessments and interviews with staff at 227 child-care centers in five cities. The researchers concluded that 41 percent of all child-care workers quit each year, many to seek better-paying jobs. In the past decade, the average day-care-center enrollment has nearly doubled, while the average salaries for child-care workers have decreased 20 percent. Typical annual wages are very low: $9,931 for full-time, year-round employment ($600 less than the 1988 poverty threshold for a family of three). Few child-care workers receive any benefits.

Parents who use other forms of day care should be concerned as well, warns UCLA psychologist Carollee Howes. Paying top dollar for au pairs, nannies and other in-home caregivers doesn't guarantee that they'll stay. Howes conducted two studies of 18- to 24-month-old children who had been cared for in their own homes or in family day-care homes and found that most had already experienced two or three changes in caregivers and some had had as many as six. In her research, Howes found that the more changes children had, the more trouble they had adjusting to first grade.

The solution, most experts agree, is a drastic change in the status, pay and training of child-care workers. Major professional organizations, such as the National Association for the Education of Young Children, have recommended standard accreditation procedures to make child care more of an established profession, for everyone from workers in large for-profit centers to women who only look after youngsters in their neighborhood. But so far, only a small fraction of the country's child-care providers are accredited. Until wide-scale changes take place, Whitebook predicts that "qualified teachers will continue to leave for jobs that offer a living wage." The victims are the millions of children left behind.

When their toddlers come home from day care with a bad case of the sniffles, parents often joke that it's "schoolitis"—the virus that seems to invade classrooms from September until June. But there's more and more evidence that child care may be hazardous to a youngster's health.

A recent report from the Centers for Disease Control found that children who are cared for outside their homes are at increased risk for both minor and major ailments because they are exposed to so many other kids at such a young age. Youngsters who spend their days in group settings are more likely to get colds and flu as well as strep throat, infectious hepatitis and spinal meningitis, among other diseases.

Here again, the state and federal governments aren't doing much to help. A survey released this fall by the American Academy of Pediatrics and the American Public Health Association found that even such basic health standards as immunization and hand washing were not required in child-care facilities in half the states. Inspection was another problem. Without adequate staff, states with health regulations often have difficulty enforcing them, especially in family day-care centers.

Some experts think that even with strict regulation, there would still be health problems in child-care centers, especially among infants. "The problem is that caretakers are changing the diapers of several kids, and it's difficult for them to wash their hands frequently enough [after each diaper]," says Earline Kendall, associate dean of graduate studies in education at Belmont College in Nashville, Tenn. Kendall, who has operated four day-care centers herself, says that very young babies have the most limited immunities and are the most vulnerable to the diseases that can be spread through such contact. The best solution, she thinks, would be more generous leave time so that parents can stay home until their kids are a little older.

Despite the compelling evidence about the dark side of day care, many experts say there's a great reluctance to discuss these problems publicly. "People think if you say anything against day care, you're saying young parents shouldn't work, or if they do work, they're bad parents," says Meryl Frank, who is now a consultant on family and work issues. "For a lot of parents, that's just too scary to think about. But we have to be realistic. We have to acknowledge that good day care may be good for kids, but bad day care is bad for kids."

There is a political battle as well. Belsky, who has become a lightning rod for controversy among child-development professionals, says "people don't want working mothers to feel guilty" because "they're afraid the right wing will use this to say that only mothers can care for babies, so women should stay home." But, he says, parents should use these problems as evidence to press for such changes as paid parental leave, more part-time jobs and higher-quality child care. The guilt and anxiety that seem to be part of every working parent's psyche aren't necessarily bad, Belsky says. Parents who worry are also probably alert to potential problems—and likely to look for solutions.

Child-Care Checklist

Questions to ask at day-care centers:

■ **What are the educational and training backgrounds of staff members?**

■ **What is the child-staff ratio for each age?** Most experts say it should be no more than 4:1 for infants, 5:1 for 18 months to 2 years, 8:1 for 2 to 3 years, 10:1 for 3 to 4 years and 15:1 for 5 to 6 years.

■ **What are the disciplinary policies?**

■ **Are parents free to visit at any time?**

■ **Are the center's facilities clean and well maintained?**

■ **Are child-safety precautions observed?** Such as heat covers on radiators, childproof safety seals on all electrical outlets?

■ **Are staff members careful about hygiene?** It's important to wash hands between diaper changes in order to avoid spreading diseases.

■ **Are there facilities and staff for taking care of sick children?**

■ **Is there adequate space, indoors and out, for children to play?**

■ **Most important of all, do the children look happy and cared for?** Trust your instincts.

The Costs of *Not* Providing Quality Early Childhood Programs

Ellen Galinsky

Ellen Galinsky served as NAEYC President from 1988 to 1990. She is Co-President of the Families and Work Institute in New York City. A noted authority on early childhood education, her work has been instrumental in shaping the emerging field of work and family issues. She is a prolific author, with publications directed to parents, researchers, the business community, as well as the early childhood field. Her work is widely respected in each of these different arenas.

The debate in this country has shifted from the issue of whether or not mothers of young children should be employed to a recognition that they are—and will continue to be in the labor force in even greater numbers. Concurrently, there has been a realization that child care responsibilities cannot be placed on families alone, but that both the private and the public sectors have a role in supporting quality early childhood programs. Rather than ask "why" they should be involved, increasingly businesses, governments, and charitable organizations are asking "how" they can help.

In these discussions, decision makers frequently turn to research to guide their efforts. If there is any one clear message to be drawn from the research on child care and early education, it is that the quality of programs has a definite and lasting effect on children's development. This chapter summarizes what is known about the ingredients of quality in early childhood arrangements and their effects on children, their parents, and their teacher-caregivers. In addition, this chapter presents what is known about the cost of *not* providing quality.

THE EFFECT OF QUALITY ON CHILDREN

The importance of relationships

The personal relationship

The most important ingredient of quality is the relationship between the child and the teacher-caregiver, whether the setting is in a center, a family child care home, or the child's home. This is why NAEYC's accreditation process for early childhood programs places great emphasis on the nature of the interactions between teachers and children. Parents also understand the importance of relationships. Parents report that the kind and quality of the attention their child receives strongly affects their decision in selecting one arrangement over another (Galinsky, 1988).

Children do form attachments to their teacher-caregivers, although Thomas Gamble and Edward Zigler (1986), in a review of this research, remind us that children's attachments to their parents are pre-eminent. Carollee Howes from the University of California at Los Angeles and her colleagues have found that children with a secure attachment to their mothers *and* their teacher-caregiver behave more competently than those with two or more insecure attachments (Howes, Rodning, Galluzzo, & Myers, 1988). Thus, it seems, the cost we could pay for poor relations between the child and the teacher-caregiver is the child's feeling that she or he is just one of the crowd and not a special, unique individual. A good self-concept is one of the foundations of emotional and social well-being. The costs may be very high, especially in terms of children's ability to form healthy relationships with others and enjoy good emotional health.

7. REFLECTIONS: The Future

The teaching relationship

No matter what the setting—center, family child care, or the child's home, teacher-caregivers are teaching children every moment, both formally and informally. The way this teaching is done makes a difference in children's development. For example, a study by Deborah Phillips, Kathleen McCartney, and Sandra Scarr (1987) found that when children are talked to, asked questions, and encouraged to express themselves, their social development is enhanced: They are more likely to be considerate. In fact, the children in this study were also rated as more intelligent and task-oriented. The teaching environment was found to be more predictive of the children's achievement than their social class background. Kathleen McCartney (1984), in a re-analysis of this same data set, found that when children were in a verbally stimulating environment, they were more likely to achieve on tests of cognitive abilities and language development.

Early childhood specialists voice concern over situations in which children are either bored or pressured. In a longitudinal study, Deborah Lowe Vandell and her colleagues found that 4-year-olds who attended programs in which they spent time aimlessly wandering around were more likely at 8 years of age to have developmental problems, including less acceptance by peers, less social competence, and poorer conflict resolution skills (Vandell, Henderson, & Wilson, 1988).

Marcy Whitebook, Carollee Howes, and Deborah Phillips, in their landmark National Child Care Staffing Study (1990), found that children were more likely to be engaged in aimless wandering in programs with high rates of staff turnover. This key signal of lower program quality was associated with programs offering lower staff salaries, fewer benefits, and poorer working conditions. These researchers detected immediate negative consequences of poorer program quality. Children in such programs did less well on tests of both social development and language development, critical areas for later achievement.

Just as children do less well when they are bored or wandering aimlessly, David Elkind from Tufts University (1987), has pointed to the potential for problems such as elementary school burnout when preschool children are overly pressured. Thus, the cost we could pay for inadequate teaching relationships in children's early years is great: diminished achievement and poorer social and language skills.

The disciplinary relationship

There has been a great deal of research indicating that the disciplinary techniques parents use have an impact on the child's subsequent development. These findings can be applied to early childhood programs. Children are more likely to develop self-control and to become more compliant, cooperative, and considerate of others if reasoning is used; if teacher-caregivers explain how a child's behavior affects others; and if problem-solving skills are taught. Vandell and Powers (1983) found that in higher quality programs, children had many more positive interactions with staff than in lower quality programs. Finkelstein (1982) showed that when teacher-caregivers are trained in behavior management techniques, the frequency of children's aggressive acts is reduced.

Such research counters the societal fear that attendance in group programs itself leads to more aggression in children. The ways that teacher-caregivers (or parents) handle young children's aggression can lead to greater or reduced aggression. The difference lies in understanding how to deal with children's aggression in appropriate ways. Lesser quality programs are more likely to have staff who do not have the knowledge and understanding to deal effectively with young children's normal assertions of prowess and power. The cost that we as a society could pay for children who grow up more aggressive seems high indeed.

The stability of relationships

With 40% of all center staff and 60% of all in-home providers leaving the field every year, it is no wonder that one 4-year-old recently said to a teacher, "I don't have to listen to you. I was here before you came and I'll still be here when you leave." Other parents report their children resist going to child care because they simply don't know who will care for them that day. According to the research of Mark Cummings from West Virginia University (1986), children have a much easier time separating from their mothers when they are cared for by well-known teacher-caregivers in small groups. Carollee Howes and her colleagues, in their studies of family child care (Howes & Stewart, 1987), found that there was a cost to children who changed arrangements frequently: They were less competent in their interactions with materials and with other children. As previously described, the National Child Care Staffing Study (Whitebook et al., 1990) documented disturbing results for children's social and language development when they were enrolled in programs with high rates of staff turnover. The Staffing Study also painted a disturbing picture of the amount of turnover in programs. Based on initial reports of program directors, the study found a 41% annual turnover rate, comparable to other nationally reported figures. However, the researchers found a 37% turnover rate in just over 6 months, based on the results of follow-up calls.

The resources of child care

The second aspect of early childhood program quality relates to the program's resources: the group size, adult-child ratio, health and safety considerations, and the professional preparation of teacher-caregivers.

Group size and staff-child ratio

The federal government funded the National Day Care

Study in the late 1970s to investigate the degree to which the regulated features of child care arrangements had an effect on children's development. One of their most important findings was that the group size made a big difference in program quality. In smaller groups the adults spent more time being with children and less time simply watching them. The children were more verbal, more involved in activities, and less aggressive. Finally, the children in smaller groups made the greatest gains in standardized tests of learning and vocabulary (Ruopp, Travers, Glantz, & Coelen, 1979).

The National Day Care Study did not find staff-child ratio as powerful as group size in predicting development for children 3 to 5 years of age. However, the range they examined was limited. As Deborah Phillips and Carollee Howes point out (1987), "The majority of studies have found that the [adult-child] ratio has a significant effect on adult and child behavior in child care." More recently the National Child Care Staffing Study (Whitebook et al., 1990) found that fewer children per caregiver was associated with more developmentally appropriate activities. Teachers in these groups were more sensitive, less harsh, and less detached when interacting with children. The number of children per adult has obvious consequences for the ability of the caregiver to be responsive to each child. The younger the children and the more dependent they are on adults, the more critical it is that the number of children per adult be limited. The crucial learning from this research is that adult-child ratios and group size must be considered together.

Health and safety

There has been a great deal of public concern about the transmission of illness in child care. Susan Aronson has been studying the health risks in group programs for the past decade. She has found a clear demarcation between those early childhood programs in which children often become ill and those in which they do not: When adults wash their hands frequently, children are healthier (Aronson, 1987). The cost of children's illness and injury are obvious in health care expenses and missed days of work for their parents.

Children's safety is another critical factor to consider. Children's safety can be improved when providers are knowledgeable and when the environment is hazard reduced. Safety is also enhanced when ratios and group size are limited. Currently 19 states permit ratios of 5 or more infants to each adult (Adams, 1990). These ratios must be questioned not only in terms of their costs on the relationships established between teacher-caregivers and children, but also for their costs in safety. The extra attention afforded by small groups and good ratios helps to prevent minor accidents and injuries. It may be a life-saver in cases of emergency evacuation. The costs of an unsafe arrangement are incalculable when children's lives are literally at stake.

The costs of an unsafe arrangement are incalculable when children's lives are literally at stake.

Teacher-caregiver preparation and training

NAEYC's experience with its accreditation system has documented that developmentally appropriate teaching practices and activities are more likely to occur when staff have a combination of formal education and specific preparation in early childhood education (Bredekamp, 1989). Other research is mixed regarding the specific characteristics of professional preparation that most contribute to program quality. The National Day Care Study (Ruopp et al., 1970) concluded that one of the most important ingredients of quality was the ongoing, relevant training of providers. In programs in which teacher-caregivers had specific early childhood training, the children behaved more positively, were more cooperative, and were more involved in the program. These children also made the greatest gains on standardized tests of learning. The National Child Care Staffing Study (Whitebook et al., 1990) suggested that the formal education of staff was a more potent predictor of program quality than early childhood training alone. While more research is needed to better define the specific relationships between different types and amounts of preparation and quality, the overall message of the importance of specialized knowledge is clear.

In summary, research on the impact of the resources of the child care program reveals a strong connection between group size, staff-child ratios, health and safety, and staff development and children's social, physical, and cognitive well-being.

Relationships with parents

Numerous studies have been conducted on the long-term effects of early childhood programs, especially model intervention programs and federally funded Head Start programs. One of the most noteworthy findings is that when early childhood programs are effective, they do much more than teach the child. The parents are affected and through this experience become better teachers, motivators, and advocates for their children (Lally, Mangione, & Honig, 1987; Weikart, 1990). This is not happenstance; providing meaningful opportunities for parental involvement has been an integral part of Head Start throughout its 25-year history.

A recent follow-up study of Head Start in Philadelphia (Copple, Cline, & Smith, 1987) is noteworthy in that it reflects typical rather than exemplary programs. In that study, Head Start children were more likely to avoid serious school problems, were less frequently retained, and had better attendance records than their counterparts who did not attend the program. The researchers suggest that the Head Start program may have reduced the helplessness these parents felt in response to the school. Instead of seeing school as a place where their children were doomed, they may have come to see it as a place where their children could hold their own, and where they, as parents, could speak out on behalf of their children's education.

The importance of establishing good working relationships with parents is not universally understood. A recent study conducted by the Families and Work Institute sounds a warning signal about this critical aspect of quality care and education. We found that the parents most likely to have the best parent-teacher relationships were the wealthier, most advantaged parents. Similarly, those least likely to have good relationships—the least advantaged, minority parents—are those who could perhaps use the support the most (Galinsky, Shinn, Phillips, Howes, & Whitebook, 1990).

Summary of the effects of quality on children

The studies described throughout this chapter have been carefully controlled. The effects of different family backgrounds have been statistically accounted for so that the researchers could determine the impact of quality on children's development. The evidence is resoundingly uniform. The quality of early childhood programs has a strong effect on children's development. Carollee Howes (1990) summarizes her numerous studies on different forms of child care by stating, "Children who entered low quality child care as infants were [the] least task oriented and considerate of others as kindergartners, had the most difficulty with peers as preschoolers, and were distractible, extroverted, and hostile as kindergartners."

THE EFFECTS OF QUALITY ON EMPLOYED PARENTS

While some of the costs of poor quality for children may not be readily apparent, we do not have to wait to assess the cost of child care problems on employed parents: The repercussions are showing up right now in diminished job performance.

An inadequate selection

It is difficult for parents to find quality child care. In a survey we conducted with 931 employees at three New Jersey companies (Galinsky, 1988), 46% of the respondents reported that locating quality arrangements was a "major problem"; 48% did not feel they had an adequate selection. Infant care was the most difficult to find—65% indicated that making arrangements for their infants was "difficult" or "very difficult."

A national study conducted by the National Council of Jewish Women (1988) of 1,927 women approximately

5 months after they had given birth found that new mothers who had problems arranging child care were more likely to experience higher levels of stress. In a nationally representative study conducted for *Fortune* magazine (Galinsky & Hughes, 1987), we found that parents who had trouble finding child care were more likely to have higher absenteeism rates.

Satisfaction

It is well known that it can be difficult for parents to admit that they are dissatisfied with the overall quality of child care even though they may admit displeasure with particular aspects of their arrangements. In the Parent/Teacher Study, conducted in conjunction with the National Child Care Staffing Study, we found that there are two sets of factors that parents use to make judgments about child care. One relates to the quality of the child's experience (the warmth of the teacher-caregiver, the activities, etc.). When parents are dissatisfied with this set of factors they are less likely to be satisfied with their child care arrangement in general. The second set of factors relates to the parents' experience with child care (hours, flexibility of scheduling, cost, location, and parents' opportunity for input). When parents are dissatisfied with these conditions, they are more likely to have higher levels of stress, more work-family conflict, and more stress-related health problems, but there is little effect on their overall satisfaction with the child care (Shinn, Galinsky, & Gulcur, 1990).

These new findings help to explain the seeming contradiction in earlier studies where overall satisfaction is reported at high levels, but considerable concern is expressed about specific factors. Parents voice the most concern with the factors that directly affect them: location, flexibility, and cost (Galinsky, 1988). The one strong exception seems to be those parents who rely on their children to care for themselves or their younger siblings. In a study conducted at Portland State University (Emlen & Koren, 1984), 57% of the sample of more than 8,000 employed parents reported dissatisfaction with latchkey arrangements as compared to 23% using family child care or centers. Taken together, these studies suggest that parents' definition of overall child care satisfaction is primarily influenced by their view of the nature of the child's experience. Parents may be dissatisfied with aspects that affect them, but as long as they feel the child's experience is satisfactory, they are satisfied with the arrangement.

One of the disturbing findings of the Parent/Teacher Study was that parents were quite satisfied with programs deemed low in quality by independent researchers. Parents were more attuned to quality when their children were preschoolers as opposed to infants and toddlers. Unfortunately, parents were more satisfied when there were more children per adult and group sizes were larger. Parents, however, did respond to the quality of the relationship between their child

Parents' definition of overall satisfaction with child care is primarily influenced by the nature of their child's experience.

and the teacher-caregiver. When these adults were judged to be more detached, insensitive, or chaotic, parents were less satisfied, lonelier, and missed their child more (Galinsky, Shinn, Phillips, Howes, & Whitebook, 1990). Thus, it seems that while parents are aware of the importance of the teacher-child relationship, they do not know that having fewer children per adult, smaller group sizes, and adequate preparation of the staff make it more likely that the teacher-caregiver will be nurturing and caring as well as able to teach in developmentally appropriate ways.

Parents in this study were very aware of the amount of staff turnover in the center. When the turnover was higher, parents were less satisfied with the program and were less likely to feel that their child benefitted from the experience. These parents also felt less adequate as parents and missed their children more while at work.

When early childhood professionals assess quality, they find a selection process at work that disadvantages the most at-risk parents. For example, Carollee Howes (Howes & Stewart, 1987) found that families who were under the most stress enrolled their children in the lowest quality child care arrangements. This finding led the National Academy of Sciences Panel on Child Care to conclude that such children are in double jeopardy, experiencing stress from their homes and from poorer child care arrangements (Hayes, Palmer, & Zaslow, 1990).

Often the reasons for selecting poorer quality arrangements are economic (Culkin, Helburn, Morris, & Watson, 1990). Sometimes, however, the results may be surprising. For example, the National Child Care Staffing Study (Whitebook et al., 1990) found that children from low-income families were much more likely to be enrolled in nonprofit programs, and children from higher income families were somewhat more likely to be enrolled in nonprofit programs. Children from middle-income families were much more likely to be enrolled in for-profit programs. In this study, auspice (nonprofit or for-profit) was the strongest predictor of quality. As a result, children from middle-income families were found to be enrolled in centers of lower quality than children from either low- or high-income families.

A patchwork system

Our studies show that parents do not use one arrangement for each child; they piece together a patchwork system. In a study we conducted several years ago, parents at Merck & Co., Inc. reported an average of 1.7

arrangements per child (Galinsky, 1988). A study by Marybeth Shinn and her colleagues (Shinn, Ortiz-Torres, Morris, Simko, & Wong, 1989) from New York University also came up with the same number—1.7. In the *Fortune* magazine study (Galinsky & Hughes, 1987), we found that 38% of the families had to contend with as many as three to four different child care arrangements.

The more arrangements the family has, the more likely they are to fall apart. The issue of child care breakdowns is of great concern because of the high turnover in child care. In the *Fortune* magazine study (Galinsky & Hughes, 1987), we found that 27% of the employed fathers and 24% of the employed mothers had been forced to make two to five special arrangements in the past 3 months because their regular arrangements had fallen apart.

Child care breakdowns are strongly associated with productivity. According to Shinn and her colleagues (Shinn et al., 1989), parents with more breakdowns are more likely to miss work. In the *Fortune* magazine study (Galinsky & Hughes, 1987), we found such parents more likely to come to work late or leave early. In fact, in that study, 72% of all employee tardiness was for family-related reasons.

Parents who face more frequent breakdowns in their child care arrangements report spending more unproductive time at work, according to the *Fortune* magazine study. A study conducted of two New England companies (Burden & Googins, 1987), found that one of every four employed parents said that they worried about their children "always" or "most of the time" while on the job. Such intense reactions to child care problems are expressed by an inability to concentrate on the job and a loss of productivity.

Our research also reveals links between child care breakdown and stress, including stress-related health problems. Parents who had to make more last minute arrangements were more likely to report such symptoms as pains in the back, head, and neck; shortness of breath; heart pounding or racing; as well as eating, drinking, or smoking more than usual (Galinsky, 1988).

It is evident that parents who cannot find quality care, who piece together multiple and tenuous arrangements, who have latchkey children, and who face frequent breakdowns in their child care systems have poorer work attendance, are less able to concentrate on the job, and have more stress-related health problems. Thus, as a nation we are paying the cost of these parents' diminished job performance right now.

THE EFFECT OF QUALITY ON TEACHER-CAREGIVERS

When we think of the impact of quality child care arrangements, we think of children or perhaps their parents, but seldom of the adults who provide care and education to young children. Although there has been a great deal of research on the working conditions of employees in most fields, there has been a notable absence of such research in the early childhood field until very recently. Perhaps this is related to the common assumption that early childhood teacher-caregivers are motivated by their love and concern for young children, so working conditions don't seem so important.

The staffing shortages that face so many early childhood programs across the country are calling this assumption into question. It has become evident that teacher-caregivers of young children can no longer afford to stay in such a low-paying field and are having to leave their jobs. Consequently, studies are beginning to be done to identify the various predictors of job satisfaction and turnover.

Job satisfaction

Paula Jorde-Bloom's research (1988) has related various job conditions to the job satisfaction of those working with young children. Among the most salient are job autonomy, relationships with one's supervisor and co-workers, and job clarity. Several studies have found that working in early childhood programs often provides high levels of satisfaction among these variables. For example, teachers in the National Child Care Staffing Study (Whitebook, et al., 1990) reported very high levels of satisfaction with the daily demands of their work. In an Indiana study, Susan Kontos and Andrew Stremmel (1988) found that the majority of child care teachers enjoy their work and want to stay in the field. Likewise, in a study of publicly funded programs in New York City, Bob Granger and Elisabeth Marx (1988) found high levels of job satisfaction among such aspects as working with children, intellectual challenge, and opportunities for creativity.

Salaries and benefits

While the high levels of intrinsic measures of job satisfaction reported by child care teachers are important, they cannot overcome the harsh realities of inadequate compensation. In a California study by Michael Olenick (1986), staff retention was higher in programs that paid higher wages. These not unexpected findings were confirmed by the National Child Care Staffing Study (Whitebook et al., 1990). Teachers' wages were the most important predictor of turnover, reported on average at 41% annually. This study found an important relationship between salaries and program quality. Programs that met recognized measures of higher quality also paid better wages and provided more benefits. Staff in these programs reported higher levels of job satisfaction and were more sensitive, less harsh, and engaged in more appropriate caregiving with children.

Similar findings were evident in the Granger and Marx study (1988). Teachers in publicly funded child

The high level of intrinsic job satisfaction in working with young children is important, but cannot overcome the harsh realities of inadequate compensation.

care and Head Start programs scored significantly lower on several measures of job stability (total years taught, years at current site, and years in current system) than teachers of preschool children in the public school. Demonstrating the relationship between stability and compensation, teachers in programs funded by the public schools received average annual salaries of over $33,000, while those in publicly funded child care and Head Start received annual salaries of just over $19,000. Only a small amount of the disparity was due to differences in education and experience. Granger and Marx estimated that if teachers in the publicly funded child care and Head Start programs were paid according to public school salary schedules, their salaries would have been approximately $31,000 and $27,000 respectively.

In subsequent research, Marx, Zinsser, and Porter (1990) analyzed the impact of 1988 state legislation in New York enacting a one-time child care salary enhancement. Before this legislation was implemented, turnover rates exceeded 30% for teachers and reached 57% for aides and assistants in upstate New York. The $12 million enhancement reached 10,270 full-time equivalent staff, each receiving just over $1,200 on average. Turnover was reduced considerably as a result. In New York City, for example, classroom teachers and supervisory staff had a turnover rate of 42% before enactment. A year following the bill's passage, turnover had dropped to 22%. Staff vacancy rates were also cut in half. Thus, not only are poor salaries linked to higher turnover, but also improved salaries lead to reduced turnover.

When early childhood teacher-caregivers broach the issue of inadequate salaries, it can sound self-serving—professionals trying to aggrandize themselves. Considering the below poverty level wages of those working in most child care and early education programs and the subsequent high rates of staff turnover, the issue must be seen as one of quality. In order to provide quality for children, the early childhood field must be able to attract and retain qualified staff. As described throughout this chapter, children and their families are paying the costs of the lack of quality that results from an insufficient pool of qualified staff.

WHAT CAN BE DONE

Slowly but surely, families and organizations within both the public and private sectors are recognizing that the costs of not providing quality early childhood

No one segment of society can solve this nation's child care crisis; all segments of society must join together.

programs are too high to pay. For example, much time and energy has been devoted to the successful passage of federal child care legislation, accomplished in the fall of 1990 after more than 20 years of effort. A number of promising approaches are also occurring at state and local levels. In addition, there are many private sector initiatives which demonstrate growing understanding of need to address quality.

While the specifics of these different efforts vary, some general principles can be applied to the efforts that show the most promise. As the chapters in this volume describe, there is a complex interplay between quality, affordability, and accessibility. Efforts must be considered in light of their effects on each of these variables.

First and foremost, efforts should be built on the idea that parents must have a choice in selecting the program option that best meets their needs. In order to provide parents with meaningful choices, it is necessary to increase and fortify the existing system of community programs. Issues of supply may be addressed by providing start-up loans or grants to potential programs or providing loans or grants for program expansion. Real choice also depends on parents being able to afford good programs. Low- and moderate-income families especially need assistance to afford the full costs of quality programs, not dependent on the hidden subsidy of inadequate staff compensation.

Efforts are needed to improve the quality of existing services. Improved regulatory standards—and effective enforcement—are essential. State licensing standards should safeguard the protection of children in settings outside their home and promote their development. In many states, rapid growth in the number of programs has outpaced the number of licensing officials. State budgetary cutbacks have in some instances led to fewer licensing officials in spite of the tremendous growth in the total number of centers and family child care homes subject to regulation.

In addition to regulatory approaches, quality can be enhanced by assisting programs and their staff to participate in professional systems of improvement and recognition. Public/private partnerships have been established to assist programs in achieving accreditation by NAEYC's Academy for centers or the National Family Day Care Association for family child care providers. Assistance may also be provided for individuals to gain professional training and credentials such as the Child Development Associate Credential, administered by the Council for Early Childhood Professional Recognition.

No one segment of our society can solve this nation's child care crisis—not the federal government, not states, not employers, and certainly not families. Instead, all segments of society must join together. The federal government must work as a partner with state and local government, business, religious groups, and social service and philanthropic organizations. Years of research knowledge about the ingredients and effects of quality make it evident that we are losing a great deal by not responding to the crisis of inadequate, tenuous, and poor quality care and education for our nation's youngest citizens. If we don't respond now, we will pay even more for our negligence in the future.

REFERENCES

Adams, G. (1990). *Who knows how safe? The status of state efforts to ensure quality child care.* Washington, DC: Children's Defense Fund.

Aronson, S. (1987). Maintaining health in child care settings. In B.M. Caldwell (Ed.), *Group care for young children: A supplement to parental care.* Proceedings of the 12th Johnson & Johnson Pediatric Round Table (pp. 163–172). Lexington, MA: Lexington Books.

Bredekamp, S. (1989). *Regulating child care quality: Evidence from NAEYC's accreditation system.* Washington, DC: NAEYC.

Burden, D., & Googins, B. (1987, August). *Boston University— Balancing Job and Homelife Study: Summary of results.* Paper presented at the Annual Convention of the American Psychological Association, New York, NY.

Copple, C.E., Cline, M.G., & Smith, A.N. (1987). *Path to the future: Long-term effects of Head Start in the Philadelphia School District.* Washington, DC: U.S. Department of Health and Human Services.

Culkin, M., Helburn, S., Morris, J., & Watson, B. (1990). *Colorado's children: An economic profile of early childhood care and education.* Denver: University of Colorado at Denver, Economics Department.

Cummings, E.M. (1986, April). *Caregiver stability in day care: Continuity vs. daily association.* Paper presented at the International Conference on Infant Studies, Los Angeles.

Elkind, D. (1987). *Miseducation: Preschoolers at risk.* New York: Alfred A. Knopf.

Emlen, A., & Koren, P. (1984). *Hard to find and difficult to manage: The effects of child care on the workplace.* Portland, OR: Regional Institute for Human Services.

Finkelstein, N.W. (1982). Aggression: Is it stimulated by day care? *Young Children, 37*(6), 3–9.

Galinsky, E. (1988, January). *The impact of child care problems on parents on the job and at home.* Paper presented at the Wingspread Conference of Child Care Action Campaign, Racine, WI.

Galinsky, E., & Hughes, D. (1987, August). *The Fortune Magazine child care study.* Paper presented at the Annual Convention of the American Psychological Association, New York, NY.

Galinsky, E., Shinn, M., Phillips, D., Howes, C., & Whitebook, M. (1990). *Parent/teacher relationships.* New York: Families and Work Institute.

Gamble, T.J., & Zigler, E. (1986). Effects of infant day care: Another look at the evidence. *American Journal of Orthopsychiatry, 56*(1), 26–42.

Granger, R.C., & Marx, E. (1988). *Who is teaching? Early childhood teachers in New York City's publicly funded programs.* New York: Bank Street College of Education.

Hayes, C.D., Palmer, J.L., & Zaslow, M.J. (1990). *Who cares for America's children? Child care policy for the 1990s.* Washington, DC: National Academy of Sciences Press.

Howes, C. (1990). Can the age of entry into child care and the quality of child care predict behaviors in kindergarten? *Developmental Psychology, 26*(2), 292–303.

Howes, C., Rodning, C., Galluzzo, D.C., & Myers, L. (1988). Attachment and child care: Relationships with mother and caregiver. *Early Childhood Research Quarterly, 3*(4), 403–416.

Howes, C., & Stewart, P. (1987). Child's play with adults, toys, and peers: An examination of family and child care influences. *Developmental Psychology, 23*(3), 423–430.

Jorde-Bloom, P. (1988). *A great place to work: Improving conditions for staff in young children's programs.* Washington, DC: NAEYC.

Kontos, S., & Stremmel, A.J. (1988). Caregivers' perceptions of working conditions in a child care environment. *Early Childhood Research Quarterly, 3*(1), 77–90.

Lally, J.R., Mangione, P.L., & Honig, A.S. (1987). The Syracuse University Family Development Research Program: Long range impact of early intervention on low-income children and their families. San Francisco: Center for Child & Family Studies, Far West Laboratory for Educational Research and Development. [Summary appears in *Zero to Three*, April, 1988, as "More pride, less delinquency: Findings from the ten-year follow-up of the Syracuse Family Development Research Program," newsletter published by the National Center for Clinical Infant Programs, Arlington, VA.]

Marx, E., & Zinsser, C., with T. Porter. (1990). *Raising child care salaries and benefits: An evaluation of the New York state salary enhancement legislation.* New York: Bank Street College and the Center for Public Advocacy Research.

McCartney, K. (1984). The effect of quality of the day care environment upon children's language development. *Developmental Psychology, 20*, 244–260.

National Council of Jewish Women (1988). [Mothers in the workplace]. Unpublished raw data.

Olenick, M. (1986). *The relationship between day care quality and selected social policy variables.* Dissertation submitted to the UCLA School of Education.

Phillips, D.A., & Howes, C. (1987). Indicators of quality in child care: Review of research. In D.A. Phillips (Ed.), *Quality in child care: What does research tell us?* Washington, DC: NAEYC.

Phillips, D., McCartney, K., & Scarr, S. (1987). Child care quality and children's social development. *Developmental Psychology, 23*, 537–543.

Ruopp, R., Travers, J., Glantz, F., & Coelen, C. (1979). *Children at the center: Final report of the National Day Care Study.* Cambridge, MA: Abt Associates.

Shinn, M., Galinsky, E., & Gulcur, L. (1990). The role of child care centers in the lives of parents. New York: Families and Work Institute.

Shinn, M., Galinsky, E., & Gulcur, L. (1990). [The parent/teacher study.] Unpublished raw data.

Shinn, M., Ortiz-Torres, B., Morris, A., Simko, P., & Wong, N. (1989). Promoting the well-being of working parents: Coping, social support, and flexible job schedules. *American Journal of Community Psychology, 17*, 31–55.

Vandell, D.L., Henderson, V.K., & Wilson, K.S. (1988). A longitudinal study of children with varying day care experiences. *Child Development, 59*, 1286–1292.

Vandell, D.L., & Powers, C.P. (1983). Daycare quality and children's free play activities. *American Journal of Orthopsychiatry, 53*(3), 493–500.

Weikart, D.P. (1990, February 26). Testimony at the Subcommittee on Education and Health, Joint Economic Committee, U.S. Congress, Washington, DC.

Whitebook, M., Howes, C., & Phillips, D. (1990). *Who cares? Child care teachers and the quality of care in America. Final report of the National Child Care Staffing Study.* Oakland, CA: Child Care Employee Project.

Index

Credits/ Acknowledgments

Cover design by Charles Vitelli

1. Perspectives
Facing overview—Elaine M. Ward.

2. Child Development and Families
Facing overview—United Nations photo.

3. Appropriate Educational Practices
Facing overview—United Nations photo by Marta Pinter.

4. Guiding Behavior
Facing overview—WHO photo.

5. Curricular Applications
Facing overview—United Nations photo.

6. Teaching
Facing overview—United Nations photo by Y. Nagata.

7. Reflections
Facing overview—United Nations photo.

ANNUAL EDITIONS ARTICLE REVIEW FORM

■ NAME: _____ DATE: _____

■ TITLE AND NUMBER OF ARTICLE: _____

■ BRIEFLY STATE THE MAIN IDEA OF THIS ARTICLE: _____
_____
_____
_____
_____
_____

■ LIST THREE IMPORTANT FACTS THAT THE AUTHOR USES TO SUPPORT THE MAIN IDEA:
_____
_____
_____
_____
_____
_____
_____

■ WHAT INFORMATION OR IDEAS DISCUSSED IN THIS ARTICLE ARE ALSO DISCUSSED IN YOUR
TEXTBOOK OR OTHER READING YOU HAVE DONE? LIST THE TEXTBOOK CHAPTERS AND PAGE
NUMBERS:
_____
_____
_____
_____
_____
_____
_____
_____

■ LIST ANY EXAMPLES OF BIAS OR FAULTY REASONING THAT YOU FOUND IN THE ARTICLE:
_____
_____
_____
_____
_____
_____

■ LIST ANY NEW TERMS/CONCEPTS THAT WERE DISCUSSED IN THE ARTICLE AND WRITE A
SHORT DEFINITION:
_____
_____
_____
_____
_____
_____

*Your instructor may require you to use this Annual Editions Article Review Form in any number of ways:
for articles that are assigned, for extra credit, as a tool to assist in developing assigned papers, or simply
for your own reference. Even if it is not required, we encourage you to photocopy and use this page;
you'll find that reflecting on the articles will greatly enhance the information from your text.

ANNUAL EDITIONS:
EARLY CHILDHOOD EDUCATION 91/92
Article Rating Form

Here is an opportunity for you to have direct input into the next revision of this volume. We would like you to rate each of the 44 articles listed below, using the following scale:

1. **Excellent: should definitely be retained**
2. **Above average: should probably be retained**
3. **Below average: should probably be deleted**
4. **Poor: should definitely be deleted**

Your ratings will play a vital part in the next revision. So please mail this prepaid form to us just as soon as you complete it.
Thanks for your help!

Rating	Article	Rating	Article
	1. A New Code of Ethics for Early Childhood Educators!		24. Children's Self-Esteem: The Verbal Environment
	2. Children of Poverty		25. Avoiding "Me Against You" Discipline
	3. Economic Issues Related to Child Care and Early Childhood Education		26. Understanding and Altering Aggression
	4. Early Care and Education: Beyond the Schoolhouse Doors		27. Learning to Play: Playing to Learn
	5. Head Start: The Nation's Pride, A Nation's Challenge		28. Creative Play
	6. Schools and Classrooms as Caring Communities		29. "Put Your Name on Your Painting, But . . . the Blocks Go Back on the Shelves"
	7. Identification of Preschool Children With Mild Handicaps: The Importance of Cooperative Effort		30. Thinking, Playing, and Language Learning: An All-in-Fun Approach With Young Children
	8. First Year Milestones		31. Emergent Literacy: How Young Children Learn to Read and Write
	9. First Friends		32. Early Childhood Physical Education: The Essential Elements
	10. Guns and Dolls		33. The State of American Preschool Playgrounds
	11. What Birth Order Means		34. Transition Time: Make It a Time of Learning for Children
	12. Working Parents		35. Conceptualizing Today's Kindergarten Curriculum
	13. Single-Parent Families: How Bad for the Children?		36. How Good Is Your Kindergarten Curriculum?
	14. Where Are the Parents?		37. Who Cares? Child Care Teachers and the Quality of Care in America
	15. NAEYC Position Statement on Developmentally Appropriate Practice in Programs for 4- and 5-Year-Olds		38. The Child Development Associate Program: Entering a New Era
	16. Developmentally Appropriate Practice: Philsophical and Practical Implications		39. Learning to Read in New Zealand
	17. Quality Infant/Toddler Caregiving: Are There Magic Recipes?		40. Excellent Early Education: A City in Italy Has It
	18. Why Not Academic Preschool? (Part 1)		41. Learning, Chinese-Style
	19. Now, *Which Kind* of Preschool?		42. A Promise at Risk
	20. What's Missing in Children's TV		43. The Day Care Generation
	21. Synthesis of Research on Grade Retention		44. The Costs of *Not* Providing Quality Early Childhood Programs
	22. How Well Do We Respect the Children in Our Care?		
	23. Nurturing Success		

(Continued on next page)

ABOUT YOU

Name_____ Date_____

Are you a teacher? ☐   Or student? ☐

Your School Name _____

Department _____

Address _____

City _____ State _____ Zip _____

School Telephone # _____

YOUR COMMENTS ARE IMPORTANT TO US!

Please fill in the following information:

For which course did you use this book? _____

Did you use a text with this Annual Edition?   ☐ yes   ☐ no

The title of the text? _____

What are your general reactions to the Annual Editions concept?

Have you read any particular articles recently that you think should be included in the next edition?

Are there any articles you feel should be replaced in the next edition? Why?

Are there other areas that you feel would utilize an Annual Edition?

May we contact you for editorial input?

May we quote you from above?

ANNUAL EDITIONS: EARLY CHILDHOOD EDUCATION 91/92

BUSINESS REPLY MAIL

First Class   Permit No. 84   Guilford, CT

Postage will be paid by addressee

**The Dushkin Publishing Group, Inc.
Sluice Dock**
DPG **Guilford, Connecticut 06437**

No Postage
Necessary
if Mailed
in the
United States